The Marshall Cavendish

ILLUSTRATED ENCYCLOPEDIA OF

# PLANTS

AND

EARTH SCIENCES

# The Marshall Cavendish ILLUSTRATED ENCYCLOPEDIA OF PLANTS AND EARTH SCIENCES

## VOLUME TWO

EDITOR-IN-CHIEF
Professor David M. Moore

SPECIALIST SUBJECT EDITORS
Professor V. H. Heywood
*Botany*
Professor A. Hallam
*Earth Sciences*
Dr S. R. Chant
*Botany*

ADVISORY EDITORS
Professor W. T. Stearn
*Flowering Plants*
Dr I. B. K. Richardson
*Flowering Plants*
Dr Peter Raven
*Plant Ecology*
Professor Lincoln Constance
*Special Consultant*

EDITORIAL DIRECTOR
Dr Graham Bateman

Marshall Cavendish
New York · London · Sydney

# CONTENTS




**Reference Edition Published 1988**

Published by:
Marshall Cavendish Corporation
143 West Merrick Road
Freeport N.Y. 11520

AN EQUINOX BOOK

Planned and produced by:
Equinox (Oxford) Ltd
Littlegate House
St Ebbe's Street
Oxford OX1 1SQ
England





Library of Congress Cataloging-in-Publication Data
The Encyclopedia of plants and earth sciences.
Bibliography: p.
Includes index.
1. Botany—Dictionaries. 2. Botany, Economic—Dictionaries. 3. Crops—Dictionaries. 4. Angiosperms-Dictionaries. 5. Earth sciences—Dictionaries. 6. Ecology—Dictionaries. I. Marshall Cavendish Corporation.
QK7.E53 1988 580'.3'21 87-23927

ISBN 0-86307-901-6 (Set)
ISBN 0-86307-903-2 (Vol 2)





Printed in Italy


Previous page
*Canopy of the Kentucky Coffee Tree (see p.166).*

# Dyes and Tannins from Plants

Vegetable dyes have been used since earliest times in various parts of the world. They were, for example, used by the ancient Egyptians, Greeks, Romans and other early civilizations. *WOAD *(Isatis tinctoria)* was the imperial blue dye of Europe for many centuries and was used by the ancient Britons as a body paint. *INDIGO *(Indigofera anil, I. tinctoria* and other species) has been grown in India and Africa from time immemorial to provide another blue dye. *MADDER OR TURKEY RED *(Rubia tinctorum)* was used by the ancient Egyptians and other Middle Eastern peoples to provide a red dye. A yellow dye and food colorant has been obtained from SAFFRON *(*Crocus sativus)* since the times of the ancient Greeks. Another yellow dye is obtained from DYER'S GREENWEED or WELD *(Reseda luteola)*, one of the earliest dye plants known. Many hundreds of plants are still used for dyeing, especially in tribal societies in remoter regions of the world. They include lichens, club-mosses, mosses, ferns, gymnosperms and flowering plants and the parts used range from the bark, twigs, needles, flowers and fruits to the whole plant.

Vegetable dyes are substances which, when dissolved in water are able to color yarns, textiles, leather, wood and some foodstuffs. They are distinguished from animal dyes and, in more recent times, from synthetic dyes. There is currently a resurgence of interest in natural plant dyes as part of home or cottage industries.

Water soluble dyes have to be made insoluble to prevent them running. This is achieved by pre-treating the material to be dyed with substances known as mordants, which make the dye fast and help attain an intensive coloration. Mordants include alum (used from very early times), common salt, cream of tartar, iron, chromium and tin with which the dyes form an insoluble compound.

**Tannins and Tanning** Mention can also be made here of another group – the tannins. The term tannin describes a group of pale-yellow to light brown substances that are widely found in plants and which have been used for centuries for dyeing fabrics, making ink and in medical preparations. Their main use, however, lies in tanning leather – the process of converting animal skins into leather. This consists of steeping skins in infusions of vegetable materials such as bark, wood, leaves, nuts or galls which are rich in tannins. Putrefaction of untreated animal skins is promoted by enzymes secreted by various microorganisms. During tanning the tannins inactivate these enzymes and combine with the proteins of the skins, converting them into compounds which the enzymes cannot attack and binding together the protein fibers.

The tannins used in commerce are mainly obtained from the bark and wood of a few species which produce exceptionally high concentrations of tannins. Other materials such as leaves, galls and fruits are used less often. Few of these materials can be produced cheaply enough as a crop and most are either collected from the wild or are a by-product of some other activity.

OAK barks have been widely used for tanning for thousands of years. In Europe, *Quercus robur* and *Q. petraea* are mainly used, while in the New World *Q. montana, Q. alba, Q. prinus, Q. borealis, Q. dentata* and other species are important. Bark of HEMLOCK SPRUCES (*Tsuga canadensis* and *T. heterophylla*) is an important source of tannin in North America and is preferred for tanning heavy skins. WATTLE (*Acacia decurrens* and *A. dealbata*) bark has a tannin content of up to 40% and these fast-growing trees can be harvested at 5–10 years old. *EUCALYPTUS bark (from *Eucalyptus astringens* and *E. wandoo*) is widely used in Australia. Although *MANGROVE BARK is rich in tannins it is not so popular since the leather it produces is not of good quality. *BIRCH (*Betula*) and conifer barks are the main tannin sources in the USSR. *QUEBRACHO from South America (*Schinopsis balansae* and *S. lorentzii*) produce a wood rich in tannins. *CHESTNUT wood is also used to some extent, notably from *Castanea dentata* in North America and *C. sativa* in Europe. Tannins extracted from the autumn leaves of SUMACS (*Rhus typhina* and *R. glabra* in America and *R. coriaria* in Europe) produce fine leathers for bookbinding.

VEGETABLE DYES

| Common name | Scientific name | Color |
|---|---|---|
| CHINESE TALLOW TREE | *Sapium sebiferum* | Black |
| GUAVA | **Psidium guajava* | Black |
| *GAMBIER | *Uncaria gambier* | Black |
| *PERSIMMON | *Diospyros kaki* | Black |
| *WALNUT | *Juglans nigra* | Black, dark brown |
| KAVA | **Piper methysticum* | Black |
| *LOGWOOD | *Haematoxylon campechianum* | Black, brown, gray |
| *INDIGO | *Indigofera tinctoria, I. anil, I. arrecta* | Blue |
| *WOAD | *Isatis tinctoria* | Blue |
| DYER'S KNOTWEED | **Polygonum tinctorium* | Blue |
| FUSTIC | *Chlorophora tinctoria* | Yellow |
| LADIES' BEDSTRAW | **Galium verum* | Yellow, red |
| DYER'S BROOM | **Genista tinctoria* | Yellow |
| SAFFRON | **Crocus sativus* | Yellow |
| SAFFLOWER | **Carthamus tinctorius* | Yellow, red |
| GOLDEN ROD | **Solidago* species | Yellow |
| YELLOW CHAMOMILE | **Anthemis tinctoria* | Yellow |
| OSAGE ORANGE | **Maclura pomifera* | Yellowish-tan, gold |
| WELD, DYER'S GREENWEED | *Reseda luteola* | Yellow, gold |
| YELLOW-BARKED OAK | **Quercus velutina* | Yellow |
| *TURMERIC | *Curcuma longa* | Yellow |
| JACKFRUIT TREE | **Artocarpus integrifolius* | Yellow |
| ZEDOARY | *Curcuma zeodaria* | Yellow, green |
| *GAMBOGE | *Garcinia hanburyi* | Yellow |
| SUMAC, VINEGAR TREE | **Rhus glabra* | Yellow-tan, gray, brown |
| BUTTERNUT | *Juglans cinerea* | Tan |
| *BRACKEN | *Pteridium aquilinum* | Gray, yellow green |
| *BLACKBERRY | *Rubus* species | Gray |
| *BIRCH | *Betula* species | Gray |
| *PINEAPPLE | *Ananas comosus* | Green |
| MUNDU | **Garcinia dulcis* | Green |
| MYROBALAN | **Terminalia chebula* | Green |
| *COCONUT | *Cocos nucifera* | Green |
| BROOM | **Cytisus scoparius* | Green |
| *CHERVIL | *Anthriscus sylvestris* | Yellow-green |
| TANSY | **Tanacetum vulgare* | Yellow-green |
| *ONION | *Allium cepa* | Orange |
| *HENNA | *Lawsonia inermis* | Orange |
| COREOPSIS | **Coreopsis tinctoria* | Orange, yellow |
| *JUNIPER | *Juniperus communis* | Brown |
| *CUTCH, CATECHU | *Acacia catechu* | Brown |
| *ASH | *Fraxinus excelsior* | Brown, green |
| *ALDER | *Alnus glutinosa A. incana* | Brown, gray, black, yellow |
| *BLACKTHORN | *Prunus spinosa* | Reddish brown |
| RED STONE-LICHEN | **Parmelia omphalodes* | Brown |
| REINDEER MOSS | **Cetraria* species | Brown |
| | **Cladonia* species | Yellow |
| WILLOW | **Salix pentandra* | Brown |
| ORSEILLE | *Roccella tinctoria* | Red |
| *ALKANET | *Alkanna tinctoria* | Red |
| CROTTLE, CROTAL | **Parmelia saxatilis* | Brownish red |
| BRAZIL WOOD | **Caesalpinia brasiliensis* | Red, purple |
| BRAZIL WOOD, CAPPAN | **Caesalpinia sappan* | Red |
| *ANNATTO | *Bixa orellana* | Red, yellow |
| BLOODROOT | **Sanguinaria canadensis* | Red |
| *MADDER | *Rubia tinctorum* | Red |

**Durian** the common name for *Durio zibethinus*, one of the most famous trees of the East, widely distributed and cultivated in Malaya and the East Indies, and to a small extent in the New World tropics, for its delectable fruit. The tree attains a height of about 100ft, with buttresses, and bears massive spiny fruits, with leathery walls containing several large seeds, each embedded in a creamy yellow, or white, aromatic and strongly flavored pulpy aril. The fruits fall mainly at night and have to be collected very quickly, as they decay so rapidly that the pulp becomes rancid and inedible within four days. The flavor is likened by some to onion-flavored custard and the smell to a malfunctioning sewerage works.
BOMBACACEAE.

*The rose-like flowers and feathery fruits of* Dryas × suendermannii. ($\times \frac{1}{2}$)

**Dyckia** a genus of succulent plants from South America. Several species are grown for their foliage as indoor pot plants or greenhouse plants, or, in the tropics and subtropics, for bedding. The flowers are small and usually yellow, orange or red, borne on spikes, racemes or panicles. The commonly cultivated species include *D. altissima*, *D. brevifolia* and *D. frigida*.
BROMELIACEAE, about 70 species.

**Dyes** see p. 126.

**Dysoxylum** a genus of trees mainly of Indomalayasia and the Pacific. Many are locally important timber trees, such as *D. fraseranum* [AUSTRALIAN MAHOGANY, ROSEWOOD, PENCIL CEDAR], used in cabinet-making. Other commercially exploited species include *D. malabaricum* [WHITE CEDAR] of India, used in barrel-making, and the Australian *D. muelleri* [TURNIP WOOD, PENCIL CEDAR], used for furniture. A few are cultivated for ornament, such as *D. lessertianum* of Australia. The leaves of some species have been used as an onion substitute in Malaysian cooking.
MELIACEAE, about 60 species.

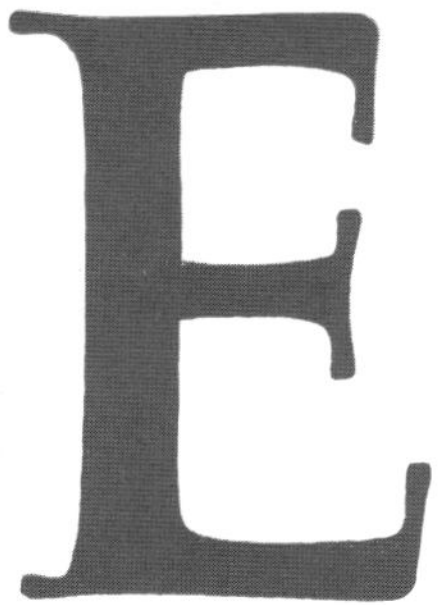

**Earth balls** the common name for certain gasteromycete fungi, such as *Scleroderma aurantium*, possessing tuberous fruit bodies which rupture irregularly to release masses of spores.
SCLERODERMATACEAE.

**Earth stars** the common name for the fungal genus *Geastrum*. The powdery spore mass of the mature fruit body is enclosed within a double wall. The thick tough outer wall breaks into lobes at maturity, bending backward in a characteristic star shape to expose the inner spore sac.
GEASTRACEAE, about 30 species.

**Ebony** the heavy, hard, dark heartwood derived chiefly from species of the genus **Diospyros* such as *D. ebenum* [MACASSAR EBONY], the source of the best ebony, and *D. dendo* [GABOON EBONY, CALABAR EBONY]. It takes a high polish and is now used principally for small objects such as piano keys, knife handles and chessmen, hairbrushes and walking sticks. Although the word is synonymous with black, ebony wood can be other colors such as that of *D. hirsuta* [COROMANDEL EBONY], which has brown or gray mottling. Other genera, such as **Dalbergia*, **Bauhinia*, **Caesalpinia* and **Jacaranda*, have been used for ebony, and *HOLLY and *HORNBEAM have been dyed to make false ebony.

**Ecballium** a genus represented by a single species, *E. elaterium* [SQUIRTING CUCUMBER], a prostrate, perennial herb with stout, fleshy stems. It is native to the Azores, the Mediterranean, the Middle East and the southwestern USSR. The mature fruit detaches itself from its stalk at the slightest touch and the fruit contents are violently expelled through the resultant hole. The juice is exceedingly bitter and highly irritant to the eyes. The plant yields the drug, elaterium, a powerful purgative and cathartic used in local medicine and produced commercially in Malta.
CUCURBITACEAE, 1 species.

**Eccremocarpus** a small genus of evergreen climbers native to Peru and Chile. *E. scaber* [CHILEAN GLORY FLOWER], which bears tubular orange-scarlet flowers is cultivated to cover walls and pergolas. It is cultivated as an annual or perennial according to the climate.
BIGNONIACEAE, 4–5 species.

**Echeveria** [HEN-AND-CHICKENS] a genus of perennial leaf-succulents from Mexico extending into the southernmost USA and southwards to the Andes. Many species are cultivated for their attractively colored leaves arranged in flower-like rosettes at the ends of usually short stems, and for their graceful loose inflorescences of bell-shaped red to yellow flowers. Popular species, cultivated as house or greenhouse plants for their attractive leaf habit and color, include *E. agavoides* [MOULDED WAX], with large rosettes of thick, apple-green pointed leaves, *E. derenbergii* [PAINTED LADY], with broad concave pale green leaves with red margins, and its hybrid with *E. elegans*, *E.* 'Fallax', with bluish shell-like leaves with pallid margins.

Species which in addition to attractive leaves are grown for their flowers include

*The colorful inflorescence of waxy flowers of* Echeveria secunda *var* glauca, *one of the many ornamental succulents from Mexico.* ($\times 1\frac{1}{2}$)

*E. derenbergii*, with orange flowers, *E. gibbiflora* (and several cultivars), with scarlet flowers, and *E. setosa* [MEXICAN FIRECRACKER], which enjoys considerable popularity for its showy red, yellow-tipped flowers.
CRASSULACEAE, about 150 species.

**Echinacea** [PURPLE CONE FLOWERS] a genus of three species of perennial herbs native to North America. *E. purpurea* is commonly cultivated, in a range of cultivars, for its daisy-like, purple flower heads about 4in in diameter on stems up to 40in tall.
COMPOSITAE, 3 species.

**Echinocactus** a genus of large thick, ribbed, hemispherical to cylindrical cacti from the southwestern USA and Mexico. Among these are the largest of the aptly-named BARREL CACTI, which form a solitary main stem of great age and bulk up to 4ft in diameter. One of these is *E. ingens* [MEXICAN GIANT BARREL]. By far the finest is *E. grusonii* [GOLDEN BALL CACTUS, GOLDEN BARREL], which

*Echinocactus polycephalus, one of the barrel cacti, forming a mound of several heads in the South Nevada Desert, USA. (× 1/20)*

has bright glossy green stems, numerous ribs and radiating stout yellow spines. This is one of the easiest cacti to cultivate and one of the most popular. The name "MOTHER-IN-LAW'S ARMCHAIR" is also popularly applied to it.
CACTACEAE, about 10 species.

**Echinocereus** a genus of cacti from Mexico to the northern USA. They are all low-growing and decumbent, clump-forming or rarely solitary, with soft-fleshed, short, columnar or globose, ribbed stems. The flowers are mostly showy, up to 4–5in in diameter and ranging in color from intense magenta or purple through pink, orange, yellow to brownish and lime-green. The fruits have a pleasantly acid taste. The frost-hardy *E. triglochidatus* (= *E. paucispinus*) [CLARET-CUP CACTUS] has brilliant claret-colored funnel-shaped blooms from stout but very soft ribbed stems which cluster and, in old age, form mounds. *E. pectinatus* var *rigidissimus* [RAINBOW CACTUS, COMB HEDGEHOG], from Arizona, is so-called from the successive rings of pink, white and straw-colored spines circling the stem. Many species withstand freezing, and a few such as *E. viridiflorus* [TORCH CACTUS] survive many years unprotected outdoors in milder areas. A few species, including *E. enneacanthus* [STRAWBERRY CACTUS] and its variety *stramineus* (= *E. stramineus*) [MEXICAN STRAWBERRY] produce edible fruits.
CACTACEAE, about 70 species.

*Close-up of the Barrel Cactus (Echinocactus grusonii) showing the swollen stem, with numerous ribs covered with radiating yellow spines. (× 1/3)*

**Echinops** [GLOBE THISTLE] a genus of biennial or perennial herbs occurring in open, often dry habitats from the Mediterranean east to Ethiopia and India. They are rather thistle-like, usually whitish-woolly plants with large globose heads of blue, pink or white flowers and an involucre of stiff, colored bracts. Several species are grown as border plants, especially *E. ritro* (= *E. ruthenicus*) and *E. sphaerocephalus*, with blue and silvery-gray flowers respectively.
COMPOSITAE, about 70 species.

**Echinopsis** a genus of South American globose to oblong, prominently ribbed cacti. Nearly all species bloom at night, with large white or pink, often sweetly scented flowers that last for a few hours only. The habit in cultivated forms ranges from dwarf solitary stems broader than wide, through large clumps as in *E. multiplex* [EASTER LILY CACTUS], to species such as *E. houttii* with cylindrical stems making offsets. The dwarf globular species include *E. eyriesii*, *E. oxygona* and *E. tubiflora*, which is often seen under glass. Globular *Echinopsis* species and hybrids are among the toughest and most trouble-free of cacti grown as houseplants.

Crosses with *Lobivia* species (× *Echinobivia*), notably the "Paramount Hybrids" from California, have large blooms in shades from pure white through yellow, orange, apricot and pink to red.

*E. pachanoi* contains hallucinogenic alkaloids used in religious ceremonies in Peru.
CACTACEAE, about 35 species.

**Echium** a genus of herbaceous annuals, biennials, perennials or shrubs found mainly in the Mediterranean region, North Africa and Macaronesia. The plants have tubular or bell-shaped flowers and a complex series of spines and hairs on the stems and leaves. Among several ornamental species are the biennial *E. plantagineum* (also a serious weed in many countries, particularly Australia) and *E. vulgare* [VIPER'S BUGLOSS, BLUE WEED, BLUE DEVIL] from Europe. Also cultivated in warmer climates such as California are some of the spectacular shrubby Canary Island species such as *E. candicans*, *E. simplex* and *E. wildpretii*, the latter with red flowers.
BORAGINACEAE, about 50 species.

**Ectocarpus** a genus of small branched filamentous brown algae with a worldwide distribution. The filaments are often interwoven to form narrow spongy strands. Many of the species such as *E. tomentosus* are epiphytic on larger seaweeds.
PHAEOPHYCEAE.

**Edelweiss** the German/Swiss name for *Leontopodium alpinum*, a small alpine plant which has been much sought after by collectors. The flower stems and undersides of the leaves are covered in dense white woolly hairs and each flower head is surrounded by petal-like, white, woolly bracts.
COMPOSITAE.

**Edraianthus** [GRASSY-BELLS] a small genus of compact tufted perennial herbs native from Italy to the Caucasus and mainly centered in the Balkan peninsula. Some species are grown as rock-garden plants. Most cultivated species, including *E. pumilio*, *E. graminifolius* (= *E. caricinus*) and *E. tenuifolius* have bell-shaped or trumpet-shaped, blue to purple or violet flowers (white in *E. graminifolius* subspecies *niveus*), similar to those of *Campanula*.
CAMPANULACEAE, about 10 species.

**Egg fruit** the common name given to the fruits of two unrelated species: *Solanum melongena* (Solanaceae) (see AUBERGINE) and *Pouteria campechiana* (= *Lucuma nervosa*) [CANISTEL, SAPOTE AMARILLO, SAPOTE BORRACHO] (Sapotaceae), a slender tree which reaches a height of 52ft in its native tropical America. The fruit is pear-shaped to globose in shape, with sweet, orange or yellow, mealy pulp with a musky flavor, eaten fresh. The plant is also the source of the spice canistel and is sometimes grown as a garden

*The cactus Echinopsis macrogona, showing the funnel-form flowers and ribbed stems that are typical of the genus. (× 1/30)*

*Water Hyacinth (*Eichhornia crassipes*) and Peacock Hyacinth (*E. azurea*) colonizing a stream in the Lower Amazon Basin.*

tree in the Caribbean. A related species, also with edible fruits, is *P. sapota* (see SAPOTE).

**Eichhornia** a small genus of freshwater aquatic herbs. All species, except the African *E. natans*, occur naturally in tropical South America where they commonly form a conspicuous component of the aquatic vegetation of shallow pools, lakes and rivers. Depending on water depth, species such as *E. azurea* [PEACOCK HYACINTH] and *E. crassipes* (= *E. speciosa*) [WATER HYACINTH] can exhibit either an emergent or free-floating life form. The spike-like or paniculate inflorescence is composed of blue or lilac flowers. In *E. crassipes* and *E. azurea* these flowers are large and attractive and thus they are cultivated ornamentally in garden ponds and greenhouses.

A major problem is represented by the WATER HYACINTH which in the past century has spread throughout the world – often with the help of Man. It is now considered one of the world's most menacing aquatic weeds, and large sums of money are spent annually in attempts to eradicate its extensive mats from reservoirs, rivers and canals. The most important factor responsible for the success of *E. crassipes* as a weed is its spectacular powers of vegetative growth, coupled with the buoyancy provided by its inflated petioles. It has been estimated that in suitable growing conditions 10 plants can produce a solid acre of plants within eight months.
PONTEDERIACEAE, 5–7 species.

**Elaeagnus** a genus of hardy evergreen or deciduous shrubs and small trees native to Europe, Asia and Australia, with one species, *E. commutata* [SILVERBERRY] in North America. The densely hairy leaves are sometimes attractively variegated (eg *E. pungens* 'Maculata'). Several species are cultivated as ornamental shrubs for their attractive foliage and inconspicuous fragrant flowers. One of the most widely grown is *E. angustifolia* [OLEASTER], a deciduous shrub with narrow silver-green leaves, silver-white flowers and yellow fruits. *E. umbellata* and *E. orientalis* are other deciduous shrubs grown as ornamentals, while *E. glabra*, *E. macrophylla* and *E. pungens* are among the evergreen cultivated species. The fruits of some species, especially *E. multiflora*, are consumed as preserves or as jelly.
ELAEAGNACEAE, about 45 species.

**Elaeis** a very small genus of palms, comprising the tropical American *E. oleifera* [AMERICAN OIL PALM] and the very important West African *E. guineensis* [OIL PALM]. These tall palms are grown in the wet tropics, principally West Africa and the Malay peninsula for their clusters of red fruits from which is extracted palm oil and palm kernel oil, which are extensively used as lubricants and for soap and margarine production. Palm toddy is extracted from the tender parts of the stem (see Arrack). They are also grown as ornamentals in the tropics.
PALMAE, 2 species.

**Elaphomyces** [FALSE TRUFFLES] a genus of widespread saprophytic fungi with subterranean, globose, nut-like fruiting bodies 0.4–1.2in across, often associated with deciduous tree roots. The fruiting bodies of certain species, notably *E. cervinis*, are used in veterinary medicine.
ELAPHOMYCETACEAE, about 20 species.

**Elemi** the name applied to a group of resinous substances and to a group of tropical forest trees from some of which the resin is obtained. The resin is soft and translucent, becoming yellow on exposure to the air and is used in the pharmaceutical and paint industries. The trees are mainly members of the Burseraceae such as *Canarium schweinfurthii* [AFRICAN ELEMI], *C. luzonicum* [MANILA ELEMI], *C. commune*, *Bursera gummifera* [WEST INDIAN or AMERICAN ELEMI], *B. jorullensis* [MEXICAN ELEMI] and species of *Protium*, *Amyris* and *Dacryodes*.

*Inflorescence of the Peacock Hyacinth (*Eichhornia azurea*) showing the conspicuous yellow "nectar guides" on the flowers.* ($\times \frac{1}{2}$)

**Eleocharis** a genus of small perennials and tufted annuals, cosmopolitan but mainly found in wet places in the temperate zones, particularly the colder regions. *E. palustris* [SPIKE RUSH] is typical of many members of the genus with tufted stems and small inconspicuous flowers confined to a terminal congested spike. *E. dulcis* (= *E. tuberosa*) [MATAI, CHINESE WATER CHESTNUT], from tropical East Africa, the Pacific, Africa and Madagascar has starchy tubers which are eaten cooked in Chinese dishes. It is grown like rice in flooded fields and some of the crop is canned and exported. *E. acicularis* is widely grown in aquaria and several species, including *E. austro-caledonica*, are used in basketwork.
CYPERACEAE, about 200 species.

**Elettaria** see CARDAMOM.
ZINGIBERACEAE, 6–7 species.

**Eleusine** a small genus of annual or perennial grasses native to Africa, with one species in South America (*E. tristachya*). The annual *E. indica* [CROWFOOT, GOOSE GRASS, WIREGRASS, YARDGRASS] is now a pernicious pantropical weed. The most important species economically is *E. coracana* [FINGER MILLET, AFRICAN MILLET, RAGI, KORAKAN] (see MILLET).
GRAMINEAE, about 9 species.

**Elm** the common name for members of *Ulmus*, a genus of deciduous trees widespread throughout the north temperate zone but with three species extending south to the tropics. Elms are widely grown as shade and avenue trees, and as specimen trees for parks. They are mainly hardy and of easy cultivation. On the other hand, they are susceptible to insect attack as well as Dutch elm disease (see below).

Some of the better-known cultivated species are: *U. americana* [AMERICAN or WHITE ELM], with several cultivars; *U. minor* (= *U. carpinifolia*) [EUROPEAN FIELD ELM], with several cultivars and distinctive local populations, such as var *cornubiensis* [CORNISH ELM], which are sometimes treated as separate species; *U. glabra* (= *U. montana*) [SCOTCH or WYCH ELM]; *U. × hollandica* [DUTCH ELM], a hybrid of *U. glabra* and *U. minor*; *U. procera* [ENGLISH ELM]; *U. rubra* [SLIPPERY or RED ELM]; *U. serotina* [SEPTEMBER ELM]; and *U. × vegeta* (*U. minor* × *U. glabra*) [HUNTINGDON or CHICHESTER ELM].

Elm timber has some valuable characteristics, especially as it is cross-grained and resists splitting. Consequently it has been the timber of choice for wheelwrights for the hubs of spoked wheels. It has also been much

*A flowering shoot of the Common Elm (*Ulmus procera*). The projecting stamens and small perianth are adaptations to pollen-dispersal by wind.* (×1)

used for furniture-making and for posts, barrels and handles for tools. Among the most important species for these purposes are *U. procera, U. americana, U. rubra, U. thomasii* [ROCK ELM] and *U. glabra*. The polished wood of elm shows a beautiful zigzag pattern, the so-called partridge-breast grain. The fact that the timber is resistant to decay under continuously waterlogged conditions accounts for its use for underwater piles.

The one known medicinal product of the elms is the mucilaginous bark of the SLIPPERY ELM, which is used as a soothing poultice for inflammations and internally as a treatment for diarrhea and other disorders. The foliage of the western Himalayan *U. wallichiana* is still important as animal fodder.

The fungus *Ceratocystis ulmi* is the causal agent of Dutch elm disease, which became prevalent in the 1920s and 1930s whence it was introduced into North America. In Europe, the disease attenuated after this outbreak, but another flare-up began after 1965, apparently through reintroduction of virulent strains from North America, where *U. americana* is particularly susceptible. The fungus kills by inducing blockage of the vessels. It is distributed by bark-boring beetles, mainly *Scolytus* species.
ULMACEAE, about 30 species.

**Elodea** a genus of submerged freshwater herbaceous plants. They are native to the New World but one species from temperate North America, *E. canadensis* [CANADIAN WATER-WEED], has been naturalized throughout Europe since 1836 in slow-flowing fresh water. A number of species, notably *E. canadensis, E. nuttalli* (North America), *E. densa* (South America) and *E. callitrichoides* (South America) are used in aquaria. In Europe usually only female plants of *E. canadensis* are found as reproduction is almost entirely vegetative.
HYDROCHARITACEAE, 10 species.

**Elymus** a widespread genus of mostly perennial Northern Hemisphere and particularly American grasses. *E. arenarius* [SEA LYME GRASS] is a widespread European species growing in sand dunes along the coasts of Britain and northwestern Europe. It is an effective sand-binder, spreading by its extensively creeping rhizomes. In North America, other species, such as *E. aralensis* and *E. racemosus*, both from the USSR, have been introduced for dune stabilization. *E. chinensis*, from China, is grown in the USA in wind-eroded areas.

In North America many species are good forage grasses: *E. glaucus* [SMOOTH BLUE WILD RYE] is one of the most valuable crops in the northwestern USA. *E. sibiricus* is cultivated in the Great Plains and intermountain district, *E. canadensis* and *E. virginicus* are common in the eastern states and *E. triticoides* [ALKALI RYE GRASS] occurs in the alkaline soils of the west.
GRAMINEAE, about 70 species.

**Embothrium** a small genus of evergreen shrubs or trees from the central and southern Andes of South America. The best-known is *E. coccineum* [CHILEAN FIRE TREE]. In its native habitat it forms a magnificent tree up to 50ft high with dark glossy green leaves and striking, brilliant crimson-scarlet, axillary and terminal racemes of flowers.
PROTEACEAE, about 8 species.

**Emilia** a small genus of annual and perennial herbs widespread through tropical Asia, China, Polynesia and Africa, with a few naturalized in the New World tropics. The only species which appears to be cultivated is *E. javanica* (= *E. sagittata, E. flammea, Cacalia sagittata, C. flammea*) [TASSEL FLOWER]. It is an erect annual, bearing loose heads of scarlet flowers – golden-yellow in cultivar 'Lutea' (= *Cacalia aurea*).
COMPOSITAE, about 30 species.

**Empetrum** a small genus of dwarf evergreen procumbent or low growing heath-like shrubs widespread and often dominant in oceanic heathlands of cool temperate areas in the Northern Hemisphere, southern South America and Tristan da Cunha. They are regarded by some authorities as three species, *E. nigrum* (= *E. eamsii, E. scoticum*) [CROWBERRY, ROCKBERRY, CRAKEBERRY], *E. rubrum* and *E. hermaphroditum* [CROWBERRY], others as only one. The black or red fleshy fruits are used locally for making jellies and preserves, and are eaten by birds.
EMPETRACEAE, 1–3 species.

**Encephalartos** the second largest genus of *cycads distributed in tropical and southern Africa. Meal can be prepared from the starch-rich pith tissues of the stem of a number of species, including *E. caffer* [KAFFIR BREAD] and *E. altensteinii* [BREAD TREE]. Some are grown for their ornamental foliage.
ZAMIACEAE, about 20–30 species.

**Endive** the common name given to **Cichorium endivia*, an annual or biennial herb grown as a salad plant for its stocky head of pale green crisp leaves which when young and tender are used in salads and other dishes. A related species is *C. intybus* [WILD *CHICORY], which is grown as a salad vegetable [WITLOOF] and whose dried roots are roasted, ground and mixed with coffee.
COMPOSITAE.

**Endothia** an ascomycete fungal genus, the best-known species being *E. parasitica*, the cause of chestnut blight or canker. After its introduction into the USA from China in about 1900 it virtually destroyed the forests of *Castanea dentata* [AMERICAN *CHESTNUT]. It was introduced into Italy in 1938, and has caused great damage to *C. sativa* [SWEET CHESTNUT].
DIAPORTHACEAE, 10 species.

**Endymion** see *Hyacinthoides*.

**Enhalus** a marine genus represented by a single species, *E. acoroides*, an aquatic herb which grows at and below low-water level on the shores of Indomalaysia and Australia. The species forms underwater "meadows" which provide the chief source of food for the

*The Chilean Fire Tree (*Embothrium coccineum*) can be grown in temperate regions.* ($\times\frac{1}{30}$)

dugong, a herbivorous sea mammal of Indian seas. *Enhalus* fibers are used to make fishing nets, and the fruits are edible.
HYDROCHARITACEAE, 1 species.

**Enkianthus** a genus of deciduous shrubs native to the Himalayas, China and Japan. Several species, including *E. campanulatus* and *E. cernuus*, are cultivated for the small white or cream, bell- or urn-shaped flowers which are produced in great profusion in spring, and for their colorful orange or red autumnal foliage.
ERICACEAE, 10 species.

**Ensete** a genus of large perennial herbs found in tropical Africa, Madagascar, southern China, Southeast Asia and Indomalaysia. They flower once and then die. *E. ventricosum* [ABYSSINIAN BANANA] is cultivated for the pulpy starch content of the swollen pseudostem and corms, which is eaten as bread, and for the young shoots which are eaten cooked. The seeds are also eaten. Fibers of the pseudostems are used for cordage and sacking.
MUSACEAE, 6–7 species.

**Enteromorpha** a genus of very common green algae found in marshes and watercourses near the sea. The genus can be a considerable nuisance as it tends to foul the bottoms of ships. Some species are consumed as a vegetable, including *E. prolifera* [locally called LIMU ELEELE] in the Hawaiian Islands.
CHLOROPHYCEAE.

**Entomophthora** a fungal genus (frequently known as *Empusa*) the members of which are all parasitic upon insects. *E. muscae* parasitizes flies, and dead flies attached to window panes, surrounded by a white halo of discharged fungal spores are a familiar sight. *E. grylli* is an important cause of death of grasshoppers in the USA.
ENTOMOPHTHORACEAE, about 40 species.

**Ephedra** a genus of gymnosperms widely distributed in warm temperate regions of the Northern Hemisphere and South America. Species tend to inhabit semi-arid or seasonally dry regions. They are mostly low creeping shrubs with slender green stems but a few are climbers and small trees. Some species, including *E. distachya*, from southern Europe and Asia, and *E. equisetina*, from Asia, are the source of vasoactive drug, ephedrine.
EPHEDRACEAE, about 40 species.

**Epidendrum** a large genus of American epiphytic and terrestrial orchids native to tropical and subtropical areas southwards from Florida but commonly cultivated and introduced into most parts of the Old World tropics. They exhibit a considerable range of plant form: many are pseudobulbous with a few apical, leathery leaves of varying shapes and sizes, but others have reed-like stems bearing many leaves.

Flower color varies with the predominant hues being whites (such as *E. nocturnum*), yellows, and greens (such as *E. ciliare*), but several species bear brilliant magenta, purple, scarlet and crimson inflorescences, as in hybrids of *E. ibaguense* (= *E. radicans*). Often, many contrasting complementary colors coexist in a single flower as in *E. cochleatum* [COCKLE-SHELL or CLAM-SHELL ORCHID].

*Epidendrum* species enter into the pedigree of many inter-generic hybrids such as × *Epicattleya* (*Epidendrum* × *Cattleya*).
ORCHIDACEAE, about 1 000 species.

*The Abyssinian Banana (*Ensete ventricosum*) produces inedible fruits but the pseudostem and corms yield a starch-rich pulp.*

**Epilobium** a diverse genus mainly of erect or creeping, annual to perennial herbs in cool temperate areas of both hemispheres and on mountains in the tropics, usually in open habitats. Several species are aggressive weeds, while some of the creeping New Zealand species, such as *E. glabellum* and *E. pedunculare*, are grown for ornament in rock gardens. ROSEBAY WILLOWHERB or FIREWEED, also known as *E. angustifolium*, is here considered as a species of **Chamaenerion*.
ONAGRACEAE, about 200 species.

**Epimedium** a genus of rather woody perennial herbs from the north temperate Old World. They are hardy ornamental species of the semi-shade, grown for their heart-shaped leaflets (often beautifully veined and tinted) and the reds, yellows and whites of the flowers, and include *E. alpinum* [BARREN WORT, BISHOPS HEAD], *E. grandiflorum* (= *E. macranthum*) and their hybrid *E.* × *rubrum*, *E. pinnatum*, and *E.* × *versicolor* (*E. grandiflorum* × *E. pinnatum*).
BERBERIDACEAE, about 25 species.

**Epipactis** a genus of orchids most of which are north temperate, but with representatives in tropical Africa, Thailand and Mexico. Some species have been grown horticulturally, including two marsh plants with conspicuous open flowers. These are *E. gigantea* [GIANT HELLEBORINE, GIANT ORCHID, CHATTERBOX], from the western USA and Mexico, with yellowish and red flowers, and *E. palustris* [MARSH HELLEBORINE], a European species with rosy flowers.
ORCHIDACEAE, about 24 species.

*The Cockle-shell Orchid (*Epidendrum cochleatum*) has twisted pale green sepals and an erect shell-like purple labellum.* (×2)

*Epimedium × versicolor, one of the Barrenworts, is often cultivated for its yellow flowers and attractively veined leaves.* (×⅕)

**Epiphyllum** a genus of mostly tropical American epiphytic cacti. The true species have long, jointed, three-winged or flattened, green leaf-like stems with aerial roots. *Epiphyllum* species have typically cactus-like flowers: usually large, white and nocturnal, and commonly intensely fragrant. There are numerous hybrids, many ascribed to *E. ackermannii* (= *Nopalxochia ackermannii*) but are probably hybrids of this species with *Heliocereus*. Commonly cultivated greenhouse species include *E. anguliger* [FISHBONE CACTUS] and *E. oxypetalum* [DUTCHMAN'S PIPE CACTUS]. In tropical countries, species of *Epiphyllum* are sometimes planted as hedges and make a magnificent sight when in bloom. It should be noted that the name *Epiphyllum* has been misused for the CHRISTMAS and EASTER CACTI now classified under **Schlumbergera*.
CACTACEAE, about 16 species.

**Episcia** a genus of showy-flowered tropical American herbs, often grown under glass, in hanging baskets and as houseplants. Commonly cultivated species include the scarlet-flowered *E. cupreata*, from Colombia and Venezuela, and the white or pale-lilac-flowered *E. lilacina* (= *E. chontalensis*), especially cultivar 'Panama'.
GESNERIACEAE, about 10 species.

**Equisetum** see Horsetails, p. 180.

**Eragrostis** [LOVE GRASSES] a large cosmopolitan genus of temperate and tropical, annual and perennial grasses. Species of *Eragrostis* occupy a wide range of different habitats. In South Africa, for example, there are many important veld species, such as *E. curvula* [WEEPING LOVE GRASS], while others occur in the desert, such as *E. cyperoides*, and a few even occur by water, such as *E. nebulosa*. In the USA the principal species include *E. pectinacea*, a pernicious perennial tumbleweed, which readily drops its panicles at maturity. *E. chloromelas*, *E. curvula* and *E. lehmanniana* (all from South Africa) have been introduced into the USA for erosion control.

Few species have economic value. However, *E. tef* [TEFF] is grown as a millet in Ethiopia, where it is the most important crop, the grain being ground into a brownish flour called "ingera". Elsewhere in Africa, and in Australia, it is grown for hay. *E. curvula* has been introduced as a forage grass into North and South America. *E. amabilis*, *E. curvula*, *E. superba* and *E. obtusa*, are valuable ornamentals.
GRAMINEAE, about 300 species.

**Eranthemum** a genus of shrubs and perennial herbs, native to tropical Asia, some of which are cultivated as ornamentals. *E. pulchellum* (= *E. nervosum*), a small shrub with blue flowers is normally grown under glass in cooler temperate zones. *E. cinnabarinum* is a tropical garden flowering shrub with reddish flowers.
ACANTHACEAE, about 30 species.

**Eranthis** a genus of small, tuberous, herbaceous, spring-flowering perennials from the north temperate Old World. *E. hyemalis* [WINTER ACONITE], *E. cilicica*, from Asia Minor, and the hybrid *E. × tubergenii* are all commonly cultivated for their large solitary yellow flowers.
RANUNCULACEAE, 7 species.

**Eremurus** [FOX-TAIL LILY, DESERT CANDLE] a genus of perennial herbs with narrow leaves in rosettes or tufts, native to the dry steppes of western and Central Asia. Some, including *E. stenophyllus* (= *E. bungei*), *E. himalaicus* and *E. robustus* and many hybrids, are cultivated for their spectacular flowering racemes, up to 10ft high, bearing white yellow or pale pink flowers depending on the species.
LILIACEAE, about 50 species.

**Ergot** a term applied to (i) a fungal disease of grasses and sedges caused by a species of *Claviceps*, (ii) the fungus causing such a disease and (iii) the sclerotia formed by *Claviceps* species, especially *C. purpurea*. Essentially, the sclerotium is a hard compact mass of fungal mycelium which forms after *Claviceps* parasitizes the ovary of grasses (notably RYE) and develops in place of the normal grain.

The sclerotia of *Claviceps* species contain toxic alkaloids which, if eaten by animals or man, can cause serious poisoning (ergotism) and even death. The arterioles are contracted with the result that the supply of blood to the extremities is impaired, and gangrene and loss of limbs may follow. They also cause convulsions and hallucinations. In the Middle Ages human ergotism was called "St. Anthony's Fire" and resulted from eating rye bread infected with *C. purpurea* (particularly toxic). With routine screening of cereal grain for impurities, ergotism in humans has become more or less unknown although serious outbreaks occur occasionally, the last being in 1953 in Belgium and France.

The same alkaloids from *C. purpurea*, purified and, in some cases chemically modified, are today used in obstetrics and in the treatment of migraine and high blood pressure. Ergot alkaloids required by the pharmaceutical trade were formerly obtained from rye crops naturally or artificially infected with *C. purpurea*, but these sources are being rapidly replaced by preparations produced in fermentation tanks using selected strains of *Claviceps* species.

**Eria** a genus of epiphytic orchids native to tropical Asia, with strikingly colored flowers. Unlike most orchids, the whole plant is covered with a mat of hairs.
ORCHIDACEAE, about 375 species.

**Erianthus** is a genus of large grasses found mainly in the warmer regions of the world. *E. ravennae* [PLUME OR RAVENNA GRASS] from southeast Europe, is cultivated for its ornamental large, silvery, plume-like inflorescences. The genus is now included within **Saccharum*.
GRAMINEAE, about 30 species.

*'Maiden Erlegh' is typical of the group of hybrids commonly called epiphyllums, although they are of polygeneric origin.* (×⅕)

**Erica** a genus of evergreen shrubs and occasionally dwarf trees which are commonly called HEATHS. However, the term "HEATHER" is also applied to a number of *Erica* species as well as the true HEATHER, **Calluna vulgaris*.

Ericas have an unusual distribution in two distinct regions of the world: most species are native to the Cape region of South Africa [CAPE HEATHS] and the remainder to Europe [HARDY HEATHS]. Their leaves are small and needle-like and the flowers are either solitary or in terminal umbels, panicles or racemes, with usually bell-shaped corollas, variously colored pink, white or red.

Once very popular as cool greenhouse and conservatory plants, very few species of CAPE HEATHS are now grown in cultivation. However, the HARDY HEATHS remain popular rock-garden subjects, often blooming in winter and early spring. The hardiest are *E. tetralix* and *E. cinerea*. *E. tetralix* [BOG HEATHER, CROSS LEAVED HEATH] is native to bogs and wet heaths in Western Europe. The stems, like those of *Calluna*, root at the base, but there are no short axillary shoots. A number of varieties are in cultivation, usually growing best on lime-free soils, eg 'Con Underwood' (red flowered) and 'Mollis' (white flowered). This species has hybridized with other species in the genus, eg with *E. ciliaris* [FRINGED HEATH] to give *E.* × *watsonii* and with *E. vagans* [CORNISH HEATH] to give *E.* × *williamsii*.

*E. cinerea* [BELL OR PURPLE HEATHER] is another low-growing shrub, with profusely branched stems rooting at the base, and many short, leafy axillary shoots. This species is more usually found on dry moors in its native Europe: A number of varieties are in cultivation, including 'Atrorubens' (red flowered), 'Carnea' (pale lavender flowered) and 'Alba Minor' (white flowered). Other hardy species include *E. vagans* [CORNISH HEATHER OR HEATH] and *E. carnea* [SPRING HEATH, SNOW HEATHER] which has many cultivars that vary in leaf and flower color.

*E. arborea* [TREE HEATH] from southern Europe is the source of the *briar root used in the manufacture of pipe bowls, while the stems of *E. tetralix* and *E. cinerea* as well as those of *Calluna* species, are the source of a yellow dye used for dyeing wool in the Scottish Highlands.
ERICACEAE, 500 species.

**Erigeron** [FLEABANE] a large genus of annual, biennial and perennial herbs, worldwide in distribution in temperate and mountainous regions, especially in North America. Most cultivated species flower in late spring or early summer.

Some of the perennial species are grown as garden-border plants, notably the perennial, fibrous-rooted *E. speciosus*, whose varieties, including *macranthus*, grow to a height of 2ft, and bear pink, blue, or purple ray florets. Another, taller (5ft), popular garden species is the coarse-leaved annual or perennial *E. annuus* [DAISY FLEABANE, SWEET SCABIOUS, WHITE-TOP], with clusters of flower heads with normally white ray florets. A number of the lower-growing species are grown in rock gardens. These include the hairy perennial *E. alpinus* with large pink to violet flower heads, the attractive bright-orange-flowered *E. aurantiacus* [DOUBLE ORANGE DAISY], the white-, pink- or blue-flowered *E. flagellaris* [RUNNING FLEABANE], and cultivars of the somewhat succulent *E. glaucus* [BEACH ASTER, SEASIDE DAISY] and *E. thunbergii* (= **Aster japonicus*).

Medicinal extracts have been obtained from the roots of the Mexican *E. affinis* and from the leaves and stem tips of the North American *E. canadensis* [CONYZA].
COMPOSITAE, about 200 species.

*The tall yellow flower-spikes of* Eremurus stenophyllus, *one of the Fox-tail Lilies, a native of eastern Iran and Afghanistan.*

**Erinacea** a genus represented by a single species, *E. anthyllis* (= *E. pungens*) [HEDGEHOG BROOM, BRANCH THORN], a tough, spiny shrub native to southwest Europe in dry, hilly areas. It bears racemes of rather large bluish-violet flowers and is occasionally cultivated for ornament.
LEGUMINOSAE, 1 species.

**Erinus** a genus consisting of one variable alpine and Pyrennean species *E. alpinus*, a tufted dwarf perennial herb cultivated in rock gardens with clusters of white (cultivar 'Albus'), carmine ('Carmineus'), lilac ('Lilacinus') or pink ('Roseus'), starry flowers.
SCROPHULARIACEAE, 1 species.

**Eriobotrya** a genus of evergreen shrubs and trees mainly distributed in East Asia. They have large leathery leaves and panicles of whitish flowers. *E. japonica* [LOQUAT, JAPANESE MEDLAR], from China and Japan, is a very important fruit tree in Japan and northwestern India and is widely cultivated for its edible yellow plum-sized fruits. The wood of this species and of *E. bengalensis* is of economic value. *E. japonica* is also widely cultivated as a subtropical ornamental.
ROSACEAE, about 30 species.

**Eriogonum** [WILD BUCKWHEAT] a genus of annual and perennial herbs or shrubs native to western and southeastern USA and Mexico. Two perennial species, *E. umbellatum* [SULPHUR FLOWER] and *E. ovalifolium*, are cultivated as ornamental garden plants. Both bear clusters or umbels of yellow flowers, the latter with pinkish veins on the sepals. The leaves and stems of some species such as *E. longifolium* [INDIAN TURNIP] are used as food by some Indian tribes.
POLYGONACEAE, about 150 species.

**Eriophorum** [COTTON GRASS] a genus of mainly north temperate and Arctic, tufted or creeping, perennial herbs characteristic of wet peat moorland. The perianth of the flower is made up of bristles which elongate and become cottony after flowering and act as a means of seed dispersal. The "cotton hair" was once used as pillow stuffing.
CYPERACEAE, about 21 species.

**Eriophyllum** a small genus of herbs and subshrubs, all native to western North America. Their stems and leaves are covered in dense hairs which give them a woolly appearance. *E. lanatum* (= *E. caespitosum*, *Bahia lanata*), an erect perennial herb, is occasionally cultivated in garden borders for its attractive daisy-like yellow flower heads.
COMPOSITAE, about 11 species.

**Erodium** [STORKSBILL, HERON'S-BILL] a genus of hardy annual to perennial herbs distributed from Europe to southern Asia, as well as temperate Australia and tropical South America. They bear white, pink or purplish flowers with long-beaked carpels.

*Fruiting heads of the Narrow-leaved Cotton Grass (*Eriophorum angustifolium*), a common colonizer of acid peaty bogland.* ($\times 1\frac{1}{2}$)

The beaks twist spirally with the carpels attached at the base separating from each other.

Many of the compact species make popular rock-garden or border plants. They include *E. corsicum* (pink flowers), *E. macradenum* (light purple flowers, but rose-pink in cultivar 'Roseum'), the densely-tufted, white-flowered *E. chamaedryoides* [ALPINE GERANIUM] and *E. petraeum* subspecies *lucidum* (white-flowered with red veins). A few species are valuable forage plants, notably the annual *E. cicutarium* [ALFILARIA, RED-STEMMED FILAREE, WILD MUSK, PIN CLOVER, PIN GRASS], which is native to the Mediterranean region but is now widely naturalized in North and South America, as is *E. moschatum* [WHITE-STEMMED FILAREE, MUSK CLOVER]. *E. hirtum* and *E. malacoides* are both used as food in North Africa, the former for its edible roots, the latter as a leaf-salad.
GERANIACEAE, about 90 species.

**Eryngium** a large genus of cosmopolitan perennial herbs with spiny-toothed leaves and small flowers arranged in dense hemispherical to cylindrical heads subtended by spiny bracts at the base. Hardy cultivated rock garden and border plants include cultivars 'Grandiflorum' and 'Superbum' of *E. alpinum*, with attractive blue or white flowers and deeply cut leaves, *E. giganteum*, a tall biennial or perennial Caucasian species with silvery-blue or greenish flowers, and the blue-flowered Eurasian *E. planum* (pink flowered in cultivar 'Roseum').

Another well-known species is *E. maritimum* [SEA HOLLY, SEA HOLM, SEA ERYNGIUM], with its glaucous-blue leaves and pale blue flowers. Although native to Europe this species is naturalized on the Atlantic coast of the USA. One of the better-known North American species is *E. yuccifolium* [RATTLESNAKE-MASTER, BUTTON SNAKEROOT], which grows to a height of about 1m and bears whitish flowers. Most material cultivated in the USA under the name of *E. aquaticum* is in fact *E. yuccifolium*. The roots of both the latter species and of the European *E. campestre* [SNAKEROOT] have medicinal uses.
UMBELLIFERAE, about 200 species.

**Erysimum** [FAIRY WALLFLOWER, BLISTER CRESS, TREACLE MUSTARD] a genus of annual to perennial herbs from the north temperate zone. Many of the species are cultivated in borders or rock gardens for their showy flowers in various shades of yellow to orange, purple or reddish, but the identity of many of the cultivated plants is not known. Most of them are probably hybrids between various *Erysimum* and **Cheiranthus* species.

Cultivated forms include the yellow-flowered European *E. helveticum* and *E. decumbens* (= *E. ochroleucum*) and the North American *E. suffrutescens* [BEACH WALLFLOWER], *E. torulosum* and *E. asperum* [WESTERN WALLFLOWER, PRAIRIE ROCKET]. Cultivated purple-flowered species include the rather dwarf Asian perennial *E. purpureum* and the European *E. linifolium* (pink and white flowers in cultivar 'Bicolor').
CRUCIFERAE, about 80 species.

**Erysiphe** a most important cosmopolitan genus of powdery mildews, including the devastating parasite of cereals and wild grasses, *E. graminis*, and *E. polygoni*, which has more than 500 hosts. In barley, *E. graminis* can cause crop losses as high as 40% in a season. The pathogen produces cottony white to brown mycelial mats on the surfaces of the leaves. Badly infected leaves turn brown and die, and the plant may be dwarfed with consequent failure to produce flower heads and grain.
ERISYPHACEAE, about 10 species.

**Erythrina** a genus of tropical and subtropical, quick growing, often spiny trees and shrubs, rarely herbs, bearing conspicuous red, pea-like flowers. Some are grown as ornamentals in warm climates or under glass in cooler temperate zones. For example *E. crista-galli* [CORAL TREE], native to Brazil and neighboring countries, is renowned for its ornamental red flowers and seeds. The seeds of many species, including *E. herbacea* (= *E. arborea*) [CHEROKEE BEAN, RED CARDINAL], from Florida and Mexico, *E. tahitensis* (= *E. monosperma*) [HAWAIIAN CORAL TREE, WILWILLI] and *E. caffra* [KAFFIR BOOM] are used as beads and are often highly poisonous. The seeds of *E. herbacea* are used as rat poison in Mexico.

Several species are used as shade trees because of their large crowns, including *E. lithospermum* in Southeast Asia and Indonesia over tea and coffee, and *E. glauca* in Venezuela and Guyana over cacao. Other species called IMMORTELLE are grown in cacao and coffee plantations, including *E. mitis* (= *E. umbrosa*), *E. fusca* [SWAMP IMMORTELLE] and *E. poeppigiana* [MOUNTAIN IMMORTELLE]. In Asia and Australia *E. variegata* (= *E. indica*) provides support as well as shade for the weak-stemmed pepper plants.

The flowers and buds of some species such as the Central American *E. rubrinervia* are eaten, as are the leaves of the Indonesian *E. fuseda*. Several species yield extracts from the leaves, seeds and bark with various local medicinal uses such as febrifuges and diaphoretics. The wood of *Erythrina* species is soft and light: that of WILWILLI is used for surfboards and fishing net floats. The bark of *E. suberosa* is used as a cork substitute.
LEGUMINOSAE, 80–100 species.

**Erythronium** a genus of erect hairless perennial herbs from southern Europe and temperate Asia, but mainly from temperate North America. The nodding white, yellow, pink or purplish flowers are either solitary or

Erysimum suffruticosum *is a commonly cultivated perennial used in rockeries or herbaceous borders.* ($\times \frac{1}{5}$)

*The Coral Tree (*Erythrina crista-galli*), from Brazil, is a shrubby species grown for its waxy brilliant red flowers.* (×½)

in racemes. *E.dens-canis* [DOG-TOOTH VIOLET] is known in cultivation in a range of cultivars including the white-flowered 'Album' and the purple-violet flowered 'Purpureum'. Popular cultivated North American species include *E. albidum* [WHITE DOG-TOOTH VIOLET, BLONDE LILIAN], with long, solitary, bluish to purplish flowers, *E. grandiflorum* [AVALANCHE LILY] with flowers solitary or several, large and golden-yellow in cultivar 'Robustum', and white with yellow centers in cultivar 'Album', and *E. americanum* [YELLOW ADDER'S TONGUE, TROUT LILY, AMBERBELL], which bears solitary yellow flowers up to 2.5in long.
LILIACEAE, about 25 species.

**Erythroxylum** a genus of shrubs and trees occurring in subtropical and tropical countries, mainly in tropical America. The most important economic plants are *E. coca* and *E. novagranatense* (see COCAINE).
ERYTHROXYLACEAE, about 250 species.

**Escallonia** a South American (mainly Andean) genus of deciduous or evergreen shrubs, a number of species and hybrids of which are in cultivation as ornamentals in parks and gardens. The inflorescences of white, purplish or red flowers are sometimes showy and fragrant.

*E. rubra* (= *E. punctata*) is a widely cultivated and very variable species containing such varieties as *macrantha* (= *E. macrantha*), which is tolerant of salt-laden winds and forms a good hedge on the western coasts of Europe. It hybridizes in cultivation with most of the other species. One of the best-known hybrids is the generally low-growing shrub *E.* × *langleyensis* (= *E.* × *edinensis*), which is the result of cross between *E. rubra* and *E. virgata*. The latter, from Chile and Argentina, is the hardiest of all the cultivated species of this genus. The extent of interspecific hybridization between garden species is such that many of the specimens in cultivation are hybrids which have replaced the original species.
SAXIFRAGACEAE, about 40 species.

**Escherichia** a non-spore-forming Gram-negative rod-shaped bacterium. Its major species, *E. coli*, is found in the intestinal tract of Man and other mammals. *E. coli* is extensively used in experimental work by biochemists and microbial geneticists.
ENTEROBACTERIACEAE.

**Eschscholzia** a genus of poppy-like annual or perennial herbs from western North America to northern Mexico, and widely naturalized in warm, dry areas elsewhere. The genus has provided gardeners with some of the most brilliant and easily grown hardy annuals. The species are of variable flower color: the widely cultivated *E. californica* [CALIFORNIAN POPPY], the state flower of California, has white and cream to yellow, orange, pink and scarlet forms. It is an annual or a perennial which flowers in its first year and, in mild areas, may overwinter after flowering.
PAPAVERACEAE, about 10 species.

**Esparto** a fiber used for the manufacture of cordage, shoes and paper, known in Arabic as "halfa", in French as "alfa", in German as "afriemengras" and in the USA as Spanish grass. It is derived from the leaves of two unrelated western Mediterranean grasses, *Stipa tenacissima* and *Lygeum spartum*. *S. tenacissima* [ALFA] can be divided into two commercial varieties – cordage alfa and papermaking alfa. *L. spartum* [FALSE ALFA] yields a long fiber that is useful only for making cordage.
GRAMINEAE.

Escallonia rubra *var* macrantha, *from South America, showing its glossy leaves and pinkish-red flowers.* (×1)

*The Dog-tooth Violet (*Erythronium dens-canis*) is not a true violet but a member of the lily family (Liliaceae).* (×⅓)

**Essential oils** see p. 136.

**Eucalyptus** a large, important genus of evergreen trees and shrubs, chiefly native to Australia and Tasmania with a few extending to New Guinea, eastern Indonesia, Timor and the Philippine Islands. They range in height from less than 3ft to over 320ft, as in *E. regnans* [MOUNTAIN ASH, SWAMP GUM, AUSTRALIAN OAK], the tallest of flowering plants. By far the greatest part of natural forest and woodland in the non-arid regions of Australia from the tropics to cool-temperate southern Tasmania is dominated by species of *Eucalyptus*, usually unaccompanied by any other genus in the upper story.

Eucalypts constitute the major hardwood timber resource of Australia: among the particularly valuable species for bridge, ship and house construction are *E. marginata* [JARRAH], *E. pilularis* [BLACKBUTT], *E. obliqua* [MESSMATE], *E. delegatensis* (= *E. gigantea*) [ALPINE ASH], *E. botryoides* [BLUE GUM, BASTARD MAHOGANY], *E. diversicolor* [KARRI GUM], *E. regnans*, *E. resinifera* [RED MAHOGANY] and *E. robusta* [SWAMP MAHOGANY]. Recently, emphasis has swung to pulp for paper and similar products, and especially for chipwood for hardboard production. Among minor products derived from the genus the best-known is a terpenoid essential oil (cineole or eucalyptol) used medicinally, as an antiseptic and to relieve colds, and in flavoring. Species which yield such an oil include *E. citriodora* [LEMON-SCENTED GUM], *E. dives* [BROAD-LEAVED PEPPERMINT] and *E. dumosa* [MALLEE, CONGOO MALLEE]. However, perhaps the major commercial source of eucalyptus oil is from the fresh leaves of *E. globulus* [TASMANIAN BLUE GUM]. Several species, including *E. leucoxylon* [WHITE IRONBARK] yield a kino, an astringent resin-like substance used in medicine and tanning. The bark of *E. astringens* [BROWN MALLEE] con-

# Essential Oils

Essential oils are a class of vegetable oils which are made up of complex mixtures of volatile organic chemicals, usually responsible for pleasant odors or tastes. They are distinguished from fixed or fatty oils such as palm oil, groundnut oil and maize oil (see Oil Crops, p. 250).

Essential oils occur in a wide variety of plants – herbs, trees and shrubs – drawn from some 60 families of gymnosperms and flowering plants, notably the Myrtaceae, Labiatae, Umbelliferae, Lauraceae and Compositae. They frequently occur as droplets in the cells of glandular hairs or in secretory cavities or ducts or in canals which permeate the tissues. They can occur in most organs of the plant, especially the leaves, flowers, fruits and stems. Often, for a single species, production is confined to a single organ but in some cases oils are produced by different organs, as in citrus fruits where they are found in the sap hairs, the rind and seed.

IMPORTANT ESSENTIAL OILS

| Common name | Source |
|---|---|
| **Perfume Oils** | |
| GERANIUM | **Pelargonium* spp |
| *BERGAMOT | *Citrus aurantium* var *bergamia* |
| *ATTAR (OTTO) OF ROSES | *Rosa damascena, R. centifolia R. moschata* |
| *YLANG-YLANG | *Cananga odorata, C. latifolia* |
| TUBEROSE | **Polianthes tuberosa* |
| CITRONELLA | **Cymbopogon nardus* |
| LEMON GRASS | *C. citratus* |
| PATCHOULI | **Pogostemon patchouly* |
| VETIVER, KHUS-KHUS | **Vetiveria zizanioides* |
| SCENTED BORONIA | **Boronia megastigma* |
| LAVENDER | **Lavandula latifolia, L. angustifolia* |
| JASMINE | **Jasminum officinale, J. niloticum, J. odoratissimum* |
| GARDENIA | **Gardenia florida* |
| **Wood Oils** | |
| CADE | **Juniperus oxycedrus* |
| *CAMPHOR | *Cinnamomum camphora* |
| CEDAR WOOD | **Juniperus virginiana* |
| EUCALYPTUS | **Eucalyptus dives, E. globulus* |
| *SANDALWOOD | *Santalum album* |
| SASSAFRAS | **Sassafras albidum* |
| PINE NEEDLE | **Pinus sylvestris* |
| **Flavoring Oils** | |
| *PEPPERMINT | *Mentha × piperita* |
| SPEARMINT | **Mentha spicata* |
| STAR ANISE | **Illicium verum* |
| *CELERY | *Apium graveolens* |
| *CLOVES | *Syzygium aromaticum* |
| *LEMON | *Citrus limon* |
| *ORANGE | *Citrus aurantium, C. sinensis* |
| *LIME | *Citrus aurantifolia* |
| CARAWAY | **Carum carvi* |
| *NUTMEG | *Myristica fragrans* |
| *THYME | *Thymus vulgaris, T. capitatus* |
| ANISEED, *ANISE | *Pimpinella anisum* |

The essential oils contain a great variety of terpenes and terpenoids which are hydrocarbons basically derived from a branched 5-carbon unit, isoprene. Their function in plants is still not clear and as by-products of secondary metabolism they have been regarded as waste-products or even demonstrations of the plant's biochemical virtuosity! There is accumulating evidence, however, that they play a significant part in attracting pollinating agents to flowers, in encouraging animals to eat their fruits and thereby aid in seed dispersal, and in defence mechanisms against predators.

Essential oils are used extensively in perfumes, flavorings and medicines. They can be conveniently divided into perfume, wood and flavoring oils, although some particular oils come under more than one of these categories.

### Perfume oils

The use of essential oils as perfumes and scents dates from earliest times and they were known to have been used by the ancient Egyptian, Hebrew, Greek and Roman civilizations. Despite the increasing use of synthetic chemicals in perfumery today, there is still a flourishing trade in a wide array of naturally produced essential oils for use in scents, cosmetics, detergents, polishes etc. Today the perfume industry is centered around the town of Grasse in the south of France. There is extensive cultivation of species such as MIMOSA *(*Acacia dealbata)*, JASMINE *(*Jasminum officinale)*, *NARCISSUS, VIOLETS *(*Viola* species), TUBEROSE *(*Polianthes tuberosa)*, and DAMASK ROSE from which essential oils are extracted for use in perfumes. Geranium oil is obtained from the leaves of several **Pelargonium* species, such as *P. graveolens* [ROSE GERANIUM] and *P.* × *asperum (= P. graveolens × P. radens)* grown in France, Spain and East Africa. *Attar or otto of Roses is obtained by distillation of the oil obtained from the flowers of the DAMASK ROSE *(*Rosa damascena)* and to a lesser extent from the CABBAGE ROSE *(R. centifolia)* and the MUSK ROSE *(R. moschata)*, which are grown for this purpose in Bulgaria, Italy, France, North Africa and India. Lavender oil is obtained from the flower tops of **Lavandula angustifolia (= L. officinalis)* and *L. latifolia*, grown in France, Spain and England.

Grass oils are obtained from the leaves of several species of **Cymbopogon*, such as *C. nardus*, grown in Java and Ceylon, which yields oil of citronella, and *C. citratus*, cultivated widely in India, tropical Africa and tropical America, which gives lemongrass oil. The roots of another grass, **Vetiveria zizanioides* [*KHUS-KHUS], are used in the production of oil of vetiver, widely used in perfumery.

### Wood oils

Several well-known essential oils are obtained mainly from the wood of a wide range of plant genera. Examples include *camphor and camphor oil, obtained by steam distillation of the wood, twigs and leaves of **Cinnamomum camphora*. Cedar wood oil is obtained, not from cedars, but from **Juniperus virginiana*. Sandalwood oil, used in perfumery and medicine, comes from **Santalum album*, whose fragrant wood is also made into cabinets, while several species of **Eucalyptus*, notably *E. dives* and *E. globulus*, are the source of eucalyptus oil, which is used in medicine and in the refinement of mineral oils by flotation.

### Flavoring oils

Numerous essential oils are used for flavoring in the food and confectionery industries, such as *mint oils from *Mentha* species, eg *M.* × *piperita* [*PEPPERMINT] and *M. spicata* [SPEARMINT], and umbelliferous oils such as caraway from **Carum carvi*, and aniseed from *Pimpinella anisum* and from **Illicium verum* [STAR ANISE]. *Clove oil, obtained from the CLOVE TREE *(Syzygium aromaticum)* and *nutmeg oil from the NUTMEG TREE *(*Myristica fragrans)* are also widely used. (See also Flavorings from Plants, p. 147.)

*A scene from the back of the throne of Tutankhamum depicts the Queen holding a salve-cup and spreading perfumed oil on her husband's collar. (Egypt: 18th dynasty – 1567–1320BC).*

*The Alpine Snow Gum (*Eucalyptus pauciflora *ssp* niphophila*) is one of the hardiest members of its genus.* ($\times\frac{1}{12}$)

tains 40–50% tannin and was formerly much used in tanning processes.

Eucalypts are widely planted (eg in Brazil, North Africa, the Middle East, southern and tropical Africa, the Mediterranean, California, India and on the Black Sea Coast of the USSR) for timber, pulpwood, firewood, shelter, erosion control, essential oil production and ornament.

About 200 species have been introduced into cultivation but the most important species grown outside Australia number only 30 or 40 and are often different from those of greatest importance for timber in Australia. They include *E. camaldulensis* [MURRAY or RIVER RED GUM], *E. globulus*, the most widely cultivated species in the world, especially as the cultivar 'Compacta', *E. microtheca* [COOLABAH, FLOODED BOX], *E. sideroxylon* [RED IRONBARK], and *E. tereticornis* [FOREST RED GUM]. *E. viminalis* [MANNA GUM] is also widely cultivated for its timber, used mainly for house construction, while its bark produces a manna eaten by the natives. Species cultivated for their ornamental value include *E. polyanthemos* [SILVER-DOLLAR GUM] and *E. pulverulenta* [SILVER-LEAVED MOUNTAIN GUM, MONEY TREE]. The leaves of juvenile trees of both these species are used in decorative flower arrangements.
MYRTACEAE, about 550 species.

**Eucharis** a small genus of bulbous, highly fragrant perennials native to tropical Central and South America, mainly Colombia. *E. grandiflora* [AMAZON LILY], from the Andes of Colombia and Peru, with flowers 4–5in across, in umbels of four to six flowers, has been extensively cultivated in hothouses in Europe and elsewhere for its very beautiful and fragrant flowers.
AMARYLLIDACEAE, 10 species.

**Euchlaena** see MAIZE.
GRAMINEAE, 2 species.

**Eucomis** a tropical and southern African genus of bulbous perennials. All the species make good pot plants; the more commonly cultivated include *E. comosa* (= *E. punctata*) [PINEAPPLE FLOWER], with purple-spotted leaves, *E. autumnalis* (= *E. undulata*), with green flowers and undulate leaf margins, and *E. bicolor* with purple-edged flowers and crisped leaf margins.
LILIACEAE, about 14 species.

**Eucryphia** a genus of evergreen (rarely semievergreen or deciduous) trees and shrubs from Chile and Australasia, which bear numerous cup-shaped white flowers. They provide useful timber and are also cultivated for the ornamental value of their flowers and leaves. Among the most widely grown are the Chilean tree *E. cordifolia* and the shrub *E. glutinosa*, and the Tasmanian tree *E. lucida*. A number of hybrids are also valued as ornamentals, notably *E.* × *intermedia* (*E. glutinosa* × *E. lucida*).
EUCRYPHIACEAE, 5 species.

**Eugenia** a large tropical and warm temperate genus of evergreen trees and shrubs. Edible fruits are obtained from *E. uniflora* [FLUTED or RED SURINAM CHERRY], *E. brasiliensis* [BRAZIL CHERRY], *E. pitanga* [PITANGA] and other, chiefly Brazilian, species. Among species formerly ascribed to *Eugenia* and now transferred to other genera are the Old World species now placed in *Syzygium*, including *S. aromaticum* (= *E. aromatica*, *E. caryophyllata*) [CLOVE TREE], *S. jambos* (= *E. jambos*) [YELLOW ROSE APPLE] and *S. cuminii* (= *E. jambolana*) [JAVA PLUM, JAMBOLAN].
MYRTACEAE, about 1 000 species.

*The spectacular midsummer display of* Eucryphia × nymansensis, *a garden hybrid originating in England.* ($\times\frac{1}{12}$)

**Euglena** the most common algae genus; it is often called a "plant-animal" because of the presence of chloroplasts in an organism which has a marked animal-like movement. Members of this genus are mainly found in fresh water and are particularly abundant in richly nitrogenous effluents.
EUGLENOPHYCEAE, about 50 species.

**Eulophia** a predominantly African genus of mainly terrestrial orchids with a few tropical American and tropical Asian species. The majority have tuberous, underground stems. The flowers, which are borne on a long erect spike, vary in color but are usually bright with yellows and reds, although many of the species, especially those from Asia, have muted reds, browns, greens, and dingy creams. The pseudobulbous species from drier areas, such as *E. quartiniana* can be cultivated in a succulent house.
ORCHIDACEAE, about 200 species.

**Euodia** a genus of evergreen or deciduous trees and shrubs occurring in East Asia, Australasia and Madagascar, of which several, including *E. daniellii* and *E. velutina* are cultivated as ornamentals. An infusion of the flowers and leaves of some species, such as *E. lunuankenda*, is used as a tonic.
RUTACEAE, about 50 species.

**Euonymus** a genus of deciduous and evergreen trees and shrubs (rarely creeping) native to Europe, Asia, North and Central America and Australia, but with the greatest concentration of species occurring in the Himalayas and East Asia. Many species are cultivated for their foliage, especially for the autumn colors of leaves and fruits.

The evergreen *E. japonica* is a popular hedging plant often seen in towns and by the seaside. Golden- and variegated-leaf forms are known in cultivation, such as cultivar 'Albomarginata' and cultivar 'Aureovariegata'. The deciduous *E. europaea* [EUROPEAN SPINDLE TREE], which grows to a height of 6m, has several cultivars including 'Aldenhamensis' with bright pink fruits and 'Burtonii' with orange-red fruits. The Asian *E. hamiltoniana* (= *E. sieboldiana*) is another deciduous tree species with several cultivars. Most of the numerous cultivars such as 'Acuta' and 'Vegeta' of the evergreen *E. fortunei* have a low trailing or climbing habit. *E. alata* [WINGED SPINDLE TREE] is one of the most valuable and spectacular autumn-coloring shrubs.

Several species have particularly unusual fruits for which they are cultivated as in the case of *E. americana* [STRAWBERRY BUSH, BURSTING-HEART], which has red, spiny, warty fruits. *E. nanus*, a dwarf species, is cultivated in rock gardens. Apart from the economic value in cultivation, the wood from members of the genus has been used for making spindles, clothes pegs and skewers. The powdered leaves of *E. europaea* have been

used to eradicate lice from children's hair.
CELASTRACEAE, about 175 species.

**Eupatorium** a very large genus of mainly perennial herbs or shrubs, with a few annuals, mostly from Mexico, the West Indies and tropical South America, but a few from Europe, Asia and Africa. The white, pink or purple flowering heads are borne in terminal clusters.

Many species have local medicinal uses. *E. cannabinum* [HEMP AGRIMONY, WATER HEMP] contains the glucoside eupatorin and was once used to treat dropsy. *E. ayapana* from Brazil is cultivated for medicinal Ayapana tea, a stimulant and cure for dyspepsia. A few species, such as *E. coelestinum* [MIST FLOWER], and *E. purpureum*, are ornamentals grown in wild gardens, borders and in temperate climates for autumn flowers. *E. glandulosum* and *E. micranthum* are cultivated in cool greenhouses and *E. atrorubens* and *E. macrophyllum* in warm greenhouses.
COMPOSITAE, about 1200 species.

*Extreme habits of the genus* Euphorbia. *Below* Poinsettia (E. pulcherrima). *Bottom The columnar* E. canariensis *and cushions of* E. aphylla. ($\times \frac{1}{50}$)
(See also p. 768.)

**Euphorbia** a large and important genus distributed throughout the world, with heavier concentrations in certain areas, for example Mexico, the Mediterranean region, southwest Asia and South Africa. The genus includes prostrate annual herbs, biennial and perennial herbs, spiny cushion-plants, shrubs, trees and cactiform succulents ranging from small subglobose types to large candelabra-like arborescent forms. They all, however, share a common type of inflorescence known as a cyathium – a cup-shaped structure bearing glands (four or five) around the rim and containing numerous male flowers surrounding a single female flower. Furthermore, all species exude a poisonous milky latex when cut or damaged.

The most popular cultivated species is *E. pulcherrima* (= *Poinsettia pulcherrima*) [*POINSETTIA, CHRISTMAS FLOWER], a pot shrub with beautiful crimson floral bracts. Some of the smaller succulent euphorbias have become popular pot plants in recent years. *E. milii* [CROWN OF THORNS], native to Madagascar, with bright scarlet or cream-colored leaves subtending the cyathia, is widely cultivated in the tropics. *E. marginata* ["SNOW-ON-THE-MOUNTAIN"], native to the USA, is often cultivated in northern gardens for its green and white banded upper leaves. *E. lactea* [CANDELABRA CACTUS] is cultivated in the open in warmer climates. Other favorite garden species include the perennials *E. griffithii*, *E. sikkimensis*, *E. tirucalli* and *E. wulfenii*.

Although of no great economic importance some species yield locally useful substances. For example *E. antisyphilitica* [CANDELILLA], a shrub of Mexico and South western USA is the source of candelilla wax which when refined is used for polishes and varnishes and incorporated into an assortment of products which require waterproofing. Medicinally useful extracts are obtained from many species including *E. ipecacuanhae* [IPECACUANHA SPURGE] and *E. lathyris* [CAPER SPURGE]. The latex of the Mexican *E. calyculata* [CHIPIRE] and *E. fulva* has been used as a source of rubber. Several species, including *E. lathyrus* and *E. esula* [LEAFY SPURGE], are troublesome weeds.
EUPHORBIACEAE, about 2 000 species.

*The brilliant autumn foliage of the Winged Spindle Tree (*Euonymus alata*), a deciduous species from China and Japan.* ($\times \frac{1}{2}$)

**Euphrasia** [EYEBRIGHTS] a taxonomically difficult group of semiparasitic annual herbs (rarely perennials), mainly in the temperate zone. The name "eyebright" may be derived from the former use of extracts of the leaves of *E. officinalis* as an eyewash.
SCROPHULARIACEAE, 200 or more species.

**Eurhynchium** a genus of mosses of mat-forming or weft-forming habit.
HYPNACEAE, about 45 species.

**Euterpe** a genus of tall, ornamental and graceful palms from tropical Central and South America. The fruits of *E. edulis* [ASSAI PALM] yield a thick, plum-colored liquid. It makes a very popular beverage and is used to flavor ices and sweetmeats. The terminal buds of *E. oleracea* [ASSAI PALM, CABBAGE PALM] and other species are used as a source of "palm hearts", which are eaten fresh or canned, especially in Brazil.
PALMAE, about 20 species.

**Exacum** a subtropical and tropical genus of annual, biennial or perennial herbs and shrubs from Africa and Asia, some of which are grown as ornamentals under glass, especially *E. affine* [GERMAN VIOLET], with fragrant purple flowers, and *E. macranthum*, with showy, rich blue flowers.
GENTIANACEAE, about 20–30 species.

**Exochorda** a genus of hardy deciduous flowering shrubs native to China, Korea, Manchuria and the southern USSR. They are cultivated for their showy white flowers, up to 2in across, which are produced in great profusion in early spring, as exemplified by *E. korolkowii* [PEARL BUSH].
ROSACEAE, 5 species.

**Fagopyrum** [BUCKWHEATS] a genus of perennial and annual herbaceous species of leafy plants often with succulent stems, native to temperate regions of Eurasia. Best-known are *F. esculentum* (= *F. sagittatum*) [COMMON BUCKWHEAT] and *F. tataricum* [INDIAN WHEAT, TARTARY OR SIBERIAN BUCKWHEAT], which are cultivated mainly for their grain in many regions of the world. POLYGONACEAE, about 6 species.

**Fagus** see BEECH.
FAGACEAE, 8–10 species.

× **Fatshedera** a bigeneric hybrid: **Fatsia* × **Hedera*. × *F. lizei* is derived from a cross between *Fatsia japonica* 'Moseri' and *Hedera helix* var *hibernica*. A trailing evergreen shrub with deeply lobed palmate leaves, it originated in cultivation in France.
ARALIACEAE.

**Fatsia** a genus consisting of a single widely grown ornamental evergreen shrub species, *F. japonica* (= *Aralia sieboldii*) [FORMOSA RICE TREE, PAPER PLANT], native to Japan. It produces dark green shiny leaves and umbels of white flowers in large terminal panicles.
ARALIACEAE, 1 species.

*Common Buckwheat (*Fagopyrum esculentum*) is a minor crop in many parts of the world.* ($\times \frac{1}{10}$)

**Faucaria** [TIGER JAWS] a genus of dwarf succulent, almost stemless perennial herbs all native to South Africa. Each plant has several pairs of leaves united at the base, keeled underneath and interlocking when young by their toothed margins, hence the popular name. The daisy-like flowers are mainly yellow in the most commonly cultivated species, *F. felina*, *F. tigrina* and *F. tuberculosa*, but there are one or two white-flowered varieties. Normally cultivation is confined to the greenhouse in the cooler temperate regions.
AIZOACEAE, about 36 species.

**Feijoa** a genus comprising two species of shrubs or small trees native to subtropical South America. *F. sellowiana* [PINEAPPLE GUAVA] is cultivated as an ornamental and for its edible fruits. It has glossy green leaves (whitish beneath) and ovoid fruits whose fleshy pulp may be eaten raw, stewed or as a preserve.
MYRTACEAE, 2 species.

**Felicia** a genus of annual or perennial shrubby herbs from tropical and southern Africa. They are prized for their daisy-like flowers and are often grown in rock gardens. A favorite is *F. bergerana* [KINGFISHER DAISY] with its mass of small azure blue flower heads. Taller species, such as *F. amelloides* [BLUE DAISY, BLUE MARGUERITE] make good pot or bedding plants.
COMPOSITAE, about 60 species.

**Fennel** the common name for **Foeniculum vulgare*, a commonly cultivated herb. Both leaves and seeds have a pleasant aniseed flavor and are often added to fish, and to soups, poultry, salad and vegetable dishes. *F. vulgare* var *azoricum* [FINOCCHIO, FLORENCE FENNEL OR SWEET FENNEL] is a shorter plant with swollen leaf-bases. These are eaten in salads, and the so-called bulbs used as a vegetable in their own right, or simply as a flavoring. *F. vulgare* var *dulce*, which does not have swollen leaf-bases, is cultivated for the essential oils in the fruits.

The name GIANT FENNEL is given to species of another genus of the carrot family, **Ferula*. In addition LOVE-IN-A-MIST (**Nigella*, family Ranunculaceae) is often called FENNEL FLOWER.
UMBELLIFERAE.

**Ferns** see p. 140.

**Ferocactus** a genus of cacti from the deserts of Mexico and the southern USA popularly known as BARREL OR HEDGEHOG CACTI. They are large globose to cylindrical cacti with prominently ribbed stems covered in large, straight or hooked spines. They produce long bell-shaped yellow, pink or red flowers. Many species are grown as indoor or greenhouse pot plants, such as *F. acanthodes* (= *Echinocactus acanthodes*) with yellow flowers and

*Giant Fennel (*Ferula communis*) growing on the Aegean Island of Patmos.* ($\times \frac{1}{10}$)

*F. latispinus* [DEVIL'S TONGUE] with red to purple flowers.
CACTACEAE, about 30 species.

**Ferula** a genus of stately herbaceous perennials, native to the Mediterranean, western and Central Asia. *Ferula* species, such as *F. communis* [GIANT FENNEL], make handsome garden plants, providing fine foliage in the larger herbaceous border, or specimen plants in isolation. The roots of *F. foetida* and *F. narthex* yield the resin asafoetida, used as an antispasmodic in medicine and as a condiment in Iran, where it is popularly known as "food of the gods". *F. galbaniflua* exudes galbanum, an oleo-gum-resin used medicinally as an expectorant and antispasmodic.
UMBELLIFERAE, about 130 species.

**Fescue** the common name for *Festuca*, a genus of annual or perennial grasses mostly from temperate regions of the Northern Hemisphere. The most interesting and horticulturally important species are those upland fine-textured species that have been selected for use in cultivated turf and lawn grass mixtures.

*F. rubra* [CREEPING OR RED FESCUE] is a fine-leaved, hard-wearing species with many new strains emerging for use in amenity turf. *F. ovina* [SHEEP'S FESCUE] is a delicate, tufted species for cold, acidic and dry soils. *F. glaucescens* is an exceptionally fine, dwarf species of blue-green color found in marsh turf in Cumbria, England. Other species, such as *F. ovina* var *glauca* [BLUE FESCUE], have considerable ornamental value and are used in contemporary landscape planting for ground cover. Several species, such as *F. elatior*, *F. ovina* and *F. rubra*, are cultivated as meadow and forage grasses.
GRAMINEAE, about 100 species.

**Fibers** see p. 144.

# Ferns

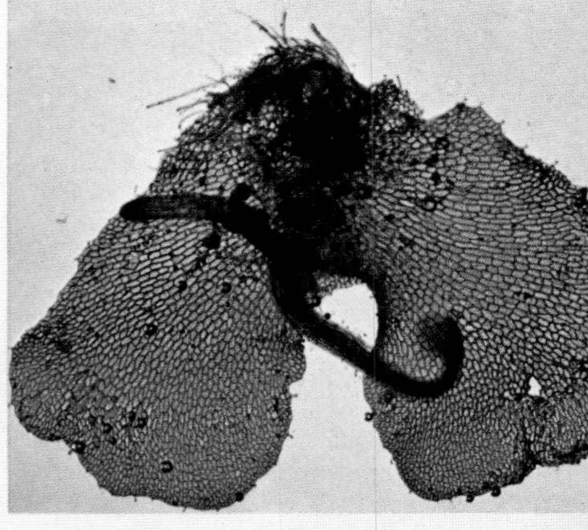

*The prothallus of a fern. This is the sexual (or gametophytic) stage of the life cycle.* (×25)

THE FERNS ARE THE MOST ADVANCED OF THE spore-producing plants and today represent the largest class (Filicophytina) of the lower vascular plants (pteridophytes), which also includes the *club mosses and *horsetails. They are, however, unique among the pteridophytes in that they, mostly, bear large photosynthetic leaves (fronds) which more closely resemble those of the more advanced seed plants (*conifers and *angiosperms).

The fossil record of true ferns is generally accepted as beginning with the Carboniferous Period (see pp. 738–739), although fossils with fern-like characteristics have been found as early as Devonian times. Today, for the most part, ferns are mesophytic plants, with thin leaf tissue, preferring moist shady habitats such as those found in woods and forest undergrowth, and beside rocky streams and in gorges. They are most abundant in the everwet climate of the tropical rain forest or the warm-temperate oceanic areas, eg New Zealand and the Canary Isles. In such climates they not only form the dominant herb layer in the forest but are also abundant as epiphytes on the trees or festooning rock walls. However, by no means all have a typical fern-like appearance and form. Some, such as *Cyathea* and **Dicksonia* reach the stature of small trees, while others, such as **Azolla*, are minute and aquatic. So-called filmy ferns (family Hymenophyllaceae) have very flimsy, almost transparent leaves. They inhabit moist areas, such as rain forests and cloud zones on mountains, and many tropical species are epiphytic. Some species of fern are specially adapted to drier ecological niches, eg exposed rockfaces, but these species require a deep crevice or seasonal wet periods for sexual reproduction to take place. So-called nest ferns, such as members of the genus **Platycerium* [STAGHORN FERNS], produce a mantle of leaves which cling closely around tree branches. Humus and water collect in these structures, thus providing a substrate of nutrient and moisture for the roots of the plant.

Polypodium injectum *is an epiphytic fern that grows in bark crevices.* ($\times \frac{1}{4}$)

**Economic Uses.** Ferns have limited uses in the modern world and even primitive peoples who rely on wild plants for food, medicines and building materials have few uses for them. Mature ferns are mostly poisonous or at least contain alkaloids that cause sickness and diarrhea; in their young stages, however, some species may be eaten. In New Guinea and other places in Southeast Asia a common species on river banks and open places is *Diplazium esculentum* (known in Malay as PAKU); this is commonly eaten boiled like spinach, which it resembles in taste. The same species – called NINGRO in Sikkim – is used there as a vegetable.

Young fronds of tree ferns (*Cyathea* spp) are eaten in New Guinea in a similar way and in the United States fronds of the OSTRICH FERN (**Matteuccia struthiopteris*) are sold deep-frozen or in cans. Very young unfurling croziers of *BRACKEN (*Pteridium aquilinum*) may be blanched and the cortical tissue eaten although mature bracken contains carcinogenic chemicals and for this reason this species should be avoided. The ripe sporocarps (nardoo) of **Marsilea* species are pounded and mixed with water by Australian aborigines to make a starchy "bread". The bulbous tubers of **Nephrolepis cordifolia* are similarly used by tribes in Sikkim.

Medicinal uses of species are no longer important. Both the MALE FERN ( **Dryopteris filix-mas*) and the POLYPODY (**Polypodium vulgare*) were used by early apothecaries as kidney flushes and vermifuges. Primitive tribes in New Guinea and South America utilize the vascular strands of the SUN FERN (**Gleichenia* spp) and of the CLIMBING FERN (**Lygodium* spp) to weave armlets and neck ornaments and today such skills are redirected to make trays, place-mats and coasters for the tourist trade. The trunks of tree ferns (*Cyathea* spp) are prized as long-lasting house posts throughout New Guinea. Tree ferns in Central and South America are in danger of extinction through overexploitation for use as hanging baskets and as a source of fiber.

In many parts of the world there has been in recent years an upsurge of interest in ferns as desirable plants for cultivation. They fill the need for restful greens as a contrast to the bright colors of flowers and in the garden they usefully occupy shady places and can be grown in light woodland, on banks, along the margins of ponds and streams and in wall crevices.

**Structure and Reproduction.** Ferns have two distinct stages in their life-cycle: firstly there is the sporophyte (or spore-producing stage)

*The nest fern* Platycerium bifurcatum *(Staghorn Fern).* ($\times \frac{1}{5}$)

which is the typical fern that we recognize and secondly there is the gametophyte (or sexual stage), which is difficult to find by the untrained eye.

For the most part the stem of the sporophyte generation is confined to a rootstock or rhizome. This should not be confused with

*Various forms of sori (clusters of sporangia) found in some common temperate ferns.*
Left Top Dryopteris filix-mas: *round, mixed sori covered by a kidney-shaped indusium.* Left Bottom Asplenium *sp: a marginal sorus covered by a flap-like indusium.* Right Top Platycerium *sp: this lacks true sori, the sporangia being widely distributed over the whole leaf.* Right Middle Phyllitis scolopendrium*: a linear sorus bordered by a long narrow indusium.* Right Bottom Pteridium *sp: a linear mixed sorus that lacks an indusium (ie is naked), but is protected by the inrolled edges of the leaflets.* (×5, ×5, ×1, ×6, ×5)

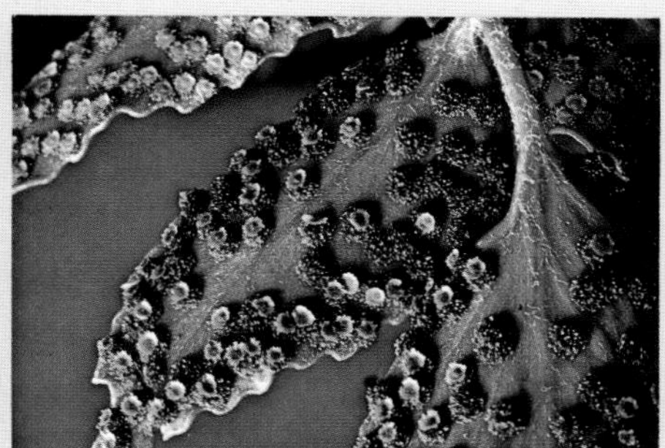

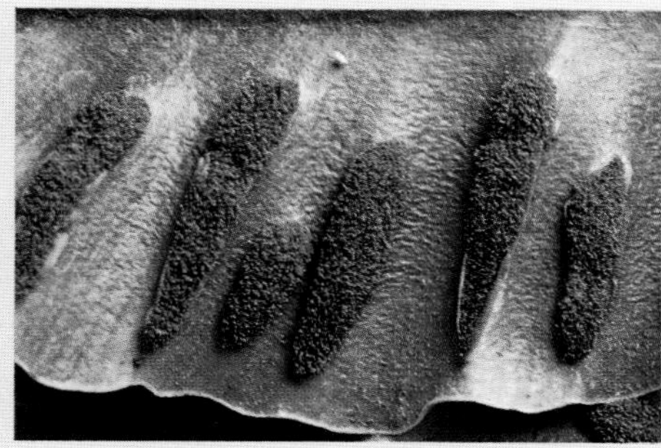

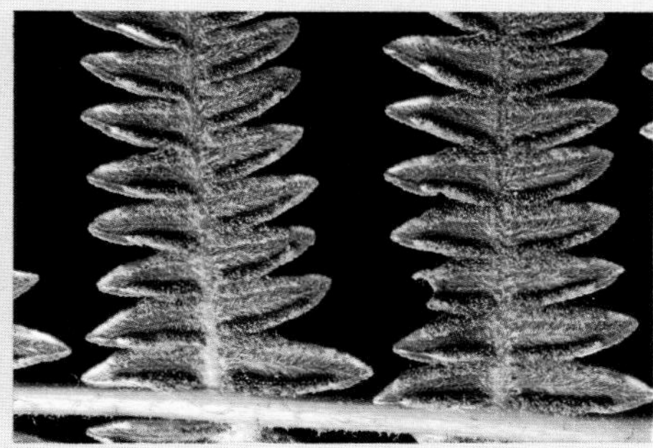

the upright stalk-bearing compound leaves as seen in bracken or the central stalk (rachis) of other ferns; these are midribs of the compound leaf system, not stems. The creeping rhizome may be a thin, wiry, branched system as in the tropical filmy ferns or the EUROPEAN OAK FERN (*Gymnocarpium* spp) or it may be thicker as in *Polypodium vulgare* or the NARROW BUCKLER FERN (*Dryopteris carthusiana*). The rhizome is normally horizontal, but may be more upright. This upright form is seen fully developed in the tree ferns of the tropics and the warm temperate zones of the Southern Hemisphere. These belong mainly to the genus *Cyathea* or *Dicksonia*. Some species of **Blechnum* may also have short stems 3–6.5ft high. Tree ferns may reach over 60ft.

Ferns can usually be distinguished from seed plants in having no secondary growth and therefore no wood or bark. The single exception to this is the genus **Botrychium* [MOONWORT and GRAPE FERN] which may form a vascular cambium. The traditional leaf shape of the fern, as seen in the LADY FERNS (**Athyrium* spp) or BUCKLER FERNS (*Dryopteris* spp), is compound, twice or three-times pinnately dissected. Such leaves, each with a central axis (rachis) and side leaflets, which themselves may be feather-like, are by no means the dominant kind, although the immediate ancestors of ferns may well have had this kind of leaf. Many species characteristically found festooning the trunks of tropical rain forest trees have simple leaves. Yet other fern leaves are palmate or dichotomously divided. Size of leaf may vary from a fraction of an inch in *Didymoglossum* to 6.5ft or more in some tree ferns.

The spore-bearing structures (sporangia) may be borne on the underside of foliage leaves, on modified leaves or on separate stalks. Sporangia form is one of the major characters in classification. In what is known as eusporangiate forms the sporangia walls comprise two layers or more, often over 0.04in across and are without stalks. In these cases the sporangia may be fused in clusters (synangia) or fused into a column as in the characteristic "adders tongue" of **Ophioglossum*. In *Botrychium* they are not fused but are globose and sessile on a branched organ (sporophore) and resemble a bunch of grapes. In leptosporangiate forms the sporangia are minute, stalked, globose structures, with walls only one cell thick. In intermediate forms the sporangia tend to be separate and thin-walled but sessile. Dehiscence of the sporangia also varies: in the eusporangiate and intermediate forms the wall cells simply dry and shrink, the capsule finally opening along a predetermined line of weaker cells (stomium). In the leptosporangiate forms a specialized row of cells (annulus) possess thickened walls, which on drying straighten out, thus breaking the cells at its weakest point. The inner cell walls of this "hinge" retain enough moisture to contract again and act as a spring, pulling the sporangium shut and projecting the spores into the surrounding air currents. In many ferns the sporangia arise usually in clusters (sori) from a pad of cells (receptacle) on the underside of the leaf. The structure positioning and arrangement of sori can vary greatly, but there are three basic types. In the simple type the sporangia are the same age and mature together. In the gradate sorus those at the apex of the receptacle mature first, while in the mixed sorus the receptacle continues to produce sporangia randomly over a period.

The dispersed spores germinate to produce the gametophyte. This varies in morphology but is always small and insignificant and most often heart-shaped. The gametophyte tends to be overlooked by the average person or thought to be a liverwort. The fern gametophyte (prothallus) produces motile sperm-cells within the male sex organs (antheridia), which are released and swim to fertilize the enveloped egg-cells which are produced in the female sex organs (archegonia). The fertilized egg germinates to give rise to the next sporophyte stage.

*Ferns used as houseplants. From left to right* Pteris cretica *(Ribbon Fern),* Adiantum capillus-veneris *(Common Maiden-Hair Fern),* Pteris *sp,* Asplenium nidus *(Bird's Nest Fern),* Adiantum *sp,* Platycerium bifurcatum *(Staghorn Fern).* ($\times\frac{1}{10}$)

**Ficus** a large pantropical genus of small shrubs, large trees up to 145ft tall and woody, root-clinging climbers. They are frequently evergreen in tropical zones, but tend to become deciduous in temperate zones. Some species are glabrous, as in *F. elastica* [INDIA RUBBER FIG, CAOUTCHOUC], others hairy, or with stinging hairs (*F. minahassae*) or with silica bodies in the leaves (*F. scabra*). The presence of latex vessels is universal throughout the plant and, in fact, the latex of *F. elastica* was used extensively in rubber manufacture up to the mid-19th century.

Figs have a characteristic inflorescence, termed a syconium, a flask-shaped fleshy container with many minute flowers densely arranged on the inner walls. Fertilization is achieved by gall wasps (*Blastophaga* spp) which enter the syconium to lay their eggs, the newly-hatched adults carrying pollen to another syconium.

Several species of fig are classed as "stranglers": here the fig grows around a host plant, slowly enclosing it and often eventually killing it. This strange habit is common in tropical species, for example *F. pertusa* and *F. cordifolia*. The strangler fig begins from a seed dropped in the fork of a twig by a fig-eating mammal or bird. As the seed germinates it begins to grow downwards, the roots wrapping round the host. The effect is to crush the bark, thus ringing the tree and destroying its food-bearing vessels. Eventually the fig survives as a free-standing tree.

Other species are called *banyans, the best-known being *F. benghalensis* [BANYAN TREE, EAST INDIAN FIG, INDIAN BANYAN]. This species is a large tree which, though indigenous to the Himalayan foothills, is now widespread throughout India, as for centuries it has been planted in many villages for the excellent shade it provides. The Hindus also regard it as sacred, for it is said that Buddha once meditated beneath a banyan tree. Perhaps its most interesting botanical features are pillar-like aerial roots which grow vertically downwards from the branches and, once established in the ground below, quickly thicken, so that the tree assumes the unusual appearance of being supported by pillars. By this manner of growth the tree is able to spread outwards almost indefinitely, and many examples are of immense size and great antiquity. The timber is fairly hard and durable but light in weight. It is used for a variety of purposes in India, including furniture, door panels and cart shafts. A type of paper is made from the bark. The COMMON or EDIBLE FIG (*F. carica*) has a long history of cultivation, beginning in Syria probably before 4 000 BC. Since then it has held an important place in folklore and literature. The art of fig culture was first documented by the Greek poet Archilochus, around 700 BC, and there are many references to the fig in the Bible. It grows successfully in many tropical and some temperate habitats, usually on dry, higher ground. The main areas of cultivation are California, Turkey, Greece and Italy. The COMMON FIG is a small tree, less than 33ft tall, with large palmately lobed leaves 4–8in long. There are two fruiting types, Adriatic and Smyrna. The more common ADRIATIC FIG does not have male flowers and the fig fruits develop from the female flowers without the need for pollination and fertilization. Its seeds are undeveloped and infertile. The SMYRNA FIG also has no male flowers, but differs in that the female flowers require pollination. To achieve this, branches of WILD FIGS with male flowers are attached to SMYRNA FIG trees at the time fig wasps are expected to emerge, thus allowing cross-pollination. The WILD FIG with male flowers is known as the CAPRIFIG, and the process described is known as caprification. All fig cultivars produce a main crop which develops on the current season's growth and matures in August to November. However, in some cultivars, syconia emerge on the previous autumn's shoots, producing a first or "breba" crop in June to July.

There are many other species of *Ficus* with edible fruits, for example *F. racemosa* [CLUSTER FIG], a common tree of East Asia. Although edible, the fruits are hardly palatable by Western standards, the figs being full of insects or hard seeds. *F. religiosa* [PEEPUL or PEEPAL TREE], venerated by Hindus and Buddhists, is often planted as a shade tree because of its dense, spreading crown. Several species are used as host trees for the lac insect, for example *F. semicordata* (= *F. cunia*) and *F. rumphii*. The insect secretes a resinous substance (*lac) which in its purified form (shellac) is used for several purposes, particularly in the manufacture of varnish and for electrical insulation. In temperate zones, some species are grown as houseplants. The commonest is the RUBBER PLANT, which is a sapling of *F. elastica* var *decora*. Also grown are *F. pumila* [CLIMBING FIG] and *F. benjamina* [WEEPING FIG or JAVA WILLOW].

MORACEAE, about 2 000 species.

Fissidens serrulatus *is a mainly western Mediterranean species with a distribution extending into southern England.* (×4)

*Inflorescence of the Meadowsweet (*Filipendula ulmaria*), which is common in damp meadows and is also cultivated.* (×1)

**Filipendula** a genus of hardy herbaceous perennials of the north temperate region, often grown as garden ornamentals. *F. ulmaria* [MEADOWSWEET, QUEEN OF THE MEADOW], common in wet meadows and woods, is characterized by its crowded irregular clusters of creamy white flowers and sweet scent. Oil of meadowsweet is distilled from the flower buds and used in perfumery. The yellow cultivar 'Aurea' and the double-flowered cultivar 'Plena' are grown in gardens. Varieties of *F. vulgaris* (= *F. hexapetala*, *Spiraea filipendula*) [DROPWORT], *F. purpurea* (= *Spiraea palmata*) and *F. rubra* [QUEEN OF THE PRAIRIE] are also cultivated.

ROSACEAE, 10 species.

**Fissidens** one of the largest genera of mosses, cosmopolitan but with the chief concentration of species in the tropics. Most are small delicate plants and some are almost microscopic. The leafy shoots are instantly recognizable as *Fissidens* because in contrast with most mosses, the leaves are strictly two-ranked.
FISSIDENTACEAE, about 1 000 species.

**Fittonia** a small genus of creeping perennial herbs with attractive foliage, native to South America but sometimes cultivated in greenhouses. Both *F. gigantea* and *F. verschaffeltii* have broad, entire leaves with colored or white veins.
ACANTHACEAE, 2–3 species.

**Fitzroya** a genus represented by a single species, *F. cupressoides* [PATAGONIAN CYPRESS], a large evergreen tree with reddish bark, native to Chile. It yields a valuable timber, particularly useful for general carpentry and construction as well as for musical instruments and pencils.
CUPRESSACEAE, 1 species.

**Flavorings from plants** see p. 147.

**Flax** the common name for **Linum usitatissimum*, an annual plant which is grown widely in Canada, the USA, the USSR, Europe, Argentina, Uruguay and India for its stem fiber (fiber flax) which is spun to produce linen threads and yarns for weaving into pure linen cloth, or to be mixed with other fibers in production of other materials. Its particular value lies in its strength and durability compared to other natural fibers such as cotton or wool.

The plant is also grown for its seed oil [OIL FLAX, SEED FLAX, *LINSEED], a drying oil used in paints, varnishes, putty and linoleum. The residue, linseed cake, is a valuable animal feed. Although flax may be grown for both fiber and oil (dual purpose flax) it is mainly grown for oil production in warmer drier regions. The best quality flax for fiber is grown in Belgium and Northern Ireland, as it is suited to moist soils and damp climates.

"Flax" is a name given to many other species of *Linum*, eg *L. narbonense* [BLUE FLAX], *L. catharticum* [FAIRY FLAX], *L. pubescens* [PINK FLAX], and to species of other genera, eg **Daphne gnidium* [SPURGE FLAX], **Phormium tenax* [NEW ZEALAND FLAX] and **Camelina sativa* [FALSE FLAX].
LINACEAE.

**Flour** is usually understood to be a very finely pounded form of WHEAT (**Triticum aestivum*), but other foodstuffs may be milled into flour, namely *potato, *rice, *maize, *rye, *barley, *oats, *soybean, *peas and *beans. When whole wheat grain is pounded, a brown whole wheat or 100% extraction flour is produced. If part of the germ (embryo in the grain) and bran (pericarp, testa and aleurone) are removed the flour formed is called pale brown wheat meal or 85–95% extraction. However, consumer preference is for white flour or 72–76% extraction, which has improved baking and keeping qualities because it is only ground from the starchy endosperm.

Bread flour has a protein content of 11–12%, with a high level of good-quality gluten proteins which are required to produce well-risen bread with a fine internal crumb structure. Wheat varieties inherently containing good breadmaking proteins are termed "strong", whereas "weak" wheats contain poor breadmaking proteins. Bread flour must contain low levels of enzymes that degrade carbohydrates and proteins because these enzymes can ruin bread texture, making it coarse and sticky. Bread flour is milled so that it contains a high level of damaged starch grains, which are required to make non-sticky doughs with a high water content. Household flour, used for cakes and pastries, and biscuit flour are milled from weak low-protein wheats that have low enzyme activity. Soup flours must have good gelling characteristics in the starch and also low enzyme activity.

In several countries, all types of flour, except wholemeal, have to contain certain minimum quantities of iron, vitamin B and nicotinic acid. Calcium is added to all except self-raising flour and wholemeal flours.

*Reaping Flax (*Linum usitatissimum*). The fiber-producing varieties are sown close together and have tall unbranched stems.*

*Flax plants (*Linum usitatissimum*) in flower. The flowers can be blue or white, the blue-flowered varieties producing the finest yarn. An oil is also extracted from the seed. (×1)*

**Foeniculum** a genus of tall biennial or perennial herbs native to Europe and the Mediterranean. The leaves are dissected into narrow segments which with the umbels of yellow flowers make them easily recognizable. (See also FENNEL.)
UMBELLIFERAE, 2–3 species.

**Fodder crops** see p. 149.

**Fomes** a fungal genus characterized by having tough, bracket-shaped fruiting bodies. Most species are actively wood-rotting, and several cause serious diseases and economic losses of trees and shrubs. One of the commonest is *F. annosus*, which attacks a wide variety of conifers. It enters stumps either through the freshly cut surface by means of air-borne spores or through roots already infected at the time of felling. Stumps then act as sources of infection to surrounding trees, the fungal hyphae passing from root to root.

There are several tropical representatives, such as *F. noxius*, which attacks the roots of important crops, including cocoa, coffee, tea and rubber.
HYMENOCHAETACEAE, about 100 species.

# Fibers from Plants

The use of plant fibers antedates civilization. Perhaps torn strips of bark first "held things together" for emerging *Homo sapiens*, and braided palm fronds might have sheltered him as he subsisted a million or more years ago on the inland African lakes. There is little archaeological evidence regarding the use of fibers as they do not preserve very well, but diggings of sites dating back to ten thousand years or even earlier, have revealed the use of many plant fibers, often in a very sophisticated manner. **Agave* fibers 8 000 years old are known from excavations in the Tehuacan Valley, Mexico and remains of woven palm-leaf fabric about 12 000 years old have also been found in Mexico.

Xylem (wood) of trees is the world's most prolific source of fiber. Wood fiber can be separated to make paper (see later) or be dissolved and restructured to make synthetic fibers such as rayon (viscose). Plant cells from seed, bark, and monocotyledon leaves, used for textiles, cordage and stuffing, are more "conventional" fibers. Like wood fibers they consist of cellulose cell walls with some lignin and other substances. Cellulose is fiber material par excellence. Lignin is more resistant to decay than cellulose, but is generally unwanted because it makes fibers harsh and prone to discoloration; it is normally dissolved away in the making of chemical paper pulps.

A wide assortment of plants belonging to 44 families yield useful vegetable fibers. They fall more or less naturally into three categories: (1) surface fibers, borne externally, the most important of which are *COTTON and *KAPOK; (2) "soft" or bast fibers, from dicotyledonous bark, of which *FLAX, RAMIE, *HEMP and *JUTE are the most important; and (3) "hard" or structural fibers, the fibrovascular bundles in foliage of monocotyledons, such as *ABACA and *SISAL. Surface fibers are used chiefly for textiles and as stuffing materials, soft fibers mostly for weaving, and hard fibers mostly for cordage (twines and ropes). A miscellaneous assortment of twigs, split stems, sectioned palm leaves and so on are used for brooms, brushes, baskets, and for coarse weaving into mats.

In recent years the production of synthetic fibers exceeded that of natural fibers, but following the dramatic increase in oil prices and conservationist policies, there is a renewed interest in natural fibers.

**Paper.** The biggest and most important use of vegetable fibers is in the manufacture of paper. PAPYRUS, in use as early as 3500 BC, can be described as the forerunner of paper. It consisted of strips of water reeds (**Cyperus papyrus*) laid in a network, soaked with water and beaten flat. Papyrus was the staple writing surface until it gradually lost its popularity to animal parchment after 200 BC.

A chinese eunuch named Ts'ai Lun has been accredited with the invention of paper in the year AD 105, but a further 700 years elapsed before the secrets of the technique

COMMERCIAL VEGETABLE FIBERS
*(excluding wood fibers and those used for paper making)*

| Family and Scientific name | Popular name | Principal growing areas | Uses |
|---|---|---|---|
| **AGAVACEAE** | | | |
| **Agave cantala* | MAGUEY | SE Pacific, SE Asia | Cordage, sacking |
| *Agave fourcroydes* | HENEQUIN | Mexico | Cordage, sacking |
| *Agave heteracantha* | *ISTLI FIBER | Mexico | Brooms |
| *Agave sisalana* | *SISAL (HEMP) | E Africa | Cordage, sacking |
| *Furcraea gigantea* var *willemettiana* | MAURITIUS HEMP | Mauritius | Cordage, mats |
| **Phormium tenax* | NEW ZEALAND FLAX | New Zealand | Cordage |
| **Sansevieria cylindrica* | BOWSTRING HEMP | Africa, Asia, Florida | Cordage |
| *Sansevieria trifasciata* | SNAKE PLANT | | Cordage |
| *Sansevieria hyacinthoides* (= *guineensis*) | AFRICAN BOWSTRING HEMP | Africa, Asia | Cordage |
| *Sansevieria roxburghiana* | INDIAN BOWSTRING HEMP | India | Cordage |
| *Sansevieria zeylanica* | CEYLON BOWSTRING HEMP | Africa, Asia | Cordage |
| **APOCYNACEAE** | | | |
| **Apocynum cannabinum* | INDIAN HEMP, HEMP DOGBANE | N America | String, cloth |
| *Apocynum venetum* | HEMP DOGBANE | N America | String, fishing nets |
| **ASCLEPIADACEAE** | | | |
| **Asclepias incarnata* | SWAMP MILKWEED, OZONE FIBER | N America | Cordage |
| *Asclepias syriaca* | MILKWEED | N America | Cordage |
| **BOMBACACEAE** | | | |
| **Bombax ceiba* | RED SILK COTTON TREE, WHITE KAPOK | India, SE Asia | Stuffing |
| **Ceiba pentandra* | *KAPOK, SILK COTTON TREE | Asia | Stuffing |
| **Ochroma pyramidale* | *BALSA, CORKWOOD | C America, W Indies | Packing, insulation |
| **BROMELIACEAE** | | | |
| **Aechmea magdalenae* | PITA | Colombia | Cordage, sacking |
| *Ananas comosus* | *PINEAPPLE | Philippines | Cordage, sacking |
| *Neoglaziovia variegata* | CAROA | Brazil | Cordage, basketry |
| **Tillandsia usneoides* | SPANISH MOSS | Tropical America | Packing |
| **CYCLANTHACEAE** | | | |
| **Carludovica palmata* | PANAMA HAT PALM | C America | Panama hats, mats |
| **GRAMINEAE** | | | |
| **Bambusa* and many other genera (eg **Arundinaria*, **Dendrocalamus*, *Melocanna*, *Ochlandra*, **Phyllostachys*, **Sasa*) | *BAMBOO | Pantropical | Mats, baskets, cordage, paper |
| **Lygeum spartum* | *ESPARTO | N Africa | Cordage, paper |
| **Stipa tenacissima* | ESPARTO | N Africa | Cordage, paper |
| **LEGUMINOSAE** | | | |
| **Crotalaria juncea* | *SUN HEMP | Tropical Asia | Cordage |
| **Sesbania aculeata* | | Africa, Asia | Fishing nets |
| *Sesbania aegyptica* | | Tropical India | Cordage |
| **LINACEAE** | | | |
| *Linum usitatissimum* | *FLAX, LINEN | Europe | Textiles |
| **MALVACEAE** | | | |
| **Abutilon avicennae* | *CHINA JUTE, INDIAN MALLOW | China, USSR | Sacking, tough cloth |
| *Gossypium* spp | *COTTON | N America, Africa, Asia | Textiles |
| **Hibiscus cannabinus* | KENAF | India | Sacking, tough cloth |
| *Hibiscus sabdariffa* | ROSELLE | India | Sacking, tough cloth |
| **Pavonia bojeri* | | Madagascar | Cloth |
| *Pavonia shimperiana* | | Africa | Cloth |
| **Sida cordifolia* | QUEENSLAND HEMP | India, China | Ropes, cloth |
| *Sida rhombifolia* | QUEENSLAND HEMP | India, China | Ropes, cloth |
| *Urena lobata* | *ARAMINA, CONGO JUTE | S America, Africa | Ropes, sacking |

left China and reached the Arabs. The Moors introduced paper making to Spain in the 12th century and it was a further 300 years before it was in use in the rest of Europe.

The basic principles of paper making have not been changed since their inception.

| | | | |
|---|---|---|---|
| **MORACEAE** | | | |
| **Broussonetia papyrifera* | TAPA (KAPA) | E Asia, Polynesia | Cloth, rope |
| **Cannabis sativa* | *HEMP | Asia | Rope, sacking |
| **MUSACEAE** | | | |
| **Ensete ventricosa* | ABYSSINIAN BANANA | African, SE Asia | Cordage, sacking |
| **Musa textilis* | *ABACA, MANILA HEMP | Philippines, C America | Rope, cordage |
| **PALMAE** | | | |
| **Arenga saccharifera* | SUGAR PALM | | Rope, thatch, brushes |
| *Attalea funifera* | *BAHIA PIASSAVA | Brazil | Brooms, brushes |
| **Borassus flabellifer* | PALMYRA PALM | Africa | Brooms, baskets, fencing |
| *Calamus* spp | *RATTAN CANE, *MALACCA CANE | SE Asia | Baskets, mats, chair seats |
| **Caryota urens* | KITUL FIBER | Tropical Asia, Australia | Ropes, brushes, baskets |
| **Chamaerops humilis* | DWARF FAN PALM | NW Africa | Horsehair, cordage, baskets |
| *Cocos nucifera* | *COCONUT, *COIR | Polynesia, Tropics | Mats, brushes, cordage |
| *Daemonorops* spp | *RATTAN CANE | SE Asia | Baskets, mats, chair seats |
| *Metroxylon sagu* | *SAGO PALM | SE Asia | Thatch |
| *Nypa fruticans* | *NYPA PALM | SE Asia | Thatch, matting |
| *Raphia* spp | *RAFFIA | Africa | Twine, matting, baskets |
| *Raphia hookeri* | *RAFFIA, *PIASSAVA FIBER | Africa | Brooms, baskets, fencing |
| *Sabal palmetto* | | C America, W Indies | Thatch, baskets |
| **Trachycarpus excelsus* | CHINESE WINDMILL PALM | E Asia | Cordage, brushes |
| **STERCULIACEAE** | | | |
| **Abroma augustum* | DEVIL'S COTTON | Asia, Australia | Ropes, cordage |
| **TILIACEAE** | | | |
| *Corchorus capsularis* | *JUTE | India, Bangladesh | Sacking |
| *Corchorus olitorius* | JUTE | India, Africa | Sacking |
| **URTICACEAE** | | | |
| **Boehmeria nivea* | RAMIE, CHINA GRASS | Asia | Rope |

Paper, simply described, is a thin tissue composed of any fibrous vegetable material. The individual fibers are first separated by mechanical or chemical action and then reconstituted in a sheet form, by depositing the fibers on to a wire mesh using water.

Although any vegetable matter can be used for paper making, the principal raw materials fall into the following categories: seed hairs (COTTON, once used for high-grade writing and printing papers); bast fibers (FLAX, HEMP, JUTE and RAMIE which are particularly strong but resistant to bleaching); grass fibers (cereal straws and bagasse); leaf fibers (ESPARTO, SISAL and MANILA HEMP which have strength and are tear resistant, but hard to bleach); wood fibers (the major group, particularly the conifers of North America and Scandinavia, eg *SPRUCE, *Picea excelsa*, and PINE, **Pinus sylvestris*). The deciduous trees, the hardwoods, produce shorter fibers (0.06in compared to 0.14in of the conifers). **Eucalyptus*, *POPLAR, *CHESTNUT and *BIRCH are particularly in demand.

*Important fiber-producing plants. 1 Hemp–stem ($\times\frac{1}{4}$, $\times 1$); 2 Cotton–seed hairs ($\times\frac{1}{3}$); 3 Manila Hemp–"stem" of sheathing leaf bases (shown in cross-section) ($\times\frac{1}{100}$, $\times\frac{1}{20}$); 4 Jute–stem ($\times\frac{1}{6}$, $\times 1$); Flax–stem ($\times\frac{1}{3}$); 6 Raffia–leaves ($\times\frac{1}{300}$); 7 Kapok–seed hairs ($\times\frac{1}{5}$); 8 Dwarf Fan Palm–leaves ($\times\frac{1}{50}$); 9 Sisal–leaves ($\times\frac{1}{50}$); 10 Esparto Grass–leaves ($\times\frac{1}{4}$); 11 Ramie–stem ($\times\frac{1}{16}$); 12 Pineapple–leaves ($\times\frac{1}{20}$); 13 Coir–husk surrounding the coconut ($\times\frac{1}{300}$, $\times\frac{1}{12}$).*

1
2
3
4
5
6
7
8
9
10
11
12
13
14
15
16
17
18
19
20
21
22

# Flavorings from Plants

A wide range of plants are used to provide materials that are added in small quantities to food and beverages to give flavoring or improve their taste. Flavoring plants include all *herbs, spices and condiments and may be used fresh, dried or preserved in some way. They normally have no nutritive value. Many of them have been known since earliest times, especially in the Greek, Roman and other civilizations bordering the eastern Mediterranean and in India and the East Indies.

Spices have played an important role in the history of civilization, exploration and commerce. Most spices are tropical in origin and are mainly produced on islands. They were among the first products to be exported from the tropics to the temperate regions. They were usually very expensive. Early Arabs had the monopoly of the spice trade, obtaining the spices in India, some of which had been brought there from further east. It was largely a desire to take part in the lucrative spice trade which led to the early explorations from Spain and Portugal. Columbus went west in 1492 in the hope of reaching the spice islands of the east, but instead of discovering the East Indies he found the West Indies. In 1498, the Portuguese sent Vasco da Gama around Africa to reach India. Later the Portuguese discovered the Moluccas, the source of *CLOVES, *NUTMEGS and *MACE. The Portuguese retained the monopoly of the spice trade for 100 years, until this was taken over by the Dutch, who maintained it for 200 years.

The only spices of New World origin are CAPSICUM or CHILIES, *ALLSPICE and *PIMENTA, the latter being the only one exclusively produced there. Most spices are lowland crops of areas with relatively high rainfall of 80–100in and with an optimum temperature of about 86°F. Most spices are derived from fruits or seeds and their characteristic pungent flavors are due to the presence of *essential oils.

Some of the best-known flavoring plants are listed in the table (for Herbs see p. 174). In addition to these, there are also some curious and unexpected cases of plants providing flavor. Carragheen, with its pungent flavor due to a high potassium iodide content, comes from a seaweed. The characteristic flavor of several famous French cheeses, such as Brie, Camembert and Roquefort, is due to the presence of different molds belonging to the genus *Penicillium*. The Greek wine known as retsina is flavored with the resin from the pine casks it is stored in. The only other flavoring originating from conifers are *juniper berries, which are used in the production of gins and sometimes as a flavoring in meats, stews, roasts and in *sauerkraut. The berries are sometimes used ground as a component of mixed spices. Many fruits are used as flavorings, either eaten entire or sliced or as juices and extracts. Some are candied, notably citrus peel and angelica stems.

*Some common flavoring plants. 1 Caraway; 2 Anise; 3 Cumin; 4 Allspice; 5 Bay; 6 Capers; 7 Saffron Crocus; 8 Cloves; 9 Vanilla Orchid; 10 Turmeric; 11 Sorrel* (Rumex acetosa)*; 12 Tarragon; 13 Nutmeg; 14 Mace; 15 Ginger; 16 Cardamom; 17 Pepper; 18 Cinnamon; 19 Fenugreek; 20 Chilli; 21 Juniper; 22 Licorice. 1, 2, 3, 9, 14, 19, 20, 21, 22* $(\times\frac{1}{2})$*; 4, 6, 7, 11, 12, 18* $(\times\frac{1}{3})$*; 5, 8, 15* $(\times\frac{1}{4})$*; 17* $(\times\frac{1}{6})$*; 10, 16* $(\times\frac{1}{8})$*. Details 1, 2, 3* $(\times 2)$*; 4, 7, 15, 16, 18* $(\times\frac{1}{2})$*; 8, 17* $(\times\frac{3}{4})$*.*

The scientific basis of flavoring is highly complex and largely not elucidated, involving assessments of both taste and smell. Human tastes are grouped into four main classes: salty, sweet, bitter and sour. Sweetness of flavor and aroma is generally attractive to the palate while bitterness, acidity and astringency tend to be repellent although often welcome in some degree to counteract insipid foods. Bitterness can be an acquired taste – in beer, for example, when the responsible constituents are the hupulones and lupulones derived from hops. Mouth feelings (sensations produced by foods that are important in taste) are pain (provoked by chilli pepper, mustard, horseradish, etc), anesthesia (provoked by cloves, vanilla, etc), coolness (induced by menthol, mints, etc) and astringency (as caused by sloes, cashew fruit, etc). Some flavors may be pleasing and attractive in small quantities, at least to some people, as in the case of sulfur-containing mustard oils in numerous crucifer crops, but they become unacceptable and repellent if taken in large quantities. Likewise onion and garlic, which contain other sulfur compounds, are highly distasteful to many people while greatly appreciated by others.

Some fruit flavors may be the result of a single chemical compound as in apple and peach; others are caused by several compounds; in some, for example apricot, as many as 10 compounds are involved. In some cases it has not yet been possible to isolate and identify the chemical principles responsible for flavor, as in blackcurrants and strawberries. In coffee and chocolate over 700 compounds have been isolated but it is still not known which, if any, are responsible. In other cases trace compounds are important and contribute more to the flavor than the major compounds. In the lemon, for example, limonene makes up 70% of the oil but it is the 5% of the oil citral that is responsible for the lemon flavor.

Flavor potentiators and modifiers are naturally occuring compounds which have little effect on their own but which enhance the flavor when combined with other taste and flavor molecules. A common example is sodium chloride (salt) and more recently monosodium glutamate. More striking is the glycoprotein miracularin. This is obtained from the *MIRACULOUS BERRY *(Synsepalum dulcificum)* and has the property of eliminating sourness or acidity temporarily. Sour lemons taste as sweet as oranges if eaten after chewing the berries of *Synsepalum* but the effect wears off in about an hour.

Flavor is greatly affected by temperature; chilling may reduce flavor while heating can both enhance and destroy it as in the case of *essential oils which may be released and then dispersed. The drying of herbs causes some flavor loss although this is minimized by quick drying methods. Some flavors are only released after mixing with water as in the case of mustard which activates enzymes to release the characteristic pungent mustard oils.

COMMON FLAVORING PLANTS

| Popular name | Scientific name | Part of plant used |
|---|---|---|
| *ALLSPICE | *Pimenta dioica* | Fruit |
| *ANGELICA | *Archangelica officinalis* | Stem |
| *ANGOSTURA | *Cusparia febrifuga* | Bark |
| *ANISE | *Pimpinella anisum* | Fruit |
| *BALM, LEMON BALM | *Melissa officinalis* | Leaf |
| *BASIL | *Ocimum basilicum* | Leaf |
| BAY LAUREL | **Laurus nobilis* | Leaf |
| *CAPERS | *Capparis spinosa* | Flower bud |
| CARAWAY | **Carum carvi* | Seed |
| *CARDAMOM | *Elettaria cardamomum* | Fruit |
| CHILLI | **Capsicum* spp | Fruit |
| *CHIVES | *Allium schoenoprasum* | Leaf |
| CINNAMON | **Cinnamomum zeylanicum* | Bark |
| *CLOVES | *Syzygium aromaticum* | Flower bud |
| *CORIANDER | *Coriandrum sativum* | Fruit |
| *CUMIN | *Cuminum cyminum* | Fruit |
| FENUGREEK | **Trigonella foenum-graecum* | Seed |
| *GARLIC | *Allium sativum* | Bulb |
| *GINGER | *Zingiber officinale* | Rhizome |
| *HOPS | *Humulus lupulus* | Fruit |
| *HORSERADISH | *Armoracia rusticana* | Root |
| JASMINE | **Jasminum* spp | Flower |
| *JUNIPER | *Juniperus communis* | Fruit |
| *LEMON | *Citrus limon* | Fruit |
| *LICORICE | *Glycyrrhiza glabra* | Root |
| *MACE | *Myristica fragrans* | Aril |
| *MARJORAM | *Origanum majorana* | Leaf |
| *MUSTARD | *Brassica juncea B. nigra Sinapis alba* | Seed |
| *NUTMEG | *Myristica fragrans* | Seed |
| *PARSLEY | *Petroselinum crispum* | Leaf |
| *PEPPER | *Piper nigrum* | Fruit |
| *PEPPERMINT | *Mentha × piperata* | Leaf |
| *POPPY | *Papaver somniferum Glaucium flavum Argemone glauca* | Seed |
| ROSELLE | **Hibiscus sabdariffa* | Calyx |
| *RUE | *Ruta graveolens* | Leaf |
| SAFFRON | **Crocus sativus* | Stigma |
| SARSAPARILLA | **Smilax* spp | Root |
| SASSAFRAS | **Sassafras albidum* | Bark and wood |
| SESAME | **Sesamum indicum* | Seed |
| *TAMARIND | *Tamarindus indica* | Flower |
| *TARRAGON | *Artemisia dracunculus* | Leaf |
| *THYME | *Thymus vulgaris* | Leaf |
| *TURMERIC | *Curcuma domestica* | Rhizome |
| VANILLA | **Vanilla planifolia* | Fruit |

**Fontanesia** an Asiatic genus of deciduous shrubs, including *F. fortunei*, of Chinese origin, and *F. phillyraeoides*, from Syria. Both species bear panicles of creamy-white flowers; they resemble *PRIVET (*Ligustrum*) and are similarly used as hedging plants.
OLEACEAE, 2 species.

**Fontinalis** a genus of mainly aquatic mosses which are confined almost exclusively to north temperate regions. However, *F. antipyretica*, which is the best-known and one of the largest species, also occurs in South America. In rivers, *Fontinalis* species commonly form trailing shoot systems well over 3ft in length.
FONTINALACEAE, about 40 species.

**Forestiera** an American and West Indian genus of mainly deciduous trees and shrubs. *F. acuminata* [SWAMP PRIVET], *F. ligustrina* and *F. neomexicana* are sometimes cultivated as ornamentals for their privet-like appearance, small yellowish flowers and black or purplish fruits.
OLEACEAE, about 15 species.

**Forsythia** a small genus of hardy deciduous shrubs from Asia, some of which are cultivated in European parks and gardens. The conspicuous bright yellow flowers are carried on lateral buds on the previous season's wood and emerge very early in the growing season. The most popular cultivated species are *F. ovata*, *F. suspensa* and the hybrid *F.* × *intermedia* (= *F. suspensa* × *F. viridissima*), particularly the free-flowering cultivar 'Lynwood'.
OLEACEAE, 6–7 species.

*Ocotillo (*Fouquieria splendens*) in bloom in the southern Californian desert, USA. This species is occasionally used for hedging.* ($\times \frac{1}{50}$)

**Fortunella** see KUMQUAT.
RUTACEAE, 4–5 species.

**Fothergilla** a small genus of deciduous shrubs native to the southeastern USA and very popular as garden ornamentals. The three most popular species, *F. gardenii* (= *F. alnifolia*), *F. major* and *F. monticola*, all produce dense white or cream sweet-smelling inflorescences of bottle-brush type in spring and show a range of attractive red and orange autumn leaf colors.
HAMAMELIDACEAE, 4 species.

**Fouquieria** a small genus of spiny trees or shrubs native to Mexico, with one species extending into the southwestern USA. The best-known species is *F. splendens* [OCOTILLO] which, like other members of the genus, produces attractive inflorescences of showy red flowers. It produces long branching cane-like stems and is used as a hedging plant. A wax is obtained from the stem or bark of some species. (See also p. 848.)
FOUQUIERIACEAE, 7–9 species.

**Foxglove** the common name for members of the small but important European, Mediterranean and Macaronesian genus *Digitalis* which includes several attractive garden plants and species of major medicinal importance, such as the purple-flowered *D. purpurea* [COMMON FOXGLOVE]. The plants are mainly biennial or perennial herbs, sometimes flowering in their first year, but a few species are small shrubs, such as *D. obscura* [SPANISH RUSTY FOXGLOVE] from Spain and North Africa, and the Macaronesian group of species, such as *D. canariensis*, sometimes treated as a separate genus, *Isoplexis*.

*D. purpurea* is a highly variable species widely cultivated both for ornament and for the extraction of cardiac glycosides such as digitalin. Another widespread species, the yellow-flowered *D. grandiflora* (= *D. ambigua*) [LARGE YELLOW FOXGLOVE], is grown as a garden border plant. The hybrid named *D.* × *mertonensis* is the result of a cross between *D. purpurea* and *D. grandiflora*, followed by chromosome doubling. It has large attractive, often strawberry-colored flowers and is widely cultivated in gardens. Also widely grown are *D. lutea* [SMALL YELLOW FOXGLOVE], which has pale yellow to whitish tubular-cylindrical flowers, *D. ferruginea*, with yellowish or reddish flowers, and *D. lanata*, with a similar-shaped corolla but white or yellowish-white with brown or violet veins. The latter species is widely grown as a source of digoxin and other alkaloids used in the manufacture of heart drugs.

The *Isoplexis* group of species from the Canary Islands and Madeira are attractive small shrubs with dark green leathery leaves and racemes of striking reddish-orange or copper-colored flowers, sometimes cultivated in the open or in conservatories. The best-known species of this group is *D. canariensis* (*Isoplexis canariensis*).
SCROPHULARIACEAE, about 23 species.

*Forsythias (*Forsythia *spp) are one of the first shrubs to burst into bloom during early spring. The flowers are produced on the previous season's wood.*

**Fragaria** see STRAWBERRY.
ROSACEAE, about 15 species.

**Francoa** [BRIDAL or MAIDEN'S WREATH] a very small genus of herbaceous perennials from the temperate regions of Chile. According to some botanists it consists of only a single variable species, *F. appendiculata*, which is cultivated as a border plant for its long, slender spikes of white or pale pink flowers. Others regard it as comprising five species.
SAXIFRAGACEAE, 1–5 species.

**Frangula** a genus of shrubs or small trees, mainly American, Mediterranean and Eurasian in distribution. The bark of some species has purgative properties. Dyes are obtained from the bark, leaves and berries of *F. alnus* (= *Rhamnus frangula*) [ALDER BUCKTHORN], whose branches are also used for making charcoal.
RHAMNACEAE, about 50 species.

**Frankincense** the aromatic resin (gum olibanum) obtained from trees of the genus **Boswellia*, especially *B. carteri*, by tapping the trunks. The milky resin hardens when exposed to the air and forms irregular lumps, the form in which it is usually marketed. Frankincense burns with a pleasant odor and is used today as a constituent of incense; it is also in fumigants, and for fixatives in perfume.
BURSERACEAE.

# Fodder Crops

*Sheep grazing on Rape* (Brassica napus) *which is a valued forage crop used for late autumn and early spring pasturing. The seed is often sown after a cereal crop.*

Fodder crops or forage crops are a diverse group of plants used directly or in a preserved form (such as hay or silage) for feeding ruminant livestock and thereby to transform plant carbohydrate and protein into meat and dairy products. They play an exceedingly important role in the farming economy of most parts of the world and represent an indirect way by which Man uses vegetation.

Much of the world's grazing land (which vastly exceeds that devoted to grain or other crops) is under-utilized. Natural pasture is being increasingly improved by planting it with high-yielding cultivated fodder crops. At present most of the important forage crops are grown in the temperate countries and all the important cultivated forage or fodder plants belong to four families – the Gramineae, Leguminosae, Cruciferae and Chenopodiaceae in that order, the first two greatly exceeding the other two in importance. Many wild, as well as cultivated species of grasses and legumes, are of value as fodder plants especially on a local scale. Many are being tried out in cultivation and, in the tropics in particular, the planting of fodder crops is still a novelty in most areas, yet tropical grassland represents a major resource and supports some 500 million head of cattle as well as other grazing animals.

The oldest fodder legume is probably *LUCERNE *(Medicago sativa)*. It is native to western Asia and reached Western Europe in the mid-16th century and through the colonizing activities of the Spaniards reached Mexico in the 16th century. It did not reach the United Kingdom till 1650 and was quite unknown in the USA until the middle of the 17th century when it came in from Mexico.

The grasses (family Gramineae) are ideally suited for grazing because during vegetative growth the growing apex remains at about ground level and grazing animals only remove the leaves above the growing point.

Fodder plants used by domestic animals in the tropics embrace a vast range of species, from thorny shrubs browsed by camels and goats in the desert to the most luxuriant giant grasses and lush pastures of the humid tropics. In the natural grazings which are mainly of the *savanna (mixed tree-grass) type, dominant grasses differ from area to area. Typical genera are **Andropogon*, *Hyparrhenia* and *Themeda* in Africa, **Cynodon* and *Dichanthium* in India, and **Paspalum* in Brazil. The feeding value is frequently low as a result of human interference (eg fire) or unenlightened management (eg heavy stocking).

TEMPERATE FODDER CROPS

| Common name | Scientific name |
|---|---|
| **Grasses – Gramineae** | |
| *RYEGRASS | *Lolium perenne* |
| | *L. multiflorum* |
| TIMOTHY GRASS | **Phleum pratense* |
| COCK'S-FOOT, ORCHARD GRASS | **Dactylis glomerata* |
| *MAIZE | *Zea mays* |
| *RYE | *Secale cereale* |
| WHEATGRASS | **Agropyron fragile* subspecies *sibiricum* |
| CRESTED WHEATGRASS | *A. cristatum* |
| SLENDER WHEATGRASS | **Elymus trachycaulus* (= *Agropyron trachycaulum*) |
| BENT-GRASS | **Agrostis stolonifera* (= *A. alba*) |
| | *A. capillaris* (= *A. tenuis*) |
| BLUESTEM | **Andropogon* species |
| OATGRASS | *Arrhenatherum elatius* |
| CARPET GRASS | **Axonopus affinis* |
| BLUE GRAMA | **Bouteloua gracilis* |
| SIDEOATS | *B. curtipendula* |
| SMOOTH BROME | **Bromus inermis* |
| RESCUE GRASS, PRAIRIE BROME | *B. willdenowii* (= *B. unioloides*) |
| BUFFALO GRASS | *Buchloe dactyloides* |
| RHODES GRASS | **Chloris gayana* |
| BERMUDA GRASS | **Cynodon dactylon* |
| CANADA WILD RYE | **Elymus canadensis* |
| SIBERIAN WILD RYE | *E. sibiricus* |
| BLUE WILD RYE | *E. glaucus* |
| LOVE GRASS | **Eragrostis curvula* |
| TEFF | *E. tef* |
| TALL, REED *FESCUE | *Festuca arundinacea* |
| SHEEP'S FESCUE | *F. ovina* |
| MEADOW FESCUE | *F. pratensis* |
| CANARY REED GRASS | **Phalaris arundinacea*, *P. aquatica* var *stenoptera* (= *P. tuberosa*) |
| TEXAS BLUEGRASS | **Poa arachnifera* |
| CANADA BLUEGRASS | *P. compressa* |
| KENTUCKY BLUEGRASS | *P. pratensis* |
| **Sedges – Cyperaceae** | |
| SEDGE | **Carex lyngbyei* |
| | *C. nigra* |
| | *C. norvegica* |
| | *C. rariflora* |
| **Legumes – Leguminosae** | |
| KIDNEY VETCH | *Anthyllis vulneraria* |
| CROWN VETCH | **Coronilla varia* |
| *LUCERNE, ALFALFA | *Medicago sativa* |
| BLACK MEDICK, YELLOW TREFOIL | *M. lupulina* |
| WHITE SWEET CLOVER | **Melilotus alba* |
| YELLOW SWEET CLOVER | *M. officinalis* |
| SAINFOIN, ESPARCET | **Onobrychis viciifolia* |
| SERRADELLA | *Ornithopus sativus* |
| RED CLOVER | **Trifolium pratense* |
| WHITE CLOVER | *T. repens* |
| STRAWBERRY CLOVER | *T. fragiferum* |
| ALSIKE CLOVER | *T. hybridum* |
| CRIMSON CLOVER | *T. incarnatum* |
| SUBTERRANEAN CLOVER | *T. subterraneum* |
| *BROAD BEAN | **Vicia faba* |
| SPRING VETCH | *V. sativa* |
| HAIRY VETCH | *V. villosa* |
| **Kales – Cruciferae** | |
| KALES, RAPE (see Brassicas p. 64.) | *Brassica oleracea* |
| | *B. campestris* |
| | *B. rapa* |

TROPICAL and SUBTROPICAL FODDER CROPS

| Common name | Scientific name |
|---|---|
| **Grasses – Gramineae** | |
| BLUESTEMS | **Andropogon* species |
| DIAZ BLUESTEM | *Dichanthium annulatum* |
| BRAHMAN BLUESTEM, ANGLETON BLUESTEM | *D. aristatum* |
| | *Hyparrhenia hirta* |
| | *H. rufa* |
| RHODES GRASS | **Chloris gayana* |
| HAIRY CRAB GRASS | *Digitaria sanguinalis* |
| PANGOLA GRASS | *D. decumbens* |
| | *D. longifolia* |
| GUINEA GRASS | **Panicum maximum* |
| BROOMCORN MILLET | *P. miliaceum* |
| PARA GRASS | *P. purpurascens* |
| DALLIS GRASS | **Paspalum dilatatum* |
| BAHIA GRASS | *P. notatum* |
| VASEY GRASS | *P. urvillei* |
| PEARL MILLET | **Pennisetum americanum* |
| BUFFEL GRASS | *P. ciliare* |
| NAPIER GRASS, ELEPHANT GRASS | *P. purpureum* |
| GUATEMALA GRASS | *Tripsacum laxum* |
| — | *Themeda triandra* |
| **Legumes – Leguminosae** | |
| BUTTERFLY PEA, CONCHITA | *Centrosema plumieri* |
| | *C. pubescens* *C. virginianum* |
| SESBAN | **Sesbania sesban* (= *S. aegyptiaca*) *S. cinerascens* |
| BEGGARWEED | **Desmodium tortuosum* |
| TICK CLOVER | *D. discolor* *D. heterophyllum* |
| | *D. heterocarpon* *D. triflorum* |
| WHITE POPINAC | *Leucaena glauca* |
| | *L. leucocephala* |
| VELVET BEAN, BENGAL BEAN | **Mucuna deeringiana* |
| *INDIGO | *Indigofera arrecta* |
| | *I. pauciflora* |
| MACROPTILIUM | *Macroptilium atropurpureum* |
| | *M. geophilum* |
| KUDZU VINE | *Pueraria lobata* (= *P. thunbergiana*) |
| KUDZU | *P. phaseoloides* |
| STYLO, WILD LUCERNE | *Stylosanthes guianensis* |
| | *S. capitata* *S. humilis* |
| | *S. hamata* *S. scabra* |

Franklinia alatamaha *has camellia-like flowers and is known only in cultivation.* ( × ½)

**Franklinia** a genus consisting of a single species, *F. alatamaha*, originally discovered in Georgia in the southeastern USA. It is now only known in cultivation as an ornamental deciduous camellia-like tree or shrub with solitary, showy, attractively scented white flowers.
THEACEAE, 1 species.

**Fraxinus** see ASH.
OLEACEAE, about 60 species.

**Freemontia** see *Freemontodendron*.

**Freemontodendron** (formerly *Freemontia*) a small genus of flowering trees or shrubs, native to Mexico and California. *F. californicum* is cultivated as an ornamental shrub for its large cup-shaped golden-yellow flowers, the sepals being petal-like and the petals absent. Although *F. mexicanum* with its yellow-orange star-shaped flowers is less widely cultivated, a hybrid between these two species, 'Californian Glory', is a more popular shrub in frost-free areas.
STERCULIACEAE, 2 species.

**Freesia** a genus of cormous perennial herbs from South Africa. The leaves are two-ranked, forming a flat fan, and the richly scented flowers are borne in one-sided spikes on branched inflorescences with their flowers turned upwards. The best-known species are *F. refracta* with pale yellow flowers, and *F. armstrongii* with pink flowers. Modern hybrids, *F.* × *hybrida*, derived from these and possibly other species have a wide color range. Freesias are popular as cut flowers and are grown commercially for this purpose.
IRIDACEAE, up to 20 species.

**Fritillaria** a genus of bulbous plants from all the north temperate zones except eastern North America.

*F. meleagris* [SNAKE'S HEAD FRITILLARY] is commonly cultivated for its attractive nodding spring flowers, purple, pink or white, with checkering throughout of a darker shade.

*F. imperialis* [CROWN IMPERIAL], from southeast Turkey to the western Himalayas, has long been cultivated for its attractive, pendent, yellow, red or orange flowers on a stout stem often as much as 4ft tall. One of the best garden species is the Siberian *F. pallidiflora* which is very hardy and flourishes in any well-drained soil. The easiest species to cultivate is *F. pontica*, from the Balkans to the Pontus mountains of Turkey, with apple-green flowers suffused with brown at the tips and margins.

The bulbs of a number of Asiatic species, notably *F. verticillata*, have various uses in Chinese medicine, particularly in treating fever and dysentery. The chocolate or blackish-purple bulbs of *F. camschatcensis* [KAMCHATKA LILY, BLACK SARANA], from East Asia, Japan to North America, are eaten by the natives of southeast Alaska.
LILIACEAE, about 100 species.

**Fruits** see p. 151.

**Frullania** a large genus of liverworts of essentially warm climates; most of its species are therefore restricted to the tropical areas of all continents. A few species, however, reach the temperate zones and one or two species are able to survive beyond the Arctic Circle. Most of the species are epiphytes that grow on the trunks of trees and more rarely on leaves in tropical rain forests; many others grow on rocks.
FRULLANIACEAE, about 1 000 species.

**Fuchsia** a genus of tender to hardy woody plants with showy pendulous tube-like flowers, all of which produce copious nectar and most of which are bird-pollinated. Most members of the genus are native to mountainous regions of Central and South America and to Tahiti and New Zealand.

Fuchsias are mainly of ornamental value. Amongst the popular shrubby species are *F. corymbiflora* (Ecuador, Peru) with long crimson flowers, *F. fulgens* (Mexico) with red stems and scarlet, green-tipped flowers, *F. magellanica* (= *F. macrostemma*) (Argentina, southern Chile) in a range of varieties including *alba*, the red- and purple-flowered *gracilis variegata*, *F. procumbens* (New Zealand), a prostrate, hanging-basket species and *F. triphylla* (Haiti, St. Domingo), a subshrub with brilliant orange-scarlet flowers. Most hybrids, referred to as *F.* × *hybrida*, have been derived from crosses between *F. fulgens* and *F. magellanica*, and include numerous named varieties, such as 'Mrs Popple' and 'Mission Bells' which can be grown outdoors, and the more tender greenhouse types such as 'Cascade'.
ONAGRACEAE, about 100 species.

**Fucus** one of the most common genera of brown algae distributed on temperate and cold-water shores. The various species usually occur in a distinct zonation on the intertidal zone. The plants have tough, leathery, divided ribbon-like fronds, a short stem terminating in a disk-shaped holdfast, attached firmly to rocks. Various species, including *F. vesiculosus* [BLADDERWRACK, LADY WRACK, SEAWARE, BLACK TANG, BLADDER FUCUS], are used as a manure and as a forage for sheep and cattle. Because it is rich in iodine, it has been used as a treatment for thyroid deficiency.
PHAEOPHYCEAE.

*The Crown Imperial (*Fritillaria imperialis*), a tall Himalayan species commonly grown in gardens, in spite of its unpleasant smell.* ( × $\frac{1}{12}$)

# Fruits

The practice of fruit gathering and growing in gardens and farms stretches back into antiquity. Woodlands and hedgerows are still a major source of such fruits as *cranberries and *blackberries, while garden production of fruits is important in many countries such as Germany. Some fruit crops are grown in mixed farming systems, as in China and Korea where vegetables and cereals are grown under fruit trees, but in the West the traditional orchard with grass providing grazing for animals has almost disappeared. Most fruit entering commerce today is grown on specialist plantations ranging from those for tropical *bananas and *pineapples to those for *dates, *citrus fruits, *apples, *raspberries, and *currants. All these crops are perennials (which increases the build-up of pests and diseases), are vegetatively propagated and are of high value if they can be produced to a high standard of visual appeal as well as good eating quality. They are also highly perishable, so need special methods of storage and transportation.

Fruit crops give high returns but are expensive to produce, so the grower cannot risk using poor sites. Good drainage combined with an adequate supply of rainfall or irrigation water is very important. Freedom from spring frost, or the ability to protect against it, is also essential for citrus fruits in Florida and *peaches in New Zealand as well as apples and *pears in Europe and America. Cold-temperate fruit plants require chilling in winter to stimulate normal growth and flowering in the following year. Those that require little chilling need a long growing season and are damaged by dormant season frosts; these are classed as warm-temperate fruits. By selection and improved cultural practices, cold-temperate fruits can be grown over a wide climatic range.

In the accompanying tables are listed the main temperate and tropical fruits. The term fruit is used here in the strictly horticultural sense of the fleshy edible part developed from the flower or flowers of a perennial plant.

TEMPERATE FRUITS

| Common name | Scientific name | Family |
|---|---|---|
| *APPLE | *Malus pumila* | Rosaceae |
| *PEAR | *Pyrus communis* | Rosaceae |
| *QUINCE | *Cydonia vulgaris* | Rosaceae |
| *PEACH, NECTARINE | **Prunus persica* | Rosaceae |
| SWEET *CHERRY | *P. avium* | Rosaceae |
| SOUR CHERRY, COOKING CHERRY, MORELLO | *P. cerasus* | Rosaceae |
| *PLUM | *P. domestica* | Rosaceae |
| BULLACE, DAMSON | *P. insititia* | Rosaceae |
| GAGE, *GREENGAGE, MIRABELLE | *P. insititia* | Rosaceae |
| | var *italica* | Rosaceae |
| | var *syriaca* | Rosaceae |
| CHERRY PLUM | *P. cerasifera* | Rosaceae |
| JAPANESE PLUM | *P. salicina* | Rosaceae |
| AMERICAN PLUM | *P. americana* | Rosaceae |
| *APRICOT | *P. armeniaca* | Rosaceae |
| *MEDLAR | *Mespilus germanica* | Rosaceae |
| *RASPBERRY | **Rubus idaeus* | Rosaceae |
| AMERICAN RED RASPBERRY | *R. ideaus* var *strigosus* | Rosaceae |
| BLACK RASPBERRY | *R. occidentalis* | Rosaceae |
| *BLACKBERRY, BRAMBLE | *R. fruticosus* | Rosaceae |
| EVERGREEN BLACKBERRY | *R. laciniatus* | Rosaceae |
| CLOUDBERRY | *R. chamaemorus* | Rosaceae |
| PACIFIC DEWBERRY | *R. ursinus* | Rosaceae |
| *LOGANBERRY, BOYSENBERRY, VEITCHBERRY | *R.* × *loganobaccus* | Rosaceae |
| WINEBERRY | *R. phoenicolasius* | Rosaceae |
| *STRAWBERRY | *Fragaria* × *ananassa* (= *F. virginiana* × *F. chiloensis*) | Rosaceae |
| *GOOSEBERRY | **Ribes uva-crispa* (= *R. grossularia*) | Rosaceae |
| BLACK CURRANT | *R. nigrum* | Rosaceae |
| RED CURRANT | *R. rubrum* | Rosaceae |
| FIG | **Ficus carica* | Moraceae |
| *OLIVE | *Olea europaea* | Oleaceae |
| *MULBERRY, BLACK MULBERRY | *Morus nigra* | Moraceae |
| RED MULBERRY | *M. rubra* | Moraceae |
| *GRAPE | **Vitis vinifera* | Vitaceae |
| FROST GRAPE | *V. riparia, V. vulpina* | Vitaceae |
| BUSH OR SAND GRAPE | *V. rupestris* | Vitaceae |
| FOX OR SKUNK GRAPE | *V. labrusca* | Vitaceae |
| MUSCADINE, BULLACE GRAPE | *V. rotundifolia* | Vitaceae |
| *BILBERRY | **Vaccinium myrtillus* | Ericaceae |
| *CRANBERRY | *V. oxycoccus, V. macrocarpon* | Ericaceae |
| COWBERRY | *V vitis-idaea* | Ericaceae |
| LOWBUSH *BLUEBERRY | *V. angustifolium* | Ericaceae |
| HIGHBUSH BLUEBERRY | *V. corymbosum* | Ericaceae |
| STRAWBERRY TREE | **Arbutus unedo* | Ericaceae |
| CHINESE GOOSEBERRY KIWIBERRY | **Actinidia chinensis* | Actinidiaceae |

See also:
Marrows, Squashes, Pumpkins and Gourds p. 222
Nuts p. 244
Vegetables p. 350

TROPICAL AND SUBTROPICAL FRUITS

| Common name | Scientific name | Family |
|---|---|---|
| SWEET *ORANGE | **Citrus sinensis* | Rutaceae |
| SOUR, *SEVILLE OR BITTER ORANGE | *C. aurantium* | Rutaceae |
| *LIME | *C. aurantiifolia* | Rutaceae |
| *LEMON | *C. limon* | Rutaceae |
| RANGPUR LIME, MANDARIN LIME | *C.* × *limonia* | Rutaceae |
| *SHADDOCK, PUMMELO | *C. maxima* | Rutaceae |
| *CITRON | *C. medica* | Rutaceae |
| KING ORANGE | *C.* × *nobilis* | Rutaceae |
| *GRAPEFRUIT | *C.* × *paradisi* | Rutaceae |
| *MANDARIN, SATSUMA, TANGERINE, CLEMENTINE | *C. reticulata* | Rutaceae |
| *KUMQUAT | *Fortunella japonica* | Rutaceae |
| LOQUAT, JAPANESE MEDLAR | **Eriobotrya japonica* | Rosaceae |
| BREADFRUIT | **Artocarpus altilis* | Moraceae |
| JACKFRUIT | *A. heterophyllus* | Moraceae |
| CHERIMOYA | **Annona cherimolia* | Annonaceae |
| CUSTARD APPLE, BULLOCK'S HEART | *A. reticulata* | Annonaceae |
| SOURSOP, GUANABANA | *A. muricata* | Annonaceae |
| SUGARAPPLE, SWEETSOP | *A. squamosa* | Annonaceae |
| *BANANA, EDIBLE PLANTAIN | *Musa acuminata. M.* × *paradisiaca* | Musaceae |
| FEHI BANANA | *M. fehi* | Musaceae |
| *AVOCADO, AGUACATE, ALLIGATOR PEAR | *Persaea americana* (= *P. gratissima*) | Lauraceae |
| *COCONUT | *Cocos nucifera* | Palmae |
| *DATE | *Phoenix dactylifera* | Palmae |
| *PINEAPPLE | *Ananas comosus* | Bromeliaceae |
| *MANGO | *Mangifera indica* | Anacardiaceae |
| CASHEW APPLE | **Anacardium occidentale* | Anacardiaceae |
| GRANADILLA, PASSION FRUIT | **Passiflora edulis* | Passifloraceae |
| SWEET GRANADILLA | *P. ligularis* | Passifloraceae |
| YELLOW GRANADILLA | *P. laurifolia* | Passifloraceae |
| SWEET CALABASH | *P. maliformis* | Passifloraceae |
| CURUBA | *P. mollissima* | Passifloraceae |
| GIANT GRANADILLA | *P. quadrangularis* | Passifloraceae |
| *PAPAW, PAWPAW | *Carica papaya* | Caricaceae |
| *DURIAN | *Durio zibethinus* | Bombacaceae |
| *MANGOSTEEN | *Garcinia mangostana* | Guttiferae |
| *RAMBUTAN | *Nephelium lappaceum* | Sapindaceae |
| LONGAN | **Euphoria longan* | Sapindaceae |
| *AKEE | *Blighia sapida* | Sapindaceae |
| GUAVA | **Psidium guajava* | Myrtaceae |
| CAPE GOOSEBERRY | **Physalis peruviana* | Solanaceae |
| TOMATILLO, JAMBERRY | *P. ixocarpa* | Solanaceae |
| *MAMMEY APPLE, MAMMEE | *Mammea americana* | Guttiferae |
| SAPODILLA | **Manilkara zapota* | Sapotaceae |
| *SAPOTE | *Pouteria sapota* (= *Calocarpum sapota*) | Sapotaceae |
| *TAMARIND | *Tamarindus indica* | Leguminosae |
| CARAMBOLA, CARAMBA, BLIMBING, BILIMBI | *Averrhoa carambola* | Oxalidaceae |
| *PERSIMMON | *Diospyros kaki* | Ebenaceae |
| *POMEGRANATE | *Punica granatum* | Punicaceae |
| LITCHI, LYCHEE | **Litchi chinensis* | Sapindaceae |

1
2
3
4
5
6
7
8
9
10
11
12
13
14
15
16
17
18
19
20

Opposite *common temperate fruits:*
*1 Blackcurrant; 2 Redcurrant; 3 Bilberry; 4 Highbush Blueberry; 5 Sweet Cherry; 6 Cranberry; 7 Black Mulberry; 8 Gooseberry; 9 Raspberry; 10 Plum; 11 Strawberry; 12 Fig; 13 Damson; 14 Greengage; 15 Medlar; 16 Quince; 17 Apricot; 18 Peach; 19 Apple; 20 Pear.* ( $\times 1$ )

Below *tropical fruits: 1 Pineapple; 2 Durian; 3 Carambola; 4 Mango; 5 Papaw; 6 Soursop; 7 Persimmon; 8 Mangosteen; 9 Pomegranate; 10 Litchi; 11 Akee; 12 Cherimoya; 13 Banana; 14 Guava; 15 Sapodilla; 16 Passion Fruit; 17 Loquat; 18 Cape Gooseberry; 19 Rambutan. 1 to 6, 12, 13* ( $\times\frac{1}{3}$ ); *7 to 11, 14 to 18* ( $\times\frac{1}{2}$ ).

*Male plant of Serrated Wrack (*Fucus serratus*) growing in the intertidal zone. (×1)*

**Fumaria** a genus of annual, often climbing herbs mainly native to Europe and the Mediterranean region but with a few species further east to Mongolia and south to East Africa. There are no horticulturally important members but *F. officinalis* [COMMON FUMITORY, EARTH SMOKE] was at one time the source of a yellow dye. Like some other species, including *F. parviflora*, it is used in herbal medicine as a tonic and laxative.
FUMARIACEAE, about 60 species.

**Funaria** a genus of mosses best-known for the common cosmopolitan species *F. hygrometrica* which tends to appear in abundance after fires.
FUNARIACEAE, about 220 species.

**Fungi** see p. 156.

**Furcraea** a genus of succulent perennials similar to **Agave* and indigenous to tropical America. The best-known species is *F. foetida* (= *F. gigantea*) [GREEN ALOE], whose large fleshy leaves yield a strong fiber (Mauritius hemp) used for mats, cordage etc. It is cultivated widely in tropical America, and on a commercial scale in Mauritius, Madagascar and St. Helena. The cultivated plant is var *willemettiana*. The inflorescences are up to 26ft long and contain many thousands of flowers.
AGAVACEAE, about 20 species.

**Fusarium** a large genus of imperfect fungi widely distributed in soils, especially cultivated ones. Various species are important as seedling pathogens of cereals, causing pre-emergence killing or damping-off. Others attack more mature plants causing root rots or ear blight. Growth of fusaria in feed grain may produce toxins which are harmful to horses, pigs and Man when eaten. Other important pathogens are those that cause severe wilt, such as *F. oxysporum*, the cause of Panama disease of bananas, or storage rots, such as *F. caeruleum*, the cause of dry rot of potato tubers.
HYPHOMYCETACEAE, about 70 species.

**Gagea** a genus of low-growing, Eurasian, bulbous monocotyledonous herbs with basal leaves and solitary or few-flowered umbels of yellowish-green flowers. *G. lutea* (= *G. sylvatica*) [YELLOW STAR OF BETHLEHEM] is sometimes cultivated for ornament. It is widespread in Europe and the Mediterranean. Some species have been used as diuretics.
LILIACEAE, about 70 species.

**Gaillardia** a genus of temperate American annual and perennial leafy-stemmed herbs. The showy radiate flower heads are red, purple, orange or yellow in color, and borne on long stalks. *G. pulchella* [BLANKET FLOWER], especially var *picta*, is widely cultivated. *G. aristata* [PRAIRIE FLOWER] was formerly cultivated but is now replaced by *G.* × *grandiflora* (*G. aristata* × *G. pulchella*), of garden origin but now naturalized in several parts of the western USA. There are numerous cultivars.
COMPOSITAE, about 28 species.

**Galangal** the common name for the herbaceous perennials *Alpinia officinale* (= *A. officinarum*) [LESSER GALANGAL] and *A. galanga* [GREATER GALANGAL]. Both of these Asian species yield from the rhizome a spice used in flavoring curries and other savory dishes.
ZINGIBERACEAE.

*Inflorescences of the Blanket Flower (*Gaillardia pulchella*), which has many single- and double-flowered garden varieties. (× ¾)*

**Galanthus** see SNOWDROP.
LILIACEAE, about 15 species.

**Galega** a small genus of busy, erect perennial herbs native to southern Europe, western Asia and tropical East Africa. *G. officinalis* [GOAT'S RUE], *G. orientalis* and *G.* × *hartlandii* (= *G. bicolor* var *hartlandii*), a natural garden hybrid, are grown for their attractive white or blue pea-like flowers.
LEGUMINOSAE, 6 to 8 species.

**Galeopsis** [HEMP NETTLES], a genus of annual herbs native almost throughout temperate Eurasia. Most species, such as *G. segetum* (= *G. dubia*) [DOWNY HEMP NETTLE] and *G. tetrahit* [COMMON HEMP NETTLE] are weeds of arable land. However, *G. segetum* has been used, in the form of a leaf-decoction, for lung, intestinal and spleen complaints.
LABIATAE, about 10 species.

**Galinsoga** a small genus of New World annual herbs, bearing small daisy-like flower heads. *G. parviflora* [GALLANT SOLDIER, JOEY HOOKER] is a widespread weed in the Northern Hemisphere. Young plants are eaten as a vegetable in Southeast Asia.
COMPOSITAE, 14 species.

**Galium** a large almost cosmopolitan genus of annual or perennial herbs. *G. aparine* [CATCHWEED, GOOSEGRASS, CLEAVERS, STICKY WILLIE] is a pernicious weed with seeds and stems which cling by means of small reflexed hooks. Attractive, profusely flowered species with filmy foliage are cultivated in rockeries, such as *G. verum* [YELLOW-FLOWERED BEDSTRAW, OUR LADY'S BEDSTRAW]. Dried plants were used to stuff mattresses (hence bedstraw), and plant juices were used to curdle milk in cheese making. In Germany and Austria, *G. odoratum* (= *Asperula odorata*) [SWEET WOODRUFF] yields an extract containing coumarin, used to flavor Maiwein ("May wine").
RUBIACEAE, about 350 species.

**Galtonia** [SPIRE LILY, SUMMER HYACINTH] a small genus of attractive bulbous plants native to South Africa. The fragrant *G. candicans* (= *Hyacinthus candicans*) with racemes of pure white flowers is the species most frequently cultivated in gardens.
LILIACEAE, 4 species.

**Gambier** a climbing shrub, *Uncaria gambir* [BENGAL GAMBIER], native to tropical Asia. The leaves and young stems yield a tannin extract used in dyeing, printing and leather preparation. Extracts of the leaves, known as catechu or pale catechu (not to be confused with black catechu from **Acacia catechu*), are still included in Western pharmacopeias as an astringent used in treating the symptoms of diarrhea.
RUBIACEAE.

*The fruits and stems of Goosegrass or Cleavers (*Galium aparine*) are covered in tiny hooks, as an aid to animal dispersal.* (×3)

**Gamboge** a yellow dye obtained from the gum resin of species of **Garcinia*, particularly *G. cambogia* [GAMBOGE TREE] and *G. hanburyi* [SIAMESE GAMBOGE TREE]. The dye, being water-soluble is used by artists. It also imparts a golden tint to metal lacquers and varnishes. Gamboge is also used locally as a violent purgative and laxative.
GUTTIFERAE.

**Ganoderma** a genus of basidiomycete fungi with woody bracket-shaped fruiting bodies. The species are widely distributed in temperate and tropical regions on decayed wood. *G. adspersum* infects wounds on broadleaved trees such as beeches, causing extensive stem rot. *G. pseudoferreum* attacks roots of rubber, cacao and other tropical crops.
GANODERMATACEAE, about 50 species.

**Garcinia** a large genus of trees and shrubs confined to the Old World tropics, with the greatest diversity in Asia. Many species yield products useful to native populations, while some have special economic importance. *G. mangostana* [*MANGOSTEEN], *G. xanthochymus* (= *G. tinctoria*), *G. multiflora* and many other species bear delicious fruits. *G. cambogia*, *G. hanburyi* and other Asiatic species produce the gum resin, *gamboge. (See also GAMBOGE and MANGOSTEEN.)
GUTTIFERAE, about 400 species.

**Gardenia** a large genus of evergreen shrubs and small trees found in the Old World tropics and subtropics. The bark is often whitish and sometimes spiny-branched and the flowers are salver-shaped, white, greenish or yellow, solitary or in pairs. The most commonly cultivated species is *G. jasminoides* [CAPE JASMINE], which is grown for its showy white highly fragrant flowers.
RUBIACEAE, about 250 species.

**Garlic** the common name for **Allium sativum*, a small extremely pungent, onion-like plant which is widely used for flavoring in salads and meat and savory dishes, particularly in the Mediterranean countries, the Middle and Far East, South America etc. The garlic "bulb" consists of a cluster of swollen axillary buds ensheathed by dry foliage leaf-bases. Each swollen axillary bud or clove is a true bulb.
LILIACEAE.

**Garrya** a genus of evergreen shrubs native to southern and southwestern North America, Mexico and the West Indies. *G. elliptica* [SILK-TASSEL BUSH] with its attractive gray-green catkins appearing in winter, is the most widely cultivated. The bark and leaves of this and other species are used in local medicine to treat fevers.
GARRYACEAE, about 15 species.

*Gasterias are popular houseplants and exhibit a great diversity of leaf form – some are biseriate, others form spiral rosettes.* (×⅓)

*Wild or Wood Garlic (*Allium ursinum*) is abundant in damp, shady old woods of temperate regions of Europe and Asia. This species is also known as Ramsons, Buckrams, Gypsy Onion and Bear's or Hog's Garlic.* (×1)

**Gasteria** a genus of dwarf, more or less stemless, leaf-succulent rosette plants from the drier parts of southern and southwestern Africa. The leaves are thick and fleshy with often horny margins and usually a sharp white tip. The flowers are borne in tall, pendulous, lateral racemes or panicles; they are tubular with a markedly inflated base and are red or pinkish with usually greenish tips.

Unlike most succulents, species of *Gasteria* tolerate shade and are hence popular houseplants where full sun is not available. The most decorative are *G. batesiana*, *G. pulchra*, a miniature forming clumps, *G. armstrongii*, a miniature with a single rosette of blackish leaves in two series, and *G. obtusifolia* 'Variegata' with dramatically cream-striped leaves.
LILIACEAE, about 70 species.

**Gaultheria** a large genus of evergreen flowering shrubs, mainly in the Americas but also in India, East and Southeast Asia to Australasia. The urn-shaped flowers are usually pink or white. The low-growing *G. procumbens* [CREEPING OR SPICY WINTERGREEN, PARTRIDGE BERRY, CHECKERBERRY, TEABERRY], from northeast North America, with red berries and a spread of 3ft or more, is the original source of wintergreen oil; it is also grown for ground cover. Several species are cultivated on lime-free soils for their edible berries, for example *G. antipoda*, from New Zealand and Tasmania, with white or red berries, and *G. shallon* [SALAL, SHALLON].
(continued on p. 160)

# Fungi

FUNGI FORM A KINGDOM OF PLANTS WHICH lack the green pigment chlorophyll and reproduce by means of spores. Fungi are ubiquitous. They occur in air, water (both fresh and salt) and in the soil. As saprophytes, they are an important cause of the deterioration of stored organic products and they destroy structural timber. As parasites, they cause major diseases of plants, animals and Man. They also parasitize one another.

On the positive side, if some are poisonous, others are edible and fungi have been used since ancient times for the leavening of bread and in the preparation of a wide range of alcoholic beverages and other fermented foods. They find a use in medicine and the many metabolic fungal products commercially available include such valuable drugs as the antibiotics penicillin and the cephalosporins. As symbionts, fungi are the dominant partner in lichens and they form mycorrhizas in association with the roots of forest trees and many other plants. The most important role of fungi is as agents of decay of organic residues, an activity that makes a major contribution to the maintenance of an environment suitable for life on this planet.

*A bracket fungus* Inonotus hispidus (= Polyporus hispidus) *which causes decay on standing Common Ash (*Fraxinus excelsior*) trees and some other deciduous tree species.* (× ⅓)

To define a fungus concisely is not easy because of the diversity of fungi and uncertainties regarding the circumscription of the group. Fungi lack chlorophyll (that is, their nutrition is heterotrophic) but they are eukaryotic and therefore distinct from the prokaryotic bacteria which were at one time commonly classified as "fission fungi" or Schizomycetes. Individual fungi vary from single cells a few microns in length, with a life span measured in minutes, to centuries-old "fairy rings" hundreds of feet in diameter. Although typically non-motile, creeping (plasmodial) forms exhibiting amoeboid movement occur and motile states are not infrequent in some aquatic fungi and their terrestrial relatives. Fungi may be asexual or sexual and exhibit simple or complex life cycles. One notable characteristic is the great variation in the form and function of the spores which are more diverse than in any other group of organsims.

Fungi are basically unicellular. Some are unicells, as is a typical yeast, but in most fungi the thallus (body) is derived from a unicellular spore (or from one cell of a multicellular spore) which germinates to give a short tube (germ tube) that elongates into a filament or hypha (plural: hyphae). These hyphae by branching and rejoining (anastomosis) give rise to a mycelium (plural: mycelia) which may undergo fusions with other mycelia.

The microscopic hyphae may become aggregated to form complex and quite massive structures. The simplest condition is the twisting together of hyphae to form the mycelial strands not infrequently shown by molds in laboratory culture and it is a similar aggregation which gives rise to the macroscopic rhizomorphs of which the most familiar example is the black "boot-laces" of the HONEY FUNGUS (**Armillaria mellea*) found associated with rotten wood. To ensure survival under adverse conditions, hyphae may become aggregated and consolidated as sclerotia which may range from 0.04in or so in diameter to massive structures weighing several pounds, such as the sclerotium of **Polyporus mylittae*, known as "blackfellows bread" in Australia. The fruiting bodies (so-called mushrooms and toadstools) of larger fungi are also constructed of hyphae.

The nutrition of fungi is typically absorptive – ingestive in slime molds – but never photosynthetic. Fungi are, therefore, dependent for their carbon on a great variety of organic compounds. Carbohydrates are particularly favorable carbon sources. Almost all fungi can assimilate glucose but the acceptability of other sugars and carbohydrates varies from one group (or even species) to another. Fungi cannot utilize elemental nitrogen but many can assimilate nitrate nitrogen; for others, ammonium nitrogen or nitrogen in organic combination is needed.

*One of the most distinctive of the cup fungi is the Orange-peel Peziza (*Aleuria aurantia*).* (× ½)

**Reproduction.** Examples of the simplest methods of fungal reproduction are provided by the budding of a yeast cell to produce a new individual or the development of a hyphal fragment into a new mycelium. The usual method of reproduction among fungi is by spores which are produced in enormous numbers – it has been calculated that one fruiting body of the GIANT PUFFBALL (*Langermannia gigantea*) contains $7 \times 10^{12}$ spores. Spore types form the basis of fungal classification. They are divided into two main categories (sexual spores and asexual spores) according to whether or not their formation is preceded by a process that can be interpreted as sexual.

Sexual spores in fungi are of four main types. Oospores result from the fusion of a female gamete with a smaller male gamete which may or may not be motile. Zygospores are naked, thick-walled spores resulting from the fusion of two morphologically undifferentiated gametes. Ascospores are produced (usually in eights) inside a microscopic, sac-like organ, the ascus. Basidiospores are borne externally (typically in fours) at the apex of a structure called a basidium.

Among asexual spores the development of the spores (sporangiospores) of **Mucor* within a rounded body (sporangium), the wall of which finally ruptures to release the spores, is analagous to that of ascospores; but the development of conidia (a general term for all asexual spores other than non-motile sporangiospores and motile zoospores) is blastic, that is the spore is differentiated from part of the conidial mother cell in a manner analagous to basidiospore formation.

Spores, being the equivalent of seeds, have to fulfill several functions: to initiate a new individual in the appropriate ecological niche and to remain viable during periods unfavorable for growth. This last function is frequently effected by special thick-walled chlamydospores. For transfer to an appropriate site, passive dispersal by air currents, water and animals is usual. The first step in dispersal is frequently the active discharge of the spore. This may be to a distance of a few microns, in the case of the discharge of a basidiospore from its basidium in agarics and polypores by a "bubble mechanism", to an inch or more in the violent discharge, due to turgor, of the spores from the asci of a discomycete (cup fungus). Air-borne spores are typically small and dry and often dark in color to offset the deleterious effects of light,

Above Coprinus micaceus *(Glistening Inkcap) which grows on old stumps in dense clumps and has distinctly grooved caps.* (×1)

Left *Young fruiting bodies of the puffball* Lycoperdon perlatum. *Spores are produced inside the wall which ruptures to release them.* (×1) Right *The evil-smelling Stinkhorn* (Phallus impudicus). *The spores mature while the fruiting body is still enclosed in a membrane and are only released when the stalk elongates rapidly to its characteristic form. The strong smell attracts insects which are involved in the dispersal of the spores.* ($\times\frac{3}{4}$)

## MEMBERS OF THE KINGDOM FUNGI

The following table gives details of the distribution, structure and reproduction of the main groups of fungi.

Abbreviations for taxonomic ranks: d = Division, sd = Subdivision, c = Class, sc = Subclass, o = Order

|  |  |  |
|---|---|---|
| d | **MYXOMYCOTA** [SLIME MOLDS] | **Heterotrophic amoeboid organisms. Cells comprising naked (no cell wall), multinucleate plasmodia or pseudoplasmodia for most of the life cycle. Nutrition by ingestion.** |
| c | *Myxomycetes* [PLASMODIAL SLIME MOLDS] | *Characteristic of wet wooded habitats, frequently bright orange in color. Comprising multinucleate plasmodia that creep by amoeboid movement. Multinucleate sporangia formed giving rise to many spores. About 400 species.* |
| c | *Plasmodiophoromycetes* [ENDOPARASITIC SLIME MOLDS] | *Entirely parasitic slime fungi producing spores that give rise to biflagellate swarmers. About 50 species.* |
| c | *Acrasiomycetes* [CELLULAR SLIME MOLDS] | *A group of slime fungi that inhabit soil with a high content of decaying organic remains. They do not produce flagellate cells or multinucleate plasmodia. Population comprises mostly uninucleate amoeboid cells. About 30 species.* |
| c | *Protosteliales* | *A recently defined heterogeneous group of slime fungi, comprising a small number of species.* |
| c | *Hydromyxomycetes* | *A very small group of marine parasitic slime fungi. The uninucleate cells form a network that moves in a gliding fashion. Number of species not yet defined.* |
| d | **MYCOTA (EUMYCOTA)** [TRUE FUNGI] | **Unicellular and multicellular (basically filamentous) heterotrophic organisms. Cell wall present, cells often multinucleate. Nutrition by absorption. Both sexual and asexual phases in the life cycle.** |
| sd | **Mastigomycotina** | **Zoospores motile and sexual spores typically motile.** |
| c | *Chytridomycetes* | *Zoospores with a single posterior whiplash flagellum.* |
| o | Chytridiales [CHYTRIDS] | Mainly aquatic, some inhabit soil or organic remains, a few are parasites. Thallus either without a vegetative system (and entirely reproductive) or with specialized vegetative system bearing reproductive structures. About 750 species. |
| o | Blastocladiales | Saprophytes in soil, water or organic remains. Thallus always with a well-defined vegetative system and having a conspicuous basal cell anchored by rhizoids. Thick-walled, resistant sporangia formed. About 50 species. |
| o | Monoblepharidales | Soil- and water-inhabiting. Vegetative thallus always well-defined, but basal cell absent. No resistant sporangia formed. About 10 species. |
| c | *Oomycetes* [EGG FUNGI] | *Mainly aquatic (some parasites), with motile zoospores and oospores with two flagella.* |
| o | Saprolegniales [FISH MOLDS] | Mainly free-living in water, soil or plant debris (some parasitize fish and plant roots). About 150 species. |
| o | Leptomiales | Saprophytic aquatic and soil fungi. About 20 species. |
| o | Lagenidiales | Parasites of algae, protozoa and aquatic animals with one genus infecting roots of cereal crops. About 45 species. |
| o | Peronosporales [DOWNY MILDEWS] | Mostly parasites of higher plants. About 350 species. |
| sd | **Zygomycotina** | **Terrestrial fungi with the hyphae septate only during reproduction; non-motile, non-flagellate asexual spores and sexual resting spores called zygospores.** |
| c | *Zygomycetes* | *Comprises two orders.* |
| o | Mucorales [PIN MOLDS] | Widely found in soil and mostly saprophytic, with some parasites of other fungi. Asexual reproduction by sporangia containing one or more spores. About 300 species. |
| o | Entomophthorales | Mainly parasites of insects and other animals. Asexual reproduction by conidia. About 100 species. |
| sd | **Ascomycotina** [ASCOMYCETES] | **Terrestrial or aquatic fungi with septate hyphae. Sexual reproduction involves production of an ascus containing ascospores. Asexual reproduction by formation of conidia.** |
| c | *Hemiascomycetes* | *Ascocarp lacking. About 300 species.* |
| o | Endomycetales [YEASTS] | Saprophytes and parasites. |
| o | Taphrinales | Plant parasites forming palisade-like layer of asci on surface of diseased tissue. |
| o | Protomycetales | Plant parasites forming thick-walled spores. |
| c | *Plectomycetes* | *Ascocarps in the form of cleistothecia. About 500 species.* |
| o | Ascosphaerales | Some insect parasites asci in clusters in a spore cyst. |

|  |  |  |
|---|---|---|
| o | Eurotiales | Mostly saprophytic, including many important agents of food spoilage and decay. Asci small and globose. |
| o | Erysiphales [POWDERY MILDEWS] | Obligate parasites of flowering plants. Asci oval to club-shaped. |
| c | *Pyrenomycetes* | *Ascocarps in the form of flask-shaped perithecia. About 9 000 species.* |
| o | Sphaeriales | Saprophytes of soil and dung or weak parasites of woody hosts. Perithecia dark-colored. |
| o | Hypocreales | Mainly parasites of flowering plants (particularly grasses) and insects, some saprophytic. Perithecia brightly-colored and fleshy. About 120 genera. |
| c | *Discomycetes* [CUP FUNGI] | *Ascocarps in the form of cup-shaped apothecia. About 3 000 species.* |
| o | Pezizales | Mostly saprophytic, many growing on dung. Ascocarps conspicuous. Asci opening by a lid. |
| o | Tuberales [TRUFFLES] | Fungi with underground, strong-smelling ascocarps. Asci without a lid. |
| o | Phacidales | Parasites of higher plants. Asci without a lid. |
| o | Lecanorales | Forming symbiotic relationship with algae in lichens. Asci without a lid. |
| c | *Loculoascomycetes* | *Ascocarps in the form of pseudothecia or a stroma containing chambers with a distinct wall. About 500 genera, 2 000 species.* |
| o | Pleosporales | Saprophytes and higher plant parasites. Asci club-shaped, separated by sterile hairs. |
| o | Myriangales | Asci globose. |
| sd | **Basidiomycotina** [BASIDIOMYCETES] | **Terrestrial fungi with septate hyphae. Sexual reproduction involves formation of a basidium containing basidiospores. Dikaryotic during most of life cycle.** |
| c | *Teliomycetes* | *Parasites on vascular plants. Basidiocarps not formed and overwintering spores either grouped in clusters or pustules or dispersed in host tissue.* |
| o | Uredinales [RUSTS] | Spores forcibly discharged and borne on stalks (sterigmata). About 5 000 species. |
| o | Ustilaginales [SMUTS] | Spores not forcibly discharged and not stalked. About 1 000 species. |
| c | *Hymenomycetes* | *Mainly saprophytes with some parasites. Basidiocarps well developed, typically with spores formed on a layer (hymenium) more or less exposed to the surroundings. Spores forcibly discharged.* |
| sc | *Phragmobasidiomycetidae* | *Basidia variously septate.* |
| o | Tremellales [JELLY FUNGI] | Mainly saprophytes on wood, typically with gelatinous, yellow or orange basidiocarps. About 200 species. |
| o | Auriculariales | Mainly saprophytes, with some parasites. About 100 species. |
| o | Septobasidiales | Parasites on scale insects in the tropics and warm temperate regions. About 175 species. |
| sc | *Holobasidiomycetidae* | *Basidia not septate.* |
| o | Exobasidiales | Parasites on flowering plants. About 65 species. |
| o | Brachybasidiales | Parasites causing leaf spot diseases; basidia protruding through the stomata or bursting the epidermis. Two species. |
| o | Dacrymycetales | Saprophytes, often with yellow or orange gelatinous basidiocarps. Basidia of an unusual "tuning fork" type. About 45 species. |
| o | Tulasnellales | Saprophytes and parasites with a wide range of hosts. About 50 species. |
| o | Aphyllophorales (Polyporales) [BRACKET FUNGI] | Saprophytes and parasites with large basidiocarps with the hymenium mostly lining pores and not borne on gills. About 1 000 species. |
| o | Agaricales [GILL FUNGI AND BOLETI] | Saprophytes and parasites, typically with large umbrella-shaped basidiocarps, with the hymenium spread over radiating gills (except in *Boletus*). About 3 000 species. |
| c | *Gasteromycetes* | *Basidiocarps mostly not exposed to the surroundings. Basidia not septate and spores not forcibly discharged. About 550 species.* |
| o | Lycoperdales [PUFFBALLS AND EARTHSTARS] | Hymenium present, collapsing at maturity to form a powdery mass surrounded by skin. |
| o | Phallales [STINKHORNS] | Hymenium present, collapsing into a glutinous mass which is carried upwards as a stalk at maturity. |
| o | Sclerodermatales [EARTH BALLS] | Hymenium not present and spores forming a powdery mass. |
| o | Nidulariales [BIRD'S NEST FUNGI] | Hymenium not present and spore-mass in the form of hard seed-like pellets. |
| sd | **Deuteromycotina** [IMPERFECT FUNGI] | **Fungi in which the sexual (or perfect) phase is not known. Reproduction is by asexual spores (conidia). About 25 000 species.** |

but some spores have a moist surface when they are dispersed by rain splash or damp air. Spores dispersed by water may be motile (zoospores) or, as in certain aquatic hyphomycetes, much branched. (See p. 819.)

**Life Cycles.** In flowering plants the nuclear cycle is standardized. The plant cells are diploid. Meiosis immediately precedes the formation of pollen grains and egg, the fusion of which restores the diploid condition. In fungi there is much variation. For the assimilative thallus to be diploid (as in oomycetes) is rare. More frequently it is haploid with the diploid phase limited to the zygote, while in higher basidiomycetes during much of the assimilative phase each cell may contain two haploid nuclei of opposite mating type which undergo simultaneous (or "conjugate") division and only fuse in the basidium where a reduction division precedes basidiospore development. This last condition is called dikaryotic (each cell with its pair of complementary nuclei being a dikaryon).

Some fungi, particularly chytrids, oomycetes and certain ascomycetes, develop morphologically distinguishable sexual organs (antheridia, oogonia and ascogonia) but sometimes the individual fungus bearing both types of sex organs is self-sterile. More frequently there is no differentiation between the sexes but, as in the well-known case of the pin molds, there are two morphologically indistinguishable but compatible mating types, and when appropriate strains (+ and −) are brought together, in response to mutual stimulation by hormones, special branches develop which on fusion give rise to a zygospore. This condition is known as heterothallism, in contrast to homothallism, in which sexual fusions are possible between different branches of one mycelium.

Fungi frequently produce both sexual and asexual spores and there may be a more or less well defined alternation, as in many parasitic species where the sexual (or perfect) state constitutes the climax on dead host tissues. For others, the perfect state is of rare occurrence and for many only the asexual (or imperfect) state is known. Some of these last are certainly as yet unconnected with perfect states already described. For others, the perfect state will sooner or later be discovered, but there remains a large residue of forms that appear to have lost the ability to produce a perfect state.

The kingdom Fungi has two divisions, the Mycota (or Eumycota), in which the thallus is basically filamentous, and the Myxomycota (slime fungi) characterized by the possession of naked, multinucleate plasmodia or pseudoplasmodia. The main diagnostic characters by which the Mycota are divided are based on the types of the sexual spores. A summary of the main groups of fungi is given in the accompanying table.

*Views of the underside of the fruiting bodies of (*Below Top*) a typical gill fungus (×5) showing the gills and (*Below Bottom*) a bracket fungus (×2) showing the pores. Spores are produced on the lining (hymenium) to the gills or pores, from which they are forcibly discharged.*

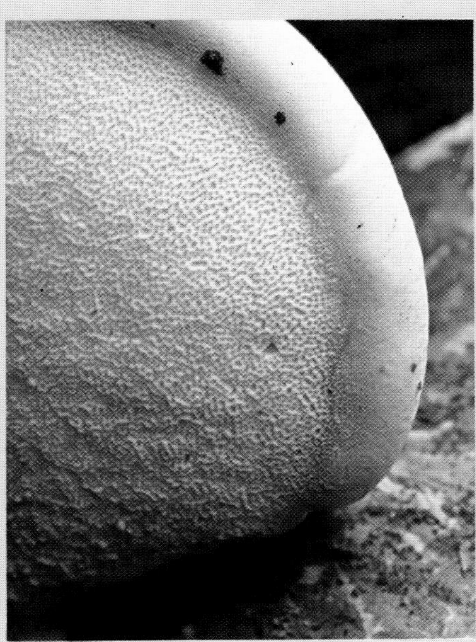

*The unmistakable cap of* Amanita muscaria *(Fly Agaric) which is dangerous because of its poisonous and hallucinogenic properties.* (×2)

from western North America, with purple-black berries.
ERICACEAE, about 100 species.

**Gaylussacia** see HUCKLEBERRY.
ERICACEAE, about 40 species.

**Gazania** a genus native to South Africa, comprising low-growing, mostly perennial herbs or subshrubs, with basal leaf rosettes and large brightly colored daisy-like flower heads borne on long leafless stalks. They are easily hybridized and several cultivars, as well as a few of the parental species, notably *G. ringens* (= *G. splendens*) [TREASURE FLOWER] are popular half-hardy garden plants in north temperate regions.
COMPOSITAE, about 25 species.

*Inflorescences of the Treasure Flower (*Gazania ringens*), a hybrid that is popular as a half-hardy garden ornamental.* (× ⅓)

**Geastrum** see EARTHSTARS.
GEASTRACEAE.

**Gelidium** a genus of red algae native mainly to the coasts of the North Pacific. It is economically important for the agar (used in the food, cosmetic, paper and textile industries) that is extracted from it by boiling. The chief producer is Japan, but it is also processed in many other countries.
GELIDIACEAE.

**Genista** a genus of shrubs or shrubby herbs, many of which are cultivated in gardens. They are native to Mediterranean regions with a few outliers in the Canary Islands and Madeira and a sparse representation in western Asia and northern Europe. The typically pea-like flowers are yellow, borne in terminal racemes or heads, or, in a few species, on short shoots in the leaf-axils. The genus as described here includes groups of species such as *Teline*, *Chamaespartium* and *Echinospartium* which are often treated as separate genera.

Species cultivated in gardens include spring shrubs such as *G. sylvestris* (= *G. dalmatica*) [DALMATIAN BROOM], a dwarf species of compact habit, *G. hispanica* [SPANISH GORSE], a much-branched, erect to decumbent, profusely flowering type, and *G. anglica* [PETTY WHIN, NEEDLE FURZE], which is erect to more or less prostrate with very spiny branches. Nonspiny cultivated species include *G. lydia* and *G. januensis* [GENOA BROOM], both of which are procumbent to erect, freely flowering forms, and *G. cinerea*, a sweetly scented erect shrub with flexuous branches. One of the most spectacular cultivated species is the tall, elegant *G. tenera* (= *G. virgata*) [MADEIRA BROOM], which bears deep yellow flowers in dense terminal racemes. *G. tinctoria* [DYER'S GREENWEED], the source of a yellow dye, is also widely cultivated under various varieties or cultivars.
LEGUMINOSAE, about 80 species.

**Gentiana** a large genus of perennial (rarely annual or biennial) herbs widely distributed in temperate regions and in mountains in the tropics. The genus is most evocative of the European Alps and is much favored by alpine gardeners. The flowers may be white, yellow, blue to purple, pinkish red, or mauve. The blue trumpet gentians of Europe include the widely cultivated *G. clusii* and *G. acaulis* (= *G. excisa*, *G. kochiana*) [STEMLESS GENTIAN]. The alpine species grow up to the snow level where few other flowering plants thrive. The North American cultivated species include the blue-flowered *G. andrewsii* [CLOSED OR BOTTLE GENTIAN] (white in var *albiflora*) and the very similar *G. clausa*, with the same common names. *G. catesbaei* (= *G. elliotti*) [CATESBY'S GENTIAN, SAMPSON'S SNAKEROOT] and *G. newberryi* [ALPINE GENTIAN] are two other North American blue-flowered species, while *G. autumnalis* (= *G. porphyrio*) [PINE-BARREN GENTIAN] has yellowish and blue flowers.

*Shoots of* Genista lydia, *a prostrate species native to southeastern Europe and Syria. It is cultivated both for its spineless gray-green shoots and bright yellow flowers that appear in the spring.* (× 1)

*The Stemless Gentian (*Gentiana acaulis*), one of the best-loved wild flowers of the European Alps.* (× 1)

*G. lutea* [GREAT YELLOW GENTIAN], is the chief commercial source of the bitter tonic, gentian bitter, and, when fermented, of the aperitif drink Suze and the liqueur Enzian. Locally, other species have been used similarly and also with, or instead of, hops in beer. In addition to the many species in cultivation, many hybrids have been raised, eg *G.* × 'Inverleith' (*G. farreri* × *G. veitchiorum*).
GENTIANACEAE, 300–400 species.

**Gentianella** a genus of annual, biennial, and rarely perennial herbs from temperate regions of both hemispheres (not Africa). Although sometimes included in **Gentiana*, it differs from that genus in not having appendages between the corolla-lobes. The flowers are blue, mauve or white. It contains several taxonomically very complex species showing great variation and hybridization. Several species are occasionally cultivated, such as *G. amarella* and *G. tenella*. Some Northern Hemisphere species, such as *G. detonsa* [FRINGED GENTIAN], are sometimes separated out as a further genus, *Gentianopsis*.
GENTIANACEAE, about 125 species.

**Geonoma** a medium to large genus of slender palms of tropical America, where they ascend to cool mountain rain forests. Although of no economic importance, the leaves of several species such as *G. interrupta* (= *G. binervia*) and *G. dominica* are used locally for thatching, and the young inflorescences for food.
PALMAE, about 75–250 species.

**Geranium** [CRANESBILLS] a genus of annual biennial or perennial herbs, often with a rhizome, tuber or rootstock. The genus is cosmopolitan but mainly found in temperate regions as far north as the Arctic Circle and south to Antarctica, while some species occur in mountains of tropical regions. The name 'Geranium' is widely applied to species and hybrids of **Pelargonium* from South Africa which are widely cultivated for ornament or for their essential oils.

The genus is not important economically and some such as *G. molle* [DOVE'S FOOT] are regarded as weeds. However, a number of the freer-flowering species are used horticulturally in herbaceous borders in rock gardens. These include the white-flowered *G. richardsonii* (with red veins on the petals), the pink-flowered *G. argenteum* [SILVER-LEAVED GERANIUM] and *G. cinereum*, the violet-blue-flowered *G. pratense* [MEADOW CRANESBILL], the purple-flowered *G. collinum* and *G. sylvaticum* (white in cultivar 'Album') and the red-to-magenta-flowered *G. robertianum* [HERB ROBERT, RED ROBIN] and *G. sanguineum* [BLOODY CRANESBILL] (white in cultivar 'Album'). The spectacular shrubby *G. maderense* with masses of carmine flowers is grown under glass.

The American species *G. maculatum* [WILD CRANESBILL, ALUM ROOT] provides a liquid extract from the roots which has astringent properties and is used to control bleeding.
GERANIACEAE, about 300 species.

**Gerbera** a genus of daisy-like perennial herbs from Africa, Asia, Madagascar and Indonesia. *G. jamesonii* [BARBERTON or TRANSVAAL DAISY] is the most hardy species. Wild forms have yellow to orange, flame-colored flower heads and many color variants exist in cultivation. *G. asplenifolia* is also attractive, with purple flower heads and fern-like foliage.
COMPOSITAE, about 70 species.

**Geum** a genus of perennial herbs found in temperate regions of both the Northern and Southern Hemisphere. Many are grown as garden plants in herbaceous borders or rockeries. The species are generally readily separable except in a few groups; in Britain, for example, *G. urbanum* [WOOD AVENS] and *G. rivale* [WATER AVENS] show extensive hybridization, usually following human disruption of the habitat. Many species are grown as garden ornamentals for the color of their large flowers; double forms are frequent. The most commonly cultivated are *G. coccineum* and *G. quellyon* (= *G. chilense*, "*G. chiloense*"), both with scarlet flowers, and

*The flowers of Water Avens (*Geum rivale*). (×1)*

*The stamens and stigmas of the Dove's Foot Cranesbill (*Geranium molle*) mature in close proximity, which assists self-pollination. (×2½)*

*G. montanum* with yellow to orange flowers, together with hybrid derivatives of these species.

The rhizomes of *G. urbanum* have been used as a flavoring for wine liqueurs and beer, as a heart tonic and as a remedy for complaints of the digestive system.
ROSACEAE, about 50 species.

**Gherkins** the warty fruits of **Cucumis anguria*, a West Indian species similar to cucumber (*C. sativus*). The "gherkins" of today, commonly bought pickled, and often flavored with *DILL, are not true gherkins but small-fruited varieties of *CUCUMBER. Less warty, they are said to be of better flavor than the fruits of *C. anguria*.
CUCURBITACEAE.

**Gigartina** a genus of red algae often found in the intertidal zone on rocky shores. In the Pacific Ocean large parenchymatous species grow in the sublittoral zone (near the sea but not on the shore). Like **Chondrus*, which grows in similar situations, this alga is collected for carrageenan extraction (see CARRAGHEEN), notably from *G. mamillosa* and *G. stellata*.
RHODOPHYCEAE.

**Gilia** a genus of annual, biennial or perennial herbs mainly from western North America, many of which make attractive ornamental bedding plants with funnel-shaped or salverform flowers. Fine examples are the annuals *G. capitata*, with terminal heads of white, blue or violet flowers, and *G. latifolia*, with long inflorescences of pink-buff flowers. Many species previously placed in the genus have been transferred to *Ipomopsis*, *Eriastrum*, *Linanthus* and *Leptodactylon*.
POLEMONIACEAE, 20–30 species.

**Gillenia** a genus of only two species of perennial herbs from North America. Both *G. stipulata* [AMERICAN IPECAC] and *G. trifoliata* [INDIAN PHYSIC, BOWMAN'S ROOT] are cultivated as ornamentals for their showy white or pink flowers with narrow petals. The roots and bark were traditionally used by North American Indians as an emetic.
ROSACEAE, 2 species.

**Gill fungi** see Fungi, p. 156.

**Ginger** the common name for the plant and the product of **Zingiber officinale*, a monocotyledonous perennial herb, native to Southeast Asia but now cultivated in many tropical regions, particularly in the West Indies, Sierra Leone, China, Japan and India. The familiar ginger condiment is derived from the fleshy rhizomes of the plant. The common white ginger is obtained by washing, boiling, peeling and blanching the rhizomes, while the rarer black ginger is merely washed and boiled before drying. The dried rhizomes are frequently ground up into a powder as a means of efficient distribution and for its use as a flavoring. Ground ginger is used mainly in flavoring cakes and drinks such as ginger beer. Preserved ginger, produced mainly in China, is derived by boiling young peeled rhizomes or stem segments, and is packed in sugar syrup, candied or crystallized. In the preserved form it is frequently used in fruit cake and for the manufacture of ginger marmalade. Ginger is also the source of an essential oil, gingerol.
ZINGIBERACEAE.

**Ginkgo** see MAIDENHAIR TREE.
GINKGOACEAE, 1 species.

**Gladiolus** a large, predominantly African genus of cormous perennial herbs, especially well represented in tropical and South Africa, but also found to the north in Europe, the Mediterranean region and western and Central Asia, with one species occurring as far north as England. The dark green basal leaves are most commonly produced all in one plane and are fairly flat in section, although a number of species have narrow cylindrical or angular leaves. The inflorescence is a spike of stalkless flowers, each produced in the axil of a pair of bracts, the whole spike being either one-sided or less frequently two-sided. The color range in *Gladiolus* species is extremely wide, virtually all colors being represented. Many species are bicolored, with a blotch of different color on

*The gladiolus is an important flower commercially. Many* Gladiolus *hybrids have been developed; cultivar 'Alderbaron' is shown here. (×⅓)*

the lower segment or segments of the flower. Several species are sweetly scented.

In cultivation in the Northern Hemisphere the southwest Cape species are not hardy since they grow and flower during the most severe weather, therefore requiring greenhouse protection. The summer-rainfall east Cape species, however, are dormant during winter and some of them will survive out of doors. It is, therefore, largely the species of this group, such as *G. natalensis*, which have been used by plant breeders to produce the large and colorful hybrid cultivars of the *G.* × *hortulanus* [GARDEN GLADIOLUS]. One of the early cultivated forms of *Gladiolus* is the summer-flowering garden hybrid, *G.* × *gandavensis* (originating from either *G. cardinalis* × *G. natalensis* or *G. natalensis* × *G. oppositiflorus*), from which most modern gladioli have been derived.
IRIDACEAE, about 300 species.

**Glaucium** a genus of annual, biennial and perennial herbs found from Europe to Central Asia. The commonest, *G. flavum* (= *G. luteum*) [YELLOW HORNED or SEA POPPY] is maritime in distribution, growing on sand, shingle beaches and cliffs. It is naturalized in the eastern USA. The flowers are bright yellow with a darker blotch at their bases. The seeds yield an oil which is used in cooking and making soap. This species, the biennial *G. corniculatum* (= *G. rubrum*) [RED HORNED POPPY], with its showy crimson or orange flowers, and *G. grandiflorum* (which is often sold as *G. corniculatum*) are commonly cultivated as border plants.
PAPAVERACEAE, about 20 species.

**Glaux** a genus represented by a single species, *G. maritima* [SEA MILKWORT, BLACK SALTWORT], which is found on the coasts, salt marshes and inland saline areas of the north temperate zone. It is a small succulent herb with creeping stems and small pinkish flowers. The young shoots are edible and are sometimes used as an emergency food.
PRIMULACEAE, 1 species.

**Glechoma** a genus of perennial herbs native to Europe and Asia. The best-known species is *G. hederacea* (= *Nepeta hederacea*, *N. glechoma*), commonly known as GROUND IVY, ALEHOOF, HAYMAIDS, FIELD BALM or GILL-OVER-THE-ROAD. A bluish-purple-flowered, prostrate, trailing, perennial herb of thin woodland and shaded banks, it can become very invasive in cultivated borders and lawns. It is widely naturalized in North America. It is used as a ground cover and a number of cultivated varieties were at one time popular ornamentals, especially the variety *variegata*, used in hanging baskets and window boxes.
LABIATAE, about 6–10 species.

**Gleditsia** (or, incorrectly, *Gleditschia*) a genus of usually spiny, deciduous trees from eastern North America, China, Japan and Iran. Many species are cultivated for their attractive fern-like foliage, for example the North American *G. triacanthos* [HONEY LOCUST, SWEET BEAN], and for shade. Cultivar 'Sunburst' has golden-yellow foliage in both spring and autumn, while 'Moraine' lacks the 12in-long spines and is sterile, thus lacking the pods which rattle when dry. Also cultivated is the spineless hybrid *G.* × *texana*, which arose naturally where populations of *G. aquatica* [WATER LOCUST] and *G. triacanthos* grew together in Texas. Some species have domestic uses. The pulp from *G. triacanthos* is sweet and pods may be fermented to make "beer" or fed to stock. Pods of *G. caspica* [CASPIAN LOCUST] and also of *G. japonica* (Japan) and *G. macracantha* (China) are used in soapmaking. Pods of the latter are also used in tanning. The wood of many species is hard and durable, and that of *G. sinensis* (China) and *G. triacanthos* is used for general carpentry, fence posts, etc.
LEGUMINOSAE, about 10 species.

**Gleichenia** [SUN FERNS] a genus of ferns native to South Africa, Malaysia and Australasia. They are all terrestrial with long creeping rhizomes. The rhizomes of *G. linearis* (= *G. dichotoma*) [SAVANNAH FERN] are used as a source of edible starch by Australian aborigines, and its leaves are woven into matting in parts of Malaysia.
GLEICHENIACEAE, about 10 species.

**Globularia** [GLOBE DAISIES] a genus of mainly blue-flowered shrubs and perennial herbs largely found in the Mediterranean region, the Alps and Macaronesia. There are no species of economic importance though *G. alypum*, from the Mediterranean region, is poisonous and violently purgative and the leaves of *G. vulgaris* yield a yellow dye. Several species including *G. alypum*, *G. cordifolia*, and *G. meridionalis* (= *G. bellidifolia*) are cultivated as ornamentals, especially in rock gardens.
GLOBULARIACEAE, about 28 species.

*Savannah Fern (*Gleichenia linearis*) here photographed in the foothills of the island of Oahu, Hawaii. These sun-loving ferns (*hence the popular name *"sun ferns") are not generally cultivated.* (×$\frac{1}{5}$)

*The Glory Lily (*Gloriosa superba*). It climbs by means of tendrils extending from the end of each leaf.* (×$\frac{1}{2}$)

**Gloriosa** [GLORY LILY] a genus of climbing or creeping tuberous perennials native to tropical Africa and Asia. The showy flowers are pendulous with yellow, orange or red reflexed perianth segments. *G. rothschildiana* and *G. superba* are easily grown in a warm greenhouse in temperate regions.
LILIACEAE, 5–6 species.

**Gloxinia** the florists' name for the tuberous-rooted herbaceous species, **Sinningia speciosa* (= *Gloxinia speciosa*), a native of Brazil which is a popular houseplant in many parts of the world. It bears oblong-ovate leaves and large showy purple, pink or violet flowers (see *Sinningia*).

*Gloxinia* is also the generic name for about 6 species of erect perennial herbs, native to Central and South America, one of which, *G. maculata*, is widely cultivated in tropical countries for its large bluish-purple flowers (lilac and red in var *insignis*). *G. perennis* and *G. gymnostoma* are cultivated particularly in the USA.
GESNERIACEAE.

**Glyceria** a genus of tall, temperate and especially North American marsh or aquatic grasses, the sweet grasses of agriculture. All species provide excellent forage for cattle in swampy places. Important species include *G. fluitans* [MANNA GRASS, SUGAR GRASS, FLOATING SWEET GRASS] and *G. maxima* [REED SWEET GRASS].
GRAMINEAE, about 40 species.

**Glycine** a small genus of perennial (rarely annual) mostly climbing herbs native to Australia, Africa and Asia. The most important economically is the annual *G. max* [*SOYBEAN], which has never been found in the wild. The WILD SOYBEAN is *G. soja*, from eastern China, the USSR, Korea, Japan and Taiwan, which hybridizes with *G. max*.
LEGUMINOSAE, 9 species.

**Glycyrrhiza** a genus of temperate and subtropical American, Eurasian, North African and southeast Australian perennial herbs characterized by their spikes of blue or violet pea-like flowers. *Licorice is obtained from the dried rhizomes and roots of *G. glabra*.
LEGUMINOSAE, about 18 species.

**Gnaphalium** a genus of yellow- or white-flowered hardy herbs or small shrubs, widely distributed throughout the world but with the main center in the mountains of Europe. *G. uliginosum* [CUDWEED, COTTONWEED] has been used locally as an astringent. They have limited horticultural value except for a few species such as *G. obtusifolium* which may be used as everlasting flowers.
COMPOSITAE, about 135 species.

**Gnetum** a genus of tropical gymnosperms most of which are climbing shrubs, the remainder being small trees. *G. gnemon* (Malaysia) and certain other species are cultivated for their edible plum-like fruits. The bark of this species and of *G. scandens* (Indochina) is used as a source of fiber.
GNETACEAE, about 30 species.

*Godetias, such as this species –* Godetia concinna *– are a common garden favorite for herbaceous borders.* ($\times\frac{1}{10}$)

**Godetia** a group of species once regarded as a distinct genus and now included in the genus **Clarkia* as a section of eight species. Many are grown as ornamental hardy annuals for their brightly colored single or double, funnel-shaped flowers, especially *C. amoena*, with pink to lavender flowers often with a central spot of bright red, and *C. concinna* (= *C. grandiflora*), with bright pink flowers; both are still often referred to under the old generic name *Godetia*.
ONAGRACEAE.

**Gomphrena** a genus of annual and perennial herbs native to tropical America, Southeast Asia and Australia, with most species in the New World. The dense chaffy flower heads of the Old World species *G. globosa* [GLOBE AMARANTH] are useful for drying as everlasting flowers. They grow in a wide range of colors from white through yellow, pink and red to purple, with yellow florets. *C. haageana*, from Texas and Mexico, with red heads and yellow florets is also cultivated.
AMARANTHACEAE, about 100 species.

**Gonyaulax** a genus of dinoflagellates which is responsible in some areas for the phenomenon known as *red tide, in which a large concentration of the algae causes the sea to appear a reddish-brown color. *Gonyaulax* produces a toxin in the cells and when the plants grow to such high densities, filter-feeding animals such as shellfish concentrate the toxin in their tissues. This may affect humans who inadvertently eat such molluscs.
DINOPHYCEAE.

**Goodyera** a cosmopolitan genus of terrestrial semi-epiphytic orchids. The terminal racemes or spikes of small white, pale green or dingy pink flowers and the usually tessellated or contrastingly veined and brittle leaves arranged in a rosette are characteristic of the great majority of species. *Goodyera* and its related genera are often called JEWEL ORCHIDS or RATTLESNAKE PLANTAINS because of the unusual leaves.
ORCHIDACEAE, about 50 species.

**Gooseberry** the common name for **Ribes uva-crispa* (= *R. grossularia*) a much-branched deciduous bush with conspicuous nodal spines along the branches, native to Europe but widely cultivated in temperate regions. In North America cultivated gooseberries are either varieties of *R. uva-crispa* or of the closely related American species *R. hirtellum* and hybrids derived from it.

Gooseberries are often picked before they are ripe and stewed or made into jam. They are also canned commercially and are an excellent fruit for domestic bottling. When ripe some varieties give excellent dessert fruits, although very few are grown commercially for this purpose.

Gooseberry varieties are usually classified by the color of the berries. Some, such as 'Whinham's Industry', are red, while others, such as 'Leveller', are yellow. 'Keepsake' has green berries, and 'Careless' and 'Whitesmith' bear whitish fruits when ripe.
SAXIFRAGACEAE.

*Gloxinias (*Sinningia speciosa*) are popular houseplants grown for their showy trumpet-shaped flowers.* ($\times\frac{3}{4}$)

**Gossypium** an economically important genus of annual or perennial herbs, shrubs or small trees native to the tropics and subtropics (see COTTON). One or two species, eg *G. arboreum* [TREE COTTON], are sometimes cultivated for their large showy flowers.
MALVACEAE, about 34 species.

**Gourd** the name given to the fruits of some members of the cucumber family, widely used in tropical countries for food, and as utensils. **Lagenaria siceraria* [BOTTLE GOURD, CALABASH] has been cultivated since prehistoric times, mainly for the hard fruit shells which are still used as containers, spoons, fishing floats, musical instruments etc; young fruits are sometimes eaten as a vegetable.

Other edible gourds include *Benincasa hispida* [WAX OR WHITE GOURD], **Cucumis anguria* [GOOSEBERRY GOURD, WEST INDIAN GOURD], **Cucurbita foetidissima* [WILD GOURD], *Momordica charantia* [BITTER GOURD], *Trichosanthes anguina* (= *T. colubrina*) [SERPENT OR SNAKE GOURD], *T. cucumeroides* [SNAKE GOURD], **Luffa aegyptiaca* (= *L. cylindrica*) [VEGETABLE SPONGE, SPONGE GOURD, DISHCLOTH SPONGE]. Some cultivars of **Cucurbita pepo* [MARROW] are grown as ornamental gourds.
CUCURBITACEAE.

**Grain amaranth** a general name for the seeds of a number of annual herbaceous species of the genus **Amaranthus*. The seeds of three species are used by primitive peoples as food, viz. *A. caudatus* [INCA WHEAT, QUIHUICHA] and its subspecies *mantegazzianus* in the Andes, *A. hypochondriacus* (= *A. frumentaceus*, *A. leucocarpus*) in Mexico and *A. cruentus* (= *A. paniculatus*) in Mexico and Central America. The small seeds of all these cultivated species are normally milled for flour. Although they are all native to the New World, grain amaranth is now widely grown in India and parts of Asia.
AMARANTHACEAE.

**Grape** the fruit of **Vitis vinifera* [GRAPEVINE]. They are eaten fresh or dried and numerous alcoholic beverages, such as wines and spirits, are derived from the grape. Dried grapes include *raisins, *sultanas and *currants.
VITACEAE.

**Grapefruit** the large, yellow, roundish citrus fruit, borne mostly in clusters on the dense, dome-shaped evergreen trees **Citrus*

× *paradisi* in warm subtropical and tropical countries. It was first noticed in Barbados around 1750, and probably originated from a chance seedling or hybrid of imported *SHADDOCK with SWEET *ORANGE. It spread to nearby Florida, where most known varieties subsequently arose.

Total world grapefruit production was 3·7 million tons in 1975. The chief growing countries are USA (60% of the world production), Israel, Cyprus and South Africa. The leading cultivated variety is the yellow 'Marsh (or Marsh's) Seedless'. Pigmented varieties include the seedless 'Thompson' ('Pink Marsh') and the seedy 'Foster'.
RUTACEAE.

**Grass pea** the common name for **Lathyrus sativus*, an herbaceous annual native to southern Europe and western Asia. Known also as VETCHLING, GRASS PEAVINE, CHICKLING PEA or, in India, where it is chiefly cultivated, as KHESARI, it is a cold-weather crop and very tolerant of drought, waterlogging and poor soils. It produces the cheapest pulse available. Although it can be eaten by humans it is more usually grown for animal fodder. There is a suggestion that the consumption of large quantities of the raw peas may cause a paralytic disease of the lower limbs, lathyrism.
LEGUMINOSAE.

**Green algae** the common name for the algae placed in the division Chlorophyta where the pigment chlorophyll *a* is usually present in much larger amounts than the other chloroplast pigments. Green algae are mainly found in freshwater environments but a few inhabit the margins of the seas. (See also ALGAE, p. 18.)

**Greengage** a type of plum believed to be derived from hybrids between **Prunus domestica* [EUROPEAN PLUM] and *P. insititia* [DAMSON PLUM] or regarded as a variety (var *italica*) of *P. insititia*. The most commonly grown variety is 'Reine Claude'.
ROSACEAE.

*Grapefruit (*Citrus × paradisi*) growing in a small plantation in Mokwa, Nigeria.* (× 1/50)

*The moss* Grimmia pulvinata *showing the 16 teeth of the single peristome.* (× 2)

**Greenheart** the common name for **Ocotea rodiaei* (= *Nectandra rodiaei*) (family Lauraceae), a large tropical forest tree, growing to 20m tall, which is exported in quantity from the Demarara River in Guiana. Its lustrous green to dark olive heartwood is very hard, dense and close-grained. It is thus immensely strong and durable and is highly resistant to attack by marine boring animals. Greenheart timber is used in the construction of marine piers, lock gates, boats and engineering work.

At least two other species are termed GREENHEART, viz. *Cylicodiscus gabunensis* [AFRICAN GREENHEART], of the family Leguminosae, and **Tecoma leucoxylon* [SURINAM GREENHEART], of the Bignoniaceae.

**Greenovia** a genus of tender leaf succulents from rocks and cliffs of the Canary Islands. All are in cultivation, and are hardy enough to thrive outdoors as far north as the Scilly Isles.
CRASSULACEAE, 4 species.

**Green peppers** the immature fruits of non-pungent cultivars of **Capsicum annuum*. Popular as salad or cooked vegetables, they are grown in most tropical and warm temperate countries and, under protection, in cool temperate regions.
SOLANACEAE.

**Grevillea** a large genus of evergreen trees and shrubs found mainly in Australia and Tasmania, extending to New Caledonia and Sulawesi. It has, however, been introduced into warm-temperate and subtropical countries throughout the world as a genus of ornamental value. In all the species the flowers are grouped together into long, usually extremely attractive racemes or panicles.

The best-known and most commonly cultivated species is *G. robusta* [SILK OAK, GOLDEN PINE], a large tree with fern-like pinnate leaves, highly prized for its golden inflorescences. It is also grown as an indoor foliage plant ("GREVILLEA") or as a summer bedding plant in cooler climates. In addition, the usually red-flowered *G. banksii*, and *G. juniperina*, with pale yellow flowers, often tinged red, are sometimes cultivated.
PROTEACEAE, about 200 species.

**Greyia** a genus of South African shrubs and small trees. *G. sutherlandii*, a shrub with showy scarlet flowers, is grown as an ornamental in warm climates, sometimes under glass.
GREYIACEAE, 3 species.

**Grimmia** a large genus of mosses most of which form neat, dark green or gray-green cushions on rocks. They are found all over the world, although sparsely in the tropics where they occur mainly at high altitudes. Several species that are well known in north temperate regions also have very wide cosmopolitan distributions, such as *G. pulvinata*, and *G. trichophylla*.
GRIMMIACEAE, about 240 species.

**Grindelia** a genus of annual, biennial or perennial, sometimes shrubby herbs from North America and South America, south of the tropics. Several species are cultivated, including *G. chiloensis* (Argentina), *G. glutinosa* (Peru) and *G. squarrosa* [GUMWEED] (North America). The leaves and flower tops of the latter contain resin, saponin, tannin, robustic acid and grindol and have been used to relieve coughs and burns.
COMPOSITAE, about 6 species.

**Griselinia** a genus of half-hardy evergreen trees and shrubs from New Zealand and South America. The leaves are leathery and

*The large rhubarb-like leaves of* Gunnera manicata *from Colombia.* (× 1/25)

Right *Green alga (*Enteromorpha*) growing in a freshwater spring on a rocky shore.*

*The canopy of the Kentucky Coffee Tree (*Gymnocladus dioica*) showing the roughened bark and large bipinnate leaves, which turn a bright yellow in the fall.*

*A species of* Gypsophila *from the Mount Ararat region of Turkey, where it forms hard round cushions on the rocky slopes.*

glossy and usually pale olive-green in color. *G. littoralis* and *G. lucida* are vigorous New Zealand evergreen shrubs that have proved very successful in southern Britain and Europe as attractive seaside hedge and screen plants. They are also grown outside in California. The timber of *G. lucida* is used in New Zealand for boat-building.
CORNACEAE, about 6 species.

**Guaiacum** a genus of tropical American and West Indian trees which have very hard, heavy wood. Two West Indian species (*G. officinale* and *G. sanctum*) are important as sources of *lignum vitae, the hardest of commercial timbers, and guaiacum resin, which has medicinal and other uses. They are planted in the tropics as ornamentals.
ZYGOPHYLLACEAE, about 6 species.

**Guarea** a genus of trees from tropical America and Africa. The African *G. cedrata* and *G. thompsonii* are trade timbers of West Africa and are much used in furniture-making. Many of the American species are small trees of the undergrowth of rain forest and exhibit the phenomenon of "evergrowing leaves". The leaves have some of the characteristics of shoots: the apex of the leaf is a naked meristem which periodically produces flushes of leaflets. In this way the leaf "bud" builds up a long pinnate leaf over several seasons. The purplish-red wood known as *acajou in the West Indies comes from *G. guara* (= *G. trichilioides*).
MELIACEAE, 35 species.

**Guizotia** a small genus of annual and perennial herbs native to tropical Africa. One species, *G. abyssinica* [NIGER SEED, NOOG], is a tall annual hairy herb, grown in Ethiopia and India as an oilseed crop. The fruits (cypselas) contain 30–50% of a pale yellow semidrying oil, mainly linoleic acid. Most niger seed oil is used locally for cooking and lighting and does not enter world trade. The protein-rich press-cake is fed to livestock. The seed is used as a food for cage birds.
COMPOSITAE, about 10 species.

**Gunnera** a largely Southern Hemisphere genus of small creeping or large, sometimes gigantic, erect herbs, with well-developed rhizomes or aerial stems and often round or kidney-shaped leaves.

The petioles of the large *Gunnera chilensis* (= *G. scabra*) [CHILE RHUBARB] are often eaten and are said to diminish fevers. The stems are used in tanning. The small mat-forming species, such as the South American *G. magellanica* and the New Zealand *G. arenaria*, are often cultivated as ground cover, while some of the large species, with enormous rhubarb-like leaves are grown around garden ponds for their striking appearance – the largest, *G. manicata* from Colombia, has leaves up to 10ft across, borne on stalks up to 8ft high.
HALORAGACEAE, about 47 species.

**Gutta-percha** a plastic gum obtained from the latex of the leaves or bark of trees mainly of the genus *Palaquium*, especially *P. gutta*, which is native to Indomalaysia. Gutta-percha has been used for insulating submarine and other electric cables, for machine belting and golf balls, and in dentistry, but is now largely superseded by plastics. *Payena leerii* (native to the same region and a member of the same family) produces a gum also called gutta-percha (gutta sundek).
SAPOTACEAE.

**Gymnadenia** a genus of tuberous, terrestrial, perennial orchids from Greenland, Europe and northern Asia. The flowers, which are usually fragrant, are borne in dense spikes. *Gymnadenia* hybridizes with other genera, eg *Anacamptis* and *Coeloglossum*; it is sometimes included in **Habenaria*.
ORCHIDACEAE, about 10 species.

**Gymnocalycium** a South American genus of low growing globose cacti, many species of which are cultivated as ornamentals for their attractive ribbed, often spiny stems and large showy, often pink flowers.
CACTACEAE, about 60 species.

**Gymnocladus** a small genus of deciduous trees with one species in eastern North America and two or three species in China. *G. dioica* (= *G. canadensis*) [KENTUCKY COFFEE TREE] grows slowly to more than 100ft producing greenish-white flowers. The flat pods contain seeds once used by settlers as a coffee substitute. Sometimes grown as an ornamental, the tree also yields a useful timber. The Chinese *G. chinensis* [SOAP TREE] has lilac-purple unisexual flowers, and smaller pods with lather-producing properties.
LEGUMINOSAE, 3–4 species.

**Gymnodinium** a genus of dinoflagellates. They have a simple form with a groove around the center of the cell and a short longitudinal furrow. *Gymnodinium* is found both in the sea and in fresh water. The disastrous Florida red tide is caused by *G. breve* (see Red tide).
DINOPHYCEAE.

*A flowering shoot of Lignum Vitae (*Guaiacum officinale*), a species grown both for its attractive flowers and hard timber.* (× ½)

**Gymnosperms** see Conifers and their allies, p. 100.

**Gynura** a genus of tropical and subtropical evergreen perennial herbs and subshrubs from Africa, Madagascar, Southeast Asia and Malaysia, some of which are cultivated under glass for their attractive foliage and stems. A popular species is *G. aurantiaca* [VELVET PLANT], with its leaves and stems covered with a dense mat of violet-purple hairs.
COMPOSITAE, about 50 species.

**Gypsophila** a genus of herbs or dwarf subshrubs from temperate Eurasia (a major center of distribution being the eastern Mediterranean), Egypt, Australia and New Zealand. The white or pink flowers, borne in cymose inflorescences, are often abundant and attract many insects. Several species and hybrids, including *G. repens* (= *G. dubia*), *G. paniculata* [BABY'S BREATH, MAIDEN'S BREATH] and *G. elegans* [BABY'S BREATH, CHALK PLANT] are cultivated in a wide range of cultivars for their ornamental value in rock gardens and borders. The latter two species are particularly valued by florists for bouquets.
CARYOPHYLLACEAE, about 125 species.

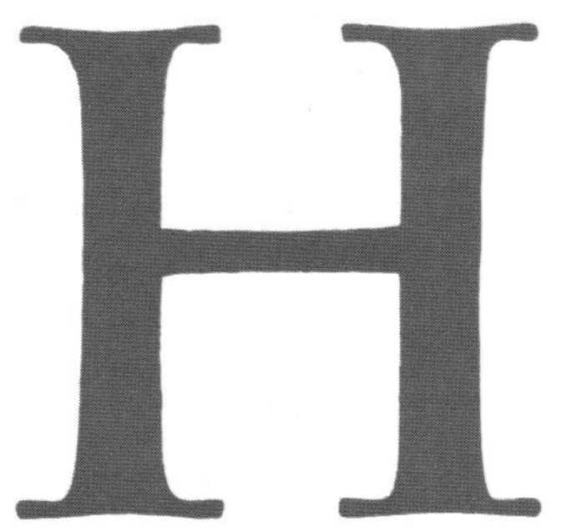

**Habenaria** a genus of widely distributed temperate and tropical, terrestrial and epiphytic orchids. The terminal inflorescence consists of dense or loose racemes of one to many flowers. The petals have a lip which may be long, lobed or fringed at the tip.

Many of the species are cultivated as ornamentals with predominantly yellowish or greenish white flowers. Among the better known temperate species are the Old World *H. bifolia* [LESSER BUTTERFLY ORCHID], with white or greenish white fragrant flowers, and the North American *H. ciliaris* (= *Blephariglottis ciliaris*) [YELLOW FRINGED ORCHID, ORANGE-PLUM, ORANGE-FRINGE], with racemes of bright yellow or orange flowers, and *H. clavellata* (= *H. tridenta, Gymnadeniopsis clarellata*) [GREEN WOODLAND ORCHID, GREEN REIN ORCHID, LITTLE CLUB-SPUR ORCHID], with greenish-white or yellowish-white flowers with a club-shaped spur, and *H. peramoena* [PURPLE FRINGELESS ORCHID, PURPLE-SPIRE ORCHID, FRET-LIP, PRIDE-OF-THE-PEAK], with showy rich purple flowers with a three-lobed lip and a club-shaped spur.
ORCHIDACEAE, about 100 species.

**Hacquetia** a genus consisting of a single species, *H. epipactis*, a small yellow-flowered herbaceous perennial of woodlands from the eastern European Alps to the Carpathians, which is sometimes cultivated in temperate rock gardens for its spring-time blooms.
UMBELLIFERAE, 1 species.

*One of the Blood Lilies,* Haemanthus multiflorus *from tropical Africa, which bears a spherical head of red flowers.* (× ¼)

**Haemanthus** [BLOOD LILY] a genus of tropical and South African evergreen and deciduous bulbous plants. The dense umbellate heads of star-shaped, red or white flowers are borne on a solid stalk and enclosed by colorful fleshy bracts. The fruits are colorful berries. *H. albiflos, H. coccineus* and *H. katherinae*, all of South African origin, and other species, are cultivated for their ornamental value.
AMARYLLIDACEAE, about 90 species.

**Haematoxylon** a small genus of trees and shrubs ranging from Central America and the West Indies to southwestern Africa. Commercially the most important is *H. campechianum* [*LOGWOOD, PALO CAMPECHIO], a small spiny spreading shrub or tree valued for its very hard heartwood and the red dye haematoxylin which it yields. It is sometimes cultivated as an ornamental.
LEGUMINOSAE, 3 species.

**Hakea** a genus of Australian and Tasmanian erect evergreen shrubs and small trees. Several species are grown as ornamental shrubs in warmer areas. *H. laurina* [PINCUSHION FLOWER, SEA URCHIN], cultivated especially on the French and Italian Rivieras, has red or pink blossoms in globular heads. The leaves are broad and the young tips are a silky golden bronze, turning red in the autumn. *H. acicularis* (= *H. sericea*) [NEEDLE BUSH] is a tall silky shrub with clusters of white, pink-tinged or rich pink flowers. *H. subera* [CORK-BARK TREE] grows in arid central Australia where its contorted form is a conspicuous feature of the landscape. The large flowers are in torch-like spikes, either cream or yellow, sweetly scented and loaded with a honey which is much relished by the Aborigines.
PROTEACEAE, about 120 species.

**Halesia** a small genus of deciduous trees native to North America and China. The showy white drooping flowers hang like snowdrops in profuse clusters in May. Best-known are *H. carolina* (= *H. tetraptera*) [SNOWDROP TREE, SILVER BELL, OPPOSSUMWOOD] from the southeastern USA, a beautiful small spreading tree which grows well in cultivation in sheltered, limefree sites, and the much taller pyramidal *H. monticola* [MOUNTAIN SILVER BELL, SNOWDROP TREE], from the mountains of the same area.
STYRACACEAE, 6 species.

**Halimeda** a genus of green algae found in tropical seas. The thallus is calcified, the breakdown of which contributes large quantities of calcareous debris to lagoons in coral atolls and along sandy tropical shores.
CHLOROPHYCEAE.

**Halimione** a small genus of plants adapted to saline habitats. One of the three species, *H. pedunculata* [STALKED ORACHE] is annual, while *H. verrucifera* and *H. portulacoides* [SEA PURSLANE] are small shrubs. They are all found in salt marshes and estuaries mainly around Europe, but also in Central and southwest Asia.
CHENOPODIACEAE, 3 species.

**Halosphaera** a genus of green algae best known as the large (up to 0.04–0.08in) spherical cysts which form one phase of the planktonic organism. It is often found in abundance floating on the surface of the sea.
PRASINOPHYCEAE.

**Hamamelis** [WITCH HAZELS] a genus of deciduous shrubs or small trees which are native to East Asia and eastern North America and are popular with gardeners for their yellow or rusty-red flowers produced from October to March. The resemblance of the leaves to *HAZELS (*Corylus* species) led early settlers in North America to use the twigs for water divining, and because of the branches' pliant properties, the popular name arose. *H. virginiana* [COMMON WITCH HAZEL] produces yellow flowers in the autumn that are particularly resistant to cold weather. The bark, leaves and twigs yield the witch hazel of pharmacy which is widely used as an astringent and coolant, and can be applied to cuts and bruises. Other cultivated species and hybrids are *H. japonica* [JAPANESE WITCH HAZEL], flowering in March, *H. mollis* [CHINESE WITCH HAZEL], *H. vernalis* [OZARK WITCH HAZEL] and the hybrid *H.* × *intermedia*, the last three flowering in January and February.

Witch Hazel is a name used also for the WITCH *ELM (*Ulmus glabra*) and WITCH *HORNBEAM (*Carpinus betulus*), the term "witch" or "wych" being an old English word used to denote any tree with particularly pliant branches.
HAMAMELIDACEAE, 4–6 species.

**Hamelia** a small genus of evergreen shrubs from tropical and subtropical America and the West Indies. The cultivated species include *H. patens* (= *H. erecta*) [SCARLET BUSH], with small tubular orange to scarlet flowers and *H. ventricosa* with tubular yellow flowers.
RUBIACEAE, about 25 species.

*Like most members of this genus,* Hakea teretifolia *has narrow leaves and axillary clusters of scented white to cream flowers.* (× ¼)

**Hancornia** a Brazilian genus represented by a single species, *H. speciosa*, [MANGABEIRA RUBBER]. This tree, which may grow to 20ft, bears yellow and red fruits, the size of a plum, which are eaten fresh or processed to make conserves and wine. The rubber is resinous and of secondary commercial quality on the commercial market. The wood is used locally for building.
APOCYNACEAE, 1 species.

**Haplopappus** a large American genus of annual and perennial herbs and shrubs widely distributed in North and South America. Most species possess either tufted or solitary inflorescences of yellow (rarely purple or saffron) daisy-like heads. Several shrubby species, including *H. croceus*, are cultivated as ornamentals in the USA.
COMPOSITAE, about 160 species.

**Hardenbergia** a small Australian and Tasmanian genus of evergreen twining shrubs. *H. comptoniana* and *H. violacea* are cultivated as ornamentals for their racemes of predominantly violet-blue or violet-purple to rose or white pea-like flowers.
LEGUMINOSAE, 3 species.

**Haricot bean** one of the common names given to the important legume **Phaseolus vulgaris*. It is a low, erect or climbing annual, native to Central and South America but now cultivated throughout temperate and tropical regions.

The varieties can be grouped by form (bush or climbers), seed colors (white, black, red, ocher or brown), or according to the use to which the fruit or bean is put and to age of harvesting. Thus FRENCH, DWARF, SNAP, GREEN or WAX, STRING and RUNNER BEANS are harvested for the entire young and tender pods which are eaten whole, sliced or snapped; FLAGEOLETS, GREEN SHELL BEANS or KIDNEY BEANS are picked for the seeds (beans) while they are still immature and therefore tender; and HARICOT or DRY SHELL BEANS are harvested when mature, and subsequently dried, when they can be stored over a long period. The latter are the basic ingredient of canned BAKED BEANS. Clearly, a single plant can yield products at all three stages, but over the years numerous cultivars have been developed which provide the best product for each need. The confusion in naming is compounded by differing national interpretations of the same names.
LEGUMINOSAE.

**Haworthia** a genus of more or less stemless leaf-succulent rosette plants from the drier parts of South Africa and Namibia. Many species are in cultivation for their attractive leaves, the surface of which has an almost infinite variety of textures and patterning, including pearl-like tubercles and incrustations, serrulate or finely haired margins and translucent "windows" which may enlarge to occupy the whole area of the truncate leaf tip. By contrast, the flowers are uniform, white or whitish, tubular and unattractive.

*Haworthia* is found naturally in the shade of shrubs and rocks and is hence suitable for shadier parts of the greenhouse. It can even be grown on sunless windowsills, provided that frost is excluded. The most commonly cultivated species are *H. attenuata*, *H. fasciata* [ZEBRA HAWORTHIA] and *H. margaritifera* [PEARL PLANT] each of which has several varieties and cultivars.

The most bizarre species are *H. maughanii* and *H. truncata*, with truncate windowed leaves in a spiral or two rows, and *H. graminifolia*, a rarity with linear grass-like leaves up to 20in long arising from a small bulb.
LILIACEAE, about 68 species.

*Flowers of the May Hawthorn (*Crataegus laevigata*). Shown here are those of the cultivar 'Paulii'. Hawthorns are popular ornamentals since they provide fine displays of color both when in bloom and when fruiting.* (×3)

*The Chinese Witch Hazel (*Hamamelis mollis*) is the most popular of the cultivated witch hazels and gives a welcome splash of color in winter.*

**Hawthorn** the common name for members of *Crataegus*, a genus of the Rosaceae comprising 200 species of deciduous, usually thorny trees also known as MAYS or QUICKTHORNS. They are distributed throughout the north temperate region. Hawthorns have fragrant blossom and are often grown as ornamentals or, being thorny, make an effective hedging material. Some species produce useful timber although this is exploited less often now than formerly. The flowers are usually white, sometimes pink or red, and the fruits (haws) are blue-black, red or yellow.

Identification of individuals of the genus is difficult, partly due to extensive hybridization and partly because the constituent species do not fall into readily distinguishable groups. However, the color of the fruits is a particularly important character, the main divisions being bluish or blackish (such as *C. chlorosarca*), red (such as *C. mollis*) or yellow (such as *C. flava*; SUMMER HAW). The commonest European species are *C. laevigata* (= *C. oxyacanthoides*, *C. oxyacantha*) [MAY HAWTHORN] and *C. monogyna* [COMMON HAWTHORN].

The wood of *Crataegus* species is very hard and has been used for engraving. *C. crus-galli* [COCKSPUR THORN], of the USA, produces a heavy wood used for tool handles and that of the European *C. laevigata* is used for a variety of articles from wheels to walking sticks. Many species are popular ornamental trees, grown for their blossom and their fruit. Best-known is the PINK MAY, a variety of *C. laevigata*. The fruits of several species are made into jellies or preserves and those of *C. cuneata* are used in China for the treatment of stomach complaints. *C. laevigata* provides a leaf-infusion tea which reduces blood pressure, a coffee substitute from the seeds and a tobacco substitute from the leaves.

Another member of the same family is

*Photinia serrulata [CHINESE HAWTHORN] while the unrelated *Aponogeton distachyus* is known as the WATER HAWTHORN.

**Hazel** the common name for members of *Corylus*, a genus of hardy decorative and economically valuable deciduous trees and shrubs from the temperate Northern Hemisphere, including Europe, Asia and North America.

The European *C. avellana* [COMMON HAZEL, COBNUT, FILBERT] is a vigorous shrub or small tree up to 23ft tall. A formerly important economic species grown in coppices, it supplied wood for making hurdles and walking sticks, and also nuts for autumn cropping. The attractive male catkins appear in early spring. It is still grown commercially, but the true filbert is *C. maxima* [FILBERT], which is grown in four main areas: Turkey, which produces 65% of the commercial crop, Italy (20%), Spain (10%), and Oregon, USA (5%). It is also grown in southeast England, where the chief commercial variety is known as 'Kentish Cob'.

*Bud-like inflorescence of the Common Hazel (*Corylus avellana*) showing the feathery red styles which catch the pollen.* (×10)

In North America the principal native cultivated species are *C. americana* [COMMON HAZEL] and *C. cornuta* (= *C. rostrata*) [BEAKED HAZEL]; *C. avellana* has also been introduced from Europe.

Also cultivated, both for their nuts and their ornamental value, are *C. chinensis* [CHINESE HAZEL], *C. colurna* [TURKISH HAZEL] and *C. tibetica* [TIBETAN HAZEL]. Ornamental cultivars include *C. avellana* 'Aurea', with soft yellow leaves, *C. avellana* 'Contorta' [CORKSCREW HAZEL], with strangely twisted branches, and *C. maxima* 'Purpurea', with purple leaves.
BETULACEAE.

**Heath** the common name given to many species of evergreen shrubs and occasionally dwarf trees which belong to the genus **Erica*.
ERICACEAE.

**Heather** a term which in the strictest sense should apply only to the genus **Calluna*, eg *C. vulgaris* [HEATHER, SCOTTISH HEATHER, LING], while the term "HEATH" is applicable only to members of the genus **Erica*. However, at least eight species of the genus *Erica* are commonly known as HEATHERS: *E. cinerea* [BELL OR PURPLE HEATHER], *E. tetralix* [BOG HEATHER OR CROSS-LEAVED HEATH], *E. vagans* [CORNISH HEATH OR HEATHER], *E. carnea* [SNOW HEATHER], *E. canaliculata* [CHRISTMAS HEATHER], *E. doliiformis* [EVER-BLOOMING FRENCH HEATHER], *E. hyemalis* [WHITE WINTER HEATHER] and *E. mediterranea* [MEDITERRANEAN HEATHER]. (See also *Cassiope*.)
ERICACEAE.

**Hebe** a genus of evergreen shrubs and small trees with opposite, four-ranked, often imbricate leaves, leathery in texture, mainly native to New Zealand, but with a few species in South America and New Guinea. Many species are cultivated in the open in warmer climates, otherwise under glass, for their attractive habit and many-flowered racemes of shortly tubular four-lobed, white, pink, reddish or bluish flowers. Members of this genus were at one time included in **Veronica* and it is also related to *Parahebe*.

Cultivated species include *H. lewisii* (= *Veronica lewisii*), an erect shrub with racemes of pale blue flowers, *H. menziesii* (= *V. menziesii*), a larger compact shrub (up to 13ft), with racemes of white or pale lilac flowers, and the popular *H. speciosa* (= *V. speciosa*), a stout shrub growing to 5ft with long racemes of reddish or bluish-purple flowers. The latter contains many varieties and cultivars (eg 'Imperialis') and hybridizes readily with other species.
SCROPHULARIACEAE, about 80 species.

**Hedera** see IVY.
ARALIACEAE, about 15 species.

Hebe *species are widely grown, particularly in mild climates, for their attractive flowers and evergreen foliage.*

*Most* Erica *species are known as heaths, but* E. cinerea, *a native of dry moors in Europe, is known as Bell Heather.* (×2)

**Hedychium** a genus of erect rhizomatous perennial herbs native to tropical Asia and the Himalayas but widely cultivated in tropical countries and under glass in temperate regions. The cultivated species normally bear attractive terminal inflorescences of fragrant showy flowers with reflexed petals, petal-like lateral staminodes and a long stamen filament.

Popular species include *H. coronarium* [GARLAND FLOWER, BUTTERFLY GINGER, WHITE GINGER, BUTTERFLY LILY, GINGER LILY, CINNAMON JASMINE], a tropical Asian species with large fragrant white flowers, which is widely naturalized in tropical America, and the Indian *H. gardneranum* [KAHILI GINGER] which bears long spikes of light yellow flowers with protruding red filaments. The

rhizome of the Indian *H. spicatum* is the source of the perfume ingredient *abir.
ZINGIBERACEAE, about 50 species.

**Hedysarum** a genus of biennial or perennial herbs or subshrubs with pea-like flowers, from the Northern Hemisphere. Several species are cultivated in rock gardens, including *H. glomeratum* (= *H. capitatum*), *H. mackenzii* [LICORICE ROOT] and *H. hedysaroides* (= *H. obscurum*), all with pink to reddish-purple (rarely white) flowers. *H. coronarium* [FRENCH HONEYSUCKLE] is taller, with fragrant flowers, and is grown as a border ornamental. It is also grown agriculturally as green fodder [SULLA CLOVER].
LEGUMINOSAE, about 150 species.

**Helenium** a genus of annual or perennial herbs with usually daisy-like flower heads, from North America and Mexico. Species such as the North American *H. amarum* [BITTERWEED] are a pest on poor pasture as they are toxic to sheep, horses and cattle, imparting a bitter flavor to the milk. *H. autumnale*, also from North America, is a popular garden perennial, as it blooms for many weeks in late summer. Many varieties exist, including 'Bishop', which has orange-yellow semidouble flower heads with a dark brown center.
COMPOSITAE, about 40 species.

**Heliamphora** a tropical genus of Venezuelan and Guianan pitcher plants growing in very wet soil and air conditions. The funnel-shaped leaf 'pitcher' with a minute lid contains, in two apical, narrow wings, nectar-secreting glands to attract insects. All species bear white, rose-tinged flowers in racemes.
SARRACENIACEAE, 6 species.

**Helianthemum** a genus of usually evergreen shrubs, rarely herbs and sometimes annuals. They are native to North and South America as well as the Old World, notably the Mediterranean region and Iran. The American species are sometimes placed in a separate genus, *Crocanthemum*.

Although the dried leaves of the North American *H. canadense* (= *C. canadense*) [FROSTWEED] are used as a tonic and to stimulate the appetite, the main use of the genus is horticultural, and several species are popular rock-garden plants. The best-known of these is *H. nummularium* (= *H. chamaecistus*, *H. variabile*) [ROCK-ROSE, SUN-ROSE], which has yellow flowers but numerous subspecies (eg *grandiflorum*) and cultivars (eg 'Aureum', 'Roseum' and 'Rubro-plenum') exist with white, pink and scarlet flowers. Two other species with yellow flowers are *H. lunulatum* and *H. oelandicum*, while *H. apenninum* (= *H. polifolium*, *H. pulverulentum*) [WHITE ROCK-ROSE] has white flowers and gray leaves.
CISTACEAE, about 100 species.

**Helianthus** see ARTICHOKE and SUNFLOWER.
COMPOSITAE, about 67 species.

*The Strawflower (*Helichrysum bracteatum*); the outer rays surrounding the disk of bisexual florets are female.* (×1)

**Helichrysum** a genus of annual to perennial herbs or shrubs ranging from southern Europe, Africa and Madagascar to southwest Asia, including southern India, Sri Lanka, Australia and New Zealand, with the center of distribution in South Africa. Many species are cultivated as ornamentals for their attractive, often gray or white, woolly foliage and for their strong colorful daisy-like flower heads, sometimes used as everlastings. Many cultivated species are half-hardy or greenhouse plants but some are quite hardy in temperate gardens.

The Australian annual *H. bracteatum* [STRAWFLOWER] and its various horticultural varieties have red, orange, yellow, pink or white petal-like bracts. Among the yellow-bracted perennials are European species such as *H. arenarium*, *H. angustifolium* [WHITE-LEAF], *H. orientale* and *H. stoechas* and South African species such as *H. splendidum*. White-bracted species suitable for rock gardens include the Corsican *H. frigidum* with a silvery mat of leaves.

Several species have aromatic foliage, some smelling strongly of curry or fenugreek, eg *H. angustifolium* and *H. italicum*. A few species have culinary uses, including *H. cochinchinense* from China, which provides tasty young leaves for flavoring rice dishes, and *H. serpyllifolium*, the leaves of which are used for tea in South Africa. The European species *H. arenarium* and *H. stoechas* have been used to combat intestinal worms and skin diseases, and as diuretics.
COMPOSITAE, about 500 species.

*One of the many garden varieties of* Helianthemum nummularium, *the best-known of the Sun-rose or Rock-rose species.* ($\times \frac{1}{2}$)

**Heliconia** a genus of perennial banana-like herbs mainly in tropical America, with a few species in the islands of the western Pacific. They are sometimes placed in the Musaceae or the Strelitzeaceae. Like *BANANA, *Heliconia* possesses a many-flowered terminal inflorescence with colored bracts. Several species, including *H. bihai* [PARROT'S CLAWS, WILD PLANTAIN, BALISIER] and *H. psittacorum* [PARROT'S FLOWER], are cultivated in the tropics for their ornamental foliage, less frequently in greenhouses in temperate countries.
HELICONIACEAE, about 50 species.

**Helictotrichon** [OAT GRASS] a genus of mainly perennial grasses forming dense tufts. They are found mainly in northern and central Europe, Asia and North America, generally in chalky grassland. *H. sempervirens* (= *Avena candida*) is an attractive ornamental species with stiff, steely-blue foliage and graceful arching flowering stems up to 3ft tall.
GRAMINEAE, about 95 species.

**Heliophila** a genus of mainly annual or rarely subshrubby perennial herbs native to South Africa. Some species are cultivated as perennial or half-hardy annual border plants, including *H. longifolia*, which bears racemes of blue flowers with a yellow or white claw to the petal, and *H. leptophylla*

with much narrower leaves and racemes of blue flowers with a yellow center.
CRUCIFERAE, about 85 species.

**Heliopsis** an American genus of annual and perennial sunflower-like herbs, some of which attain almost 1 3ft in height. The large yellow, orange or golden flower heads are borne terminally on long erect stalks. Many varieties of *H. helianthoides* are known in cultivation as border plants, including cultivars with "double" ray flowers.
COMPOSITAE, about 12 species.

**Heliotropium** [HELIOTROPES] a large genus of annual herbs, subshrubs and shrubs from tropical and temperate regions. The blue, purple, pink or white flowers are clustered in one-sided, sometimes axillary spikes. Many varieties of *H. arborescens* (= *H. peruvianum*) [COMMON HELIOTROPE, CHERRY PIE], from Peru, *H. amplexicaule* (= *H. anchusifolium*) [SUMMER HELIOTROPE], and *H. corymbosum* are grown for their clusters of fragrant, often forget-me-not-like flowers. *H. arborescens* is used in perfumery in southern Europe.
BORAGINACEAE, about 250 species.

**Helipterum** a genus of mostly xerophytic herbs and subshrubs from South Africa and Australia whose daisy-like flower heads, like those of the related *Helichrysum, often have petal-like involucral bracts which retain their color when dried and are sold as everlastings for flower arrangements. Popular cultivated species include *H. humboldtianum*, with a dense inflorescence of yellow flower heads, and *H. manglesii* (= *Rhodanthe manglesii*), with pink to reddish flower heads and a yellow center.
COMPOSITAE, about 60 species.

**Helleborine** a name that is applied generally to several species of some genera of European terrestrial orchids. It is more commonly associated with species of *Epipactis and *Cephalanthera. This is due to the superficial resemblance of their flowers to those of the genus *Helleborus (Ranunculaceae).
ORCHIDACEAE.

*The Green Hellebore (*Helleborus viridis*) produces a mass of greenish-yellow flowers during the early spring.* ($\times \frac{1}{3}$)

*Inflorescence of* Heliconia pendula *from Guatemala to Peru. Several* Heliconia *species are cultivated for their attractive flowers.* ($\times 2$)

**Helleborus** a very complex genus of perennial herbs, many of which are cultivated as garden-border plants, native from Europe to western Asia, with two outlying species in Tibet and China.

The flowers of the best-known species *H. niger* [*CHRISTMAS ROSE] are large and very showy, white or cream in color. In common with other species it flowers in early spring or in winter. *H. foetidus* [STINKING HELLEBORE, BEAR'S FOOT] has many small, pale green flowers, becoming edged with purple-red on aging. *H. orientalis* [LENTEN ROSE] has several cultivars with a range of flower color from creamy white and green to pink or purple and often spotted. The dried roots and rhizomes of *H. niger* yield a cardiac glycoside, helleborein.
RANUNCULACEAE, about 20 species.

**Helvella** [SADDLE FUNGI] a genus of mainly north temperate saprophytic terrestrial fungi with fleshy fruiting bodies consisting of a hollow stipe and a saddle-shaped, reflexed cap. The best-known species is *H. crispa*, which forms white fruiting bodies in deciduous woods.
HELVELLACEAE, about 25 species.

**Helwingia** a small genus of deciduous shrubs from the Himalayas eastwards to Taiwan and Japan. *H. japonica* is occasionally cultivated as a curiosity, but the flowers are not attractive. The leaves of this species have been eaten as a vegetable in Japan.
CORNACEAE, 3 species.

**Hemerocallis** a genus of rhizomatous perennial lily-like herbs distributed in Europe and temperate Asia from Italy to the Far East, although the majority of species are from China and Japan. The flowers, which usually last only a day, are funnel- or trumpet-shaped, yellow, orange, red or purple in color. The modern cultivated hybrids have been produced as a result of crosses between several different species, notably *H. citrina*, *H. fulva*, [ORANGE DAYLILY, TAWNY DAYLILY, FULVOUS DAYLILY], *H. lilioasphodelus* (= *H. flava*) [YELLOW DAYLILY, LEMON DAYLILY] and *H. minor* [DWARF YELLOW DAYLILY]. The fragrant flower buds of *H. middendorffii* are eaten as a vegetable in Japan.
LILIACEAE, about 15 species.

**Hemileia** a genus of rust fungi which occur on various tropical and subtropical hosts. The most important is *H. vastatrix*, the cause of coffee rust, which was probably native to East Africa but spread to Sri Lanka in the 1870s, where it wiped out the coffee industry. It has also spread to all coffee-growing parts of Africa and since 1965 has become widespread in Brazil and Central America.
PUCCINIACEAE, about 35 species.

**Hemlock** the common name for the poisonous umbelliferous herb *Conium maculatum, a tall biennial native to temperate Eurasia, though now widely naturalized in North and South America and in New Zealand. It is unique in its family in containing alkaloids that are extremely toxic to both Man and livestock, and was used by the ancient Greeks

*Hemlock (*Conium maculatum*) is notoriously poisonous and dangerous to both livestock and to Man.* ($\times \frac{1}{25}$)

*Like other hellebores, the Lenten Lily or Lenten Rose (*Helleborus orientalis*) produces its flowers in the early spring.* (× ½)

to put criminals to death. The unripe fruit has been used in medicine as an anodyne, sedative and antispasmodic.

A species of *YEW, *Taxus canadensis*, is known as GROUND HEMLOCK.

**Hemlock spruce** or **hemlock** the common names for *Tsuga*, a genus of evergreen conifers native to North America, Japan, China, Taiwan and the Himalayas. In habit they are broadly pyramidal, the branches being horizontal to somewhat pendulous. Hemlocks produce valuable timber and pulpwood as well as ornamental trees.

The wood of *T. canadensis* [COMMON or CANADA HEMLOCK] and of the western North American species *T. heterophylla* [WESTERN HEMLOCK] is used for building construction generally and the bark for tanning. The resin of the former is also useful and is known commercially as Canada pitch. In China the soft wood of *T. chinensis* [CHINESE HEMLOCK] is used for shingles as is that of *T. brunoniana* [INDIAN HEMLOCK SPRUCE] in the Himalayas. The timber of *T. sieboldii* [JAPANESE HEMLOCK] is fine-grained and has been used in cabinet-making.

A number of species are cultivated as ornamentals or as hedging plants, notably COMMON HEMLOCK (including many garden forms and cultivars), WESTERN HEMLOCK, *T. mertensiana* [MOUNTAIN HEMLOCK] and *T. caroliniana* [CAROLINA HEMLOCK].
PINACEAE, about 12 species.

**Hemp** a tall-growing slender annual herb, **Cannabis sativa*, widely cultivated for its fibers throughout the warm temperate and subtropical countries of the world, but principally in the USSR (the leading producer), southern Europe and the eastern USA. The long, stout, strongly lignified bast-fibers are used in the manufacture of coarse fabrics. The term hemp is also used for fiber-producing species of other genera, including **Musa textilis* [*ABACA FIBER, MANILA HEMP], **Crotalaria juncea* [SUNN HEMP], **Sansevieria* species [BOW-STRING HEMP], **Hibiscus cannabinus* [DECCAN HEMP], **Furcraea foetida* var *willemettiana* [MAURITIUS HEMP] and **Agave sisalana* [SISAL HEMP].

**Henna** the dye obtained from the shrub *Lawsonia inermis* (= *L. alba*) [MIGNONETTE TREE] native to the Old World tropics, cultivated since ancient times, and naturalized in tropical America. The dye is derived from the dried, ground leaves and young shoots and is used in many countries to dye various parts of the body, including the hair, an orange-brown color. It is a very fast dye for fabrics and leather. Henna is also used in local medicine for many disorders, and the fragrant flowers have been used in perfumery.
LYTHRACEAE.

**Hepatica** [LIVERLEAF] a genus of spring-flowering, low-growing, perennial herbs from the north temperate zone with long, petiolate, three- to five-lobed leaves. They are closely related to **Anemone* in which they were formerly included. *H. nobilis* (= *Anemone hepatica*), with bluish-violet, purple, pinkish or white flowers, is often cultivated in rock gardens or shaded areas. Double forms are also known. *H. americana* and *H. acutiloba* (= *Anemone acutiloba*), from North America, are closely related species.
RANUNCULACEAE, about 10 species.

**Heracleum** a genus of coarse biennial or perennial umbelliferous herbs from north temperate regions, mainly in the Old World, with a few species in North America and tropical African mountains. *H. sphondylium* [COMMON COW PARSNIP, HOGWEED, KECK] is common in grassy places and roadsides in Europe, Asia and North America. *H. mantegazzianum* [GIANT HOGWEED], from the Caucasus, grows up to 16ft tall, with a hollow stem which is purple spotted and up to 4in in diameter. It is sometimes cultivated for effect and is locally naturalized. The huge inflorescences can be up to 4ft in diameter.
UMBELLIFERAE, about 70 species.

**Herbs** see p. 174.

**Herniaria** a small genus of prostrate or mat-forming annual or perennial herbs from Europe and the Mediterranean region to Afghanistan and South Africa. Selected strains of *H. glabra* [RUPTUREWORT, HERNIARY BREASTWORT] have been used since the 19th century as the green carpeting component of formal bedding schemes in parks and gardens. It is also cultivated in rock gardens. RUPTUREWORT has been used medicinally in southern Europe as a diuretic and an antispasmodic. The only other cultivated species is *H. alpina*.
CARYOPHYLLACEAE, about 15 species.

**Hesperis** a genus of tall biennial or perennial herbs from Europe and the Mediterranean to Asia. Tall stems carry spikes of white, lilac or purple flowers with a delicate fragrance, especially in the evening. *H. matronalis* [DAME'S VIOLET, DAMASK VIOLET, SWEET ROCKET] is a perennial plant (sometimes biennial) long cultivated in cottage gardens. *H. tristis* and *H. violacea* are two cultivated biennial species. Oil from the seeds (damask oil) is used in perfumery.
CRUCIFERAE, about 30 species.

**Heuchera** a North American and Mexican genus of smallish perennial herbs with small pendent flowers in lax, delicate panicles or racemes. *H. sanguinea* [CORAL FLOWER, CORAL BELLS, ALUM ROOT], with red or white flowers, is the most widely cultivated species in borders. Other cultivated species or hybrids include *H. americana* [ROCK GERANIUM, ALUM ROOT], *H. cylindrica*, *H. micrantha*, *H. villosa* and *H.* × *brizoides*.
SAXIFRAGACEAE, about 40–50 species.

*Various cultivars of Day Lilies are grown throughout the world. This is an orange cultivar of* Hemerocallis lilioasphodelus. (× 1)

# Herbs

The term herb refers, strictly speaking, to plants that die down after flowering and do not, therefore, have persistent aboveground woody parts. In a more restricted sense it is also applied to plants used for the aromatic, savory or medicinal properties of their stems, leaves or occasionally flowers. They may be used fresh or dried. In this sense it covers potherbs, culinary herbs, condiment herbs and medicinal herbs.

Herbs and spices have been used since earliest times to add variety and flavor to foodstuffs. Plants used in this way are normally pungent or aromatic and are used sparingly since they are often unpalatable if consumed directly or used in large quantities for flavoring.

The majority of the widely used herbs grow in warm regions with dry summers, especially in the Mediterranean area where aromatic herbs such as *THYME _(Thymus_ species), ROSEMARY _(*Rosmarinus officinalis)_, *SAGE _(Salvia officinalis)_ and SAVORY _(Satureja_ species) are common components of the characteristic scrub vegetation that covers large areas of the Mediterranean where the forest cover has been removed. The cooks in the ancient Mediterranean civilizations of Rome and Greece must have learned by trial and error which plants possessed desirable properties for adding good flavor to their dishes. Most of the herbs used were found growing wild locally. These Mediterranean herbs were in due course handed on to other cultures as the Greek and Roman empires extended. Many of the herbs grown in the kitchen and herb gardens of monasteries, and later in the early medicinal or botanic gardens were introduced by the Romans and are still grown today in our herb gardens. Even today, many of the commonly used herbs are grown commercially in Mediterranean countries such as France, Spain and Italy, where they are dried and exported to other parts of Europe and elsewhere.

In a similar way, herbs were introduced from Europe to North America and other parts of the world by colonizers and these continue to be cultivated today, sometimes in preference to local species with similar properties which otherwise would have replaced them. Other parts of the world have contributed some herbs, such as *GARLIC _(*Allium sativum)_, from Central Asia, *TARRAGON _(*Artemisia dracunculus)_ and LEMON GRASS _(*Cymbopogon citratus)_, from Southeast Asia and now widely grown in the United States, South America and Africa, LEMON *VERBENA _(Aloysia triphylla)_, from the Argentine and Chile and now widely cultivated in the tropics, and *BASIL _(*Ocimum basilicum)_, from the Old World tropics and widely grown for seasoning soups and sauces such as the classic Provençal "pistou".

Most of the culinary herbs belong to the families Labiatae and Umbelliferae. Labiate herbs include *BASIL _(Ocimum basilicum)_, *MARJORAM _(Origanum_ species), *MINT _(Mentha_ species), SAGE, ROSEMARY and THYME. Their flavor and aroma are caused by the volatile essential oils present in the leaves and other parts of the plant. THYME, derived from several species of _Thymus_, notably _T. vulgaris_, is perhaps the most widely used of all culinary herbs and is used to flavor meats, stews, soups, sauces and stuffings. It is a component of "bouquet garni" and "mixed herbs". The mints _(Mentha_ species) are amongst the oldest of European herbs and are native throughout Europe and widely cultivated in other temperate zones.

Umbelliferous herbs are aromatic due to the presence, throughout the plant and fruits, of secretory canals containing aromatic essential oils. The best known is *PARSLEY _(Petroselinum crispum)_ which is widely used in the fresh state as a garnish rather than actually consumed, although it is extensively used in cooking as a mild flavoring. *FENNEL _(*Foeniculum vulgare)_, especially its finely dissected leaves, is used as a flavoring especially in fish dishes and is widely employed in Scandinavia. In

_Some of the commonly cultivated herbs. 1 Garden Thyme; 2 Sweet Marjoram; 3 Parsley; 4 Coriander; 5 Rosemary; 6 Chervil; 7 Sage; 8 Summer Savory; 9 Fennel; 10 Tarragon; 11 Peppermint; 12 Sweet Basil; 13 Dill; 14 Tansy; 15 Mint, Spearmint; 16 Lemon Balm; 17 Lovage; 18 Costmary 1 to 11, 14_ $(\times \frac{1}{2})$_; 12, 13, 15 to 18_ $(\times \frac{1}{3})$.

COMMONLY CULTIVATED HERBS

| Common name | Scientific name | Family |
|---|---|---|
| ALEXANDERS | _*Smyrnium olusatrum_ | Umbelliferae |
| *ANGELICA | _Angelica archangelica_ | Umbelliferae |
| WILD ANGELICA | _A. sylvestris_ | Umbelliferae |
| *ANISE | _Pimpinella anisum_ | Umbelliferae |
| *BALM | _Melissa officinalis_ | Labiatae |
| *BASIL, SWEET | _Ocimum basilicum_ | Labiatae |
| BAY, SWEET BAY | _*Laurus nobilis_ | Lauraceae |
| *BERGAMOT, WILD | _Monarda fistulosa_ | Labiatae |
| BERGAMOT, RED; OSWEGO TEA; BEE BALM | _*M. didyma_ | Labiatae |
| BERGAMOT, LEMON | _M. citriodora_ | Labiatae |
| BETONY | _Betonica (*Stachys) officinalis_ | Labiatae |
| BORAGE | _*Borago officinalis_ | Boraginaceae |
| BURNET, SALAD | _*Sanguisorba minor_ | Rosaceae |
| CALAMINT | _*Calamintha sylvatica_ | Labiatae |
| CAMOMILE; *CHAMOMILE | _Chamaemelum nobile_ | Compositae |
| CARAWAY | _*Carum carvi_ | Umbelliferae |
| CATMINT | _*Nepeta cataria_ | Labiatae |
| *CELERY | _Apium graveolens_ | Umbelliferae |
| CHERVIL | _*Anthriscus cerefolium_ | Umbelliferae |
| *CHIVES | _Allium schoenoprasum_ | Liliaceae |
| *CORIANDER | _Coriandrum sativum_ | Umbelliferae |
| *COSTMARY; ALECOST | _Balsamita major_ | Compositae |
| *DILL | _Anethum graveolens_ | Umbelliferae |
| *FENNEL | _Foeniculum vulgare_ | Umbelliferae |
| GARLIC MUSTARD | _Alliaria petiolata_ | Cruciferae |
| *HYSSOP | _Hyssopus officinalis_ | Labiatae |
| LEMON GRASS | _*Cymbopogon citratus_ | Gramineae |
| LEMON BALM | _*Melissa officinalis_ | Labiatae |
| LEMON VERBENA | _Aloysia triphylla_ | Verbenaceae |
| *LOVAGE | _Levisticum officinale_ | Umbelliferae |
| MARIGOLD, POT | _*Calendula officinalis_ | Compositae |
| *MARJORAM; WILD OREGANO | _Origanum vulgare_ | Labiatae |
| *MARJORAM, SWEET | _O. majorana_ | Labiatae |
| *MARJORAM, POT | _O. onites_ | Labiatae |
| MELILOT, SWEET CLOVER | _*Melilotus officinalis_ | Leguminosae |
| *MINT, LEMON, EAU DE COLOGNE or BERGAMOT | _Mentha × piperita_ var _citrata_ | Labiatae |
| *MINT, GINGER OR SCOTCH | _M. × gentilis_ | Labiatae |
| *MINT, HORSE | _M. longifolia_ | Labiatae |
| *MINT, APPLE | _M. suaveolens_ | Labiatae |
| *MINT, WATER | _M. aquatica_ | Labiatae |
| *PARSLEY | _Petroselinum crispum_ | Umbelliferae |
| PENNYROYAL | _*Mentha pulegium_ | Labiatae |
| *PEPPERMINT | _Mentha × piperita_ | Labiatae |
| *ROCKET | _Eruca sativa_ | Cruciferae |
| ROCKET, WALL | _Diplotaxis muralis_ | Cruciferae |
| ROSEMARY | _*Rosmarinus officinalis_ | Labiatae |
| *RUE | _Ruta graveolens_ | Rutaceae |
| *SAGE | _Salvia officinalis_ | Labiatae |
| SAVORY, SUMMER | _*Satureja hortensis_ | Labiatae |
| SAVORY, WINTER | _S. montana_ | Labiatae |
| SORREL, COMMON | _*Rumex acetosa_ | Polygonaceae |
| SORREL, GARDEN | _R. scutatus_ | Polygonaceae |
| SORREL, SHEEP | _R. acetosella_ | Polygonaceae |
| SPEARMINT | _*Mentha spicata_ | Labiatae |
| SWEET CICELY; *MYRRH | _Myrrhis odorata_ | Umbelliferae |
| SWEET WOODRUFF | _*Galium odoratum_ | Rubiaceae |
| TANSY | _*Tanacetum vulgare_ | Compositae |
| *TARRAGON | _Artemisia dracunculus_ | Compositae |
| *THYME, GARDEN | _Thymus vulgaris_ | Labiatae |
| *THYME, CARAWAY | _T. herba-barona_ | Labiatae |
| *THYME, LEMON | _T. × citriodorus_ | Labiatae |
| VERVAIN | _*Verbena officinalis_ | Verbenaceae |

Provençal cuisine, the dried stems are used to form a bed on which fish such as sea bass is flamed with brandy (eg loup au fenouil). *DILL *(Anethum graveolens)* is grown both for its fruits, used in pickling cucumbers and for making dill vinegar, and for its young leaves (dill weed) used fresh or dried in flavoring soups and sauces as well as in dill pickles (in addition to the seeds) especially in Scandinavia, central and Eastern Europe. The leaves of CHERVIL *(*Anthriscus cerefolium)* and *CORIANDER (Coriandrum sativum) are also used as herbs but more important are their seeds which along with FENNEL, PARSLEY, *CUMIN *(Cuminum cyminum)* and CARAWAY *(*Carum carvi)* are very extensively used as culinary spices, in curries etc.

Few members of the Compositae are used as herbs. The best-known are TARRAGON, one of the great culinary herbs, whose leaves have a very characteristic flavor, used in tarragon vinegar, WORMWOOD (*Artemisia absinthum*), a bitter aromatic herb mainly used today to flavor herb wines and aperitifs, TANSY *(*Tanacetum vulgare)*, a traditional culinary and medicinal herb now little used, and *CHAMOMILE *(Chamaemelum nobile)* whose flower heads are used to make an infusion – chamomile tea.

The leaves of several members of the genus **Allium* (Liliaceae), such as *CHIVES *(Allium schoenoprasum)* and CHINESE CHIVES or CUCHAY *(A. tuberosum)*, are used as flavorings.

SORREL *(*Rumex acetosa)* a member of the Polygonaceae, has very acid leaves which are used for flavoring. In India and the West Indies it is replaced by a malvaceous plant, **Hibiscus sabdariffa*, known as ROSELLE. From the laurel family comes the aromatic leaf of the BAY or SWEET BAY *(*Laurus nobilis)*.

Herb gardens have been grown for centuries and are still popular today. In earlier times they would include not only culinary herbs, but a selection of medicinal herbs used in tonics, lotions, potions, cough mixtures and so on. Despite the increasing tendency to return to herbal remedies, most of the herbs grown today are for culinary purposes.

Most culinary herbs are perennial and are either propagated from seed or by division. Some, such as CARAWAY, CLARY, DILL, FENNEL and SWEET MARJORAM are biennial or short-lived perennials, while a few, for example ANISE, CORIANDER, SUMMER SAVORY and SWEET BASIL, are annuals that are sown directly in the herb garden each year.

Herbs are normally distinguished from spices which are dried parts, such as roots, bark, leaves, berries or seeds, of aromatic plants found mainly in the Old World tropics. The fruits of some of the herbs, such as the umbelliferous CARAWAY, CUMIN and CORIANDER, mentioned above, are used as culinary spices.

Herbs and spices, together with other kinds of condiments, constitute the group of substances known as flavorings which are considered separately (see p. 147).

*Para Rubber (*Hevea brasiliensis*) in a west coast Malaysian rubber plantation showing the sloping tapping cuts and collecting cups.*

**Hevea** a genus of tropical American trees of which *H. brasiliensis* [PARA RUBBER] is of great economic importance as the world's major source of natural rubber (see RUBBER PLANTS). Two other related species, *H. benthamiana* and *H. guianensis*, also yield commercially acceptable latex. *Hevea* is native to the Amazon basin, and *H. brasiliensis* is grown on a commercial scale in plantations in the Old World tropics, mainly in Southeast Asia. The latex is obtained by tapping the bark. Cooked seeds of *Hevea* species are eaten by aborigines in the northwest part of the Amazon basin.
EUPHORBIACEAE, about 9 species.

**Hibbertia** a large genus of mainly Australian heath-like or climbing shrubs also occurring in Madagascar, New Guinea, New Caledonia and Fiji. The leaves are small and often needle-like. The flowers are yellow or white, solitary or in few-flowered raceme-like inflorescences. Some species are grown out of doors in warm temperate regions, such as *H. dentata*, and *H. scandens*.
DILLENIACEAE, about 100 species.

**Hibiscus** a large tropical, subtropical and warm temperate genus of annual and perennial herbs, evergreen and deciduous shrubs and small trees. It contains numerous ornamentals and some plants of economic value such as *H. esculentus* [GUMBO, OKRA, LADY'S FINGER] (sometimes placed in the separate genus *Abelmoschus*) (see OKRA). *H. cannabinus* [INDIAN HEMP, DECCAN HEMP, KENAF, BASTARD JUTE], which yields a fiber like jute and an oil from the seed, and *H. sabdariffa* [ROSELLE, JAMAICA OR INDIAN SORREL], whose calyces make a pleasing cordial, sauce or jelly. ROSELLE also produces a tough fiber used for cordage.

The most common tropical ornamental is *H.* × *rosa-sinensis* [SHOE FLOWER, ROSE OF CHINA, HAWAIIAN OR CHINESE HIBISCUS], a name loosely applied to more than 1 000 cultivated varieties of uncertain origin, but probably involving hybridization and mutation. Participating species probably include *H. schizopetalus* from East Africa, itself most attractive, *H. kokio* and *H. arnottianus*, both from Hawaii. Some of the more familiar cultivars have scarlet, pink, white or yellow flowers, pendulous or erect, up to about 6in in diameter. The habit of these bushes is normally rounded and to about 16ft tall, although they also make a good dense hedge.

Other tropical ornamentals include the African *H. trionum* [FLOWER-OF-AN-HOUR], *H. mutabilis* [COTTON ROSE] from southern China, so called because the flowers change color to darker shades with age, and *H. elatus* [BLUE MAHOE], the national tree of Jamaica, a useful forestry species growing to 80ft in the mountains and whose wood is used for cabinet-making etc. There are about 40 cultivars of *H. syriacus* (=**Althaea frutex*) [ROSE OF SHARON], a shrub native to warm temperate East Asia, with white, purple or mauve flowers borne on an erect bush. Another popular ornamental is the tall perennial herb *H. moscheutos* [COMMON OR SWAMP ROSE MALLOW, WILD COTTON], a native of the eastern and southern USA which includes the subspecies *moscheutos* (= *H. oculiroseus*) and *palustris* (= *H. palustris*) [MARSH MALLOW, SEA HOLLYHOCK]. There are numerous cultivars of progeny from hybrids of this species and *H. coccineus* and *H. militaris*.
MALVACEAE, about 250 species.

**Hieracium** [HAWKWEEDS] a large genus of very variable, often hairy, perennial herbs distributed throughout temperate regions with the exception of Australasia. Only a few species are cultivated as they soon become rampant. Among the more popular are *H. pilosella* [MOUSE EAR HAWKWEED], with hairy gray leaves and lemon-yellow flower heads, *H. aurantiacum* [DEVIL'S PAINTBRUSH], with flame-colored flower heads, and *H. villosum* [SHAGGY HAWKWEED], which is covered with silky hairs and has large bright yellow flower heads.

Many thousands of apomictic forms have been described as species.
COMPOSITAE, 700–1 000 or more species.

**Himantoglossum** a small genus of robust terrestrial orchids found across Europe and in North Africa and the Near East. The commonest species is *H. hircinum* [LIZARD ORCHID] which, like the other members of the genus, possesses foul-smelling flowers basically greenish purple in color.
ORCHIDACEAE, about 4 species.

**Hippeastrum** a genus of bulbous plants widely distributed in the New world, mostly in tropical America, with one species in West Africa. The large showy funnel-shaped flowers have made these BARBADOS LILIES or AMARYLLIS, as they are commonly known, popular as greenhouse plants in the north for winter flowering, or as garden plants in the south.

Most of the cultivated species are hybrids or variants of *H. aulicum* (= **Amaryllis aulica*) [LILY-OF-THE-PALACE], which has red flowers with a green throat, *H. elegans* (= *A. elegans*), which has long greenish-white flowers, *H. puniceum* (= *A. belladonna*) which has red flowers, green at the base, *H. reginae* (= *A. reginae*), which has red flowers with a greenish-white throat, *H. reticulatum* (= *A. reticulata*), with mauve-red flowers, and *H. striatum* (= *A. rutila*), with bright crimson flowers with a green keel.
AMARYLLIDACEAE, about 75 species.

Mare's Tail (Hippuris vulgaris) *is a widely distributed hydrophyte that grows in mud in pools and slow-moving water.* (× 1/5)

**Hippophae** a small temperate Eurasian genus of thorny deciduous shrubs or small trees covered with silvery scales, and with small inconspicuous flowers which appear before the leaves. *H. rhamnoides* [SEA BUCKTHORN] has an unusually wide distribution extending from Great Britain across Europe to Kamchatka and Japan. The bushes sucker freely and so are able to grow on loose soil, helping to stabilize it. The bright orange "berries" can be used to make a sharp-tasting jam or jelly.
ELAEAGNACEAE, 2–3 species.

**Hippuris** a genus comprising a single species, *H. vulgaris* [MARE'S TAIL], found in temperate and cold regions of the Northern Hemisphere. It is a perennial herb that normally grows in shallow water, developing erect flowering shoots from a creeping rhizome. The submerged shoots form an important winter food for many animals and for Eskimos.
HIPPURIDACEAE, 1 species.

**Hoffmannia** a genus of mainly shrubs, rarely herbs, native to Central and South America from Mexico to Argentina. A few species are grown under glass, more for their foliage than for their small tubular flowers. *H. discolor* has leaves which are purple beneath and red flowers. *H. refulgens* has leaves wine-red beneath and pale red flowers, and the leaves of *H. ghiesbreghtii* are reddish purple beneath and the flowers are yellow with a red blotch.
RUBIACEAE, about 100 species.

**Hoheria** a small New Zealand genus of shrubs or small trees cultivated as ornamentals for their attractive clusters of white flowers. A popular species is *H. populnea* [LACE BARK] an evergreen shrub which may reach a height of 33ft, the wood of which is used in cabinet-making.
MALVACEAE, 2–5 species.

**Holcus** a small genus of perennial grasses occurring in the Canary Islands, North Africa, Europe, Asia Minor and the Caucasus, with one species in South Africa. The common tufted perennial *H. lanatus* [WOODY HOLCUS, YORKSHIRE FOG, VELVET GRASS] and the closely related rhizomatous *H. mollis* [CREEPING SOFT GRASS] are often troublesome weeds in north temperate regions, and are only of minor value for grazing.
GRAMINEAE, 8 species.

**Holly** the common name for the widespread woody genus *Ilex*, found mainly in temperate and tropical regions of Asia and North and South America. They are sometimes deciduous, usually evergreen trees and shrubs, with shoots often angled, the greenish or white unisexual flowers axillary and usually borne on separate male and female plants.

*Leaves and fruit of the Sea Buckthorn* (Hippophae rhamnoides), *a suckering shrub used to stabilize soil and sand.* (× 1/3)

*I. aquifolium* [ENGLISH, EUROPEAN or OREGON HOLLY], from Europe, North Africa and western Asia, is used as a decoration during the Christmas season, as it was by the Romans during their Saturnalia. It is a tree to about 80ft tall. Its dark green spiny foliage and red winter berries have made it one of the best-known and most popular of plants and there are over 100 different cultivated varieties, some referred to *I.* × *altaclerensis* (*I. aquifolium* × *I. perado*). Some are variegated, while others have crisped or puckered leaves of diverse shape. *I. opaca* [AMERICAN HOLLY] is the best-known evergreen American species, growing to about 50ft and containing more than 110 cultivars. *I. verticillata* [BLACK ALDER, WINTERBERRY] is a large deciduous North American shrub or small tree, with several cultivars which bear copious red (rarely yellow) fruit in winter; its purple leaves turn yellow in autumn.

Asian evergreen hollies include two species each with several cultivars, *I. cornuta* [HORNED HOLLY] and the dwarf *I. crenata* [JAPANESE HOLLY] with black berries. The Chinese species *I. pernyii*, and *I. latifolia* [TARAJO HOLLY], from Japan, bear orange-red berries. *I. perado* var *perado* [MADEIRA HOLLY] and var *platyphylla* [CANARY ISLAND HOLLY] are attractive small evergreen trees native to Madeira and the Canary Islands, with dark green or yellowish-green leaves and dark red berries.

A bitter drink, cassine or the "black drink"

A Silvery Moth (Plusia gamma) feeding at night on a Honeysuckle flower (Lonicera periclymenum), which brings about pollination. (× 3)

Female flowers of the Hop (Humulus lupulus) which after fertilization develop into the typical hop cone.

of North American Indians, is prepared from the dried leaves of the North American shrub or small tree, *I. vomitoria* [CASSINA, YAUPON, CAROLINA TEA HOLLY]. Birdlime is partly made from the bark of *I. aquifolium* and *I. integra* [MOCHI TREE]. The leaves of *I. paraguariensis* [YERBA MATÉ, PARAGUAY TEA] are the source of maté, the popular South American drink.

**Hollyhock** the common name for some of the tall leafy stemmed herbs belonging to the genus *Alcea*, particularly *A. rosea* (= **Althaea rosea*) [HOLLYHOCK] and *A. ficifolia* (= *Althaea ficifolia*) [FIGLEAF HOLLYHOCK]. Many varieties of the first-named species are cultivated in temperate gardens for their large showy flowers in a wide range of colors; they are also naturalized in many parts of the world.
MALVACEAE.

**Holodiscus** a North American genus of deciduous flowering shrubs, two of which, *H. discolor* [CREAMBUSH] and *H. dumosus*, are grown as ornamentals bearing dense inflorescences of tiny creamy-white flowers.
ROSACEAE, 8 species.

The fleshy leaves and round fruit of Sea Sandwort (Honkenya peploides), common on north temperate sandy and pebbly seashores. (× $1\frac{1}{2}$)

**Honeydew melons** a name applied to a class of *melons more properly known as WINTER MELONS, fruits of cultivars of **Cucumis melo*. They are yellow or green, hard skinned, ellipsoid in shape with length greater than the diameter, smooth or shallowly corrugated. They ripen late, and can be stored for a month or more; in consequence, they are popular with growers who export to distant markets.
CUCURBITACEAE.

**Honeysuckle** the common name for members of the genus **Lonicera*, consisting of evergreen and deciduous flowering shrubs and woody climbers, often with fragrant, long-tubed flowers containing nectar (see *Lonicera*). In countries where *Lonicera* is not native, other species have become known locally as honeysuckles. Thus *Halleria lucida* is the AFRICAN HONEYSUCKLE, *Tecomaria capensis* the CAPE HONEYSUCKLE and *Lambertia multiflora* the AUSTRALIAN HONEYSUCKLE.

**Honkenya** a small genus of perennial herbs of north temperate and circumpolar regions and southern Patagonia. *H. peploides* [SEA SANDWORT], a common species of sandy and pebbly shores, has a long creeping underground stem with scale-leaves and fleshy green leaves and can endure short periods of immersion in salt water.
CARYOPHYLLACEAE, 2 species.

**Hop** the common name for the climbing perennial herb *Humulus lupulus*, which is cultivated for its use in brewing, giving to beer its characteristic bitter taste and hop aroma. The plant has a perennial rootstock but the aerial twining stems (bines) die down to ground level each winter. The fresh roots which emerge in the spring climb by twining clockwise (without tendrils), and commercially they are grown up strings or wires which are attached each year to a permanent framework of poles and wire.

Hop plants are either male or female, and it is the female inflorescences or "cones" which are the commercial product. Usually the hops are grown seedless by eliminating all male plants from the district. The constituents of brewing value are the soft resins which provide the bitterness and the essential oils which contribute the aroma characteristic to beer. Both of these are produced in lupulin glands, which constitute up to a quarter of the dry weight of the cones.

Successful plant breeding by hybridizing European and wild American hops has resulted in cultivars with an increased soft resin content in their cones. The bittering power of hops depends upon the acid fraction of the soft resins, and the acid content of the traditional cultivars is from 4–5%. The most recently produced cultivars contain as much as 10–12% acid, so that the yield of brewing material has been more than doubled without increasing the land area grown.
MORACEAE.

**Hordeum** see Barley.
GRAMINEAE, about 20 species.

**Horminum** [DRAGON MOUTH] a genus represented by a single species, *H. pyrenaicum*, which occurs naturally in mountains from the Pyrenees to the Alps. A hardy herbaceous plant, sometimes cultivated in borders or rock gardens, it has a flowering stem up to 10in long bearing numerous bluish-purple flowers. There are varieties with rose-purple or white flowers.
LABIATAE, 1 species.

**Hormoseira** an important genus of brown

algae found in Australasia. The thallus appears rather like a string of hollow beads. PHAEOPHYCEAE.

**Hornbeam** the common name for members of the genus *Carpinus*, deciduous trees distributed throughout the temperate regions of the Northern Hemisphere. The flowers are borne in unisexual catkins, with both sexes occurring on the same tree.

The spring-flowering *C. betulus* [COMMON HORNBEAM] is regularly cultivated and is one of nature's most handsome trees, ranging in height from 5–80ft in its mature state. It coppices well, retains its leaves after clipping, and because it branches profusely, like beech, it makes an excellent hedge. The wood, which is heavy and strong, is used for turning, for tool handles etc. There are several well-known cultivars, varying in color, leaf shape, tree shape and branching habit. Hornbeams are extremely hardy trees and very handsome, especially when in flower and fruit.

*C. caroliniana* [AMERICAN HORNBEAM or MUSCLE TREE, BLUE BEECH], a native of the eastern USA, is somewhat similar to the COMMON HORNBEAM, but is usually a smaller tree differing by its whitish hair-covered leaves, which turn orange yellow or scarlet in the autumn. Another well-known species, *C. japonica* [JAPANESE HORNBEAM], is a widely cultivated sturdy, pyramidal tree which grows to a height of 40–50ft. It is particularly valued for its large, handsome leaves and its pendulous female catkins. Less frequently cultivated, but nonetheless beautiful trees include *C. orientalis* [ORIENTAL HORNBEAM] *C. henryana* [CHINESE HENRY'S HORNBEAM] and *C. cordata* [CORDATE HORNBEAM]. BETULACEAE, about 35–40 species.

*Hornbeams (*Carpinus betulus*) were formerly much coppiced, both for their hard timber and for making charcoal.*

**Horseradish** the common name for *Armoracia rusticana* (= *Armoracia lapathifolia*), a vigorous rapidly spreading plant with a swollen, branching taproot and large simple leaves. The root is harvested, peeled and grated. It contains a very pungent mustard oil. The grated root can be used as a relish, but is most commonly used to make horseradish sauce, a traditional British piquant accompaniment to roast beef.

The traditional practice of growing a few aged plants in a garden to harvest periodically yields tough stringy roots. The best and most tender roots are obtained commercially by growing horseradish as an annual crop. CRUCIFERAE.

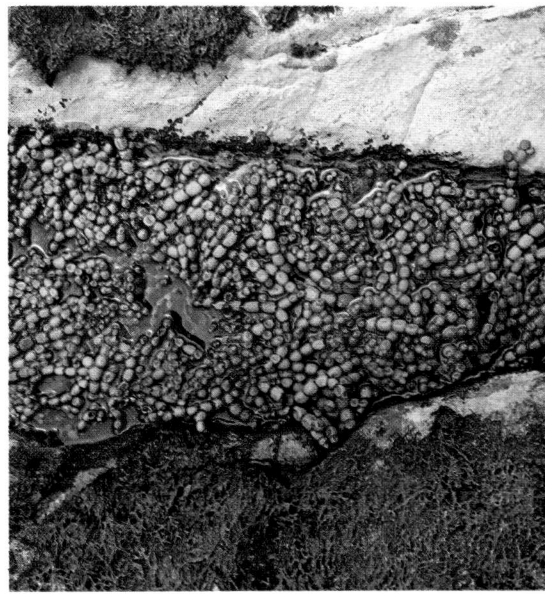

*Venus' Necklace (*Hormoseira banksii*) is a brown alga, seen here growing on South Island, New Zealand. The conspicuous "beads" contain the reproductive organs. (×1)*

**Horsetails** see p. 180.

**Hosta** (= *Funkia*) [PLANTAIN LILIES] a genus of perennial herbs with ornamental foliage and funnel-shaped white to dark violet flowers borne in erect racemes, mainly native to Japan, with a few species in China and Korea. Among the cultivated species (many of which occur in a range of cultivars) are: *H. plantaginea* [FRAGRANT PLANTAIN LILY] with a short dense raceme of upright, fragrant, white flowers subtended by large bracts; *H. ventricosa* [BLUE PLANTAIN LILY], with dark violet flowers with a narrow tube suddenly expanded into a bell-shaped mouth; *H. fortunei*, with pale lilac flowers; *H. lancifolia* (= *H. japonica*) [NARROW-LEAFED PLANTAIN LILY], with loose racemes of dark violet flowers; and *H. undulata* (= *H. lancifolia* var *undulata*), with pale lavender flowers in many-flowered racemes.
LILIACEAE, about 40 species.

**Hottentot bean** the edible seed, eaten by native peoples, of some of the 18 species of the southern African genus *Schotia*. Most are trees, such as *S. brachypetala* [TREE FUCHSIA], producing seeds with a large, rich, fatty aril. LEGUMINOSAE.

**Hottonia** a genus comprising two species of hardy perennial, floating aquatic herbs from Europe, Asia and North America. The lilac-flowered *H. palustris* [WATER VIOLET], with its finely divided submerged leaves, is a valuable oxygenating species for ponds and aquaria. The other species, the white-flowered *H. inflata*, is North American in origin. PRIMULACEAE, 2 species.

# Horsetails or Scouring Rushes

THE GENUS *Equisetum* [HORSETAILS, or SCOURING RUSHES] comprises 16 species and about the same number of hybrids. They are primitive plants and are the only members of the group known as the Sphenophytina, a subdivision of the vascular plants. They are intermediate in form between the *club mosses and *ferns. Horsetails are most frequently found in moist habitats such as marshes, flushes, dune slacks, lakesides and river banks but they also colonize drier sites such as derelict ground and railway embankments. They are often the dominant plants with colonies covering considerable areas: indeed, an unbroken stand of *E. hyemale* stretches for over 180mi along the Mississippi river. The gametophytes (sexual generation) may be found on bare mud by lakes and rivers. Although spread is predominantly by rhizomes, the high incidence of hybrid horsetails indicates that sexual reproduction is probably more frequent than is generally assumed.

Although horsetails are found throughout the world (except Australia and New Zealand) they show greatest diversity in the Northern Hemisphere. Over half the species have distributions covering the entire range of the genus. Three species are restricted to central South America and *E. diffusum* is a Himalayan endemic. The occurrence of *E. telmateia* along the western edges of Eurasia and North America and its absence on the eastern sides of these continents suggests large-scale regional extinction.

Horsetails are perhaps best known as garden weeds whose deeply buried rhizomes make them difficult to eradicate. This same property, however, renders them important guides for the siting of wells above subterranean water supplies on the American prairies. Horsetails are poisonous to herbivores in pastures but, in Japan, the young cones are regarded as a delicacy. In the past, they were widely employed for scouring pans but today their abrasive powers are restricted to polishing tools and the reeds of wind instruments. Most remarkable of all, horsetails are said to have found favor with prospectors since they apparently accumulate unusual elements including gold.

The most conspicuous features of these plants are their jointed and ridged photosynthetic stems which bear whorls of branches and fused microphyllous leaves. The stem ridges, together with the leaves lying above them, show a regular alternation from one internode to the next. Their sandpapery texture, resulting from the presence of silica bodies in the epidermis, is especially interesting since silicon is an essential element for these plants. Horsetails grow prolifically by means of subterranean rhizomes which give rise at the nodes to erect shoots, roots and, in some species, starch-filled tubers.

With stems less than 6in tall, *E. scirpoides* is the smallest species while *E. giganteum* reaches a height of 42ft. The stems of the latter, however, are only 0.8in in diameter and have to rely on the surrounding vegetation for support. Some species are unbranched whilst others, such as *E. sylvaticum*, with two orders of lateral branches, have an almost lacy appearance.

All living horsetails are herbaceous, produce just one type of spore (homosporous) and lack secondary thickening, but in the past they displayed far greater morphological diversity. Tree-like and sometimes heterosporous plants, belonging to the extinct Calamitales formed a major component of Carboniferous coal-measure swamp forest. These existed side by side with herbaceous plants which resembled extant horsetails. (See pp. 738–740, 1217.)

The spore-forming bodies (sporangia) are borne on peltate stalks (sporangiophores) grouped together in cones. In some species they occur terminally on special unbranched stems that lack chlorophyll while in others the fertile stems are green and identical with the sterile ones. Material deposited around the developing spores forms into bodies (elaters) with spoon-shaped bands. These are hygroscopic (moisture-absorbing) and coil with changes in humidity, at the same time flicking spores from the sporangia. Ripe spores contain chlorophyll and are spherical.

Above *A mass of fertile and young vegetative shoots of* Equisetum fluviatile *(Water Horsetail).* (×½)
Left *Cone of* E. arvense *(Field Horsetail) comprising a mass of brown stalks with white sporangia below. A typical vegetative shoot is shown on the right.* (×2)

The spores germinate to form the sexual (or gametophyte) generation. These are photosynthetic and surface-living. They are up to 1.2in in diameter, and consist of cushions of soft tissue bearing unicellular root-like rhizoids on the underside and green tissues above. The female sex organs (archegonia) have projecting necks and each contain an egg. The male sex organs (antheridia) are borne on upright branches of the cushion and contain coiled male gametes (spermatozoids) each with 80–120 flagella. The gametophytes may be male or bisexual with

Above *The sponge-like prothallus of* Equisetum fluviatile *(Water Horsetail) on which the sex organs form and from which, after fertilization, the next sporophytes grow – three can be seen here.* (×3)
Below *The same species growing in shallow water.*

sexuality depending on environmental conditions. The next generation of sporophytes is readily produced by either self- or cross-fertilization and over 35 new plants have been recorded from a single gametophyte.

Equisetum arvense *(Field Horsetail) can be a problematical weed of damp fields and gardens, and, because of its deep-seated rhizomes, it is difficult to eradicate. It is seen here in a newly-cultivated vegetable garden.* (× $\frac{1}{4}$)

**Houseleek** the common name for *Sempervivum*, a genus of dwarf, rosette-forming, hardy leaf-succulents. They are typical of rocky mountainous habitats in Europe, North Africa, and Asia. Each plant forms a cluster of almost stemless rosettes of tightly packed, spirally arranged fleshy leaves of green, often overlaid with purplish-red. When flowering, the stem elongates and expands above into many-flowered clusters of small starry blooms. Even after the flowers have passed, the heads of the dried fruits have a decorative value.

From early times *S. tectorum* [COMMON OR ROOF HOUSELEEK] has been credited with beneficial properties, perhaps because of its apparent coolness and longevity in hot dry situations lethal to other plants. It is often grown as a clump on the roof (hence the common name) in some rural areas of Europe, as a supposed protection from lightning. The sliced leaves were recommended as a poultice for burns or stings, and were said to cure warts and corns.

Sempervivums make ideal trouble-free rock-garden plants. Among the most popular garden species are the purplish-red-flowered *S. tectorum* with numerous cultivars, *S. arachnoideum* [COBWEB HOUSELEEK, SPIDER-WEB HOUSELEEK], whose leaves are connected by cobwebby strands, *S. montanum* with purple flowers (yellowish-white in var *braunii*), and the greenish-yellow-flowered *S. soboliferum* [HEN-AND-CHICKENS]. Numerous hybrids are in cultivation, including *S.* × *barbulatum* (*S. arachnoideum* × *S. montanum*) and *S.* × *fauconnettii* (*S. arachnoideum* × *S. tectorum*).
CRASSULACEAE, about 40 species.

**Houstonia** a genus of low-growing tufted perennial herbs native to the southern and western USA and Mexico. The genus is sometimes included in *Hedyotis*. The plants have blue, purple or white flowers, and species such as *H. serpyllifolia* (= *Hedyotis michauxii*) [CREEPING BLUETS] and *H. caerulea* (= *Hedyotis caerulea*) [BLUETS] are frequently cultivated in rock gardens.
RUBIACEAE, about 50 species.

*Male flowers of the Hop (*Humulus lupulus*). These occur on separate plants from the females and since only seedless female cones are required for brewing, great efforts are made to eliminate all male plants from a growing district. (×2)*

*The Wild Hyacinth or English Bluebell (*Hyacinthoides non-scripta*) flowers from April to June, usually forming a dense carpet in woodlands.*

**Houttuynia** a genus represented by a single species, *H. cordata* (= *Gymnotheca chinensis*), a perennial creeping rhizomatous herb native to the Himalayas, China and Japan. It is cultivated for ground cover in moist places. The flowers are borne in a terminal spike subtended by a collar of four white bracts, the whole resembling a single flower.
SAURURACEAE, 1 species.

**Howea** (= *Kentia*) a genus comprising two species of ornamental palms from Lord Howe Island in the southwest Pacific. *H. belmoreana* [CURLY PALM] and *H. forsterana* [FLAT OR THATCH-LEAF PALM, SENTRY], both with stout, erect stems and long feathery leaves, are grown as ornamentals indoors, or outside in the tropics.
PALMAE, 2 species.

**Hoya** a genus of evergreen, chiefly climbing or twining plants from China, southeast Asia, Indomalaysia and Australia, with fleshy, opposite leaves and axillary umbel-like clusters of waxy flowers. *H. carnosa* [WAX FLOWER, WAX PLANT] is a vigorous climber and has pendulous umbels of fragrant white flowers with pink centers. In temperate climates it can be grown on a wall in a greenhouse. In the tropics it does best on tree trunks. *H. bella* is more slender; it is grown in hanging baskets for its white flowers with rose, crimson or violet centers.
ASCLEPIADACEAE, 70–200 species.

**Huckleberry** the common name normally given to several species of bushy shrubs of the North and South American genus *Gaylussacia*. They usually flower in spring, producing white or pinkish flowers in axillary racemes. Many species, including *G. baccata* [BLACK HUCKLEBERRY], *G. brachycera* [BOX HUCKLEBERRY], *G. ursina* [BEAR HUCKLEBERRY] and *G. dumosa* [DWARF HUCKLEBERRY, BUSHY WHORTLEBERRY], bear edible fruits similar to blueberries or blackberries.

Some species of **Vaccinium* are also called HUCKLEBERRY. Examples include *V. vacillans* [BLUE OR SUGAR HUCKLEBERRY] and *V. hirsutum* [HAIRY HUCKLEBERRY].
ERICACEAE.

**Humulus** a small genus of perennial or annual climbing herbs widespread in the temperate Northern Hemisphere. Female plants of the perennial *H. lupulus* [*HOP] are widely cultivated for their catkins containing lupulin resins which during brewing are converted to isohumulones, the bitter principles of beer. The tender young shoots are sometimes eaten as a vegetable and the hops used in hop pillows. *H. japonicus* [JAPANESE HOP] is sometimes cultivated as a garden-twiner for its screening effect when in leaf in the summer. Although this is a perennial species it is usually grown as an annual from seed.
MORACEAE, 2 species.

**Hyacinthoides** a genus of bulbous monocotyledons native to Western Europe and northwest Africa. The genus is better known by the incorrect name *Endymion*. The flowers are bell-shaped or rotate in shape and white,

*The Spanish Bluebell (*Hyacinthoides hispanica*) is often cultivated in gardens and is often naturalized in southern and western Europe.* ($\times\frac{1}{10}$)

pink or blue in color, arranged in a raceme.

Cultivated species include the popular *H. non-scripta* (*Scilla non-scripta*) [WILD HYACINTH, ENGLISH BLUEBELL, HAREBELL] with various white (eg 'Alba'), blue (eg 'Caerulea') and pink (eg 'Rosea') cultivars, *H. hispanica* (= *S. campanulata, S. hispanica*) [SPANISH BLUEBELL, SPANISH JACINTH, BELL-FLOWERED SQUILL], again with several cultivars, and the lilac-flowered *H. italica* (= *S. italica*) [ITALIAN SQUILL].
LILIACEAE, 3–4 species.

**Hyacinthus** [HYACINTHS] a small genus of bulbous herbs native to the Mediterranean region, southwest Asia and the Middle East. The plants have a cluster of strap-shaped or linear basal leaves and a leafless stem bearing flowers in a raceme.

*H. orientalis* [COMMON HYACINTH, DUTCH HYACINTH] is a sweetly scented plant from which all the colorful, large-flowered florists' hyacinths have been raised by selection. In the wild, it is a fairly small-flowered plant with only a few blue or lilac flowers in the raceme, whereas the named cultivars have densely flowered racemes with individual flowers about three or four times the size, in a wide range of colors from white through pink and blue to deep purple and red. They are widely used, both in outdoor bedding and for forcing in pots for indoor decoration. The "ROMAN HYACINTHS" resemble more closely the original wild species with fewer, smaller flowers.

Other species, previously included in *Hyacinthus*, are now placed in *Brimeura*, *Bellevalia* and *Hyacinthella*.
LILIACEAE, 1 species.

*A white cultivar of the Common Hyacinth (*Hyacinthus orientalis*, together with Grape Hyacinths (*Muscari *sp).* ($\times\frac{1}{12}$)

**Hydrangea** a genus of deciduous and evergreen shrubs or woody climbers, mainly from East Asia, the Himalayas, the Malaysian region and North and South America. The star-shaped flowers are small and numerous, arranged in corymbs or panicles, and in most species some of them are sterile, with greatly enlarged petal-like sepals and the other floral parts abortive.

The most popular hydrangeas, especially for pot-cultures, are those usually known as "hortensias", which are all sterile-flowered. They originated in Japanese gardens where the parent species, *H. macrophylla* [FRENCH HYDRANGEA, HORTENSIA] is native. In the "lace-cap" hydrangeas the inflorescence is a corymb with only the outermost flowers sterile. Hortensias and lace-caps have flowers of various shades of red, pink, mauve or blue; this is determined partly by the genetic constitution on the plant (in some varieties the flowers are always red or pink), but partly by the soil, all varieties which have blue flowers on acid soils changing to purple or pink on neutral or alkaline soils.

Among the popular cultivated hydrangeas are the climbers, *H. anomala* (subspecies *anomala* and subspecies *petiolaris*), both with white flowers, the small shrubby white-flowered *H. arborescens* [HILLS OF SNOW, SEVENBARK], and the medium-sized to taller shrubs, *H. paniculata* (flowers white, turning pink), *H. quercifolia* (white, turning pink), *H. aspera* subspecies *sargentiana* (= *H. sargentiana*) (white and lilac), *H. aspera* subspecies *aspera* (= *H. villosa*) (violet) and *H. heteromalla* (white).

The wood of *H. paniculata*, which is fine-grained and hard, is used in Japan for making umbrella handles and pipes.
SAXIFRAGACEAE, about 25 species.

**Hydrocharis** a small aquatic genus, widespread in temperate and tropical regions of the Old world and Australia. They are free-floating herbs with long stolons bearing leaves in groups at the nodes. The best-known species, *H. morsus-ranae* [FROG-BIT], has become naturalized in North America. This species is also widely grown in large freshwater aquaria.
HYDROCHARITACEAE, 3–6 species.

**Hymenaea** a Central and tropical American genus of trees, the most important of which is *H. courbaril* [LOCUST TREE, COURBARIL] from Brazil. It attains a height of 100ft, frequently with buttress roots. This species is a major source of a yellow or red resin, *copal, which is exuded from every part of the plant. It is used in high quality varnishes. The hard, durable timber is of economic value. *H. verrucosa* [EAST AFRICAN COPAL] is often placed in the genus *Trachylobium*.
LEGUMINOSAE, about 25 species.

**Hymenocallis** a genus of bulbous perennials with shortly tubular or funnel-shaped flowers, native mainly to North and South America. Easily cultivated outside in warm regions, in cooler temperate countries they require to be kept in either hothouse or cool greenhouse conditions. The cool greenhouse species include the white-flowered *H. narcissiflora* (*H. calathina*) [BASKET FLOWER, PERUVIAN DAFFODIL] and the yellow-flowered *H. amancaes* (= *Ismene amancaes*). Hothouse species include *H. expansa* (white flowers tinged pale green) and the fragrant *H. latifolia*.

*H. littoralis* (= *H. americana*), which is native to tropical America, and *H. pedalis*, native to eastern South America, are naturalized in Africa where they have been incorrectly described as *H. senegambica*.
AMARYLLIDACEAE, 25–30 species.

*'Pencil'd flower of sickly scent' – George Crabbe's poem well describes the poisonous Henbane (*Hyoscyamus niger*).* ($\times 1$)

**Hyoscyamus** [HENBANES] a genus of herbaceous, often poisonous plants widely distributed throughout the Western Hemisphere. *H. niger* [BLACK HENBANE] is a highly poisonous, fetid, annual or biennial, sticky-hairy plant from Europe and Asia. It is grown as a source of the sedative drug hyoscyamine.
SOLANACEAE, about 10 species.

**Hypericum** [ST. JOHN'S WORTS] a large and important genus of herbs or shrubs, rarely trees, native to temperate and tropical

*The feathery shoots of the mat-forming moss* Hypnum cupressiforme *var* lacunosum, *a locally common species found on chalky grassland.* ( × 3)

regions. Best-known perhaps is the near-cosmopolitan *H. perforatum* [PERFORATED ST. JOHN'S WORT], which is poisonous to animals and contains photosensitizing compounds which can cause dermatitis.

Many species are cultivated for their attractive yellow flowers, including *H. calycinum* (= *H. grandiflorum*) [ROSE OF SHARON, AARON'S BEARD, CREEPING ST. JOHN'S WORT], an evergreen shrub, the Canary Islands *H. canariense* (= *H. floribundum*), a taller semievergreen shrub, and some smaller species, including the Asian evergreen *H. patulum*, the evergreen *H.* × *moserianum* [GOLD FLOWER], a hybrid between *H. calycinum* and *H. patulum*, the North American *H. stans* [ST. PETER'S WORT] and the Eurasian *H. androsaemum* [TUTSAN]. Useful rockery species are the prostrate shrub *H. reptans* and the low spreading perennial *H. concinnum* [GOLDWIRE].
HYPERICACEAE, about 300 species.

**Hypnum** a genus of mat-forming mosses, the best-known of which is the highly variable, cosmoplitan *H. cupressiforme*.
HYPNACEAE, about 40 species.

**Hypochoeris** [CAT'S EARS] a genus of perennial herbs, cosmopolitan in distribution. The sinuate or ovate leaves are arranged in a basal rosette and the dandelion-like, usually yellow flower heads are borne on leafless stalks. *H. scorzonerae* is used in Chile as a diuretic. The young leaves of *H. maculata* [EUROPEAN CAT'S EAR] are sometimes eaten in salads. *H. uniflora* from the Alps is sometimes cultivated in rock gardens. *H. radicata* [SPOTTED CAT'S EAR] is a weed that is naturalized in various parts of the world.
COMPOSITAE, about 80 species.

**Hypocrea** a widespread genus of ascomycete fungi. The numerous fruiting bodies (ascocarps) are enclosed in a perithecium. Characteristic habitats include rotting wood and bark, bracket fungi and soil.
HYPOCREACEAE, about 100 species.

**Hypoxis** [STAR GRASSES] a genus of perennial herbs native to America, Africa, Indomalaysia and Australia. *H. hirsuta*, from North America, is one of several species cultivated as a garden ornamental. The shortly tubular yellow flowers are borne in a few-flowered terminal cluster at the end of a leafless stalk. *H. aurea*, from Asia, yields extracts used in local medicine as a tonic.
AMARYLLIDACEAE, about 100 species.

**Hyssop** the common name given to the genus *Hyssopus*, of which *H. officinalis*, an aromatic dwarf shrub native to Central Asia, is sometimes grown as an ornamental border plant or as a culinary herb. The leaves have a somewhat minty flavor and an oil distilled from them is used in perfumery and as a flavoring for liqueurs. In North America, the related *Agastache urticifolia* is called NETTLE-LEAVED GIANT HYSSOP, and was used by Indians medicinally and as a flavoring. *A. foeniculum* is ANISE HYSSOP or FRAGRANT GIANT HYSSOP, the dried leaves of which are used for seasoning and to make a tea.
LABIATAE.

*Hyssop (*Hyssopus officinalis*) is very attractive to insects such as the hoverfly shown here. The aromatic leaves are sometimes used as a culinary herb.* ( × 3)

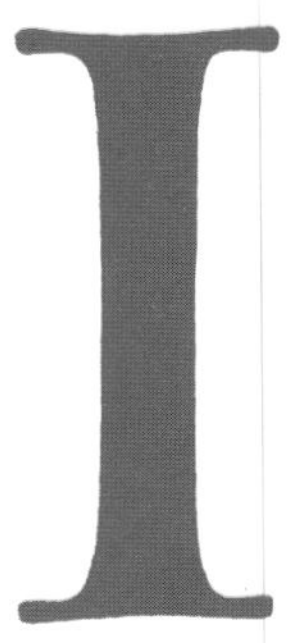

**Iberis** a genus of annual or perennial herbs, rarely dwarf shrubs, native to the Mediterranean region, some of which are cultivated in gardens for their umbel-like clusters of white, pink, red or purple flowers. *I. amara* and *I. umbellata* are the commonly grown CANDYTUFTS of gardens. They are variable, showy annuals with several cultivars. The perennial subshrubby *I. saxatilis*, *I. sempervirens* and *I. gibraltarica* are good rock-garden plants, sometimes used for edging.
CRUCIFERAE, about 30 species.

Incarvillea mairei *is a herbaceous perennial from East Asia. The pink flowers are typically tubular and two-lipped.* ( × ½)

**Ice plant** the popular name originally given to *Mesembryanthemum crystallinum*, so called from the glittering crystaline papillae covering the whole plant. The name is now loosely used for other garden ornamental species of *Mesembryanthemum* and unrelated leaf succulents of fleshy habit such as *sedums.
AIZOACEAE.

**Idesia** a genus from China and Japan represented by a single species, *I. polycarpa* [IIGIRI TREE], a deciduous tree up to 50ft tall with more or less horizontal branches. *I. polycarpa* is grown in the southern USA as a shade tree for parks or street planting and is hardy in parts of Europe, where it is occasionally cultivated in arboreta and botanic gardens for its fragrant flowers and clusters or orange-red berries.
FLACOURTIACEAE, 1 species.

Golden Samphire (*Inula crithmoides*) is usually found near the sea, growing on shingle, cliffs and rocks or on salt marshes. ($\times\frac{1}{10}$)

**Ilex** see HOLLY.
AQUIFOLIACEAE, about 400 species.

**Illicium** [ANISE TREES] a genus of evergreen trees and shrubs native to Asia, North America and the West Indies. They have red, purple, pink, white or pale yellow fragrant flowers and starlike fruits (clusters of many one-seeded follicles). Oil of anise, used for flavoring drinks and confectionery and in medicines, is obtained from *I. verum* [STAR ANISE], a native of China, and also from the American *I. parvifolium* [YELLOW STAR ANISE]. The unripe fruits of the former are used as a spice. The East Asian *I. anisatum* [JAPANESE STAR ANISE], with yellow flowers, and the North American *I. floridanum* [PURPLE ANISE, ANISEED TREE], with crimson to purplish flowers, are among the few species grown as ornamentals in warm regions.
ILLICIACEAE, about 40 species.

**Immortelle** the name given to a number of species of tropical trees used as shade trees in cacao and coffee plantations (see *Erythrina*). The name is also given to a wide variety of plants whose flowers retain their color after drying, such as **Helichrysum* species and *Xeranthemum annuum*.

**Impatiens** a large genus of annual and perennial herbs distributed through tropical and temperate Eurasia and Africa, especially Madagascar and the mountains of India and Sri Lanka. There are also a few species in North and Central America.

*I. wallerana* (= *I. holstii*, *I. sultani*), from Tanzania to Mozambique, and many cultivars derived from it, are the widely cultivated BUSY LIZZIES with pink, red, white, orange, purple or variegated flowers. *I. balsamina* [GARDEN BALSAM], an Asian species, is also widely grown, especially as double-flowered forms. *I. roylei* (= *I. glandulifera*) [HIMALAYAN or INDIAN BALSAM] is cultivated in Europe and North America and has become naturalized by rivers, lakes and other damp habitats.
BALSAMINACEAE, about 600 species.

**Imperfect fungi** see Fungi, p. 156.

**Incarvillea** a genus of annual or perennial herbs with woody or tuberous roots, native to Central and East Asia and the Himalayan region. Several species, such as *I. delavayi* and *I. mairei* var *grandiflora* (= *I. grandiflora*), are cultivated as garden-border plants, in rock gardens or under glass, for their large, showy, predominantly pink flowers.
BIGNONIACEAE, about 14 species.

**Indigo** a deep-blue and very fast natural dye obtained from leaves of the INDIGO plant, mainly from the Asian *Indigofera tinctoria* and the tropical American *I. suffruticosa*. The leaves contain the colorless glucoside, indican, which, when the water in which they are steeped is stirred, becomes oxidized and forms the permanent dye indigo. This settles out as a dark blue sediment which is then dried. Other leguminous plants are called INDIGO, including species of *Amorpha*, **Baptisia*, **Lonchocarpus* and **Swainsonia*.
LEGUMINOSAE.

**Inula** a large genus of mostly perennial herbs from Europe, Asia, Africa and Madagascar. Several species are commonly cultivated for ornament, including *I. helenium* [ELECAMPANE, SCABWORT, HORSEHEAL, YELLOW STARWORT], with daisy-like yellow flower heads, the shorter *I. ensifolia*, also with yellow flower heads and hairless leaves, and *I. orientalis* (= *I. glandulosa*), with orange flower heads and hairy leaves. The leaves of *I. crithmoides* [GOLDEN SAMPHIRE] are sometimes used as a potherb in England. The root of ELECAMPANE is used for flavoring absinthe and extracts are used medicinally to treat intestinal worm infestations. It is also sometimes used as a potherb.
COMPOSITAE, about 100 species.

**Iochroma** a genus of tropical Central and South American shrubs or small trees with large, showy, tubular or bell-shaped flowers. A number of species, including *I. coccineum* (scarlet flowers), *I. fuchsioides* (orange-scarlet flowers) and *I. cyaneum* (= *I. lanceolatum*) (blue to purplish-blue flowers) may be grown under glass or cultivated in the open in sheltered warm or subtropical areas.
SOLANACEAE, about 25 species.

Himalayan Balsam (*Impatiens roylei*) is now naturalized in many parts of Europe, especially along river banks.

**Ionopsidium** a small genus of annual Mediterranean herbs with the leaves in rosettes. *I. acaule* [VIOLET CRESS], from Portugal, is widely cultivated especially as an edging plant or in rock gardens. The whole plant is 2–4in tall, and the solitary, white lilac or purple flowers are borne on long stalks.
CRUCIFERAE, 5 species.

**Ipecacuanha** the dried root or rhizome, sometimes called "ipecac", obtained from the tropical American shrub *Cephaelis ipecacuanha* (= *Psychotria ipecacuanha*) [IPECACUANHA, IPECAC]. Its active principles are emetine and cephaeline which are alkaloids used as emetics, expectorants and in the treatment of amebic dysentery. Commercial production still continues in India and Malaya. *Psychotria emetica* [FALSE IPECAC] is a source of ipecac although of lower quality than that obtained from *Cephaelis*.
RUBIACEAE.

**Ipheion** a small genus of bulbous, onion-scented perennials native to Central and South America. The best-known cultivated species is *I. uniflorum* (= **Brodiaea uniflora*), which usually bears solitary, star-like, whitish, or pale blue to deep blue, fragrant flowers.
LILIACEAE, about 20 species.

**Ipomoea** a large genus of herbaceous annuals and perennials, or less often woody shrubs or vines, including several ornamentals and the important tropical root crop *I. batatas* [SWEET POTATO]. Some species are the source of extracts with hallucinogenic properties. For example, the seeds of the herbaceous climber *I. tricolor* were used as a hallucinogen in religious ceremonies by the Aztecs. Species occur in tropical and warm-temperate regions of the world. The usually large flowers are borne singly or in clusters,

*Flowers of the Morning Glory (*Ipomoea tricolor*) showing their distinctly trumpet-shaped purple corollas.* (× ⅓)

*Aerial view of cultivated and fallow Sweet Potato (*Ipomoea batatas*) gardens in the New Guinea forest.*

and have white or variously colored trumpet-shaped corollas.

Many of the species with more attractive flowers are cultivated for ornament, either as annuals such as *I. hederacea* and *I. purpurea* [COMMON MORNING GLORY] in temperate regions or as perennials or woody twiners such as *I. acuminata* [BLUE DAWN FLOWER], *I. nil* (which includes the IMPERIAL JAPANESE MORNING GLORIES, ascribed to the horticultural species *I. imperialis*), *I. horsfalliae* and *I. tricolor* with its numerous cultivars. Some species have flowers which remain open all day, whereas in others they open around dawn and wither before mid-day [MORNING GLORY], or open only in the evening as in *I. alba* [MOONFLOWER].

Apart from their value as ornamentals and their innumerable uses in native medicine and animal foodstuffs, some species of *Ipomoea* constitute valuable human foodstuffs. *I. batatas* [SWEET POTATO] has edible subterranean tubers. Probably originally from South America, it is now cultivated in all warm regions of the world, and in some places it is the main starch food. The young shoots and leaves of *I. aquatica* are used as a vegetable in East Asia, and in some areas *I. batatas* is treated similarly, or used as a salad. *I. purga* [*JALAP] from Central America, produces subterranean tubers which are used to prepare a purgative. The seeds of *I. muricata* have similar properties. *I. pes-caprae* [BEACH MORNING GLORY, RAILROAD ROAD] is a useful sand binder.
CONVOLVULACEAE, about 500 species.

**Iresine** [BLOODLEAF] a genus of herbs and subshrubs native to South America, the Galapagos Islands and Australia. A number of the tropical South American species are grown as bedding plants, including *I. herbstii* (= *Achryanthes verschaffeltii*), with its attractive purplish-red, crimson, green, greenish-red or bronze-colored leaves, depending on the variety.
AMARANTHACEAE, about 80 species.

**Iris** a large and very ornamental genus distributed throughout the northern temperate regions of the world. The genus can be divided into two major groups: subgenus *Iris* consists of the rhizomatous species and subgenera *Xiphium* and *Scorpiris* those that are bulbous. *I. nepalensis* is distinct from either of the above groups in possessing a very small rhizome terminating in a cluster of fleshy roots. It thus constitutes a third group or division – *Nepalenses*.

The stem in *Iris* varies from being more or less absent, as in *I. reticulata*, to extremely well-developed, as in *I. confusa*, where it grows to the stature of a small bamboo cane with a cluster of leaves at its apex. Leaves mostly arise from the stem base, are two-ranked and linear to sword-shaped.

Iris flowers are well known in their overall structure, and practically all of the species have this same basic make-up, differing from species to species in color and in size and shape of the individual perianth parts. There are three large and showy outer segments known as the "falls" because they are normally reflexed, and three inner segments which are usually smaller and erect, referred to as the "standards". The falls may be furnished with a raised crest or have a cluster of hairs on the middle and lower portion, known as the "beard". There are divergent groups which do not agree exactly with the basic flower form, notably the *Juno* group in which the standards are very small and held out horizontally or deflexed.

The rhizomatous division is further subdivided into bearded irises (*Pogon*), the beardless irises (*Apogon*), which have smooth falls without hair or crest, and the crested irises, with crests instead of beards on the falls.

These are further subdivided into many smaller groups. Although the genus as a whole has a very wide distribution, some of the sections are confined to distinct areas.

Obviously the main importance of the genus lies in its decorative value, although the dried rhizomes of *I. germanica* var *florentina* [*ORRIS ROOT] are used in perfumery to produce a violet-like scent. Most of the wild *Iris* species are extremely beautiful, but on the whole they are less popular for general garden display than the host of showy hybrids which have been raised. There is nowadays a large range of colors available in the tall bearded *Iris* group which do not occur in the original wild plants. Cultivated bearded irises include *I. × albicans*, *I. aphylla*, *I. kashmeriana* and the popular hybrid *I. × germanica* [FLAG, FLEUR-DE-LIS].

Among species of beardless irisis, several are widely cultivated, including cultivars 'Kermesina' and 'Rosea' of *I. versicolor* [WILD IRIS, BLUE FLAG, POISON FLAG], *I. spuria* [BUTTERFLY IRIS], *I. brevicaulis* [LAMANCE IRIS] with cultivars such as 'Brevipes' and 'Flexicaulis', *I. missouriensis* [WESTERN BLUE FLAG] and *I. pseudacorus* [YELLOW IRIS, YELLOW FLAG, WATER FLAG]. Important species of the crested forms include *I. cristata* [DWARF CRESTED IRIS] and *I. tectorum* [WALL IRIS, ROOF IRIS].

Cultivated bulbous species in the subgenus *Xiphium* include *I. reticulata*, *I. latifolia* (= *I. xiphioides*, *I. pyrenaica*) [ENGLISH IRIS] and *I. xiphium* (= *I. hispanica*, *I. lusitanica*) [SPANISH IRIS]. *I. persica* [PERSIAN IRIS] and *I. magnifica* are two of the much smaller number of cultivated species of the subgenus *Scorpiris*.
IRIDACEAE, about 250 species.

**Iroko** one of the common names for *Chlorophora excelsa*, a tropical African tree which produces a valuable timber suitable for furniture and building construction. It has sometimes been called FUSTIC or AFRICAN TEAK and is often used as a substitute for true teak.
MORACEAE.

Iris songarica *is a widespread species of the dry windswept lowland steppes of Iran, Afghanistan and southern USSR.*

**Ironbarks** members of the Australian genus **Eucalyptus* named for their heavily furrowed, usually dark barks. The durable hardwood of such trees as *E. fergusoni* [BLOODWOOD IRONBARK], *E. crebra* [NARROW LEAFED IRONBARK], *E. fibrosa* (= *E. siderophloia*) [BROAD LEAFED OR RED IRONBARK] and *E. nanglei* [PINK IRONBARK] is much used for heavy construction purposes, railway sleepers etc.
MYRTACEAE.

**Ironwood** a common name used locally, or more widely, particularly in commerce, for at least 24 species, from several genera, of shrubs and trees, and for their tough, hard timber, which is sometimes heavier than water. The woods are used for a variety of purposes including furniture, fine cabinet work and veneer, turnery, tool handles, floors, telegraph poles and railway sleepers. In North America, **Ostrya virginiana* [HOP HORNBEAM] and species of *Carpinus* [*HORNBEAM] are known as IRONWOOD. Central and South American IRONWOODS include *Olneya tesota* [SONORA IRONWOOD], *Cyrilla racemiflora*, *Reynosia septentrionalis* and *Rhamnidium ferreum*. Most IRONWOODS are from the Old World tropics and Australasia. From the latter come IRONWOODS of the myrtle family: *Choricarpia subargentea* [GIANT IRONWOOD], *Austromyrtus acmenoides* [SCRUB IRONWOOD], *Backhousia myrtifolia* and species of **Eugenia*. At least five tropical genera of the family Leguminosae yield timber called IRONWOOD: **Acacia*, **Afzelia*, *Copaifera*, *Cynometra* and *Intsia*. Other tropical Old World IRONWOODS are **Lophira alata* [DWARF IRONWOOD], *Eusideroxylon zwageri* [BORNEO IRONWOOD], and species of **Casuarina* [SOUTH-SEA IRONWOOD], *Hopea*, *Sideroxylon* and *Toddalia* [WHITE IRONWOOD].

**Isatis** a genus of annual, biennial or perennial herbs, native to Europe, the Mediterranean and western and Central Asia. The small yellow flowers are borne in great profusion in graceful loose panicles. Only *I. tinctoria* is commonly cultivated in gardens. This is more usually known by its common name of WOAD, OR DYER'S WOAD, and was formerly used as a deep-blue dye before it was replaced by *indigo.
CRUCIFERAE, about 45 species.

**Isoetes** see Club mosses, p.94.

**Istle** or **istli fiber** the name given to fibers obtained from the leaves of several species of the genus **Agave*, notably *A. lecheguilla* [TULA ISTLE] a large succulent stemless plant which is native to Texas and Mexico, and *A. funkiana* [JAMAUVE ISTLE]. The fiber is sometimes also called ixtle or ixtli.
AGAVACEAE.

*The pure white flowers of* Iris laevigata *'Alba' make it one of the most attractive ornamental varieties of the genus.* ($\times \frac{1}{15}$)

**Itea** a genus of deciduous or evergreen trees and shrubs mainly from tropical and temperate Asia with one species in the eastern USA. The most popular cultivated species are the North American *I. virginica* [SWEET SPIRE, VIRGINIA-WILLOW], a handsome deciduous shrub with fragrant, creamy-white flowers in erect, cylindrical racemes. *I. yunnanensis* and *I. ilicifolia* are evergreen shrubs with spiny-toothed leaves, originally native to China.
SAXIFRAGACEAE, about 10–15 species.

**Ivy** the common name for *Hedera*, a genus of mostly evergreen climbers or occasionally woody shrubs native to the northern parts of the Old World. Most cultivated ivies are

Iris afghanica *was discovered only in the 1960s in the Central Hindu Kush of Afghanistan where it has limited distribution.*

grown for their attractive heart-shaped or lobed, leathery, glossy and often variegated leaves.

*H. helix* [COMMON IVY] is found throughout Europe, western Asia, North Africa and is naturalized in the USA. It is a very hardy, adaptable species with very many cultivars of great ornamental value. *H. helix* var *hibernica* (= *H. hibernica* of horticulture) [IRISH IVY], with cultivars 'Hibernica' and 'Scotica', is a lustrous, larger-leaved, more vigorous variety making magnificent ground cover beneath trees. *H. canariensis* (= *H. maderensis*) is the strong-growing CANARY ISLAND or MADEIRA IVY. *H. colchica* [PERSIAN IVY] has an attractive variegated form, cultivar 'Dentata-variegata'.
ARALIACEAE, 6–15 species.

**Ixia** a genus of cormous herbs native to South Africa (Cape Province), with grass-like leaves and stems 12–16in high, usually unbranched, bearing spikes of flowers with slender tubes spreading out into six lobes. *I. viridiflora* has a blue-green perianth with a black throat. In *I. monadelpha* the colors range from yellow through orange to red and also blue, lilac and purple.
IRIDACEAE, about 30–40 species.

*The orange-flowered* Ixora chinensis *is an evergreen shrub from the Malay Peninsula and China. There are also varieties with white or red flowers.* ($\times \frac{1}{10}$)

**Ixora** a large genus of evergreen shrubs and small trees originally native to the tropics and now widely cultivated in greenhouses and in the open in warm climates, giving rise to a profusion of cultivars. They have showy tubular flowers usually borne in dense terminal clusters. Frequently cultivated shrubs include *I. coccinea* [FLAME-OF-THE-WOODS], with bright red flowers, *I. odorata*, with very fragrant, white, pink-tinged flowers, *I. chinensis*, with red to white flowers (dark orange in cultivar 'Dixiana'), and *I. williamsii*, with deep red flowers.
RUBIACEAE, about 400 species.

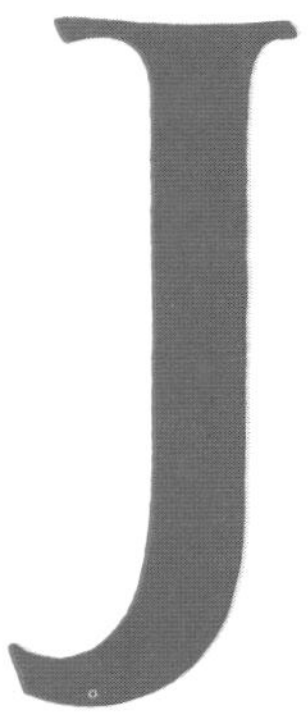

**Jacaranda** a tropical American genus of trees and shrubs with feathery leaves and beautiful panicles of blue to violet, rarely white or pink flowers. Among the most widely cultivated species used as street trees or garden ornamentals in the tropics and subtropics are *J. mimosifolia* (= *J. ovalifolia*), from northwest Argentina, with blue flowers, the blue-violet-flowered *J. cuspidifolia*, from Brazil and Argentina, *J. obtusifolia*, from Venezuela and Guiana, with blue-mauve to lilac flowers borne on older leafless branchlets, and its variety *rhombifolia* (= *J. filicifolia*).

The timber of some species, including *J. copaia*, *J. micrantha* and *J. mimosifolia*, is used for general carpentry and house building.
BIGNONIACEAE, about 50 species.

**Jalap** a purgative drug obtained as a resin from the tuberous roots of **Ipomoea purga*, a climbing plant of the Mexican Andes, and related species. The roots of the unrelated Peruvian **Mirabilis jalapa* yield a false jalap with similar properties. The name also applies to **Podophyllum peltatum* [WILD JALAP, MAY APPLE], from North America.
CONVOLVULACEAE.

**Jasione** a small genus of annual, biennial or perennial herbs native to Europe, the Mediterranean, and Asia Minor. They are usually under 12in high. The leaves are mostly in a basal rosette and the blue flowers are in a dense terminal head. *J. humilis* and *J. montana* [SHEEP'S BIT SCABIOUS] are sometimes cultivated as rockery or border-edging plants.
CAMPANULACEAE, about 10–20 species.

**Jasminum** [JASMINES] a large genus from temperate and tropical regions, excluding North America. Jasmines are evergreen or deciduous climbers or scrambling shrubs of spreading habit, with tubular white, yellow or red, often fragrant flowers usually in terminal or axillary cymes. Jasmines are easily cultivated species ranging from hardy outdoor to tropical greenhouse plants.

*J. fruticans* is a hardy, semi-evergreen shrub, with clusters of yellow flowers in early summer. One of the best winter-flowering shrubs is the deciduous *J. nudiflorum* [WINTER JASMINE], which produces solitary yellow flowers from November to February. *J. officinale* [COMMON WHITE JASMINE], from the Himalayas, is a climber, producing fragrant white flowers which contain an essential oil used in perfumery. *J. polyanthum* and *J. mesnyi* (= *J. primulinum*) [PRIMROSE JASMINE], both from China, are first-class climbing shrubs for very mild localities or cool greenhouses. *J. sambac* [ARABIAN JASMINE], long cultivated and probably of Asian origin, is used for making jasmine-scented tea, and the flowers of *J. grandiflorum* [CATALONIAN JASMINE], possibly from Arabia, yield an essential oil used in perfumery. The large fragrant flowered *J. humile* and its cultivar 'Revolutum' [ITALIAN JASMINE] have been cultivated for more than 100 years.
OLEACEAE, about 250 species.

**Jatropha** a genus of subtropical and tropical species of herbs, shrubs or small trees with milky or watery juice. *J. curcas* [FRENCH PHYSIC NUT, BARBADOS NUT, PURGING NUT], from tropical America, with yellow, purple or red flowers, is used as a hedge plant, and others such as *J. multifida* [CORAL PLANT, PHYSIC NUT], from tropical America, and *J. integerrima* [PEREGRINA], from Cuba, with scarlet to rose flowers, are grown as ornamentals for their bright flowers and fruits and variously divided or lobed leaves. A strong purgative oil, also used for candles and soapmaking, is obtained from the seeds of *J. curcas*.
EUPHORBIACEAE, about 170 species.

*Winter Jasmine (*Jasminum nudiflorum*) is a great favorite with gardeners and flowers from mid autumn to early spring.* ($\times \frac{1}{2}$)

**Jelly fungi** see Fungi, p. 156.

**Jew's ear fungus** a jelly fungus known for a long time as *Auricularia auricula-judae*, but correctly named *A. auricula*. The earlier name (*judae* = of Judas, *auricula* = ear: Judas' ear) derived from the supposed belief that Judas hanged himself on an elder tree, *Sambucus*, the commonest host for the fungus. The fruiting body is a well-known delicacy in the East.
AURICULARIACEAE.

**Joshua tree** the common name for **Yucca brevifolia*, which occurs in the desert and arid hills of the southwestern USA. The plant

forms a tree 16–48ft high with a stout stem. It has fleshy, stiletto-like fibrous leaves clustered near the ends of the branches and long branching inflorescences of greenish-white flowers.
AGAVACEAE.

**Jubaea** a genus comprising a single species, *J. chilensis* (= *J. spectabilis*) [COQUITO or CHILEAN WINE PALM]. It is native only to the coast of Central Chile but because of its massive, elegant, shiny gray trunk, up to 33ft high and 40in in diameter, it has been extensively planted for ornament in parks and along avenues in many areas with a Mediterranean climate. On evaporation the sap yields a sweet palm honey (miel de palma).
PALMAE, 1 species.

*The complexly-branched, orange-stalked inflorescence of small flowers of the Purging Nut (*Jatropha curcas*).*

**Juglans** see WALNUT.
JUGLANDACEAE, 15 species.

**Jumping beans** the small, half-round capsular fruits of a Mexican shrub, *Sebastiana pavoniana*. A small butterfly (*Carpocapsa saltitans*) lays its eggs in the young fruit. Ultimately the eggs hatch out into larvae or maggots. The rolling or jumping of the fruits ("beans") is caused by keeping them in warm conditions which makes the larvae active within them. In Mediterranean regions the beetle *Nanodea tamarisci* parasitizes the fruit of **Tamarix gallica* with similar results.

**Juncus** [RUSHES, BOG RUSHES] a genus of small, clumped herbaceous plants with underground stems producing a single leafy shoot each year, and leaves which are sometimes reduced to basal sheaths. They occur mainly in wet places of most temperate countries and rarely in the tropics. The stems of *J. acutus* [SHARP RUSH], *J. effusus* (= *J. polyanthemus*) [SOFT RUSH, JAPANESE-MAT RUSH], and *J. inflexus* (= *J. glaucus*) [HARD RUSH] are still used in many parts of the world in mats, chair bottoms and basket work. *J. effusus* is particularly valued in southwestern Japan

Jacaranda mimosifolia *from Argentina is widely cultivated in the tropics and subtropics where it grows into a gracefully branched tree.*

*The Jew's Ear Fungus (*Auricularia auricula*) is one of the larger jelly fungi, having a gelatinous fruit body. (×2)*

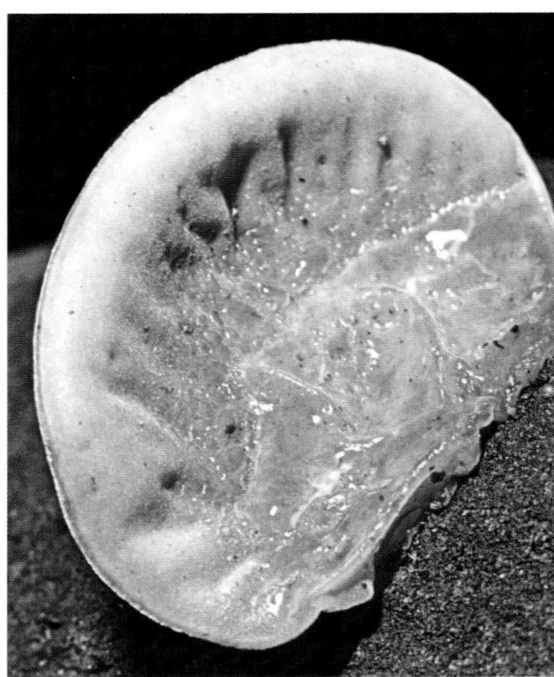

where it is used for weaving tatami, the floor covering used in many Japanese houses. Rushes sometimes serve as winter grazing on hillsides when grass becomes scarce.

Two species are hardy evergreen waterside ornamentals: *J. effusus* cultivar 'Spiralis' [CORKSCREW RUSH], with curious twisted stems, and *J. inflexus*, with needle-like leaves bending over when mature.
JUNCACEAE, about 300 species.

**Juniper** the common name for *Juniperus*, a genus of evergreen trees and shrubs widely distributed throughout the Northern Hemisphere, from the mountains of the tropics as far south as the equator and ranging as far north as the Arctic. Junipers have leaves of two kinds: the normal adult leaves are scale-like and linear; the juvenile leaves are larger and awl-shaped. Some species retain their juvenile foliage but generally only one type of leaf is present on the shoots at any given time.

Juniper wood is generally durable and easy to work; the presence of oils is probably responsible for the juniper's resistance to many insect attacks. The timber is used in general building, for roof shingles, furniture, posts and fences. In Burma, *J. recurva* var *coxii* [COFFIN JUNIPER] is the favored wood for coffins. *J. virginiana* [PENCIL CEDAR], is extensively used in the manufacture of pencils.

Cedar wood oil is obtained from a distillation of the sawdust, shavings etc and, until recently, was the main immersion oil used in high-power light microscopy. *J. oxycedrus* [PRICKLY JUNIPER] yields oil of cade or juniper tar by distillation of the wood. This oil has been used as a treatment for skin diseases, especially psoriasis, but is now largely replaced by coal-tar products, which are more effective. It is also used in the perfumery industry. Oil of juniper is distilled from the fully grown but unripe berries of *J. communis* [COMMON JUNIPER] and is responsible for the characteristic flavor of gin. Oil of savin, from *J. sabina* [SAVIN], is obtained by distilling fresh leaves and shoots. It is a powerful diuretic and has been used as an abortifacient.

Junipers are important ornamentals, with species and varieties suitable for many situations. Particularly rich in named cultivars and varieties are *J. chinensis* [CHINESE JUNIPER], *J. horizontalis* [COMMON OR CREEPING JUNIPER], *J. scopulorum* [COLORADO RED CEDAR] and *J. virginiana* [RED CEDAR]. As well as containing tree and shrub forms these species also have representatives suitable for rock gardens and ground cover, such as the *J. chinensis* var *sargentii* [SARGENT JUNIPER], *J. chinensis* var *procumbens*, *J. communis* var *depressa* [GROUND JUNIPER] and *J. virginiana*

*To produce jute fiber, fresh stalks of* Corchorus *spp are first softened by retting (prolonged soaking in water). In Bangladesh a local method makes use of the floating mats of Water Hyacinths (*Eichhornia *sp), to keep the stalks submerged.*

*The Common Soft Rush (*Juncus effusus*).*

'Prostrata', to name but a few. Similarly "color" forms are widely available; within *J. chinensis* var *chinensis* there are many such forms, for example 'Alba' with creamy-white twig tips, 'Aureo-globosa', with golden-yellow leaves and 'Variegata' with cream-colored branchlets. Other junipers cultivated as ornamentals include *J. drupacea* [SYRIAN OR PLUM JUNIPER], *J. excelsa* [GREEK JUNIPER], *J. occidentalis* [SIERRA OR CALIFORNIAN JUNIPER], *J. rigida* [NEEDLE JUNIPER] and *J. silicicola* [SOUTHERN RED CEDAR].
CUPRESSACEAE, about 70 species.

**Jurinea** a genus of thistle-like, erect herbs or subshrubs native to central and southwest Europe, southwest and Central Asia. The inflorescence is a single flower head made up of purple disk florets. A few species are cultivated in gardens.
COMPOSITAE, about 250 species.

**Justicia** a large genus of shrubs or perennial herbs, mainly native to the tropics and subtropics, but extending into temperate North America. A number of species are cultivated as ornamentals outdoors in warm countries, and under glass in cooler temperate zones. Differences between groups of species have been the basis for some authorities to segregate this genus into a number of distinct genera, including *Beloperone* and *Jacobinia*. The following, however, refers to *Justicia* in the wide sense.

*The white flower and pinkish-brown bracts of the Shrimp Plant (*Justicia brandegeana = Beloperone guttata*), from Mexico.* (×1)

One of the most widely cultivated ornamental species is *J. brandegeana* (= *Beloperone guttata*) [SHRIMP PLANT, MEXICAN SHRIMP PLANT, FALSE HOP], a rather weak-stemmed evergreen shrub with long pendent terminal flowering spikes bearing large attractive brownish-red to yellowish-green bracts.

Another popular greenhouse species is *J. carnea* (= *Jacobinia carnea*) [BRAZILIAN PLUME, PLUME FLOWER, FLAMINGO PLANT, PARADISE PLANT, KING'S CROWN] which has four-angled stems growing to 6.5ft, bearing large prominently-veined leaves and dense terminal panicles of long pink-purple flowers. The Mexican *J. spicigera* (= *J. atramentaria, Jacobinia mohintli*) [MOHINTLI] is a shrub of approximately the same size but bears smaller leaves and axillary or terminal one-sided racemes of several orange-red elongated flowers. The leaves yield a dye as well as an extract with medicinal uses.
ACANTHACEAE, about 300 species.

**Jute** perhaps the most important textile fiber of the world next to cotton, jute is derived from two annual species of the genus *Corchorus, *C. capsularis* [WHITE JUTE] and *C. olitorius* [UPLAND OR TOSSA JUTE]. *C. olitorius* is pantropical but is often an escape rather than wild and it has been regarded as primarily African. *C. capsularis* is probably native to Indo-Burma although some authorities prefer China. Although *C. olitorius* has been cultivated as a minor vegetable in Africa and the Middle East for a very long time, the domestication of it and *C. capsularis* in India is relatively recent. The domestication of both species was the result of deliberate research to find new fiber crops to replace *hemp. Jute became important in the mid 19th century when Dundee spinners learned how to spin it.

Although there are about 100 species in the genus and many that yield useful bast fibers, it is only these two species which yield commercial quantities of the fiber predominantly used for the manufacture of hessian cloth (burlap) and twine. Less widespread uses include carpet yarns, cloth backings for heavy rugs, carpets and linoleum, webbing and cable covers. About 90% of the world's jute supply comes from India and Pakistan. The most suitable soils for plantation are those which are inundated near the river banks – the largest production by far is in the Ganges-Brahmaputra delta. *C. capsularis* is the most widely cultivated species because it has a better tolerance of these conditions. There are numerous different strains which are grown to suit varying ecological conditions and fiber qualities required.

Bark fibers are obtained by retting, ie separation from the woody stems by a combined action of softening by water, microorganisms and enzymes. After retting, the bast fibers are removed from the long woody stalks by hand and then washed, dried and finally bleached in the sun before being baled up.
TILIACEAE.

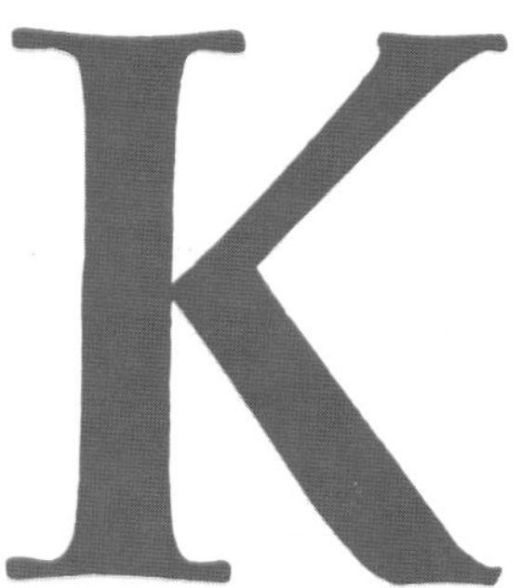

**Kaempferia** (= *Kaempfera*) a genus of more or less stemless perennial herbs native to tropical Africa and Asia. The tuberous rhizomes usually have a gingery smell and those of *K. galanga* [GALANGA] and *K. aethiopica* are sometimes used as a spice. Some species, such as *K. rotunda* from Southeast Asia [RESURRECTION LILY] and *K. atrovirens* [PEACOCK PLANT], from Borneo, are occasionally grown as ornamentals for their attractive trumpet-shaped white flowers with a lilac, pink or violet lip.
ZINGIBERACEAE, about 55 species.

Kaempferia rosea *is a common grassland ginger of East Africa. The flowers appear at ground level at the base of the stem.* ($\times\frac{3}{4}$)

**Kaki** or **kakee** the widely used Japanese vernacular name for **Diospyros kaki*, otherwise known as the CHINESE OR JAPANESE DATE PLUM OR KAKI PERSIMMON. Native to East Asia, the KAKI is a small tree with deciduous, simple leaves, extensively cultivated in warm climates for its orange- to red-skinned apple-like fruits. It is the favorite fruit of much of China and Japan.
EBENACEAE.

**Kalanchoe** a widespread genus of shrubby, tender leaf-succulents centered in tropical Africa and Madagascar. The genus is subdivided into three sections accorded separate generic status by some authorities, viz. *Bryophyllum*, *Kitchingia* and *Kalanchoe*. The flowers are erect in *Bryophyllum*, *Kitchingia* and pendent in *Kalanchoe*. The corolla in members of *Bryophyllum* is frequently constricted against the pistils, a feature not seen in members of the other sections.

*The Felt Bush (*Kalanchoe beharensis*) cv 'Nuda'. Like the wild species it has large heart-shaped leaves but without the shaggy hairs.*

Several species are popular houseplants, notably *K. blossfeldiana* and *K. flammea* and their various hybrids. *K. pumila* combines dark purple leaves covered in white powder, with dainty, deep pink flowers. This species, *K. manginii* and *K. uniflora* [KITCHINGIA] are suitable as basket plants. Many species that are grown outdoors in warmer climates are suitable for greenhouse cultivation in cooler temperate zones. These range in habit from the woody, scrambling *K. beauverdii* and the felty shrub *K. beharensis* [FELT BUSH, VELVET-LEAF, VELVET ELEPHANT EAR] to the smaller shrubs, *K. integra* [FLAME KALANCHOE], with its many red-flowered varieties, and the whitish- or yellow-flowered *K. marmorata* [PEN-WIPER KALANCHOE]. Other popular species include *K. pinnata* (= *Bryophyllum pinnatum*) [AIR PLANT, LIFE PLANT, FLOPPERS, MOTHER-IN-LAW, MIRACLE LEAF, SPROUTING LEAF], the densely felty *K. tomentosa* [PUSSY-EARS, PLUSH PLANT, PANDA PLANT] and *K. tubiflora* [CHANDELIER PLANT].
CRASSULACEAE, about 125 species.

*The Mountain Laurel (*Kalmia latifolia*) is a handsome shrub from North America that grows best in partial shade on lime-free soil. (× ½)*

**Kale** a name referring to two groups of plants allied to the common cabbage: **Brassica oleracea* var *acephala* (or Acephala group) and *B. napus* (Pabularia group). There are many types in both groups, most of which, because of their extreme hardiness, have been cultivated for thousands of years, as livestock feed for cattle during winter or as a winter vegetable. The vegetable forms [often known as CURLY, CRIMPED or COTTAGER'S KALE, or BORECOLE] are cultivars of *B. napus*, growing up to 40in high, commonly with green curly leaves, although smooth-leaved and purple-leaved varieties are also grown.

Kales for stock feeding are mainly derived from *B. oleracea* var *acephala* and have two main types: THOUSAND HEADED KALES, with many leafy shoots and MARROW STEM KALES with fewer shoots but with larger, fleshier leaves and a thickened stem. HUNGRY GAP KALE, SIBERIAN KALE and RAGGED JACK KALE are forms of *B. napus*.
CRUCIFERAE.

**Kalmia** a genus of shrubs native to North America and Cuba, with opposite or whorled, entire, leaves. A number are cultivated as garden ornamentals. *K. angustifolia* [SHEEP LAUREL] reaches a maximum of 40in in height and produces clusters of purple or crimson saucer-shaped flowers, while *K. latifolia* [MOUNTAIN LAUREL, CALICO BUSH] often grows to a height of over 10ft and produces dense clusters of saucer-shaped white-rose colored flowers. Other cultivated species are *K. microphylla* [WESTERN LAUREL] and *K. polliifolia* [BOG KALMIA].
ERICACEAE, about 6 species.

**Kapok** a fiber made from the usually white lustrous seed hairs inside the fruits of **Ceiba pentandra* [KAPOK TREE, SILK COTTON TREE], which grows to 100ft. The species is bicontinental in distribution, possibly originating in Central or South America with fruits or seeds being transported in pre-Columbian times via sea currents to Africa. It probably reached Southeast Asia via India from Africa before the 6th century.

One tree bears annually up to 400 fruits, yielding about 4.5lb of kapok which can be used for stuffing quilts, pillows, life-jackets or for insulation. Kapok is lighter than cotton, water-repellent, elastic, buoyant, durable, and has good thermal and acoustic insulation properties. Although kapok has been substantially replaced by synthetic fibers, it is still produced on a commercial scale, particularly in Thailand and Kampuchea which are the main exporters.
BOMBACACEAE.

*Numerous adventitious leaf buds are produced by* Kalanchoe daigremontiana, *earning it the popular name of Mother of Thousands.* (× 3)

**Kariba weed** the common name for the free-floating water-fern **Salvinia auriculata*. This particular species grew extensively after the construction in 1955–59 of the Kariba dam on the Zambezi River, but is now less prevalent and occurs mainly in the more sheltered parts.
SALVINIACEAE.

**Kauri** or **kauri pine** the Maori names (now universally used) for species of the genus *Agathis* especially *A. australis* a valuable and handsome coniferous tree that grows to a huge size. It is restricted to the northwestern peninsula of North Island, New Zealand. Very little of the virgin forest still remains. It is rarely cultivated. The most cultivated *Agathis* is *A. robusta* [QUEENSLAND KAURI]. Besides being a useful source of timber, most kauri pines yield a resin (kauri gum). In addition, large quantities of an amber-like fossil resin (*copal), are found preserved in peat bogs where kauri pines formerly grew.
ARAUCARIACEAE.

**Kelp** a common term for seaweeds, usually the brown algae, found in intertidal and subtidal waters and washed up on the shore. The name refers especially to the genera **Macrocystis* [GIANT KELPS], **Laminaria* [OARWEEDS] and **Nereocystis* [BULL KELPS].

**Kerria** a genus represented by a single species, *K. japonica* [JEW'S MALLOW]. It is a deciduous, spring-flowering shrub growing to a height of up to 10ft. It is much cultivated outside its native China and Japan, especially the cultivar 'Pleniflora', which has double, orange-yellow flowers.
ROSACEAE, 1 species.

**Khat, kat, chat, catta, qat** or **Arabian tea** common names for *Catha edulis*, a shrub native to Ethiopia and formerly Arabia. It is cultivated in Ethiopia, Somalia, Yemen and Zambia. The leaves and young twigs contain a stimulant and are either

chewed fresh or made into a tea-like beverage (Arabian tea).
CELASTRACEAE.

**Khaya** a genus of trees native to tropical Africa and Madagascar. They constitute the true African mahoganies, valued for their hard, reddish, insect-resistant wood. *K. ivorensis* [RED MAHOGANY], *K. senegalensis* [AFRICAN MAHOGANY] and *K. nyasica* [NYASALAND MAHOGANY] are among the most important species.
MELIACEAE, 8 species.

**Khus khus** or **khas-khas** the common name for **Vetiveria zizanioides*, a tropical Indian grass cultivated in Asia for its fragrant roots which are woven into fans, baskets and mats. The roots and sweet scented rhizomes also yield an oil on distillation (vetiver oil) which is used in the manufacture of perfumes and soaps.
GRAMINEAE.

**Kino** the name given to a number of astringent gum-resins, soluble in water and used in medicines and locally in tanning. The name is sometimes also used for the trees from whose bark the resins are derived (usually by tapping), for example the East Indian **Pterocarpus marsupium* [MALABAR KINO], *P. erinaceus* [WEST AFRICAN KINO, SENEGAL ROSEWOOD], **Eucalyptus* species, notably *E. resinifera* (Australia), **Coccoloba uvifera* (southern Mexico to South America) and **Butea monosperma* (India, Malaysia).

**Kirengeshoma** a genus represented by a single species, *K. palmata*, a robust perennial from Japan and Korea with handsome, yellow cup-shaped flowers, sometimes cultivated in moist herbaceous borders.
SAXIFRAGACEAE, 1 species.

*A Kapok Tree (*Ceiba pentandra*) growing in northern Sonora, Mexico, showing the down which is harvested as kapok.*

Kleinia semperviva, *from Tanzania and Ethiopia, showing its succulent leaves and stems and the caudex (the above-ground portion of rootstock).* ($\times \frac{1}{3}$)

**Kiri wood** the name given to wood from the Japanese tree **Paulownia tomentosa* [KARRI TREE, PRINCESS TREE]. The wood is reddish brown in color, very light in weight and is used in Japan mainly for cabinet-making and musical instruments.
BIGNONIACEAE.

**Kleinia** a genus of succulent herbs and shrubs, mainly native to southern Africa and Arabia, some of which are commonly cultivated in bowl gardens or as houseplants on account of their novel and cactus-like appearance. The flower heads consist mostly of disk florets, white or red, rarely yellow or orange, which appear in autumn and winter. Most modern authorities now include this genus within **Senecio*.

The main cultivated species can be divided into three types: (1) Subshrubs such as *K. galpinii* (orange flower heads) and *K. fulgens* (orange-red flower heads). (2) Dwarf shrublets or creeping, rooting perennials such as *K. rowleyana* [STRING-OF-BEADS PLANT], with relatively large fragrant, predominantly white flower heads. (3) Stem succulents with deciduous leaves, such as *K. anteuphorbium*, a scrub up to 5ft tall, named for its reputed value as an antidote to the poison of the cactus-like **Euphorbia* species among which it grows.

Other species in this group include *K. articulata* [CANDLE PLANT] and *K. pendula* [INCHWORM], so called because the short, fat, jointed stems arch back to the soil and progress in serpentine fashion.
COMPOSITAE, about 50 species.

**Knautia** a genus of annual, biennial and perennial herbs which, although exhibiting very showy flower heads, unlike the closely related **Scabiosa*, is rarely cultivated. It is mainly native to Europe and the Mediterranean region. The flowers show a range of colors from white or yellow to pink, purple or violet. *K. arvensis* [BLUE-BUTTONS] and *K. dipsacifolia* (= *K. sylvatica*), both extremely variable species, are sometimes cultivated, as is the yellow-flowered *K. tatarica*. DIPSACACEAE, about 50 species.

**Kniphofia** [TORCH LILY, RED HOT POKER] a genus of tufted, rhizomatous, perennial herbs from South and East Africa and Madagascar. A number are hardy in cultivation in Europe and North America but others need cool or heated greenhouse conditions. The erect many-flowered spikes of cylindrical flowers range in color from yellow to orange or scarlet. *K. uvaria*, with several cultivated forms, and the more compact *K. galpinii* are two of the most widely cultivated species. LILIACEAE, about 65 species.

**Kochia** a genus of annual and perennial herbs and subshrubs, one of which, *K. scoparia* [SUMMER CYPRESS], is grown as a bedding plant for its attractive foliage which turns reddish purple in the autumn. The Australian *K. aphylla* [SALTBUSH] is used for livestock feed in times of drought. CHENOPODIACEAE, about 90 species.

**Koelreuteria** a genus of deciduous trees native to East Asia and Fiji. The best-known is *K. paniculata* [GOLDEN RAIN TREE, PRIDE OF INDIA, VARNISH TREE], growing to about 65ft high, native to China but long cultivated and naturalized on seashores in Japan; it is also planted around temples. It is prized for its impressive panicles of yellow flowers, which are used in medicine in China. The fruits are bladder-like capsules which separate into papery, colored segments, and the seeds are used for necklaces in China. *K. elegans* [FLAMEGOLD], from Taiwan and Fiji, is also cultivated. SAPINDACEAE.

*Kohlrabi (*Brassica oleracea *var* gongylodes*).* (× ¼)

*Kola nuts are seeds from species of* Cola, *a genus of smallish forest trees from West Africa. They are consumed for their stimulatory effects.* (× ¾)

**Kohleria** [TREE GLOXINIAS] a genus of rhizomatous terrestrial herbs or shrubs from Mexico to northern South America. Several species, notably *K. amabilis*, *K. bogotensis*, *K. eriantha*, *K. digitaliflora* and *K. warszewiczii*, and hybrids derived from them, are cultivated as greenhouse ornamentals for their attractive inflorescences of tubular foxglove-like flowers. GESNERIACEAE, about 50 species.

**Kohlrabi** one of the cultivated forms of **Brassica oleracea* (var *gongylodes*), with a swollen green or purple stem which is eaten like a turnip. It is popular in some continental European countries and is occasionally grown elsewhere. It is also used as a stock feed in some European countries. CRUCIFERAE.

**Kola** the common name given to the seeds, and to certain species, of the tree genus **Cola*. The main cultivated species is *C. nitida*, which is native to the rain forests of West Africa, while *C. acuminata* is a minor crop in the rain forests and savannas of eastern West Africa. The fleshy seed coat is removed to leave the embryos, called kola "nuts", which are creamy-white, through pink, to dark purple. There is a strong social preference for white nuts. Each nut is up to 2 × 1.2in and contains 2% caffeine, traces of theobromine and a glucoside, colanin, all of which contribute to its stimulatory effects. Kola nuts are chewed to stave off hunger, thirst or fatigue. In times of scarcity, a substitute is found in the seeds of the unrelated **Garcinia kola* [BITTER KOLA].

The total production of kola nuts is an estimated 175 000 tons per year, of which the major part comes from the plantations of Nigeria. Both species were introduced to South America during the Slave Trade but production there (Caribbean Islands and Brazil) is low. There is little demand from soft drink manufacturers in America and Europe, for the "cola" ingredients commonly used by them are not extracted from kola nuts but are synthetic chemicals resembling the natural compounds. STERCULIACEAE.

**Kolkwitzia** a genus consisting of a single species, *K. amabilis*, a bushy shrub native to China. The flowers are pink with yellow throats, borne in pairs in corymbs, and the species makes an attractive bush in cultivation. CAPRIFOLIACEAE, 1 species.

**Kumquat** a name given to the four or five East Asian species of shrubs and trees of the genus *Fortunella*. They bear small edible orange-colored fruits with a thick pungent rind surrounding a pulpy center. Of the two species commonly cultivated, *F. japonica* [ROUND KUMQUAT] has round fruits and *F. margarita* [OVAL KUMQUAT] has oval fruits. Hybrids between *Fortunella* and several species of **Citrus* and with **Poncirus trifoliata* have been produced. RUTACEAE.

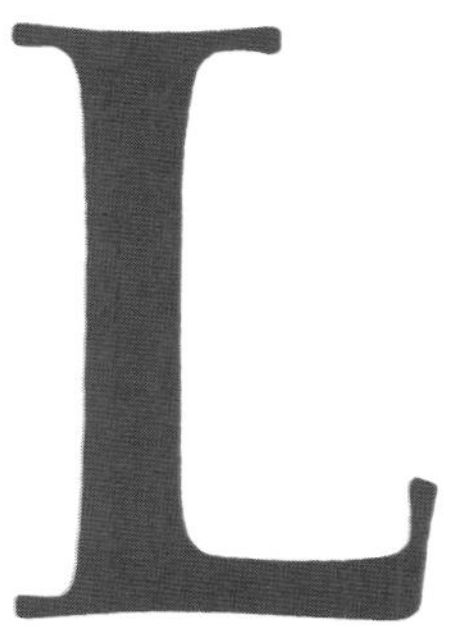

**Lablab** a common name for *Dolichos lablab* [also known as BONAVIST OR HYACINTH BEAN], an important legume, thought to be of Asian origin and long cultivated in India. It has also been introduced to Africa and other tropical countries. A strong-growing herbaceous perennial climber, it is usually cultivated as an annual. The seeds and pods are normally eaten when young and tender, boiled or in curries. The seeds contain a poisonous glucoside which can only be destroyed by cooking. The whole plant is used as fodder, or it can be plowed into the ground as green manure. Some varieties are grown as ornamentals bearing pink, purple or white flowers.
LEGUMINOSAE.

+ **Laburnocytisus** a graft chimera resulting from the grafting of a scion of *Cytisus* on the stem of *Laburnum*. + *Laburnocytisus adamii* is a small tree produced by the grafting of the purple-flowered *Cytisus purpureus* on to the yellow-flowered *Laburnum anagyroides*. *L. adamii* has purple-yellow flowers, but occasional branches with yellow or purple flowers of the parents also occur.
LEGUMINOSAE.

**Laburnum** a small central and south-eastern European genus of two species of small trees and shrubs with attractive foliage, pendulous racemes of bright yellow flowers, and poisonous leaves and seeds.

Both species, *L. alpinum* [SCOTCH LABURNUM] and *L. anagyroides* (= *L. vulgare*) [COMMON LABURNUM, GOLDEN-CHAIN, BEAN-TREE, GOLDEN RAIN TREE] are much-planted ornamentals, but their seeds (and those of their hybrid, *L. × watereri*) are freely formed and can be fatally poisonous to humans and cattle. The hybrid, although with equally poisonous seeds, forms far fewer seed pods and is therefore the most widely planted laburnum. The poisonous principles are the alkaloids cytisine and laburnine. Laburnum heartwood is used in cabinetwork and inlay.
LEGUMINOSAE, 2 species.

**Lac** or **shellac** a resinous substance secreted on the twigs of many trees of India, Burma and Thailand, including **Ficus religiosa*, *Schleichera oleosa* [LAC TREE], **Ziziphus mauritiana*, **Butea monosperma*, by the lac insect (*Tachardia lacca* = *Laccifer lacca*). Shellac is used for several industrial purposes, particularly in the manufacture of varnish and for electrical insulation.

**Lace bark** the common name for *Lagetta lintearia* (= *L. lagetto*), a small tree native to the West Indies. The inner bark is made up of fine interlacing fibers which resemble lace and are used for ornament. The name is also applied to other species, such as the New Zealand evergreen shrub **Hoheria sexstylosa* and **Pinus bungeana* [LACE BARK PINE].

**Lachenalia** a genus of bulbous perennials native to South Africa. The tubular or bell-shaped flowers are borne on spikes or racemes. Ornamental species include *L. aloides* (= *L. tricolor*) [CAPE COWSLIP], with spikes of yellow to orange or red flowers, often tinged or tipped with green or red, and *L. glaucina*, with white flowers, flushed yellow or red.
LILIACEAE, about 55 species.

*A "loose leaf" or "salad bowl" variety of the Common Lettuce (*Lactuca sativa*). Several other* Lactuca *species are grown as ornamentals.*

**Lacquer** an exudate obtained from **Rhus verniciflua* [LACQUER OR VARNISH TREE], from East Asia, employed in the famous decorative techniques of China and Japan. It is cultivated in Japan. When freshly tapped from the tree, lacquer is a thick brownish fluid but when applied to the required object, usually of wood, in many layers, it becomes dry and hard. Lacquered articles have traditionally been decorated with gold dust and gold leaf, mother-of-pearl and precious stones, and the lacquer itself sometimes colored by an admixture of pigments. Burmese lacquer is derived from *Melanorrhoea usitata*.
ANACARDIACEAE.

**Lactarius** a genus of gill fungi. Most species occur in temperate zones and although some species are poisonous, *L. deliciosus* and *L. sanguifluus* are eaten in Europe, Asia and North Africa. *L. resinus* and *L. scrobiculatus* are esteemed in the USSR after salting down.
RUSSULACEAE, about 120 species.

Lactarius subdulcis *is a common species of gill fungus often found in beech woods.* ($\times \frac{3}{4}$)

**Lactuca** a genus consisting of Eurasian and North American herbaceous biennials, perennials and shrubs, with some species in tropical and temperate southern Africa. The yellow, blue, purple or white florets are all strap-shaped and arranged in cylindrical heads. Species cultivated as ornamentals include *L. macrantha* (= *Mulgedium macranthum*) and *L. racemosa* (= *M. albanum*), both with blue flower heads. *L. sativa* is the COMMON *LETTUCE. *L. serriola* [PRICKLY LETTUCE] is a common weed in many parts of the world.
COMPOSITAE, about 100 species.

**Laelia** a genus of pseudobulbous, epiphytic orchids, widely distributed from Mexico to Brazil. They vary very much in overall size and in the shape and size of their leaves and flowers. The inflorescences are erect and bear up to five flowers which are always strikingly showy or otherwise attractive. *Laelia* species are in great demand for horticultural pur-

*A Larch (*Larix sp*) shoot in spring, showing the emerging leaves, previous year's cones (top) and new season's female cones (bottom); the latter are often called "larch noses". (×2)*

poses, being grown either as "pure" species, such as *L. anceps*, with many cultivars, *L. autumnalis* and *L. purpurata*, or in the form of intrageneric or intergeneric hybrids such as × *Brassolaeliocattleya*. The great popularity of certain species has put them in considerable danger of extinction, but *L. jongheana* from Brazil, for example, is now one of many orchid species protected by an international convention.
ORCHIDACEAE, about 30 species.

× **Laeliocattleya** a group of bigeneric hybrids resulting from crosses between the orchid genera **Laelia* and **Cattleya*. Examples include × *L.-c. albanensis* (*C. warneri* × *L. grandis*), × *L.-c. amanda* (*C. intermedia* × *L. lobata*) and × *L. -c. verelii* (*C. forbesii* × *L. lobata*).

Popular cultivated greenhouse forms include 'Aconagua' (predominantly white and purple flowers) and 'Edgard van Belle' (bright yellow flowers with red and white markings).
ORCHIDACEAE.

**Lagenaria** see CALABASH GOURD.
CUCURBITACEAE, 6 species.

**Lagerstroemia** a genus of deciduous or evergreen trees and shrubs from south and East Asia, south to New Guinea and Australia. The best-known species is *L. indica* [CRAPE MYRTLE], a very showy shrub widely cultivated in warm temperate or subtropical gardens and municipal plantings, with crinkled red, scarlet or pink flowers. The timber of a number of species, including the Asian *L. speciosa* (= *L. flos-reginae*) [QUEEN CRAPE MYRTLE] and the Indian *L. microcarpa* (= *L. lanceolata*) [BENTEAK, NANAN WOOD], is close-grained and used for general construction work such as bridge and house building.
LYTHRACEAE, about 30 species.

**Lagurus** a genus represented by a single species, *L. ovatus* [HARE'S TAIL] an annual grass native to the Mediterranean region but now widely grown as an ornamental and for use by florists. The beautiful inflorescences are very persistent and are often dried and dyed with bright colors for use in winter decorations, bouquets and floral displays.
GRAMINEAE, 1 species.

**Laminaria** [OARWEED] a genus of large brown algae normally found growing in the sublittoral fringe; they are only rarely exposed to the air. The genus is common in the colder waters of the Northern Hemisphere. They are large plants up to 10ft long and consist of an attaching organ (holdfast), a narrow stipe and a flattened and variously-shaped lamina or blade. Plants of this genus

*The White Dead-nettle (*Lamium album*) has been used in folk remedies, and the leaves and young shoots are occasionally used as a vegetable. (×$\frac{1}{2}$)*

*Brilliant in full sun, these* Lampranthus *flowers are closing in the late afternoon light, but still produce a bright display of color. (×$\frac{1}{10}$)*

are consumed for food in Asia and are also widely collected for fertilizer and for the production of alginates.
PHAEOPHYCEAE.

**Lamium** [DEAD-NETTLES] a genus of herbaceous species from Europe, Asia and Africa. The flowers usually have a hooded upper lip, and the two lateral corolla lobes on the lower lip are reduced to small teeth. *L. album* [WHITE DEAD-NETTLE] and *L. purpureum* [RED DEAD-NETTLE] are common weeds, especially in Europe. *L. galeobdolon* [YELLOW ARCHANGEL], a tall garden ornamental with yellow flowers, is now placed in its own genus and called *Lamiastrum galeobdolon* (= *Galeobdolon luteum*). Cultivars of *L. maculatum* [SPOTTED DEAD-NETTLE], particularly the white-flowered 'Album' and pink flowered 'Roseum', and the species *L. garganicum* and *L. orvala* [GIANT DEAD-NETTLE] are cultivated in shady sites in gardens.
LABIATAE, about 50 species.

**Lampranthus** a genus of South African leaf-succulents forming small, much-branched shrublets. Cultivated species are hardy only in exceptionally sheltered areas but are much propagated for summer bedding as they produce brilliant displays of glossy, daisy-like flowers in all colors except blue.
AIZOACEAE, possibly 100 species.

**Landolphia** a tropical African genus of woody shrubs and climbers, which are the source of the *rubber known commercially as AFRICAN or *MADAGASCAR RUBBER. The latex is chiefly obtained from *L. owariensis*, *L. heudelotii* and *L. kirkii*. *Landolphia* fruits are globose or pea-shaped and about the size of an orange; they are edible raw and are also made into an alcoholic beverage. A blue dye is obtained from the leaves and flowers of

*L. comorensis*. A few species, including *L. florida* and *L. owariensis* are cultivated in warm greenhouses for their large white or yellowish salver-shaped flowers.
APOCYNACEAE, about 50 species.

**Lantana** a genus of evergreen shrubs or herbs mainly native to tropical and subtropical America and the West Indies, with a few species in the Old World. A number of species are cultivated as greenhouse ornamentals for the attractive red, golden or white flowers. They include *L. camara* (= *L. aculeata*) [YELLOW SAGE] a prickly-stemmed shrub with many varieties. The aromatic leaves of this species are used in tropical America to make a tea-like beverage.
VERBENACEAE, about 150 species.

**Lapageria** a genus consisting of a single species, *L. rosea* [COPIHUE, CHILEAN BELL-FLOWER], an evergreen creeper confined to the cool temperate forests of southern central Chile. This handsome plant, with red or occasionally white flowers up to 6in long, is the national flower of Chile.
LILIACEAE, 1 species.

**Lapeirousia** a genus of cormous herbs from tropical and southern Africa. The leaves are arranged in opposite ranks to form a fan, and the long tubular flowers spreading out into six lobes are borne in spikes or racemes opening to one side. Of several cultivated species, *L. laxa* (= *L. cruenta*) has red flowers with darker blotches on the three lower lobes, and *L. anceps* and *L. corymbosa* both have deep violet or purple flowers.
IRIDACEAE, about 60 species.

**Lapsana** a genus of annual and perennial temperate Eurasian herbs. The inflorescence comprises numerous small yellow flower heads borne in loose clusters. *L. communis* [NIPPLEWORT] has been used as a salad plant.
COMPOSITAE, 9 species.

*Beds of Kelp* (Laminaria *spp*)*, such as those shown here from Plymouth, England, only become visible at low tide and very rarely become completely exposed to the air.*

*Sheets of crude latex from the Para Rubber Tree* (Hevea brasiliensis) *are pounded into sheets and hung up to harden before processing.*

**Larch** the generally accepted popular name of the coniferous genus *Larix*, which consists of graceful deciduous trees native to north temperate regions. A number are cultivated as ornamentals, both for their attractive shape and for their foliage which turns golden-brown in late autumn.

Widely cultivated species include *L. decidua* (= *L. europaea*) [EUROPEAN LARCH], *L. laricina* [TAMARACK, EASTERN LARCH] and one of the tallest species (to 200ft), the North American *L. occidentalis* [WESTERN LARCH]. Two other widely grown species are *L. kaempferi* (= *L. leptolepis*) [JAPANESE LARCH] and its hybrid with *L. decidua*, *L.* × *eurolepis*. One of the smaller cultivated larches is the East Asian *L. gmelinii* [DAHURIAN LARCH].

The timber of many species, notably EUROPEAN, EASTERN and WESTERN LARCH is valued for its durability and strength and is therefore widely used in constructional work as well as for interior furnishings. The bark of some species has medicinal uses and that of EUROPEAN LARCH is the source of Venice or Venetian turpentine. (See also p. 912.)

**Larix** see LARCH.
PINACEAE, about 12 species.

**Larrea** [CREOSOTE BUSH] a small genus of evergreen shrubs native to the southwestern USA, Mexico and South America. Characteristically, the stems are jointed and swollen at the nodes, the leaves are pinnate and the yellow flowers are solitary and terminal. All species are resinous, as in the case of *L. tridentata* (= *L. mexicana*), a strongly-scented shrub which grows to a height of 10ft. The flower buds are pickled in vinegar and eaten as *capers. Extracts of this species are used medicinally in parts of Mexico for treating rheumatism, and leaf decoctions are used for fomentations. (See also p. 848.)
ZYGOPHYLLACEAE, 3–4 species.

**Lasthenia** a small herbaceous genus native to western North America and central Chile, all but one species of which are spring-flowering annuals. *L. chrysostoma* [GOLDFIELDS] and, less often, *L. glabrata* (= *L. californica*) and *L. coronaria* are cultivated for their showy yellow flower heads.
COMPOSITAE, 16 species.

**Latania** a genus of large solitary fan palms originally from the Mascarenes but now (especially *L. loddigesii* from Mauritius) cultivated throughout the tropics and subtropics.
PALMAE, 3 species.

**Latex** the name given to the juice, usually white but sometimes colored, which exudes when certain plants are cut or wounded. Poppy and lettuce are familiar examples. The ramifying system which contains it is made up of living cells or tubes called laticifers or laticiferous ducts. Commercially, latex is very important, since both medicinal drugs like the morphine alkaloids and structural material like rubber are provided by it.

A wide range of different substances may be present in the fluid depending on the parent plant. In true solution are sugars, organic acids, mineral ions, alkaloids (eg morphine) and other small molecules; in colloidal solution are proteins, enzymes (eg papain), mucilages and, perhaps most characteristically, the hydrophobic (lacking affinity for water) particles which impart the usual opaque milky appearance. Among materials composing the colloids, the most important are hydrocarbons belonging to the family of the isoprenoids, which includes such substances as rubber, resins, steroids and essential oils.

Commercially, latex reaches its greatest importance in *rubber, the particles of which may comprise about 35% of the latex. Important families are Euphorbiaceae (**Hevea brasiliensis* is the source of rubber), Papaveraceae (**Papaver somniferum* yields the opium alkaloids), Apocynaceae, Araceae, Asclepiadaceae, Compositae, Moraceae, and Sapotaceae.

**Lathraea** a genus of wholly parasitic herbaceous perennials with leaves reduced to scales and lacking chlorophyll, occurring naturally through temperate Europe and Asia.

*L. squamaria* [TOOTHWORT] is a fleshy, white to purple colored plant bearing violet to dark purple flowers, parasitic mainly on the roots of species of **Corylus*, **Fagus* and **Alnus*. *L. clandestina* [PURPLE TOOTHWORT], which parasitizes the roots of species of **Salix*, **Populus* and *Alnus* (rarely of other trees) is a most attractive spring-flowering plant with bright mauve flowers up to 2in long, arising in the axils of the scales on the rhizomes, at or just below the soil surface. Both species are cultivated for their showy flowers.
OROBANCHACEAE, 5 species.

**Lathyrus** a genus of annual and perennial, frequently climbing herbs with branched tendrils, native to temperate regions of Eurasia and the New World. Economically the most important genus is *L. sativus* [CHICKLING or GRASS PEA], which is cultivated, chiefly in India, mainly for animal fodder [see GRASS PEA]. Experimental breeding of *L. odoratus* [SWEET PEA] has produced every flower color except yellow, and a new shape (the 'Spencer' form) in which the standard is wavy-margined. Other ornamentals, some used locally as food or fodder, are *L. latifolius* [EVERLASTING PEA], *L. tingitanus* [TANGIER PEA], *L. tuberosus* [GROUNDNUT PEA VINE, EARTHNUT PEA] and *L. aureus*, a bushy plant without tendrils.

*The Everlasting or Perennial Pea (*Lathyrus latifolius*) is native to southern Europe, but is naturalized elsewhere as a garden escape. It is widely cultivated in gardens where it will produce a magnificent show of flowers each year. Several cultivars are in cultivation.* ($\times \frac{1}{10}$)

A few perennials are widespread in north temperate regions; examples are *L. pratensis* [MEADOW VETCHLING] which inhabits meadows and scrub, and *L. japonicus* [SEA PEA] which colonizes maritime sands, shingle and lake shores in Asia, Europe and North America.
LEGUMINOSAE, about 130 species.

**Laurel** a general name applied to various shrubs or small trees, particularly those of the family Lauraceae. The most notable examples are **Laurus nobilis* [BAY LAUREL, SWEET BAY] and **Umbellularia californica* [CALIFORNIA LAUREL]. Some species of other families are also known as laurels. Examples are **Calophyllum inophyllum* [ALEXANDRIAN LAUREL], **Kalmia angustifolia* [SHEEP LAUREL], **Prunus laurocerasus* [CHERRY LAUREL], **Aucuba japonica* [JAPANESE LAUREL or SPOTTED LAUREL], **Daphne laureola* [SPURGE LAUREL] and **Magnolia virginiana* [SWAMP LAUREL].

**Laurelia** a genus consisting of two species of aromatic trees. *L. novae-zelandiae*, from New Zealand, provides a commercial timber, and *L. aromatica* [PERUVIAN NUTMEG], from Peru and Chile, produces seeds which are used locally as a spice. *L. novae-zelandiae* is sometimes grown as an ornamental.
MONIMIACEAE, 2 species.

**Laurus** a genus consisting of two species of aromatic evergreen trees, the better-known being the evergreen *L. nobilis* [BAY LAUREL, SWEET BAY], native to the Mediterranean region and widely cultivated. In ancient times it was associated with victory and nobility. The dried leaves are used as a condiment to flavor meat and fish dishes, especially in France. The leaf oils and an oily extract from the seeds (bay fat or laurel berry fat) are used in perfumery and medicine. The other species, *L. canariensis* [CANARY ISLAND LAUREL], is restricted to the forests of the Canary Islands and Madeira.
LAURACEAE, 2 species.

**Lavandula** a genus of perennial herbs, shrubs and subshrubs mainly native to warm temperate regions from the Canary Islands to India. Several species are cultivated for ornament, for their pleasant aromatic scent, as honey plants and for the extraction of oil from the flowers.

Some species of *Lavandula* are used in the preparation of lavender oil, which is obtained by steam distillation of the flower heads. The commonest is *L. angustifolia* [COMMON LAVENDER], a mainly Mediterranean species which is widely cultivated, especially in France, Italy and England for perfumery and as an ornamental. The names FRENCH or SPANISH LAVENDER are applied to another species, *L. stoechas*, which has been used since classical times as a medicinal plant and as a toilet preparation. Lavender oil is also obtained from *L. latifolia* [SPIKE LAVENDER] (formerly called, incorrectly, *L. spica*, as was *L. angustifolia*).

*Young leaves of the Bay Laurel (*Laurus nobilis*), which when dried are used as a flavoring for meat and fish dishes.* ($\times 1$)

Lavender oil is often obtained from wild plants and distilled *in situ* but the quality is inferior to that of *L. angustifolia*. French lavender is also sold as bunched flowers and the dried flowers are powdered for sachets and used in potpourris. Various medicinal properties have been attributed to lavender since classical times. Poor-quality oils are used in the manufacture of lacquers and varnishes and in cheap perfumery.
LABIATAE, about 28 species.

**Lavatera** a genus of herbs and shrubs mostly from the Mediterranean region, but some also from the Canary Islands, Asia, Australia and California. Several species are cultivated, including *L. olbia* [TREE LAVATERA], a western Mediterranean shrub with solitary axillary red-purple flowers 2in across, and *L. arborea* [TREE MALLOW], a European biennial with clusters of pale purple flowers 2in across. Large white- and pink-flowered varieties of the annual *L. trimestris* (= *L. rosea*) flower throughout the summer.
MALVACEAE, about 25 species.

**Lavender** the common name for a number of species of the genus **Lavandula*, particularly for *L. angustifolia* [COMMON LAVENDER]. However, species of other genera are also called LAVENDER, eg **Limonium vulgare* [SEA LAVENDER] and **Heliotropium curassavicum* [WILD LAVENDER].

**Laver bread** a food made from boiled, pulped and pressed algae of the genus **Porphyra*. It is eaten in various parts of Europe, particularly in South Wales. Laver bread has a jelly-like consistency and is usually mixed or coated with oatmeal and fried.
RHODOPHYCEAE.

**Lawsonia** see HENNA.
LYTHRACEAE, 1 species.

**Layia** a small genus of hairy annual herbs mainly from western North America (California). Their daisy-like flower heads have yellow disk florets and ray florets which may be white, golden-yellow or yellow with white tips. *L. platyglossa* (= *L. elegans*) [TIDY-TIPS], a bushy plant, is commonly cultivated as an ornamental.
COMPOSITAE, about 12 species.

**Leek** the common name for **Allium porrum*, a popular winter vegetable, especially in northern Europe. The edible portion consists of a false stem of concentric leaf-bases. It is a cultivated form of *A. ampeloprasum* along with the very similar KURRAT (*A. kurrat*). It was known as far back as 3200 BC in ancient civilizations of the Middle East and was popular as a vegetable in the Middle Ages. It is also used as a flavoring.
LILIACEAE.

**Legumes and pulses** see p. 200.

**Leiophyllum** [SAND MYRTLES] a small genus of evergreen shrubs native to eastern North America, two of which are cultivated as spring-flowering ornamentals. Both the prostrate, short, upright *L. buxifolium* and the prostrate *L. lyonii* (= *L. buxifolium* var *prostratum*), sometimes treated as a single variable species, produce attractive white or pink terminal inflorescences.
CYPERACEAE, 1 or 3 species.

*The Purple Toothwort (*Lathraea clandestina*) is a parasite of trees and shrubs, particularly willows (*Salix spp*). As a total parasite, it produces no green leaves, just short stems enclosed in white scales, gaining its nourishment from the host. (× ½)*

*A grove of lemons (*Citrus limon*) in Greece, along the shore of the Corinthian Gulf. This scene is in great contrast to the vast and highly mechanized plantations of California, which is second only to the Mediterranean as a center of production.*

**Lemna** see DUCKWEED.
LEMNACEAE, about 9 species.

**Lemon** the common name for the fruit and tree of **Citrus limon*. The species is considered to be of Himalayan or Southeast Asian origin, but is cultivated in areas of Mediterranean climate such as Spain, Italy, Cyprus and California. The pulp of the yellow fruits is juicy (minimum 28%) and acid (5–7%), mainly citric but also malic and other acids.

Lemons are the most important acid fruit. Acid and non-acid cultivars are cultivated, the rind producing lemon oil. In 1971, together with limes, they accounted for 10% of the total world citrus production, ranking second to oranges. Mediterranean countries accounted for 37% of production, the USA and Argentina being the other major producers.
RUTACEAE.

**Lentil** the common name given to the genus *Lens*, which contains five species of climbing herbs native to the Mediterranean region and southwestern Asia. The wild species are unimportant apart from *L. orientalis*, which is probably the progenitor of the valuable pulse *L. culinaris* (= *L. esculenta*). This is a small pea-like annual herb with white, blue-tinged flowers developing into short flattened pods containing two seeds (lentils).

Two main forms exist: lentils 0.25–0.35in in diameter belong to a group known as *macrosperma*, while smaller forms 0.12–0.25in in diameter) belong to the *microsperma* group. These types have existed for several thousand years. There is also great variation in color, from pale straw or greenish through light brown to dark brown. Lentils are mainly grown in the Mediterranean area, Ethiopia, southwestern Asia, the Indian subcontinent, Chile, Argentina and the USA. World production in 1975 was estimated at over 1.2 million tons.

Lentils have a high food value and contain about 25% protein, 50% carbohydrate and 2% vegetable oil. They are usually cooked in boiling water as an ingredient of soups, stews or, in India, as "dal" or "dhal", a thick lentil sauce used with curry dishes. The young pods of some varieties may also be cooked as a vegetable dish. After harvesting, the pods, stems and leaves may be used as fodder. Lentil meal, prepared from milled lentils, may also be used as animal fodder and for making a type of bread.
LEGUMINOSAE.

*Mature Leek plants (*Allium porrum*) ready for harvesting. (× ⅙)*

# Legumes and Pulses

The family Leguminosae (see p. 499) is second only to the grass family in its importance to Man. The term legume refers to the characteristic fruits of the family – basically a dehiscent pod that develops from a single carpel and splits into two valves, although there are many deviations from this general structure, some fruits in the family being indehiscent and drupe-like, others transversely divided, and they may be dry or fleshy, winged or not. The name legume is also applied to those members of the family which are edible – either the pods themselves or the seeds (when they are called pulses, grain legumes, or beans), or both. The leaves are rarely eaten by Man, as in the case of species of **Pterocarpus* grown in parts of Nigeria, but several species are important fodder crops (see p. 149). Members of the Leguminosae also provide important timber trees, sources of dyes and tannins, gums and resins, oil seed crops, medicinal and insecticidal species as well as numerous well-known ornamental species. They are also an important component of the vegetation in many parts of the world. Here, however, we are only concerned with edible legumes and pulses.

*Common temperate legumes and pulses: 1 Scarlet Runner Bean; 2 Kidney Bean; 3 Haricot Bean; 4 French; 5 Lentil; 6 Broad Bean; 7 Garden Pea; 8 Asparagus Pea; 1 to 8 (× ½); whole plant (× 1/10)*

Nutritionally, legumes are very important, second only to cereals as a source of human food. They are two or three times richer than cereals in protein, some are rich in oil, such as *SOYBEANS *(Glycine max)*, and GROUND NUTS *(*Arachis hypogaea)*, and in terms of their amino-acid composition they complement the cereals, so that a mixed diet of pulses and cereals is nutritionally well balanced and traditional in several civilizations.

Legume grains or pulses are still major components of the diet in the Indian subcontinent (especially *LENTIL, *Lens culinaris*; *PIGEON PEA, *Cajanus cajan*; and *CHICKPEA, **Cicer arietinum*), the Far East (particularly *SOYBEAN), and Latin America (particularly the BEAN, **Phaseolus vulgaris*).

Only about twenty species of legumes (out of the thousands that are known to science) are widely used for food, such as *PEAS *(Pisum* species*)*, *BEANS *(Phaseolus* species*)*, LENTIL, GROUND NUT, *COWPEA *(Vigna unguiculata)*, GRAMS *(*Vigna* species*)*, *MUNG BEAN *(Phaseolus aureus)* and *PIGEON PEA *(*Cajanus cajan)*. Many tropical species have great potential, such as the BAMBARA GROUNDNUT *(Voandzeia subterranea)* and the *LABLAB OR HYACINTH BEAN *(*Dolichos lablab)*, and efforts are being made to exploit them more fully as human food. In temperate climates, PEAS, BEANS, LENTILS and LUPINS *(Lupinus* species*)* are the main edible legumes. The COMMON OR GARDEN *PEA *(Pisum sativum)* probably originated in the Near East and is now cultivated in most temperate regions and at high altitudes in the tropics. It is one of the four most important grain legumes and in the dried state was once a staple food of Western Europe, as pea meal or split peas. The immature pods are traditionally harvested for the young seeds which are used as the vegetable, fresh peas. They are also grown for canning, but a very large part of the crop is now harvested immature for freezing, garden peas being one of the frozen foods most in demand.

Beans derived from species of the genus *Phaseolus* are cultivated in both the Old and New Worlds. In tropical countries, the seeds are used largely as dry beans, whereas in temperate and Mediterranean countries, although there is some consumption of dry beans, cultivars have been developed for use as green vegetables such as the immature pods of *Phaseolus vulgaris* [FRENCH OR SNAP BEAN]. The dried seeds of this species are the haricot beans of commerce used in stews and in sauce as canned baked beans. *P. coccineus* [SCARLET RUNNER BEAN], a Middle American species, is also grown in Europe for its fleshy immature pods. The tropical species *P. acutifolius* [TEPARY BEAN] is a drought-resistant crop which is grown for its dry beans which have a high protein content, but it is hardly ever grown outside its native America.

The FIELD OR BROAD BEAN *(*Vicia faba)* is an important legume in many parts of the north temperate zone and in some subtropical areas at higher altitudes. The seeds are large and rich in protein and are consumed green and immature or ripe and dried.

The most important grain legume in terms of world trade and production is the SOYBEAN. The leading producer is the United States, where the rise to prominence of the SOYBEAN crop in the last 50–60 years has been spectacular, to the extent that it is now the most important cash crop in the United States and a major export. The main use of

## LEGUMES AND PULSES

**I. Cool Temperate and Warm Temperate**

| Common name | Scientific name | Part consumed |
|---|---|---|
| GARDEN *PEA | *Pisum sativum* | Seeds, young pods |
| FIELD PEA | *P. arvense* | Seeds |
| ASPARAGUS PEA, WINGED PEA | *Tetragonolobus purpureus* | |
| FRENCH, KIDNEY, *HARICOT, GREEN, RUNNER, STRING, SALAD, WAX BEAN | **Phaseolus vulgaris* | Young pods, seeds |
| RUNNER, SCARLET RUNNER | *P. coccineus* | Young pods |
| BUTTER, SIEVA, CIVET, MADAGASCAR, CAROLINA SEWEE BEAN | *P. lunatus* | Seeds |
| LIMA BEAN | *P. limensis* | Seeds |
| *SOYBEAN | *Glycine max (G. soja)* | Seeds, sprouts, oil |
| *LENTIL | *Lens culinaris* | Seeds |
| BROAD BEAN | **Vicia faba* | Seeds |
| LUPIN | **Lupinus albus* *L. pilosus, L. luteus, L. mutabilis* | Seeds |
| *CAROB BEAN, LOCUST BEAN, ST JOHN'S BREAD | *Ceratonia siliqua* | Pods |

**II Tropical**

| Common name | Scientific name | Part consumed |
|---|---|---|
| TEPARY BEAN | **Phaseolus acutifolius* var *latifolius* | Seeds |
| CLUSTER BEAN, GUAR | *Cyamopsis tetragonolobus* | Young pods, seeds |
| GOA BEAN, *ASPARAGUS PEA, WINGED PEA | *Psophocarpus tetragonolobus* | Young pods |
| | *P. palmetti-orum* | Young pods |
| *YAM BEAN, CHOPSUI POTATO | *Pachyrhizus erosus, P. tuberosus* | Young pods, roots |
| *LABLAB, HYACINTH BEAN | **Dolichos lablab* | Pods, seeds |
| MADRAS GRAM, HORSE GRAM | *D. biflorus* | Seeds |
| CHICK PEA | *Cicer arietinum* | Seeds |
| BAMBARA GROUNDNUT, KAFFIR PEA | *Voandzeia subterranea* | Seeds |
| KERSTING'S GROUNDNUT | *Kerstingiella geocarpa* | Seeds |
| *TAMARIND | *Tamarindus indica* | Pulp from pods, seeds |
| MOTH BEAN | **Vigna aconitifolia* | Seeds |
| ADZUKI BEAN | *V. angularis* | Seeds |
| *COWPEA | *Vigna unguiculata* | Seeds |
| BLACK-EYED PEA | subspecies *unguiculata* | Seeds |
| YARD LONG BEAN | subspecies *sesquipedalis* | Pods |
| BLACK GRAM | *Vigna mungo (Phaseolus mungo)* | Seeds, young pods |
| GREEN GRAM, *MUNG BEAN | *V. radiata (Phaseolus aureus)* | Seeds Pods, sprouts |
| RICE BEAN | *V. umbellata* | Seeds |
| JACK BEAN | **Canavalia ensiformis* | Young pods, seeds |
| SWORD BEAN | *C. gladiata* | Young pods, seeds |
| GROUNDNUT | **Arachis hypogaea* | Seeds, oil |
| *PIGEON PEA, CAJAN, CONGO PEA, RED GRAM | *Cajanus cajan* | Seeds |
| AFRICAN LOCUST BEAN | **Parkia filicoidea, P. biglobosa* | Seeds, pulp of pod |
| *YAM BEAN | *Sphenostylis stenocarpa* | Seeds |

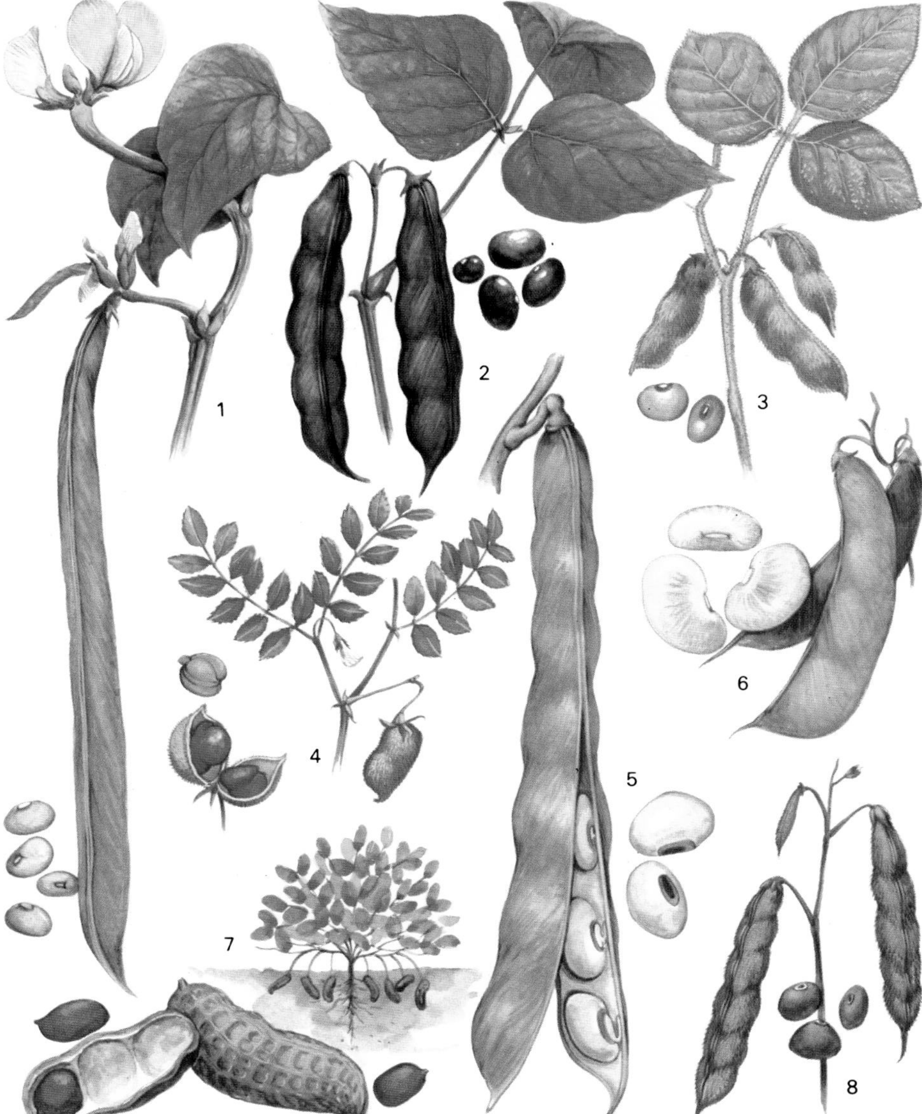


*Common warm temperate and tropical legumes and pulses: 1 Cowpea; 2 Lablab; 3 Soybean; 4 Chick-pea; 5 Jack Bean; 6 Butter Bean; 7 Groundnut; 8 Pigeon Pea. 1, 2 ($\times\frac{2}{3}$); 3, 6, 7, 8 ($\times\frac{1}{2}$); 4, 5 ($\times\frac{1}{3}$); whole plant ($\times\frac{1}{10}$).*

the beans is the production of protein-rich meal and oil. They are also consumed fresh, as bean sprouts and in liquid or curd form, especially in the Far East.

LENTILS are one of the oldest legume pulse crops of the New World and were involved in the origins of agriculture in the Near East along with wheat and barley. The seeds contain a high percentage of protein and are widely consumed in the Indian subcontinent, the Middle East and the Mediterranean. It has also been introduced into the New World, in Argentina, Chile and parts of the United States.

Tropical legumes used for human food are many and various, but few are cultivated on a major scale. The most widely cultivated crop species are the COWPEA, grown as a vegetable or as a pulse throughout the tropics and subtropics, the GROUND NUT, grown in warm temperate and tropical regions around the world, for vegetable oil or as an appetizer, the PIGEON PEA, a pulse crop grown by small farmers mainly in India, but with some production in Southeast Asia and equatorial Africa, and the SOYBEAN already mentioned. Minor tropical crop species are listed in the table.

It is often not realized that lupins have been in cultivation as agricultural crops, particularly in South America, since earliest times, being used for animal forage and as a source of grain. *L. mutabilis* was once a major source of protein in the Andes. The seeds, however, have a high alkaloid content and as agricultural practices improved and better legumes became available, they dropped out of favor. Interest in them as a protein source has now revived and research is being carried out into alkaloid-free varieties.

Legumes are additionally important in cultivation because of the association in their root nodules with nitrogen-fixing bacteria which are able to convert free atmospheric nitrogen into nitrates. Their value as green manure which can be ploughed in to enhance the nitrogen levels in the soils is especially important in shifting cultivation in the tropics.

**Leontodon** a genus of annual, more usually perennial herbs, common in Europe and southwest Asia. Although a number of species bear attractive yellow, orange, pink or purple flower heads, none appears to be cultivated.
COMPOSITAE, 50–60 species.

**Leontopodium** a genus of tufted, downy-woolly, perennial herbs found in the mountains of Europe and Asia, with two species in Andean South America. The best-known species is *L. alpinum* [EDELWEISS], which is widely grown as an alpine rock-garden plant.
COMPOSITAE, about 30–40 species.

**Lepidium** a cosmopolitan genus of annual to perennial herbs. The most important species is *L. sativum* [COMMON or GARDEN CRESS], a native of western Asia and Egypt, which is used as a garnish or a salad. It is the long, succulent hypocotyls of the seedlings which are used.
CRUCIFERAE, about 130 species.

**Leptospermum** a genus of evergreen shrubs and trees mainly from Australia but with some in New Zealand, Malaysia and the Caroline Islands. The New Zealand species *L. scoparium* [MANUKA, TEA TREE, BROWN TEA TREE] is an ornamental tree to 23ft in height with small white flowers. Pink or reddish-flowered cultivars are also grown. The leaves of *L. scoparium* and *L. thea* have been used locally as a tea substitute. The hard durable timber of *L. ericoides* [HEATH TEA TREE] is used locally in New Zealand for spokes and wheels. *L. petersonii* (= *L. citratum*), native to Australia, is grown commercially in Kenya and Guatemala for the lemon-scented essential oil obtained from its leaves.
MYRTACEAE, about 50 species.

Leontodon autumnale, *photographed in a dry meadow in September. Each strap-shaped "petal" is in fact a separate flower (floret).* (×1)

Leptospermum flavescens, *photographed after a rainstorm in the usually dry Pilliga scrub area in New South Wales, Australia.*

**Lespedeza** [BUSH CLOVERS] a genus of annual and perennial herbs and shrubs from the Himalayas, East Asia, Australia and North America. *L. bicolor* is cultivated for the ornamental value of its rosy-purple flowers. The annuals *L. striata* [JAPANESE CLOVER] and *L. stipulacea* [KOREAN CLOVER] and the perennial *L. cuneata* (= *L. sericea*) are Asiatic species grown also in North America for fodder, hay and green manure.
LEGUMINOSAE, about 100 species.

**Lettuce** the common name for many of the species of the herbaceous genus *Lactuca* including the cultivated *L. sativa* and the closely related *L. serriola* [PRICKLY LETTUCE], *L. saligna* [WILLOW-LEAVED LETTUCE] and *L. virosa* [POISON, OPIUM or BITTER LETTUCE]. The three latter species are weeds of roadsides and waste places and originated around the Mediterranean, from where they have spread to most parts of the world. *L. sativa* does not occur in the wild except as an escape from cultivation and probably originated by Man's selection from its close relative *L. serriola*.

Lettuce is cultivated almost exclusively for fresh consumption as a salad vegetable and occurs in a number of forms, of which the most important are the cabbage lettuces and the cos or Romaine. In the cabbage lettuces, which include both the crisp-head and the butterhead, the relatively broad, succulent leaves overlap to form, when mature, a roughly spherical heart or head. The crisp-head type has leaves which are more crinkled and frilled at the edges, and of a more brittle texture than those of the somewhat limp-leaved butterhead type. Together these main types include several hundred cultivars.

Other types of lettuce include the "loose-leaf" in which relatively small leaves are copiously produced in a completely open rosette, and the asparagus or stem lettuce grown in and around China for consumption of the young fleshy stems.
COMPOSITAE.

*Commercially cultivated Lettuce (*Lactuca sativa*) growing under glass ready for out-of-season marketing.*

**Leucanthemum** a genus of mainly perennial herbs with conspicuous flower heads of yellow disk and white ray flowers, mostly native to Europe and northern Asia. The commonest and most widespread species is the extremely variable *L. vulgare* (= *Chrysanthemum leucanthemum*) [OX-EYE DAISY, MOON DAISY, MARGUERITE]. Cultivated forms are grown in gardens in borders and used as cut flowers. The OX-EYE DAISY has traditionally been used as a medicinal herb and has properties similar to those of chamomile.

*L. maximum*, from the Pyrenees, is also widely cultivated in gardens for ornament. Several very large-headed forms, such as the

SHASTA DAISY, have been derived from it. These sometimes have double white centers or serrated or fringed strap-shaped flowers. Another related species, *L. atratum*, is also cultivated in borders. Like *L. vulgare* it is highly variable in the wild and contains several distinct subspecies.
COMPOSITAE, 20–50 species.

**Leucobryum** a genus of mosses, mainly tropical in distribution. The plants mostly form dense cushions which hold water like a sponge. The leaves, unlike those of most mosses, are several cell layers thick and when the moss becomes dry the water-holding layers become air-filled, thus imparting a characteristic whitish appearance.
DICRANACEAE, about 120 species.

**Leucojum** [SNOWFLAKES] a genus of bulbous perennial herbs from southern and central Europe and Morocco, closely related to the SNOWDROPS. *L. vernum* [SPRING SNOWFLAKE], from central Europe, has solitary flowers. *L. aestivum* [SUMMER SNOWFLAKE], from central and southern Europe, is more robust with stems 20in high. The flowers are borne in umbels of two to nine flowers in April. *L. autumnale*, a Mediterranean species, has very narrow leaves, and pale pink flowers, one to three (usually two) per stem, in the autumn just before the leaves appear.
AMARYLLIDACEAE, about 12 species.

**Leucothoe** a genus of evergreen and deciduous shrubs from North and South America, East Asia and Madagascar. They bear crowded racemes of white, pink or greenish-white, urn-shaped flowers. Several species are known in cultivation, such as the deciduous shrub *L. racemosa* (= **Andromeda racemosa*) [SWEETBELLS] and *L. fontanesiana* (often offered as *L. catesbaei* in cultivation) [DOG-HOBBLE], a spreading evergreen shrub up to 6.5ft in height, both from North America.
ERICACEAE, about 44 species.

Leucobryum glaucum *growing in a wood. The gray-green cushions of this moss are often collected for decoration.*

**Lewisia** a genus of highly xerophytic, perennial, leaf-succulent rosette plants from the western USA through Mexico to Bolivia. The leaves are flat or cylindric and sometimes deciduous in the resting period and the flowers are often showy. Most of the plants in cultivation are of hybrid origin. *L. rediviva* [BITTER ROOT] is the State flower of Idaho.
PORTULACACEAE, about 16 species.

**Leycesteria** a small genus of Himalayan shrubs of which *L. formosa* is the most widely cultivated. It is a vigorous, deciduous, hollow-stemmed shrub with arches or drooping spikes of flowers, used in woodland coverts and as background planting.
CAPRIFOLIACEAE, 6 species.

**Liatris** [BLAZING STAR, GAY FEATHER, BUTTON SNAKEROOT] a genus of perennial, cormous or rhizomatous herbs native to North America. *L. spicata* is frequently cultivated in the herbaceous border for its dense spikes of bright purple, reddish-purple or white, thistle-like flower heads on stout stems up to 3ft tall. Other cultivated species are *L. graminifolia* and *L. scariosa*, both with purple or white spikes.
COMPOSITAE, about 40 species.

**Libertia** a genus of tufted perennial herbs native to New Guinea, Australia, New Zealand and Chile. The leaves are arranged in fans and the flowers are white or pale blue, borne in dense clusters in the axis of sheathing bracts, as in *L. grandiflora*. Although they are fine garden plants, they are not commonly cultivated.
IRIDACEAE, about 12 species.

**Libocedrus** a small genus of evergreen coniferous trees with scale-like leaves, native to New Zealand and New Caledonia. These trees, especially *L. decurrens* [CALIFORNIA INCENSE CEDAR], sometimes placed in a separate genus, *Calocedrus*, *L. chilensis* [CHILEAN INCENSE TREE], sometimes placed in *Austrocedrus*, and *L. plumosa* [KAWAKA] are valuable sources of close-grained timber, which is soft but durable and used in general construction.
CUPRESSACEAE, about 5 species.

*A columnar form of* Libocedrus decurrens *(=* Calocedrus decurrens*), a native of western North America where it normally has a conical form.*

**Lichens** see p. 204.

**Licorice** or **liquorice** a medicinal and flavoring material extracted from the roots of **Glycyrrhiza glabra*, a perennial herb from southern Europe and Asia. Licorice has been valued since ancient times for medicinal purposes, not least for disguising the taste of nauseous prescriptions, but also as a demulcent and expectorant. It is also used to color and flavor confectionery, tobacco and beer, in shoe polish and in metallurgy. It contains glycyrrhizin, many times sweeter than sugar, and the waste fibers of the plant are used in wallboard. Today, it is mainly obtained from the USSR, Spain and the Middle East.

*G. lepidota*, from North America, is known as WILD LICORICE. Other leguminous plants known as LICORICE include **Abrus precatorius* [INDIAN OR WILD LICORICE], **Astragalus glycyphyllus* [WILD LICORICE] and **Hedysarum mackenzii* [LICORICE ROOT].
LEGUMINOSAE.

# Lichens

LICHENS ARE SLOW-GROWING PLANTS THAT consist of an intimate association between a fungus and an alga. In most lichens the bulk of the plant body is composed of the fungus, with the algae restricted to a thin layer near the surface. The algae are green or blue-green and are either unicellular or form simple short filaments. In nature, lichen fungi never occur free-living. Approximately 18 000 species of fungi occur in lichens, so they are a large group comprising about 25% of the known species of fungi. The commonest alga, found in about 70% of species, is the green unicellular *Trebouxia*. This alga is not found outside lichens, although all the other 26 genera of algae found in lichens may also be found free-living.

Most lichens occur as crusts either closely adhering to or actually within the surface of their substrate – typically rock or wood, but occasionally very stable soil surfaces. Much more prominent as components of the vegetation are the minority of lichens that are less closely attached to the substrate and are leafy, shrub-like or filamentous. Shrub-like forms such as REINDEER MOSS and ICELAND MOSS cover large areas of ground in the tundra regions. (See also p. 855.)

Lichens have a worldwide distribution. They extend farther towards the poles and higher up mountains (up to 25 000ft) than any other plants of comparable size, but may also feature prominently on trees in tropical and equatorial forests. Very few species live permanently submerged and these grow mostly on shallow rocks in freshwater streams. On rocky seashores, they occur almost down to the low water mark, but rarely grow below it. (See p. 829.)

Lichens are very slow-growing plants. Those existing as surface crusts rarely have a radial growth exceeding 0.04in per year (and often much less than this), while even the leafy or shrubby kinds rarely grow more than 0.4in per year. Because lichens grow so slowly, and because of the difficulty of continuously observing them over long periods of time in nature, it is not easy to observe how they reproduce. Many lichens have small powdery areas on their surface, each individual grain of powder consisting of an algal cell or short filament surrounded by fungal hyphae. In the few cases studied, these grains appear capable of slowly developing into new plants. Other lichens produce numerous fruiting bodies of the fungus. However, the germinating fungal spore must encounter the appropriate alga in nature before a new lichen can be formed, but such syntheses have only rarely been observed.

Very few lichens are found in urban areas because they are particularly sensitive to atmospheric pollution, especially sulfur dioxide. Indeed, they are totally absent from the centers of the more heavily polluted areas. It is only at relatively long distances from large conurbations that the full complement of lichen species can be found. One reason why lichens may be so sensitive to atmospheric pollution is that they have developed very efficient mechanisms for absorbing nutrients from the liquids passing over their surface – usually rainwater. Such an adaptation is

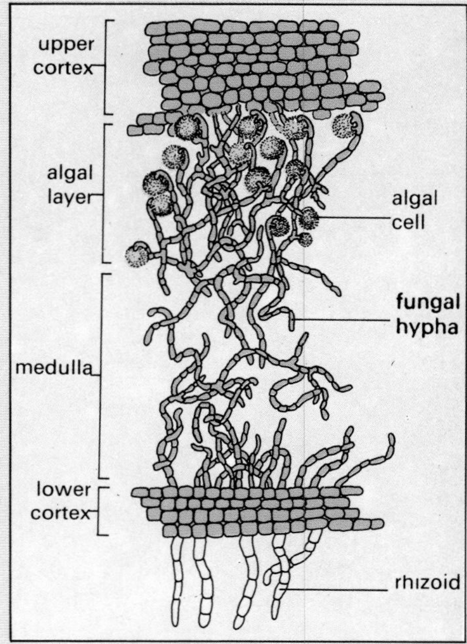


The bulk of the body is fungal (orange), while the algal cells (green) are confined to a layer below the upper surface.

Above Right *Cross section of the thallus of a lichen.*

*The hanging lichen,* Usnea longissima, *growing from a tree, near Mount Everest, at an altitude of nearly 8 000ft.* ( × $\frac{1}{15}$)

Below *A mosaic of gray lichens growing on a rock in Australia.* ( × $\frac{1}{2}$)

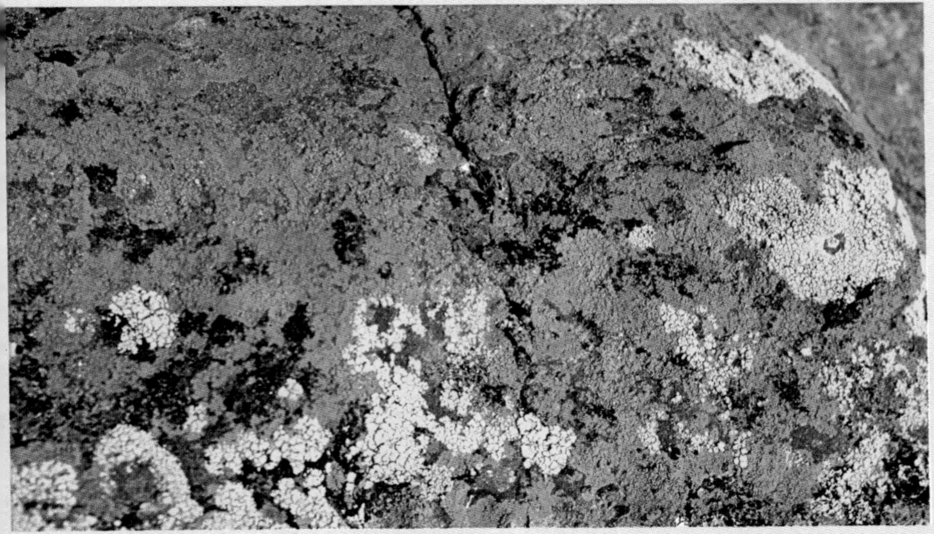

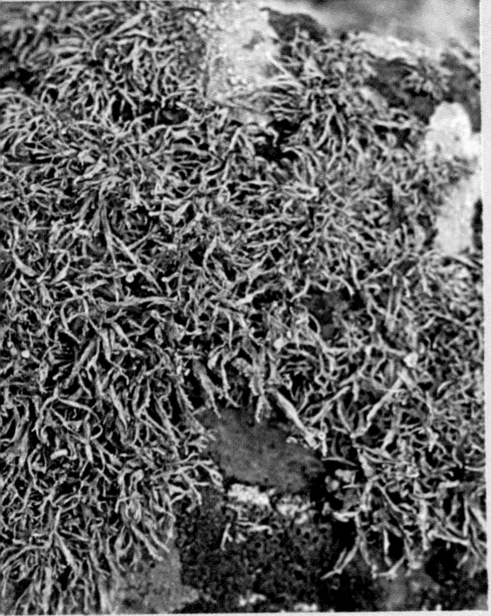

Above *A mosaic of orange and yellow crustose lichens growing on a bare rock surface in California. Lichens are often the first colonizers of bare surfaces, slowly building up an organic-based surface which other plants can later colonize.* (×1)
Left *The fruticose (shrubby) lichen* Ramelina siliquosa *growing on rocks by the sea. This species thrives within the salt spray zone.* (×2)

presumably important for their existence in barren and nutrient-poor habitats. But this adaptation has its Achilles heel. (See p. 943.)

Although very sensitive to atmospheric pollution, lichens are very tolerant of other environmental extremes, withstanding weeks and months of drought. They also tolerate extremes of temperature, as indicated not only by their luxuriant growth in arctic regions, but also by the fact that those in hotter regions can tolerate long periods of quite high temperatures when dry – over 140°F for several hours.

Both the fungal and algal components of lichens can be grown free-living in laboratory culture but neither bear any resemblance to the parent lichen. Clearly, there must be a remarkable interaction between the two components to produce the distinctive appearance and structure of the lichen plant. One aspect of the interaction is that the alga continuously supplies to the fungus 70–80% of the carbohydrates it manufactures by photosynthesis. This rapid and substantial supply of nutrients enables lichens to live in their characteristically barren habitats removed from the supplies of external organic food normally needed for fungal growth. Many researchers also believe that the lichen alga must receive some "benefit" in return for supplying the fungus with an abundance of carbohydrate, although this has never been proved experimentally.

Lichens cover more of the Earth's surface than all other fungi, but their economic value to Man is negligible. In arctic and antarctic regions, lichens of the reindeer moss type (*Cladonia* and **Cetraria* species) provide fodder for animals such as reindeer and caribou. However, most other animals (including human beings) gain little nutritive value from eating lichens since they do not have the digestive enzymes necessary for breaking down the unusual carbohydrates they contain. Additionally, many lichens contain substances generally called "lichen acids", some of which irritate the stomach unless the lichen is first boiled. Nevertheless ICELAND MOSS (*Cetraria islandica*) has been used as a substitute for flour during hard times in Scandinavia and Iceland.

Lichens have in the past had extensive use in dyeing. Litmus was originally produced from the lichen *Roccella*. They also have a long history in providing ingredients in certain kinds of perfumes, and the ability of powdered lichens to absorb and retain perfumes made them valuable as constituents of hair powders in the times when wigs were worn widely and bodily hygiene was less adequate than in modern times. More recently, lichens have been explored as a source of antibiotics. Many lichen antibiotics proved unsuitable for clinical use but a few (especially the common usnic acid) have had some use in combating tuberculosis and certain skin diseases.

Below Parmelia perlata, *a foliose (leafy) lichen found on trees and rocks.* (×1) Right *A crustose lichen* (Rhizocarpon) *growing on a stone in Alaska.* (×2) *Lichens are very tolerant of temperature extremes (though not of pollution).*

**Lignum vitae** the common name given to *Guaiacum officinale* and *G. sanctum*, attractive evergreen trees from tropical and subtropical America. They are grown for ornament and bear attractive blue or purple flowers. The wood yields a hard resin with medicinal properties called guaiacum, once used as a stimulant and purgative, and, in conjunction with mercury, as a treatment for syphilis. The very heavy durable wood (the hardest commerical timber) is pale brown outside, chocolate colored inside. It is used for fine carving and for making objects such as pulley blocks, where extreme toughness is required.
ZYGOPHYLLACEAE.

**Ligularia** a widespread temperate Eurasian genus of herbaceous perennials. Cultivated species include *L. dentata* (= *L. clivorum*, **Senecio clivorum*), with kidney-shaped leaves and orange-yellow flower heads, and *L. macrophylla* (= *S. ledebourii*), a massive species with 6–10ft stems, leaves up to 40in long and bright yellow flower heads.
COMPOSITAE, about 120 species.

**Ligusticum** a genus of perennial herbs occurring naturally all over the Northern Hemisphere. *L. scoticum* [SCOTCH LOVAGE] was once cultivated as a potherb, its roots, leaves and seeds used for medicinal purposes and the young stems candied and used like angelica.
UMBELLIFERAE, about 60 species.

**Ligustrum** see PRIVET.
OLEACEAE, about 50 species.

**Lilac** the common name for *Syringa*, a genus of deciduous shrubs or small trees from Asia and Eastern Europe with showy panicles of waxy, fragrant flowers ranging from white to deep purple in color. Cultivated species include *S.* × *persica* (*S. afghanica* × *S. laciniata*) [PERSIAN LILAC] and *S. vulgaris* [COMMON LILAC], of which there are over 500 named cultivars, many originating in France. These hardy, large, easily grown shrubs thrive in towns and industrial areas. There are a number of excellent species from China and central Europe, such as *S.* × *chinensis*, *S. reflexa*, *S. villosa* and *S. josikaea* [HUNGARIAN LILAC], which have been used as parents for a great many hybrids.
OLEACEAE.

Lilaea scilloides *showing the stalked inflorescences bearing male and bisexual flowers, with the long styles of the female flowers projecting from the axils.* (× ½)

Ligustrum lucidum *is an evergreen privet from China, where a wax secreted in response to insect damage is used commercially.*

**Lilaea** a genus consisting of a single species, *L. scilloides*, a tufted, grass-like annual living in shallow water in western North and South America and in Victoria, Australia (where it was probably introduced). It has no known economic use.
LILAEACEAE, 1 species.

**Lilium** [LILIES] a horticulturally well-known genus of bulbous perennials spread throughout the north temperate region, although there are a few outlying species, such as *L. neilgherrense* which inhabits the mountains of southern India.

The inflorescence is a raceme with the flowers on long stalks, but in some species the flower is solitary and in others the axis of the inflorescence is condensed so much that the flowers appear to arise all at the same point, so giving an umbellate appearance. The flower consists of six, usually equal segments, free from each other but arranged in various ways to give a wide range of shapes to the different species. For example, in *L. martagon* [TURK'S CAP LILY, MARTAGON LILY] the flowers are pendulous with the segments curled right back, in *L. umbellatum* they are erect with the segments forming an upright cup, while in *L. regale* they are horizontal with the segments held together to form a long tube. Size varies from 1in to as much as 10in across.

Lilies are highly prized ornamental flowers, and are intensively cultivated and hybridized for indoor and garden display. Enthusiasts and growers recognize nine divisions for exhibition purposes: Asiatic hybrids; martagon hybrids; candidum hybrids; American hybrids; longiflorum hybrids; trumpet and aurelian hybrids; oriental hybrids; all other hybrids; true species and their botanical forms and varieties.

Among the most important species, both in their own right and as a source of hybrids, are *L. auratum* [GOLDEN-RAYED LILY], *L.* × *aurelianense* (= *L. henryi* × *L. sargentiae*), *L. bulbiferum* [ORANGE LILY], *L. canadense* [CANADA LILY], *L. candidum* [MADONNA LILY], *L. chalcedonicum* [SCARLET TURK'S CAP LILY], *L. formosanum* [FORMOSA LILY], *L. hansonii*, *L. henryi*, *L.* × *imperiale* (= *L. regale* × *L. sargentiae*), *L. japonicum*, *L. lancifolium* (= *L. tigrinum*) [TIGER LILY], *L. longiflorum* [EASTER LILY], *L.* × *maculatum*, *L. martagon* [TURK'S CAP LILY], *L. pardalinum* [PANTHER LILY], *L. pyrenaicum*, *L. regale*, *L. superbum* and *L.* × *testaceum* (= *L. candidum* × *L. chalcedonicum*) [NANKEEN LILY].
LILIACEAE, about 90 species.

**Lily of the valley** the common name for *Convallaria*, a north temperate genus represented by a single species, *C. majalis*, a perennial plant with a creeping rhizome which grows in dry woods on chalky soils. Leafless stalks arise from the axils of the paired leaves and bear inflorescences of fragrant, bell-shaped flowers. Cultivated varieties include the white flowered 'Fortin's Giant' and the pink flowered 'Rosea'. The plant yields convallatoxin, a cardiac glycoside. Var *keiskei* from Japan is sometimes treated as a separate species.
LILIACEAE, 1 species.

**Lima bean** one of the common names [BUTTER BEAN is another] for the annual climbing herb *Phaseolus lunatus*, a number of varieties of which are commonly cultivated in the tropics. A native of tropical and subtropical Central and South America, it requires a higher humidity for growth than most beans. The varieties are divided into the larger 'Lima' group containing both climbing (pole) and dwarf varieties, and the smaller 'Sieva' group. While the short, flat pods may be eaten as a green vegetable, it is the usually pale green seeds which are eaten fresh, canned or frozen. Variety *limenanus* [DWARF SIEVA BEAN] is a dwarf bush form.
LEGUMINOSAE.

*Flower of the Golden-rayed Lily* (Lilium auratum), *an outstanding species from Japan. This is a typical lily flower, having six perianth segments, six stamens and a single style.* ( × ½)

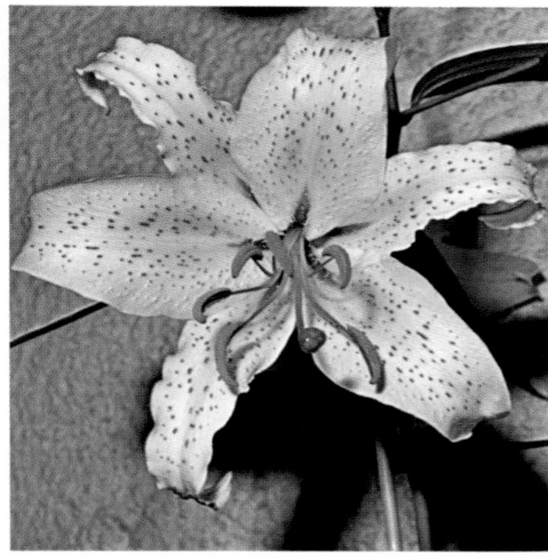

**Lime** a very acid yellow citrus fruit, resembling the *lemon except for its greenish-yellow flesh. **Citrus aurantiifolia* [LIME TREE] is native to northeastern India and Malaysia but is widely cultivated throughout the tropics, especially in the West Indies, Mexico and India, for juice and for the oil which can be expressed from the rind. Limes may contain an acid or a sweet pulp.

The WEST INDIAN OR KEY LIME fruits all the year round. It is highly acid, usually oblong or ovoid with a small nipple, while the PERSIAN OR TAHITI LIME (= *C. latifolia*) is sweeter, larger, broadly ovoid with a broad nipple, and fruits only in autumn and winter. Historically, acid limes were the first citrus fruits to be used by sailors against scurvy.
RUTACEAE.

**Limnanthes** a genus of annual herbs from the west coast of North America, one of which, *L. douglasii* [POACHED EGG FLOWER], is grown as a border plant or as a greenhouse pot plant for its 1in-wide flowers which have white-tipped petals sometimes yellow at their base.
LIMNANTHACEAE, 7 species.

**Limonium** [SEA LAVENDER, STATICE] a large genus of annual and perennial herbs and subshrubs widely distributed in coastal habitats throughout all the continents of the world. The flowers are small, carried in many branched panicles, pink to lavender in color, and persist in the dried form. Some species are used for decoration as everlasting flowers. Cultivated ornamental species include the annual yellow-flowered *L. bonduellii*, the rose-pink flowered *L. suworowii* (= *Psylliostachys suworowii*) and the perennial, lavender-blue flowered *L. latifolium*. *L. carolinianum* is a powerful astringent, formerly used to treat dysentery.
PLUMBAGINACEAE, about 300 species.

**Linaria** [TOADFLAX] a genus of annual and perennial herbs and subshrubs occurring mainly in Europe and the Mediterranean region. Many are found in gardens, perhaps the best-known being the yellow-flowered European *L. vulgaris* [TOADFLAX] or the purple *L. repens* [PALE OR STRIPED TOADFLAX], both notorious as weeds. Similar to the latter, *L. purpurea* [PURPLE TOADFLAX] is grown for its dense purple or pink spikes. The annuals frequently cultivated for their variously purple, red, yellow or white flowers under the name *L. maroccana* are North African and perhaps of hybrid origin. *L. triornithophora* from Spain and Portugal is a tall perennial with large, showy, bluish-purple and yellow flowers, often found in cultivation. The commonest cultivated alpine species are the pale yellow *L. supina*, the yellow and brown *L. tristis* and the purple and orange *L. alpina* [ALPINE TOADFLAX]. All are short-lived perennials with masses of snapdragon-like flowers. *L. vulgaris* is now widely naturalized in North America.
SCROPHULARIACEAE, about 150 species.

*Inflorescences of Sea Lavender or Statice* (Limonium vulgare), *a common inhabitant of muddy salt marshes, where it forms a carpet of color.* ( × 1)

Lilium nepalense, *a large-flowered lily native to the humid Himalayas at altitudes around 6 500–9 000ft. It is grown in cultivation, but is slightly frost-tender.* ( × ⅓)

**Lindera** a genus of aromatic trees or shrubs mainly native to Asia and North America. The most widely cultivated decorative species is the eastern North American *L. benzoin* [SPICEBUSH], a shrub which may grow to a height of 16ft and whose aromatic bark also has medicinal uses. Other cultivated species include *L. mellissifolia* [JOVE'S FRUIT], *L. obtusiloba* and *L. umbellata*, the former North American, the latter two from China and Japan.
LAURACEAE, about 100 species.

**Linnaea** [TWIN FLOWER] a small genus of evergreen prostrate or trailing subshrubs, circumpolar in distribution. The common name derives from the arrangement of the flowers in pairs at the ends of long stalks. *L. borealis* is cultivated as a rock-garden or ground-cover plant bearing fragrant bell-shaped rose or white flowers from late spring.
CAPRIFOLIACEAE, 1–3 species.

**Linseed** the seed of **Linum usitatissimum* [*FLAX]. Linseed oil is the most important vegetable drying oil (ie when exposed to air it slowly oxidizes and becomes hard). It is used as an ingredient of emulsions, varnishes, putty (a mixture of chalk and linseed oil) and linoleum, which consists of the oil with resins and powdered cork on a jute backing. The residual oil-cake is a valuable cattle food. When extracted cold, it is important as an artists' medium for grinding oil colors. The seed is employed in medicine as a demulcent.
LINACEAE.

**Linum** a large genus of annual, biennial and perennial herbs and subshrubs found in temperate and subtropical regions of all continents. The annual *L. usitatissimum* [*FLAX], is the source of both *linseed oil and linen fiber. A number of other species are grown as ornamental border or rockery plants, including the yellow-flowered, eastern Mediterranean *L. arboreum* and the pale blue-flowered, European *L. austriacum*, both rather shrubby perennials, and the attractive annual North African *L. grandiflorum*, with large saucer-shaped, reddish-colored flowers (white in cultivar 'Bright Eyes', crimson in cultivar 'Rubrum' and purplish-blue in cultivar 'Caeruleum').
LINACEAE, about 230 species.

**Lippia** a large genus comprising perennial herbs and shrubs, mainly from the tropics of the New World, but with a few species in Africa and Asia. The genus is not often seen in cultivation, except for *L. citriodora* (= *Aloysia triphylla*) [LEMON OF SWEET-SCENTED VERBENA], a shrub from Argentina and Chile up to 5ft tall, which is grown for its fragrant lemon-scented foliage.
VERBENACEAE, about 200 species.

**Liquidambar** [SWEET GUMS] a small genus of trees from North America, southwestern Asia and southeastern China and Taiwan. SWEET GUMS are grown mostly as ornamentals for their autumn colors, and for their wood, but also for the fragrant gum known as American storax (or styrax) from *L. styraciflua* and liquid storax from *L. orientalis*, used in perfumery, primarily to scent soap, as an expectorant in cough pastilles, and as a fumigant in the treatment of skin diseases such as scabies. The Chinese *L. formosana* is another species cultivated for ornament. A reddish heartwood (satin walnut or red gum) is obtained from *L. styraciflua*; the white sapwood is sold as hazel pine.
HAMAMELIDACEAE, 3 species.

*Perennial Flax (*Linum perenne *spp* anglicum*), a rare wild flower photographed in limestone grassland in northeastern England. (× ½)*

Livistona rotundifolia, *a handsome palm tree with hanging branches of fruits, is widely cultivated throughout the tropics.*

**Liriodendron** see TULIP TREE.
MAGNOLIACEAE, 2 species.

**Liriope** an East Asian genus of stemless perennial herbs with linear, tufted leaves and racemes of purple or white flowers. *L. muscari* (= **Ophiopogon muscari*) and *L. spicata* are grown in gardens for ground cover.
LILIACEAE, 6 species.

**Listera** a small genus of orchids native to the north temperate zone. They are characterized by having a pair of broad flat opposite leaves, and consequently are often known as TWAYBLADES, particularly *L. ovata*. This, like most other species of the genus, has a slender spike of rather insignificant greenish or purplish flowers.
ORCHIDACEAE, about 30 species.

**Litchi** a small genus of trees and shrubs from southern China, Southeast Asia and western Malaysia to India. The most important species is *L. chinensis* (= *Nephelium litchi, Dimocarpus litchi*) [LITCHI, LYCHEE, LEECHEE], an evergreen tree which yields an edible fruit. It is a native of southern China and has been widely introduced throughout the tropics, although it only flourishes well at high altitudes. The red-brown globose fruits (drupes) are borne in clusters. The white edible juicy aril of the fruit is eaten fresh or canned in syrup. The aril is also dried and is known then as litchi nuts. The tree is also grown for its ornamental value and its timber.
SAPINDACEAE, about 12 species.

**Lithops** [LIVING STONES, PEBBLE PLANTS] a remarkable South African genus of leaf-succulents in which the entire body is reduced to one pair of opposite, pebble-like leaves forming a top-shaped growth which lies buried in the soil with only the flat leaf tips exposed. Each leaf pair is renewed annually, and some species form a cluster of heads with age. Daisy-like white or yellow flowers arise from the fissure separating the two leaves and are large for the size of the plant.

*Lithops* leaves are never plain green, but shades of gray-green and brown and variously mottled or striped. The colors and

*The flower of the Tulip Tree (*Liriodendron tulipifera*), showing the cone-like mass of narrow carpels; it is closely allied to the magnolias. (× ⅓)*

patterns of each species closely resemble those of the natural rock background of the habitat and have the effect of disruptive camouflage. *Lithops* species, especially *L. optica* and *L. fulleri*, are among the most popular of greenhouse succulents.
AIZOACEAE, about 37 species.

**Lithospermum** a genus of perennial herbs or small shrubs with hairy leaves and usually blue flowers, native to Europe and Asia. Several are cultivated as perennials in flower borders and rock gardens and have been extensively hybridized. *L. diffusum* (= *Lithodora diffusum*) and *L. oleifolium* (= *L. oleifolia*), from Europe, bear blue flowers, while *L. canescens* [PUCCOON, RED ROOT] from North America, has yellow flowers. The European *L. purpuro-caeruleum* (= *Buglossoides purpurocaerulea*) [BLUE GROMWELL] has flowers which are at first red and then turn blue.
BORAGINACEAE, about 50 species.

**Littorella** [SHOREWEEDS] a genus of creeping, perennial aquatic herbs with two species, *L. uniflora* in northern and central Europe and *L. australis* in southern Patagonia and Tierra del Fuego. The plants often form extensive turf in freshwater lakes and ponds down to depths of about 13ft.
PLANTAGINACEAE, 2 species.

*The upper slopes of Mount Kenya support certain unique species, eg the spiky Lobelia plants (*Lobelia deckenii *ssp* keniensis*), and the giant tree-like Groundsels (*Senecio *sp) with rosettes of large leaves.*

*A Living Stone (*Lithops olivacea*) in flower. The pebble-like double leaves blend remarkably with the stony ground on which they grow.* (× ½)

**Liverworts** see Mosses and Liverworts, p. 234.

**Livistona** a genus of tall, elegant solitary fan palms occurring from Assam and southern China to the Solomon Islands, New Guinea and Australia. Several species, especially *L. chinensis* and *L. rotundifolia* are widely cultivated as ornamentals throughout the tropics. The leaves of several species, for example *L. australis*, *L. saribus* and *L. jenkinsiana*, are used locally for thatching and the young leaves and buds of *L. australis* are eaten as a vegetable but only locally.
PALMAE, about 24 species.

**Lobelia** a large cosmopolitan genus of annual and perennial herbs, subshrubs and sometimes trees, some of which are familiar in temperate gardens. There are the fascinating giant lobelias, native to the East African highlands, as well as more conventional garden plants such as the North American *L. purpuro-caèruleum* (= *Buglossoides purpurocaeruleum*), the Chilean *L. tupa* growing to 6.5ft high with deep red flowers, and the graceful *L. laxiflora*, from Arizona to Mexico and Colombia, with red and yellow flowers.

The most commonly cultivated species is the dwarf annual or perennial *L. erinus* [EDGING LOBELIA], with blue flowers with a white or yellowish throat. There are several varieties differing in flower color, as well as double-flowered forms. *L. inflata* [INDIAN TOBACCO] yields the alkaloid lobeline, used medicinally.
LOBELIACEAE, about 350 species.

**Locust** or **locust bean** a name given to the species of a number of different genera, including **Parkia filicoidea* [WEST AFRICAN LOCUST BEAN], **Robinia pseudacacia* [BLACK LOCUST], **Hymenaea courbaril* [LOCUST TREE] and **Gleditsia triacanthos* [HONEY LOCUST], but most commonly to the *CAROB TREE, *Ceratonia siliqua*, extensively cultivated in the Mediterranean area for its large sweet pods.

**Lodoicea** see DOUBLE COCONUT.
PALMAE, 1 species.

**Loganberries** large, edible, purplish-red fruits produced by the widely cultivated shrub **Rubus* × *loganobaccus* (= *R. ursinus* var *loganobaccus*). The plant is generally considered to be a natural fertile hybrid of the AMERICAN BLACKBERRY (*R. vitifolius*) and an unreduced gamete of the EUROPEAN RASPBERRY (*R. idaeus*).
ROSACEAE.

**Logwood** or **haematoxylin** a dye produced from the red-brown heartwood of a large tree [also known as LOGWOOD], **Haematoxylon campechianum*, found growing wild in Central America and sometimes cultivated elsewhere in the tropics. Imported first into Elizabethan England, it was used for dyeing wool and silk. The heartwood provides the basis of several useful stains used in microscopy, such as haematoxylin.
LEGUMINOSAE.

**Lolium** see RYEGRASS.
GRAMINEAE, 10–12 species.

**Lonas** a genus represented by a single species, *L. annua*, an annual herb with yellow discoid flower heads, found in southern Europe and North Africa.
COMPOSITAE, 1 species.

**Lonchocarpus** a large tropical genus of climbers, shrubs and trees, some of which (eg *L. sericeus* and *L. latifolius*) yield useful timber. The Peruvian *L. utilis* is one of the major sources of rotenone, a powerful and commercially important insecticide extracted from the roots (see also Derris). Leaves of the West African vine *L. cyanescens* yield a blue dye, Yoruba indigo.
LEGUMINOSAE, about 150 species.

**London pride** the common name for *Saxifraga umbrosa* and *S.* × *urbium* (= *S. spathularis* × *S. umbrosa*), perennial herbs widely cultivated in gardens for their attractive fleshy leaves (in basal rosettes) and loose inflorescences of small pink or white flowers.
SAXIFRAGACEAE.

Lophophora williamsii *is one of the few completely spineless cacti. This is the fabulous Peyote which yields the hallucinogenic alkaloid mescaline, used by Mexican Indians for centuries.* (×1)

**Lonicera** a large genus of erect or twining shrubs with opposite, simple leaves, widespread in the Northern Hemisphere, extending southwards to Mexico in the New World, and into North Africa from Europe; from Asia it extends southwards as far as southwestern Malaysia and into the Philippine Islands, and it is well represented in the Himalayan region.

The genus is popular in gardens where many shrubs and climbers are exploited as ornamentals. Most species and hybrids are hardy and deciduous although some are more or less evergreen. The genus can be divided into three sections, each of which provides a different group of garden plants. The first, including such well-known species as the European, North African and west Asian *L. periclymenum* [COMMON HONEYSUCKLE, WOODBINE], the yellow-flowered European and west Asian *L. caprifolium* [GOAT-LEAF HONEYSUCKLE, PERFOLIATE WOODBINE, ITALIAN WOODBINE] and the Mediterranean *L. etrusca*, with yellow and purple flowers, are climbers and often deciduous.

The second section, with *L. xylosteum*, a Eurasian species, *L. pyrenaica*, from the Pyrenees, and others, comprise upright shrubs ["BUSH HONEYSUCKLES"]. This section includes the evergreen Chinese *L. nitida*, a common hedging plant, and the numerous cultivars of the widely grown *L. tatarica* [TATARIAN HONEYSUCKLE], native from Russia to Turkestan.

The third section comprises mostly evergreen climbers, exemplified by the fragrant East Asian *L. japonica* [JAPANESE HONEYSUCKLE, GOLD AND SILVER FLOWER], with red and white flowers, the hairy *L. giraldii*, from China, and *L. hildebrandiana* [GIANT HONEYSUCKLE], from Burma, growing to 60–80ft, with flowers more than 4in long and yellow turning orange. Another popular species in this group is *L. sempervirens* [TRUMPET HONEYSUCKLE, CORAL HONEYSUCKLE], native to North America, cultivars of which include the yellow-flowered 'Sulphurea' and the scarlet-flowered 'Superba'.
CAPRIFOLIACEAE, about 200 species.

*The Common Honeysuckle (*Lonicera periclymenum*), frequently found growing wild in woods and hedgerows.* Below Left *The fragrant flowers are often pollinated at night by moths.* (×½) Right *The brightly colored berries extend the period of ornamental display.* (×2)

**Lopezia** a genus of erect herbs and shrubs native to Mexico and Central America. Although not extensively cultivated some species, especially *L. hirsuta* (= *L. lineata*), with pink to rose flowers, make attractive ornamentals in subtropical and warm-

*A bee visiting the flower of the Bird's Foot Trefoil (*Lotus corniculatus*). It is a common plant in European meadows and is grown as a forage crop in Europe and North America. (×2)*

temperate gardens or grown under glass in temperate regions.
ONAGRACEAE, about 17 species.

**Lophira** a genus represented by a single variable species, *L. lanceolata* (= *L. alata*) [AFRICAN OAK, RED IRON, DWARF IRONWOOD], a tropical West African tree which provides a commercial heavy red hardwood, mainly used locally for construction purposes. The seeds when pressed yield an edible oil (meni oil or niam fat).
OCHNACEAE, 1 species.

**Lophocolea** a large genus of leafy liverworts most of which occur in the tropics and subtropics, particularly in the Southern Hemisphere, although a few extend into the boreal climates of the Northern Hemisphere. They grow in moist habitats on soil, stones, tree trunks and decaying wood. The large dorsal "leaves" are commonly two-lobed, but in some species may also be entire or fringed.
HARPANTHACEAE, about 200 species.

**Lophophora** [PEYOTE, DUMPLING CACTUS, MESCAL BUTTON] a genus of dwarf, top-shaped, soft-bodied, gray, spineless cacti perhaps consisting of a single species, *L. williamsii*, from South Texas to North Mexico, although a second species, *L. diffusa*, from central Mexico, is recognized by some authorities. *L. williamsii* is the sacred cactus of Mexico and has achieved fame and notoriety for its hallucinogenic alkaloids (notably mescaline), used by Mexican Indians for over 2 000 years (as peyote or peyotl) in rituals. A ban was imposed on its cultivation in certain states in the USA and elsewhere when the scare over LSD plants was at its height.
CACTACEAE, 1–2 species.

**Loranthus** a large genus of woody parasites of the Old World tropics with a few in Eurasia and Australia. They usually parasitize trees by means of suckers, which are modified adventitious roots. One species, *L. europaeus*, is sometimes deliberately cultivated by growing it on **Castanea* or **Quercus*. It produces terminal racemes of yellowish-green flowers.
LORANTHACEAE, about 600 species.

**Lotus** a term embracing two entirely separate groups of plants. The genus *Lotus* belongs to the family Leguminosae, while LOTUS is also the popular name for the genus *Nelumbo* (Nymphaeaceae) (see *Nelumbo*). *Lotus* [BIRD'S FOOT TREFOILS] is a genus of annual and perennial herbs and some subshrubs, native mainly to North America, Australia, temperate Asia and Africa, and the Mediterranean region. Perhaps the best-known species is the Eurasian *L. corniculatus* [BIRD'S FOOT TREFOIL], a more or less spreading hairless perennial with yellow pea-like flowers streaked with red. It is widely found in European meadows and pastures and is grown there and in North America as a forage crop. *L. tenuis* [SLENDER BIRD'S FOOT TREFOIL] is similar but the stems are more wiry, slender and more profusely branched than *L. corniculatus*.

Species cultivated as ornamentals include *L. berthelotii* [PARROT'S BEAK, WINGED PEA, CORAL GEM], a silvery, scarlet-flowered shrub from the Cape Verde and Canary Islands, and *L. creticus* [SOUTHERN BIRD'S FOOT TREFOIL], a yellow-flowered perennial from the Mediterranean region. The European WINGED PEA formerly known as *L. tetragonolobus* is now placed in *Tetragonolobus* as *T. purpureus*.
LEGUMINOSAE, about 60 species.

*A field of irrigated Lucerne or Alfafa (*Medicago sativa*) being mown on a new agricultural development in Saudi Arabia. It is used as a forage crop.*

**Lovage** or **lovage angelica** the common names for *Levisticum officinale*, a tall perennial herb native to southern Europe and cultivated for its aromatic fruits and nuts which are the source of an oil used in flavoring. The stems may be eaten after blanching, like celery, and were once candied, like those of **Angelica*. SCOTCH LOVAGE is **Ligusticum scoticum*.
UMBELLIFERAE.

**Lucerne** [ALFALFA] the longest cultivated and the world's most important forage crop, with an ancient origin in southwestern Asia, but now grown from Norway to New Zealand. **Medicago sativa* [COMMON LUCERNE, COMMON ALFALFA] is the most widely grown species. It is a strong-rooted perennial usually persisting for three to five years depending on conditions. The flowers are violet in color and the pods are coiled in tight spirals. *M. falcata* [YELLOW-FLOWERED ALFALFA, SICKLE MEDICK] is a perennial which is very common in many countries, although it only produces one cut per year. It bears yellow flowers and sickle-shaped pods. Some of its forms are drought and cold resistant, and so it has been useful in breeding improved lucernes. *M. arabica* and *M. orbicularia*, both annuals, are sometimes grown as alfalfa.

Both *M. sativa* and *M. falcata* are related to the wild species *M. coerulea*. Hybrids between *M. sativa* and *M. falcata* show intermediate features between the two parents and were at one time ascribed to a specific rank as *M. media* or *M. varia*. Some forms of cultivated alfalfa may well be hybrids of either *M. sativa* or *M. falcata* with *M. glutinosa* or *M. glomerata*. Lucerne produces a good yield of nutritious fodder. This can be grazed, but is often cut for hay, producing a very valuable feed containing some 90% dry matter, about

half of which is digestible dry matter with 12–18% protein. Most of the protein is in the leaves, and haymaking methods should aim to lose as few leaves as possible. A feed with higher protein content can be produced by cutting the young foliage, which is then dried and usually ground into meal.
LEGUMINOSAE.

**Ludwigia** a genus of slender herbs, often floating or creeping, or large shrubs largely restricted to the Old and New World tropics but extending to eastern North America, temperate Eurasia and Hawaii in aquatic or moist habitats. Most species, such as the pantropical weed *L. hyssopifolia*, have been widely distributed as a consequence of human activity. A few species are grown as ornamentals as marsh plants or in aquaria. The stems of *L. repens* are eaten as a vegetable in parts of China.
ONAGRACEAE, about 75 species.

**Luffa** a genus of tropical herbaceous tendril-bearing climbers containing the economically important annual species, *L. aegyptiaca* (= *L. cylindrica*) [SPONGE GOURD, LOOFA], whose large fruit (8–24in long) yields a fibrous skeleton on retting, used for bath sponges. The young fruits of *L. acutangula* [TOWEL or DISH-CLOTH GOURD] are used as a curry vegetable.
CUCURBITACEAE, about 6 species.

**Lunaria** a small herbaceous genus of central and southeast European origin. Two of the species, *L. rediviva* [PERENNIAL HONESTY] and *L. telekiana*, are perennial, and *L. annua* (= *L. biennis*) [HONESTY, BOLBONAC, SILVER DOLLAR, PENNY FLOWER] is a biennial. The white- or purple-flowered *L. annua*, as well as the cultivar 'Variegata', with red flowers and variegated leaves, and the white-flowered *L. rediviva*, are popular garden-border plants. *L. annua* is also grown for its nearly orbicular fruits with a flat, silvery-white, papery septum, which are used as a winter decoration.
CRUCIFERAE, 3 species.

*Ragged Robin or Cuckoo Flower (*Lychnis flos-cuculi*) is a common and attractive inhabitant of damp places.* (×2)

*The cucumber-like fruits of Loofa (*Luffa aegyptiaca*). The familiar loofas used as sponges are the "skeletons" left behind when the fleshy part has been retted away.* (×⅛)

**Lunularia** a genus of thallose liverworts consisting of a single species, *L. cruciata*. Although restricted naturally to warmer and drier climates, especially in the subtropics, this species has been remarkably successful in extending its geographic range by becoming a conspicuous weed in moist greenhouses.
MARCHANTIACEAE, 1 species.

**Lupinus** [LUPINS] a large genus of annual or perennial herbs and some subshrubs mostly concentrated in western North America, but also distributed in other temperate regions, including the Andes and the Mediterranean. Several including *L. polyphyllus*, *L. perennis* [SUNDIAL LUPIN], *L. mutabilis* [PEARL LUPIN], are valuable herbaceous ornamentals. The best-known of the subshrubs is *L. arboreus* [TREE LUPIN]. The renowned lupin hybrids, the RUSSELL LUPINS, are amongst the most spectacular and colorful of all garden plants. They probably arose as hybrids between *L. hartwegii* and *L. polyphyllus*.

The five species cultivated for forage and as a green manure are of Mediterranean origin, with the exception of the South American *L. mutabilis*. *L. albus* [WHITE LUPIN] and *L. mutabilis* have been in cultivation for at least 3000 years. Other commonly cultivated species are *L. angustifolius* [BLUE LUPIN], and *L. luteus* [YELLOW LUPIN]. Although normally poisonous, low-alkaloid forms are now generally available in cultivation, and improved varieties, especially of WHITE LUPINS, are increasingly being recognized as a rich source of oil (12–17%) and protein which may be used both as animal and human food.
LEGUMINOSAE, about 300 species.

**Luzula** [WOODRUSHES] a cosmopolitan genus of tufted grass-like perennials occurring chiefly in cold temperate regions in the Northern Hemisphere. A few species, including *L. albida*, *L. campestris*, *L. sylvatica* and *L. lutea* are cultivated in woodland situations.
JUNCACEAE, about 50 species.

**Lycaste** a genus of tropical American and West Indian pseudobulbous epiphytic or terrestrial orchids. Their appealing flower colors and often strong scents (such as *L. aromatica*) have led to a number of species being culti-

*The green thallus of the liverwort* Lunularia cruciata *bearing disk-shaped gemmae within crescent-shaped gemmae cups.* (×3)

*Almost mature fruiting bodies of the puffball* Lycoperdon perlatum, *showing the warty scars that are the remains of the spines.* (× ⅓)

vated. These include *L. cruenta*, with bright yellow and rich apricot-colored flowers tinged with olive green and flecked with red. The wild white-flowered form of *L. virginalis* [NUN ORCHID] is the national flower of Guatemala; its cultivars have flowers that are white suffused with yellow, rose-white, purple, crimson or maroon.
ORCHIDACEAE, 40–50 species.

**Lychnis** a small genus of erect perennial herbs from north temperate Eurasia. Several species are cultivated, including *L. flos-cuculi* [RAGGED ROBIN, CUCKOO FLOWER] which grows in damp areas. Its cultivars include 'Pleniflora' with its double rose-colored flowers. *L. chalcedonica* [JERUSALEM CROSS], with dense inflorescences of scarlet flowers, has many varieties. Two attractive plants are *L. coronaria* [ROSE CAMPION], which has purplish or occasionally pale or white flowers, and *L. flos-jovis* with purplish or scarlet (rarely white) flowers.
CARYOPHYLLACEAE, 8–12 species.

**Lycium** a genus of temperate and subtropical shrubs from both hemispheres but mainly in America. Useful species include *L. afrum* [KAFFIR THORN], which is grown as a hedge plant in South Africa, and *L. chinense* [CHINESE WOLFBERRY, MATRIMONY VINE or TEA TREE], whose leaves are used as a vegetable. The fruits of a number of species, including those of *L. arabicum* [ARABIAN WOLFBERRY], *L. andersonii* [ANDERSON WOLFBERRY] and *L. pallidum* [RABBIT THORN] are eaten, either raw or cooked, locally in Arabia, Arizona, and Mexico respectively.
SOLANACEAE, about 100 species.

**Lycoperdon** a cosmopolitan genus of gasteromycete fungi which comprises the true puffballs. The powdery spore mass is contained in a sac which opens at maturity by an apical mouth, so that when the elastic sides of the sac are struck by a raindrop a puff of spores emerges. The fruiting bodies of *L. fuligineum* and *L. gemmatum* are eaten in tropical Asia and the USA respectively.
LYCOPERDACEAE, about 50 species.

**Lycopersicon** see TOMATO.
SOLANACEAE, about 7 species.

**Lycopodium** [CLUB MOSSES] a genus of herbaceous prostrate creeping or erect perennial fern-allies widespread in temperate and tropical regions. The spores of *L. clavatum* [STAG'S-HORN MOSS, COMMON CLUB MOSS] are used as a dusting powder and for coating pills. (See Club mosses and their allies, p. 94.)
LYCOPODIACEAE, about 450 species.

**Lygeum** a genus comprising a single species, *L. spartum* (see ESPARTO).
GRAMINEAE, 1 species.

**Lygodium** a small tropical and subtropical genus of ferns which possess leaves with a twining habit. The sporangia lie singly in double rows on fertile leaflets and are not organized into sori. The stems of the tropical *L. scandens* are used for making hats and the stems of *L. circinatum*, from the Malayan peninsula, for basketwork. *L. japonicum* is cultivated for ornament.
SCHIZAEACEAE, about 40 species.

**Lyonia** a small genus of evergreen or deciduous shrubs native to North America and Asia, three of which are cultivated as ornamental shrubs, with axillary or terminal clusters of pink or white flowers. The early-flowering evergreen *L. lucida* [TETTERBUSH] and the deciduous *L. mariana* [STAGGERBUSH] grow to a height of about 6.5ft, while the deciduous *L. ligustrina* [MALE BERRY] may reach 13ft.
ERICACEAE, about 30 species.

*The Yellow Loosestrife or Garden Loosestrife (*Lysimachia vulgaris*), an attractive waterside perennial, native to Europe but now also naturalized in North America. It is also cultivated as an ornamental in gardens.* (× ½)

*The tall purple inflorescences of the Purple Loosestrife or Spiked Loosestrife (*Lythrum salicaria*) are a familiar sight along river banks and the edges of lakes. A number of ornamental cultivars and varieties are now in cultivation.* (× $\frac{1}{10}$)

**Lysichiton** a small genus of two robust perennial stemless herbs which are cultivated in wet soil for their large ovate leaves and arum-like inflorescences. *L. americanum* [SKUNK CABBAGE] is native to western North America and bears leaves up to 5.7ft long and an inflorescence enclosed by a bright yellow spathe. The other species, *L. camtschatcense* from East Asia, is similar but somewhat smaller with a white spathe. The latter is sometimes included in *L. americanum*.
ARACEAE, 2 species.

**Lysimachia** a large genus of erect or creeping herbaceous perennials, widespread in temperate and subtropical regions, especially East Asia and North America. *L. nummularia* [CREEPING JENNY, MONEYWORT] is an excellent trailing ground cover plant with cup-shaped yellow flowers. *L. vulgaris* [YELLOW LOOSESTRIFE] is a tall, 28–32in, waterside perennial. Cultivated species include *L. clethroides* [GOOSENECK], with white-flowered spikes, and *L. ephemerum*, with white- or purple-flowered spikes. Various species, including *L. nemorum* [YELLOW or WOOD PIMPERNEL] were formerly used in healing wounds.
PRIMULACEAE, about 200 species.

**Lythrum** a small genus of annual and perennial herbs and small shrubs, usually found in damp places. *Lythrum* is centered round the Mediterranean and in western Asia, but extends into North America and East Asia, and is found in Australia and New Zealand. *L. salicaria* [PURPLE LOOSESTRIFE] is a common plant of reed-swamps with tall spikes of crinkly-petaled purple flowers. Although in nature living by water, it grows well in gardens and there are several cultivars, such as 'Roseum Superbum' with pink flowers. *L. virgatum* is a more slender species and also contains several cultivars with purple, pink or rose-pink flowers. *L. flexuosum* is a small trailing pink-flowered species sometimes grown in baskets.
LYTHRACEAE, 30–35 species.

**Macadamia** or **Australia nut** the seeds of two small ornamental evergreen trees, *Macadamia integrifolia* (= *M. ternifolia* of some authors) ["SMOOTH SHELL MACADAMIA"] and *M. tetraphylla* ["ROUGH SHELL MACADAMIA"]. The oily seeds which are expensive and highly prized are grown commercially mainly in Australia (New South Wales, Queensland), where they are endemic, and in California (USA) and Hawaii. They are eaten raw, roasted or fried.

A third species, *M. ternifolia* [MAROOCHY NUT], bears small bitter fruits which are inedible. Naturally occurring interspecific hybrids occur and several high-yielding cultivars are characterized also by their large kernels.
PROTEACEAE.

**Macassar oil** an oil obtained from the seeds of *Schleichera oleosa* (= *S. trijuga, S. trijugata*) [LAC TREE], a tree native to Southeast Asia. The oil is used in making ointments and candles, as an illuminant and as a hair-dressing.
SAPINDACEAE.

**Mace** the dried orange to scarlet aril of **Myristica fragrans* [*NUTMEG], from the Moluccas and widely cultivated in the tropics. This spice is used ground or whole to flavor meat, fish, cheese and vegetable dishes.
MYRISTICACEAE.

**Macleaya** a genus of two large, glaucous, stately perennials up to 8ft tall, native to China and Japan. *M. cordata* [PLUME POPPY, TREE CELANDINE] has palmately lobed leaves up to 1.2in wide and large showy panicles, up to 12in long, of creamy or pink petal-less feathery flowers. Both it and *M. microcarpa*, with yellowish flowers, are cultivated in temperate gardens.
PAPAVERACEAE, 2 species.

**Maclura** see OSAGE ORANGE.
MORACEAE, 1 species.

**Macrocystis** a genus of brown algae commonly known as GIANT KELPS and often growing to a length of 100–160ft. It is found mainly in the Southern Hemisphere but extends into the northern Pacific Ocean along the west coast of America. A sturdy holdfast attaches the plant to the bottom of the sea in water of up to 100ft in depth. *Macrocystis* is important for production of alginates, plants being cut and collected from the kelp beds by special harvesting boats.
PHAEOPHYCEAE.

**Macrozamia** a genus of cycads inhabiting temperate regions of Australia. Some species, including *M. plumosa, M. miquelii, M. communis* and *M. lucida* are cultivated as greenhouse ornamentals. *M. hopei*, a native of Queensland, and sometimes placed in the genus *Lepidozamia*, is reputed to be the tallest of the cycads growing to about 65ft.
ZAMIACEAE, about 14 species.

*Many white-flowered magnolias are in cultivation. Shown here is the magnificent* Magnolia kobus, *from Japan.* (× $\frac{1}{40}$)

*The outstanding pink flowers of* Magnolia campbellii *spp* mollicomata *produce a magnificent display in early spring.* (× $\frac{1}{3}$)

**Madagascar rubber** a type of *rubber obtained from the latex of a number of species of trees, shrubs and vines native to Madagascar. They include species of the genera **Landolphia, *Marsdenia* and *Cryptostegia*. The latex is inferior in quality and yield to that of **Hevea brasiliensis*, and Madagascar rubber is no longer commercially important. (See also RUBBER PLANTS.)

**Madder** the common name for **Rubia tinctoria* and also for the red dye, alizarin, once obtained from its roots. The name is also given to other members of this genus, including *R. peregrina* [WILD MADDER, LEVANT MADDER], *R. cordifolia* [INDIAN MADDER], and to *Sherardia arvensis* [FIELD MADDER].
RUBIACEAE.

**Madia** a genus of annual, biennial or perennial Pacific American herbs which are usually glandular, strongly scented and hairy. The best-known is *M. sativa* [TARWEED], native to Chile and the west coast of North America but cultivated in many countries for the seeds which yield the sweet, edible madia oil.
COMPOSITAE, about 20 species.

**Magnolia** a genus of evergreen and deciduous trees or shrubs, native to Asia from the Himalayas to Japan and Java, and to North and Central America and Venezuela. They provide some of the most popular ornamentals, being unsurpassed in beauty when in full bloom. The solitary, showy flowers are usually large and star- or bowl-shaped, in a range of colors, with white, cream and rose predominant. The flower parts are arranged on the central axis with an outer perianth of two or more whorls of petaloid tepals, subtending numerous free, spirally arranged stamens with stout filaments. There are numerous spirally arranged carpels which are fused into a cone. The red or orange seeds are large, suspended when mature by a single thread-like attachment.

The ever-increasing popularity of magnolias as garden subjects is due mainly to the striking beauty of such deciduous precocious-flowering species as *M. acuminata* [CUCUMBER TREE], whose numerous cultivars include 'Cordata' (= *M. cordata*) [YELLOW CUCUMBER TREE] and 'Aurea', *M. campbellii* with such cultivars as the rose-purple-flowered 'Darjeeling' and the white-flowered 'Maharanee', *M. dawsoniana*, *M. heptapeta* (= *M. conspicua*, *M. denudata*) [YULAN], the white-to-pink-flowered *M. kobus*, the large-leaved, white-flowered, fragrant *M. macrophylla* [LARGE-LEAVED CUCUMBER TREE, GREAT-LEAVED MAGNOLIA], *M. quinquepeta* (= *M. discolor*, *M. liliiflora*, *M. purpurea*), *M. salicifolia*, *M. sargentiana*, with very large showy rose-purple flowers in the shrubby var *robusta*, *M. sieboldii* (= *M. parviflora*), *M. stellata* (= *M. halleana*) [STAR MAGNOLIA], of compact habit with many showy flowers as in cultivars 'Rosea' and 'Rubra', *M. tripetala* [UMBRELLA MAGNOLIA] and *M. virginiana* (= *M. glauca*) [SWEET BAY] which is evergreen in mild areas. Other evergreens include *M. delavayi* and *M. grandiflora* [BULL BAY, SOUTHERN MAGNOLIA].

Hybrids are now being cultivated in increasing numbers. Some have arisen spontaneously by accident, others by deliberate cross-fertilization. The most frequently grown hybrid is *M.* × *soulangiana* (= *M. heptapeta* × *M. quinquepeta*) [CHINESE MAGNOLIA, SAUCER MAGNOLIA], a small tree with numerous cultivars including 'Alba Superba' with large white flowers, 'Candolleana' with flowers tinged purple at the base and 'Lennei' with very large saucer-shaped flowers, white inside and purple on the outside.

Many authorities consider that the floral, vegetative and anatomical features of the genus are relatively unspecialized, and accordingly species of *Magnolia* could be regarded as some of the most primitive living examples of flowering plants.
MAGNOLIACEAE, about 85 species.

**Mahogany** a commercially important timber which is valued for its reddish-brown color, luster, strength and figuring. Over 200 types of wood are traded under the name, but true mahoganies are restricted to the tropical American and West Indian genus *Swietenia* and the African genus **Khaya*. *S. mahagoni* [TRUE, CUBAN OR WEST INDIES MAHOGANY] was the original source of commercial mahogany but has now been largely replaced by *S. macrophylla* [HONDURAS, MEXICAN OR BIG LEAVED MAHOGANY], although *S. candollea* [VENEZUELAN MAHOGANY] is also a source of timber.

Of the AFRICAN MAHOGANIES, the best-known are *Khaya nyasica* [RED OR NYASALAND MAHOGANY], *K. senegalensis* [SENEGAL MAHOGANY], *K. ivorensis* [IVORY COAST MAHOGANY] and *K. grandiflora*. The timbers vary in weight, color and figuring. The color of the wood varies with the species and also changes with age. The timber of *K. grandiflora* is pale at first and then darkens to a deep brown, while *S. macrophylla* becomes paler.

Other genera containing species whose wood often goes under the name of mahogany include **Cedrela*, **Dysoxylum*, **Guarea*, **Melia*, *Entandrophragma* and **Ptaeroxylon obliquum* [CAPE MAHOGANY].

Macrozamia riedleri, *one of some 14 species of this Australian genus of cycads, showing the typical palm-like form of the class.*

*The glossy spiny, divided leaves and clusters of bright yellow flowers make mahonias attractive ornamentals. Shown here is* Mahonia *'Charity'.* ($\times \frac{1}{15}$)

**Mahonia** a genus of evergreen shrubs and trees native to Asia, from the Himalayas to Japan and Sumatra, and to North and Central America. The leaves are odd-pinnate, usually with spiny-toothed leaflets. Ornamental species include *M. bealei* and *M. japonica* (often confused in cultivation), and *M. aquifolium* [OREGON GRAPE], with bright yellow flowers in crowded racemes in spring, standing out against the shining dark foliage, followed by black berries. *M. lomariifolia*, with fragrant deep-yellow flowers in erect dense racemes up to 12in long, is sometimes grown.
BERBERIDACEAE, about 100 species.

**Maianthemum** a small genus of low perennial herbs, native to north temperate regions, bearing very small white flowers followed by

Pounding maize (Zea mays) into flour in an African village. Maize is a staple food in Africa and widely used throughout the world as animal feed.

brown or red berries in a terminal raceme. *M. bifolium* [MAY LILY] occurs extensively in Europe and parts of Asia in shady woodland habitats and, like the North American *M. canadense* [FALSE LILY OF THE VALLEY], is sometimes cultivated for ornament.
LILIACEAE, 2–3 species.

**Maidenhair tree** the common name for *Ginkgo biloba*, a tall deciduous tree sacred to the Buddhist religion and cultivated for many centuries in both China and Japan, especially in the grounds of temples. It also probably occurs in the truly wild state in eastern China. Within the last 200 years the tree has been planted widely and has been grown successfully under many different conditions of soil and climate. It is also remarkably free of disease and resistant to pests. The mature seed has a soft outer fleshy layer which has the unpleasant odor of rancid butter. Male trees are usually preferred for avenue planting. (See also p. 914.)
GINKGOACEAE, 1 species.

**Maize or corn** the common names for *Zea mays*, one of the most important cereal crops in the world. It is the only cereal of American origin and it formed the staple diet of the American Indians [INDIAN CORN]. The USA produces nearly 50% of the world's maize but the crop is now grown widely in southeast Europe, Brazil, Argentina, Mexico, Africa and Indonesia. In some areas of Asia and Africa it forms the major part of the diet. There is evidence from pollen samples that maize and the closely related annual *Euchlaena mexicana* (= *Z. mexicana*) [TEOSINTE], or their possible common ancestor, were in existence 60 000 to 80 000 years ago in Mexico.

The grain is an important animal feed, particularly for poultry and pigs. For industrial purposes, maize is used in starch manufacture and for whisky distilling. Maize is also an important forage crop and is favored as a silage crop particularly in dry areas where grass growth may be poor. SWEET CORN, used for eating as "CORN ON THE COB", is a form of maize, var *rugosa*, in which the change of sugars to starch in the kernel is reduced, so keeping the grain sweeter and more tender. Other cultivars of maize belong to such varieties as *indurata* [FLINT CORN], in which the grain is hard and smooth, and *indentata* [DENT CORN], the principal commercial corn cultivated for grain fodder and silage.

Recent developments include the northward spread of maize for grain production into northwestern Europe, even as far as southeast England (51°N) and also into southern Ontario in Canada. This trend has followed the breeding of early hybrids that not only mature in short growing seasons but are tolerant of cold spring conditions and resistant to stalk-rot caused by **Fusarium* species in the autumn. Breeding can also improve the protein content in maize grain, thus producing a more balanced food for livestock and Man. There is also a modern tendency to breed from plants which produce more numerous small cobs with an overall increase in yield.
GRAMINEAE.

**Malacca cane** the stems of some species of **Calamus* [*RATTAN PALMS], notably *C. scipionum* and *C. bacularis*. Some species of *Licuala* are additional sources. The stems of these plants are used for walking sticks and for making baskets.
PALMAE.

**Mallow** the common name for several species, mainly of the genera **Malva* and **Abutilon*, such as *M. sylvestris* [COMMON EUROPEAN MALLOW], *M. crispa* [CURLED MALLOW] and *A. indicum* [INDIAN MALLOW]. The name is also used for species of other genera including **Althaea officinalis* [MARSH MALLOW], **Lavatera maritima* [SEA MALLOW] and others.
MALVACEAE.

The Common European Mallow (Malva sylvestris) brings its bright color to hedgerows and waste places in early summer. (× $\frac{1}{2}$)

*Young maize crop (*Zea mays*) in Wisconsin, USA. Half of the world's maize is grown in the United States and most of this is used as animal feed or as a forage crop.*

**Malope** a genus of colorful annual herbs native to the Mediterranean region. Horticultural forms of *M. malacoides* and *M. trifida* are cultivated for their showy, mallow-like rose, pink, purple or white flowers.
MALVACEAE, 3–4 species.

**Malpighia** a tropical American and West Indian genus of evergreen trees and shrubs. Cultivated ornamental species include shrubs such as *M. coccigera* [SINGAPORE HOLLY], a small evergreen shrub with holly-like leaves and red fruits, and *M. glabra*, which has small pink or purple flowers and edible fruits with a high vitamin C content, resembling cherries but of poor flavor in comparison. The fruits of *M. punicifolia* [WEST INDIAN CHERRY] are of better quality and are used in preserves and sauces. The BARBADOS CHERRY, often referred to *M. glabra*, is probably a hybrid between this species and *M. punicifolia*.
MALPIGHACEAE, about 35 species.

**Malus** a genus of deciduous fruit-bearing trees and shrubs, some of which are known as crab apples. The genus also includes the many varieties of edible apples. (See APPLE and CRAB APPLE.)
ROSACEAE, about 35 species.

**Malva** [MALLOWS] a genus of annual, biennial or perennial herbs native to southern Europe, temperate Asia and North Africa. Most species are weedy and not cultivated. *M. sylvestris* [COMMON MALLOW] is common on roadsides and waste places; *M. moschata* [MUSK MALLOW], with attractive pink flowers and deeply divided leaves, and *M. alcea* are two of the species cultivated in herbaceous borders.
MALVACEAE, about 40 species.

**Mammee** the common name for *Mammea americana* [also known as MAMMEE APPLE, MAMEY, ST. DOMINGO APRICOT], a small tree native to the West Indies and widely cultivated in the Caribbean and Central and South America. It bears large, leathery, showy leaves, white, scented flowers and a globose, russet-colored fruit about the size of an orange. The tough rind encloses a sweet, scented, yellow, edible flesh. An aromatic liqueur (eau de creole) is distilled from the flowers in parts of the West Indies, while the fine-grained timber is valued for its use in cabinet-making.
GUTTIFERAE.

**Mammillaria** a large genus of cacti from Mexico and the southwestern USA, with a few species in the West Indies and northern South America. Most are dwarf, round or cylindrical stem succulents with spirally arranged tubercles tipped with the spine-bearing areole. The flowers are small but profusely borne in rings around the tops of the stems. They are followed by elongated red berries, often persistent.

*Mammillaria* is the most popular cactus genus in cultivation. The compact plants are ideal subjects for a specialist collection, taking up little space. Thus, *M. magnimamma* (= *M. centricirrha*), from Mexico, is almost hardy, pest-free and some would say indestructible, demanding a larger pot each year and eventually forming massive clumps. At the other extreme, *M. goldii* and *M. saboae* are at home in a 2in pot although their blooms are larger than those of *M. magnimamma*.

*M. hahniana* [FEATHER CACTUS] and *M. plumosa* [OLD LADY CACTUS] look as if covered in white wool; in *M. candida* [SNOWBALL PINCUSHION] the whiter-than-white effect is due to the presence of multitudinous densely packed white spines. *M. spinosissima* is also heavily armed with spines which range in color from white through yellow to ruby red. The flowers are bright carmine. Hooked central spines are a feature of *M. magnifica*, where they are long and pale brown, and of *M. bombycina*, where the dark central spines contrast with the white radial spines and axillary wool. *M. deherdtiana*, *M. dodsonii* and *M. theresae* can be recommended for collectors who require tiny plants with comparatively large flowers.

The small but plentiful red fruits of *Mammillaria* are edible and are called chilitos.
CACTACEAE, about 220 species.

**Mandarin** or **mandarin orange** the collective name for the small, loose-skinned, orange-colored citrus fruits which are steadily gaining in popularity because of their easy-peeling properties. All mandarin oranges are generally regarded as belonging to a single species, **Citrus reticulata*, but there are many types and hybrids. Important varieties include SATSUMAS, TANGERINES and CLEMENTINES. Mandarin hybrids include *TANGELO and *UGLI (both crosses with *GRAPEFRUIT) and ORTANIQUE, a cross with SWEET *ORANGE. *C.* × *nobilis* (*C. reticulata* × *C. sinensis*) cultivar 'King' is the KING MANDARIN.
RUTACEAE.

Mammillaria prolifera *(=* M. pusilla*) produces abundant yellow flowers and red berries.* ($\times \frac{1}{2}$)

**Mandevilla** a Central and tropical South American genus of tall climbing shrubs with racemes of large, showy, white, yellow or violet, funnel-shaped flowers expanding into five lobes. They are often cultivated in warm greenhouses in temperate regions. Popular species and hybrids include *M.* × *amabilis* (= *Dipladenia* × *amabilis*) (rose-colored flowers), *M. boliviensis* (= *D. boliviensis*) (white flowers with yellow throat), *M. sanderi* (= *D. sanderi*) (rose-pink flowers), and *M. laxa* (= *M. suavolens*) [CHILEAN JASMINE].
APOCYNACEAE, about 100 species.

**Mandrake** the common name for members of the genus *Mandragora*. All are herbs with narcotic or other medicinal properties and are native to the Mediterranean region. They have large fleshy roots and large bell-shaped flowers which are pale blue-violet, white or purple. Mandrakes have long had mythical associations with witchcraft and sorcery. Under the "doctrine of signatures" their root system was held to resemble the human form, and legend relates that anyone pulling up a mandrake will be driven mad by a terrible shriek coming from the root. *M. officinarum* and *M. autumnalis* both contain alkaloids that are pharmacologically useful.
SOLANACEAE, about 6 species.

**Manettia** a genus of evergreen twining shrubs and herbs, native to Central and tropical South America and the West Indies. Some of the species are grown as decorative ornamental plants in the greenhouse or in sheltered areas in warm temperate regions. One of the most widely cultivated species is the small twining shrub *M. inflata* (= *M. bicolor*), from Uruguay and Paraguay, which has tubular, reddish flowers, yellow at the tip where the lobes are expanded. *M. cordifolia* [FIRECRACKER VINE], a herbaceous vine, is also cultivated.
RUBIACEAE, about 130 species.

**Mangel-wurzel, mangold** or **field beet** the common names for a variety of **Beta vulgaris* which is cultivated for its swollen roots used as an important animal feed.
CHENOPODIACEAE.

**Mangifera** is a genus of tall evergreen trees from Southeast Asia, with the greatest concentration in the Malayan peninsula. Several species yield edible fruit but the most important by far is *M. indica* [MANGO] which is cultivated throughout the tropics, especially in India, where it is known wild in the northeastern part.

The celebrated fruit is a very variable fleshy, ovoid drupe 3–12in long, sometimes with a beak at the proximal end, usually yellow or green at first and becoming reddish when ripe. The outer skin is thick and glandular, enclosing the orange or yellow flesh which varies from soft, sweet and juicy to somewhat fibrous and coarse. The ripe fruits are eaten raw, or canned or used in the manufacture of juices, squashes and jellies. Other mangoes are pickled for use in chutneys or curries. The fruits are also sliced, dried and seasoned with turmeric to produce "amchur", which is ground to a powder and added to soups, chutneys and curries. The kernels are removed from the stones and dried, roasted and eaten, or ground to produce a flour.

The leaves of *M. indica* provide a yellow dye and are also used as cattle fodder. The bark yields a tannin and the timber is used in shipbuilding.
ANACARDIACEAE, about 40 species.

**Mangosteen** the highly esteemed fruit of **Garcinia mangostana*, a Southeast Asian village tree fruit rarely grown elsewhere in the tropics. The fruit is depressed-globose in shape and about 2in across. Inside the thick, leathery, purple-brown pericarp lie a number of edible fleshy white segments, each enclosing a small seed.
GUTTIFERAE.

**Mangrove bark** the source of an important tanning material. All species of the mangrove genus **Rhizophora* contain tannin, and *R. mangle* [RED MANGROVE] and *R. mucronata*, both native to the coastal zones of the tropics, are the best sources. Most commercial supplies come from East Africa and Central and South America, yielding up to 40% tannin from the dried bark. Other mangrove genera whose bark yields quantities of tannin include *Avicennia*, especially *A. officinalis* [WHITE MANGROVE], *Ceriops*, especially *C. can-*

*A Mangrove (*Avicennia marina*), colonizing the mud of a rocky shore on the coast of southeastern Australia, showing the aerial roots.*

*The thallose liverwort* Marchantia polymorpha *is a common weed, particularly in soil disturbed by Man and by fire.* (×3)

*dollaeanum*, and *Kandelia*, especially *K. rheedei*. (See also p. 891.)
RHIZOPHORACEAE.

**Manihot** a genus of shrubs and trees, all of which are native to subtropical and tropical areas, distributed from the southern USA through Central and South America as far as central Argentina. A number of shrubs and trees, including *M. glaziovii* and *M. dichotoma*, which are endemic to Brazil, contain latex in the stems and large fleshy roots which yield a high-quality *rubber (ceara and jequie rubber, respectively). Ceara rubber is grown commercially in Sri Lanka, India and other tropical countries. However, the trees are not as resilient as **Hevea brasiliensis* to continual tapping of the bark.

*M. carthaginensis* is a shrub, found from Mexico to Venezuela, with edible roots, and seeds which contain an oil with emetic and purgative properties. *M. dulcis* has sweet roots which are used as a vegetable in Brazil but the most important species commercially is *M. esculenta* (= *M. utilissima*) [see CASSAVA], which can produce more starch per hectare in a year than almost any other crop. The roots form an important staple food in many parts of Africa, India and South America, as well as providing a source of starch for many commercial purposes, for example in the paper and textile industries.

Plant breeders have successfully crossed *M. saxicola*, *M. dichotoma*, *M. melanobasis* and *M. glazovii* with *M. esculenta*, with the aim of producing cassava hybrids resistant to various virus, bacterial and fungal pathogens.
EUPHORBIACEAE, 98 or 128 species.

**Manilkara** (= *Achras*) a genus of evergreen trees native to tropical America and the West Indies. *M. zapota* [SAPODILLA, MARMALADE PLUM, BEEF APPLE, NASEBERRY, NISPERO, CHIKU] is cultivated throughout the tropics for its edible fruit which is pear-shaped or spherical, 2–4in in diameter, with a thin, rough, rusty-brown skin and translucent brownish pulp containing several hard black seeds. Fully mature sapodillas are extremely sweet and are considered by some to be among the finest of dessert fruits. The trunk of the tree yields a latex, *chicle, the original main ingredient of chewing gum. *M. bidentata* is the main source of nonelastic rubber, *balata. The timber is hard, durable and commercially valuable.
SAPOTACEAE, about 85 species.

**Manna** a general term referring to plant exudates, usually sugary, which harden when dry and can be collected and eaten. Three types of manna are mentioned in the Bible. One has been tentatively identified as a sweet, gummy exudate from species of the genera **Tamarix* or *Alhagi*, while it has been suggested that the types that appeared on the damp ground and were sent from heaven may have been species of algae (**Nostoc*) or lichen (*Lecanora*). Manna from **Fraxinus ornus* [MANNA ASH] is commercially collected in Sicily.

**Manzanilla** a name applied in Spain to a number of aromatic composite herbs and to the infusion made from their flower heads, especially **Matricaria aurea* (= **Chamomilla aurea*), *M. chamomilla* (= *Chamomilla recutita*) and **Chamaemelum nobile* [ROMAN CHAMOMILE]. Highly prized is **Artemisia granatensis* [MANZANILLA REAL], from the Sierra Nevada of Spain, which is greatly endangered through overcollection.

MANZANILLA is also the common name of several Central and North American **Crataegus* species such as *C. stipulosa* and *C. mexicana*, whose fruits are used as preserves or jellies. The name MANZANILLA means little apple and refers to the fruits.

**Maranta** a genus of herbaceous perennials native to tropical America. Some species such as *M. arundinacea* [ARROWROOT] are rhizomatous, while others such as *M. bicolor* are tuberous. The former produces erect branching leafy stems, while the latter and some other species, eg *M. leuconeura* [PRAYER PLANT] and varieties such as *kerchoviana*, grown as ornamentals for their attractive marked foliage, are nearly stemless.

*M. arundinacea* is found wild in Brazil, northern South America and Central America. It is cultivated in the tropics of the Old and New Worlds (with the main center of production in the Caribbean, especially St. Vincent) for the starch contained in its large fleshy rhizome (see ARROWROOT).
MARANTACEAE, about 25 species.

**Maraschino cherry** the cultivated fruit of and common name for **Prunus cerasus* cultivar 'Marasca'. It is used in canning and for desserts and jam as well as being the base of cherry brandy and the Italian liqueur maraschino.
ROSACEAE.

**Marattia** a genus of mainly tropical ferns with stout stems and pinnate leaves. Species cultivated for ornament include *M. alata* and *M. salicifolia*. The stem pith of *M. fraxinea* [KING FERN] was a source of starch for the New Zealand Maoris.
MARATTIACEAE, about 60 species.

**Marchantia** a very widely distributed genus of liverworts. The most common, *M. polymorpha*, is a cosmopolitan weed that extends from the tropics to the arctic regions. It is especially prevalent in areas that have been disturbed by the activities of Man, particularly by fire. It can be a pernicious weed in greenhouses because of the rapidity with which it covers soil.
MARCHANTIACEAE, about 50 species.

**Marigold** the name given to **Calendula officinalis* (also called COMMON or POT MARIGOLD), a hardy erect annual which is cultivated in many varieties. AFRICAN and FRENCH MARIGOLDS belong to the genus **Tagetes*; the BUR MARIGOLD is **Bidens tripartita*; **Chrysanthemum segetum* is the CORN MARIGOLD; **Dimorphotheca* species are the CAPE MARIGOLDS; and *Baileya multiradiata* is the DESERT MARIGOLD. All of the above mentioned belong to

*Manioc or Cassava (*Manihot esculenta*) under cultivation in a recently cleared plot at Rio Casiquiare, southern Venezuela.*

the Compositae. However, **Caltha palustris* (MARSH MARIGOLD) is a member of the Ranunculaceae.

*Pot Marjoram (*Origanum vulgare*) used in flavoring meats, stews and stuffings and for bouquets garnis.* (× ⅓)

**Marjoram** the name given to some species of culinary herbs in the genus **Origanum*. *O. majorana* (= *Majorana hortensis*) [SWEET MARJORAM], from southern Europe, is cultivated for the leaves which are used to flavor meat dishes. Oil of marjoram, obtained by steam distillation, is used for the same purposes. *O. vulgare* [POT MARJORAM] yields a similar but not so sweet flavoring.
LABIATAE.

**Marram grass** the common name for **Ammophila arenaria* (= *A. arundinacea*), a widespread perennial grass, abundant and often dominant along the coasts of Western Europe, and introduced to North America and Australia as a sand binder.
GRAMINEAE.

**Marrows and squashes** see p. 222.

**Marrubium** a genus of herbaceous perennials native to Eurasia and the Mediterranean region. *M. vulgare* [HOREHOUND] was once popular for home remedies. The leaves and young shoots were used in syrups and teas to counteract sore throats and colds. Essential oils from the leaves are used in liqueurs. *M. incanum*, with white-woolly leaves and stems and whitish flowers, is sometimes cultivated.
LABIATAE, about 40 species.

**Marsdenia** a small genus of tropical and subtropical African or Asian shrubs with small flowers usually in panicles or umbellate inflorescences. *M. roylei*, with yellow flowers, is one of several species sometimes grown for ornament, usually under glass. Some species, especially *M. tenacissima*, from the lower Himalayas and Bengal are a source of fiber and latex.
ASCLEPIADACEAE, about 70–100 species.

**Marsilea** [WATER CLOVERS] a genus of tropical and temperate aquatic or marsh ferns. The leaves and branches arise from a slender creeping rhizome. Individuals of a single species may be either aquatic or amphibious. In the former, the leaf-stalks are long, flexible and weak with the four leaf-lobes floating on the surface of the water. In the amphibious forms the leaf-stalks are shorter and thicker and stand erect. Some species vegetate during the dry season but others (eg *M. vestita*), which grow in areas with a distinct dry season, die down and persist in the form of bean-shaped sporocarps. Species cultivated in pools, aquaria etc include *M. drummondii* and *M. quadrifolia*.
MARSILEACEAE, about 60 species.

**Martynia** a genus represented by a single species, *M. annua*, a herb native to Mexico. The best-known "martynia", *M. proboscidea*, from southern North America to tropical America, is now referred to the genus *Proboscidea* as *P. louisianica*, commonly called the RAM'S HORN or UNICORN PLANT on account of its horned fruit. It is sometimes cultivated as an oddity, or for the young fruits which are used as pickles.
MARTYNIACEAE, 1 species.

**Masdevallia** a large genus of tropical American epiphytic or terrestrial orchids found growing mainly at high altitudes. The plants are without pseudobulbs, and the thick, sometimes succulent leaves grow in tufts usually evenly spaced along a creeping rhizome. The inflorescences are erect and bear up to 12 flowers. They are frequently grown for the bizarre somewhat funnel-shaped flowers, some of which have a "shot-silk" look. *M. chimaera* and *M. coccinea*, with various cultivars, are among the most popular species.
ORCHIDACEAE, about 300 species.

*Marsilea, the Water Clovers, are in fact ferns. Shown here is M. mutica with the four leaf lobes floating on the surface; the leaf stalks are attached to a slender creeping rhizome.* (× ¾)

**Mastic** a resin which has two principal uses: as a varnish and as a chewing gum. American mastic is tapped from **Schinus molle* [PEPPER TREE], Bombay mastic from **Pistacia mutica*, and Chios mastic, an ancient resin, obtained from *Pistacia lentiscus*, from the eastern Mediterranean. The Turks chew mastic to sweeten the breath, to aid digestion and to preserve the gums. Indeed, mastic has been used as a temporary stopping for teeth. In Europe it is used as a varnish for coating paint and in lithography.

**Maté** or **yerba de maté** the leaves of **Ilex paraguariensis*, an evergreen tree, cultivated and wild, from South America (Paraguay, Argentina, Brazil), used as a tea in many parts of that continent. It was originally a native drink which was taken up by settlers and has since become widespread and second only to coffee, tea or cocoa. The oven-dried and threshed product is called, in diminishing size of the greenish leaf fragments, maté grosso, maté entrefino and maté fino.
AQUIFOLIACEAE.

**Matricaria** the name formerly used for species of the genus **Chamomilla*.
COMPOSITAE.

**Matteuccia** a genus of large ferns with stout rootstocks, native to temperate regions of the Northern Hemisphere. The leaves are of two forms: the fertile leaves are smaller and less dissected than the sterile bipinnatifid leaves. The most commonly cultivated species is *M. struthiopteris* (= **Onoclea germanica*, *Struthiopteris germanica*) [OSTRICH FERN], with sterile leaves up to 5.7ft long.
ASPIDIACEAE, 3–5 species.

**Matthiola** a genus of gray-pubescent herbs and subshrubs from Europe, southwest Asia and North Africa. The flowers, which may be purple, brown-purple, reddish, bluish, yellow or white, are borne in cylindrical racemes

Melaleuca preissiana *growing at the edge of a dried-out lake in Western Australia.*

and are often scented. The best-known is *M. incana* [GARDEN STOCK, GILLYFLOWER], variants of which are grown as short-lived perennials, biennials [BROMPTON OR IMPERIAL STOCKS] or as annuals [TEN WEEK STOCKS]. An intermediate form [WINTER STOCK] is sown at the same time as TEN WEEK STOCKS but is hardier and blooms later even during cold weather. *M. longipetala* subspecies *bicornis* [NIGHT-SCENTED STOCK] is less showy than the previous species, but its lilac or purple flowers open in the evening and are sweetly scented throughout the night.
CRUCIFERAE, 30–50 species.

**Maxillaria** a genus of pseudobulbous epiphytic and terrestrial orchids occurring from southern Florida throughout Central and tropical South America and the West Indies to Argentina. Many of them are found at high altitudes and can be grown easily in a cool greenhouse. The inflorescences arise from among the leaves and bear one to a few flowers. Varying greatly in size, up to 6in in diameter, the flowers can be either of one color or variously spotted, speckled or blotched in contrasting colors. The tepals are usually long and narrow and the overall effect can be very spider-like, as in *M. arachnites*.
ORCHIDACEAE, about 300–400 species.

**Mealies** a common name for *MAIZE (*Zea mays*). The term is used mainly in South Africa.
GRAMINEAE.

**Meconopsis** a genus of annual, biennial or perennial herbs, one of which, *M. cambrica* [WELSH POPPY], is native to Western Europe, the rest to the Himalayas and the region across to western China. They are popularly known as HIMALAYAN OR TIBETAN POPPIES.

They are handsome garden plants when given rich soil and cool shady conditions. The yellowish or orange-flowered *M. cambrica* is not nearly so demanding. *M. baileyi* [BLUE POPPY] has flowers up to 4in in diameter, sky-blue in color if the conditions are right, otherwise a washy mauve. *M. grandis* bears one or more spectacular dark blue or purple flowers, 5in in diameter, on stout stalks from the axils of the upper leaves. *M. regia* and *M. integrifolia* [YELLOW CHINESE POPPY] produce yellow flowers up to 4.5in in diameter. The winter basal rosette of *M. regia*, often 40in in diameter with silver or golden-haired leaves, is extremely attractive.
PAPAVERACEAE, about 43 species.

**Medicago** a genus of mostly weedy annual or perennial herbs, from Europe, the Mediterranean and South Africa. *M. sativa* [ALFALFA, LUCERNE] is the world's most important forage crop, growing in both temperate and subtropical climates (see LUCERNE).

*M. lupulina* [BLACK MEDICK] is also a highly nutritious fodder plant but in gardens it is regarded as a weed. However, a few species are cultivated in gardens, eg *M. echinus* [CALVARY CLOVER], in which the coiled pods are covered with long interlocking spines like a crown of thorns. It has clusters of small yellow pea-type flowers and leaflets with a reddish spot in the center which in var *variegata* is more prominent.
LEGUMINOSAE, about 50 species.

*Garden Stock (*Matthiola incana*) has dense racemes of heavily scented flowers.* ($\times 1$)

Meconopsis horridula, *one of the brilliant blue Himalayan Poppies; this species is covered with distinctive straw-colored spines.* ($\times \frac{1}{6}$)

**Medicinal and narcotic plants**
see p. 226.

**Medlar** the common name for *Mespilus germanica*, a small spreading tree that is found in southeastern Europe extending eastwards to Central Asia. It is the only species in the genus *Mespilus*. Medlars often persist in cultivation as old, gnarled, but attractive specimens. The brownish apple-shaped fruits are traditionally eaten with wine after frosting or bletting (rotting) has softened the hard fruit tissues. Jellies and preserves can also be made from the fruits.
ROSACEAE.

**Melaleuca** a tropical genus of shrubs and medium-sized evergreen trees from Australia and the Pacific Islands, with one species extending to Indomalaysia. The latter, *M. leucadendron* [CAJUPUT TREE, RIVER TEA TREE], has a thick spongy bark, and its leaves are a source of a green medicinal aromatic oil, cajuput oil, used (mainly locally) as a stimulant and tonic, and in soothing ointments. The tree also produces a very durable red-violet timber, suitable for posts, piles, roofing and shipbuilding. *M. minor* also yields cajuput oil.

Ornamental species include *M. quinquenervia* [PAPERBARK TREE] (often incorrectly called *M. leucadendron* in cultivation) as well as such attractive and graceful shrubs as *M. incana*, with spikes of yellowish-white flowers, and *M. huegelii* [CHENILLE HONEY-MYRTLE], with spikes of creamy-white flowers.
MYRTACEAE, about 100 species.

**Melampsora** a mainly north temperate genus of rust fungi parasitic on angiosperms. The most important species is *M. lini* [FLAX RUST] which has all the stages of its life cycle on *FLAX.
MELAMPSORACEAE, about 80 species.

# Marrows, Squashes, Pumpkins and Gourds

Marrows, *squashes and *pumpkins are the edible fruits of *_Cucurbita pepo, C. mixta, C. moschata_ and _C. maxima_ (family Cucurbitaceae; see p. 465). The application of the common names of these species is very confusing and varies from region to region, and country to country. Cultivars known as pumpkins and others known as winter squashes occur in all four species. In the United States, the cultivars used for pies, stock feed and lanterns are commonly called pumpkins. The name marrow is normally restricted to cultivars of _Cucurbita pepo_ although _C. maxima_ is sometimes known as ORANGE MARROW.

The term *gourd is applied to fruits, usually with hard durable rinds, related to the pumpkins, squashes, *cucumbers and *melons. The yellow-flowered gourds of North America are _Cucurbita pepo_ var _ovifera_ and the MALABAR GOURD is _C. ficifolia_ but the white-flowered and other kinds of gourd belong to *_Lagenaria, Trichosanthes_ and other genera.

They are all trailing or climbing herbs, with tendrils, and with large, alternate, often palmately lobed leaves, and large, usually yellow, unisexual flowers. The fruit is a large berry, known as a pepo, sometimes with a tough rind or "shell". The edible species are all annuals. Marrows, squashes and gourds probably all originated in the New World, mainly around the Mexico–Guatemala border area. They were domesticated in pre-Columbian times by American Indians and were an important part of their diet along with maize and beans, but their detailed history is not known. _C. maxima, C. moschata, C. pepo, C. mixta_ and _C. ficifolia_ are of cultivated origin and do not occur in the wild state. Marrows, squashes and pumpkins are cultivated on a commercial scale in the United States, Soviet Russia and parts of Europe, and they are widely grown on a local scale especially in the tropics. _C. moschata_ and _C. mixta_ are more adapted to tropical conditions than _C. maxima_ and _C. pepo_, which grow best in temperate areas. The young shoots and flowers are eaten (as in marrow flower soup) as well as the fruits, and the seeds (known as pepitos) are highly appreciated when fried and salted. Marrows or vegetable marrows _(C. pepo)_ are divided into "bush" or "trailing" cultivars and are green, whitish-green or striped. Squashes can be divided into summer or winter: summer squashes are fruits of _C. pepo_ which are eaten when immature (from the day of flowering until the rind becomes hard). They occur in a wide range of shapes and types, including 'Summer Crookneck' with bright yellow or orange warty club-like fruits, scallop or pattypan squashes, which have white disc-shaped and ribbed joints, and the cylindrical or globular *courgettes or zucchini which are solid green or striped. Vegetable marrows also come under the heading of summer squashes. Winter squashes are fruits of _C. pepo, C. maxima, C. mixta_ and _C. moschata_ which are eaten when mature or are stored for winter consumption as table vegetables, or for making pies, jam and as feed for livestock. They include the Turban and Chioggia squashes. Winter squashes usually have darker flesh, are less fibrous, contain less water, are higher in sugar and dry matter,

_A wide range of hard-shelled ornamental gourds belonging to_ Cucurbita pepo _var_ ovifera [YELLOW-FLOWERED GOURDS]. _(× ¼)_

## MARROWS, SQUASHES, PUMPKINS AND GOURDS

| Scientific name | Common name |
|---|---|
| *_Cucurbita pepo_ | VEGETABLE MARROW; SUMMER AND AUTUMN PUMPKIN OR SQUASH; BRAZILIAN OR AMERICAN PUMPKIN; CUSTARD MARROW; SCALLOP GOURD; SUMMER CROOKNECK; COURGETTE; ZUCCHINI; VEGETABLE SPAGHETTI; ACORN SQUASH; PATTYPAN SQUASH; COCOZELLE SQUASH; BUSH SQUASH. |
| var _ovifera_ | YELLOW-FLOWERED GOURDS |
| *_Cucurbita maxima_ | AUTUMN AND WINTER SQUASH OR PUMPKIN; TURBAN SQUASH; ORANGE MARROW; BANANA SQUASH; HUBBARD SQUASH; SEA SQUASH; CHIOGGIA SQUASH; OHIO SQUASH. |
| *_Cucurbita mixta_ | WINTER SQUASH; WINTER PUMPKIN; CUSHAW PUMPKIN; SQUASH; SILVER SEED GOURD; TENNESSEE SWEET POTATO. |
| *_Cucurbita moschata_ | PUMPKIN; CANADA PUMPKIN; CROOKNECK, BUTTERNUT OR WINTER SQUASH; NAPLES SQUASH. |
| *_Cucurbita ficifolia_ | MALABAR GOURD, FIG-LEAF GOURD; MALABAR MELON; SIAMESE GOURD. |
| *_Cucurbita foetidissima_ | MISSOURI GOURD; CALABAZILLA; FETID WILD PUMPKIN. |
| *_Citrullus lanatus (Citrullus vulgaris, Colòcynthis citrullus)_ | WATER MELON; CITRON; PRESERVING MELON. |
| *_Citrullus colocynthis_ | COLOCYNTH |
| *_Cucumis anguria_ | WEST INDIAN GHERKIN; BUR GHERKIN; GOOSEBERRY GOURD; GOAREBERRY GOURD. |
| *_Cucumis dipsaceus_ | HEDGEHOG GOURD; TEASEL GOURD. |
| *_Cucumis melo_ | |
| var _cantalupensis_ | *CANTALOUPE; ROCK MELON |
| var _chito_ | MANGO MELON; ORANGE MELON; GARDEN LEMON; MELON APPLE; VEGETABLE ORANGE; VINE PEACH. |
| var _conomon_ | ORIENTAL PICKLING MELON. |
| var _dudaim_ | DUDAIM MELON; POMEGRANATE MELON; QUEEN ANNE'S POCKET MELON; STINK MELON. |
| var _flexuosus_ | SNAKE MELON; SERPENT MELON. |
| var _inodorus_ | WINTER MELON; CASABA MELON. |
| var _reticulatus_ (var _scandens_) | MUSK MELON; NETTED MELON; NUTMEG MELON; PERSIAN MELON. |
| var _saccharinus_ | HONEYDEW MELON. |
| *_Cucumis metuliferus_ | AFRICAN HORNED MELON. |
| *_Cucumis sativus_ | *CUCUMBER, "GHERKIN". |
| _Lagenaria siceraria_ | WHITE-FLOWERED GOURD; *CALABASH GOURD; DIPPER GOURD; SUGAR-TROUGH GOURD; HERCULES'-CLUB GOURD; BOTTLE GOURD; KNOB-KERRIE GOURD; TRUMPET GOURD. |

| | |
|---|---|
| *Trichosanthes anguina* (*T. cumeraria*) | SERPENT GOURD; SERPENT CUCUMBER; SNAKE GOURD; CLUB GOURD; VIPER'S GOURD. |
| *Trichosanthes cucumeroides* | SNAKE GOURD. |
| *Benincasa hispida* (*B. cerifera*) | WHITE GOURD; WAX GOURD; ASH GOURD; TUNKA; CHINESE WATER MELON. |
| *Sicana odorifera* | CURUBÁ; CASSABANANA. |
| *Sechium edule* | *CHAYOTE; SOU-SOU; CHRISTOPHINE. |
| **Ecballium elaterium* | SQUIRTING CUCUMBER. |
| **Luffa aegyptiaca* (*L. cylindrica*) | TOWEL GOURD; SPONGE GOURD; DISHCLOTH GOURD; LUFFA; LOOFA. |
| *Luffa acutangula* | ANGLED LOOFA. |
| *Coccinea grandis* | IVY GOURD. |

(See also Melons, Gourds)

richer in protein, fats and vitamin A than summer squashes. They are usually baked rather than boiled.

Pumpkins and squashes are inexpensive and highly digestible vegetables. They do not have a pronounced flavor and are low in nutritive value, being 90–95% water and 3–6% carbohydrate. The seeds on the other hand are rich in oil and protein. Some of the gourds are grown for food, such as the MALABAR OR FIG GOURD (*Cucurbita ficifolia*), which is cultivated both in the Old and New Worlds. Its flesh is eaten candied and its ripe seeds are edible. It differs from other edible species of *Cucurbita* in being perennial. The SNAKE or SERPENT GOURD (*Trichosanthes anguina*), an Indomalaysian species with fruits up to 6.5ft in length, cultivated in tropical Asia, and the WAX GOURD (*Benicasa hispida*), from Southeast Asia, with large oblong to cylindrical fruits, are also eaten when immature. Other species such as *Lagenaria siceraria* [WHITE-FLOWERED CALABASH, BOTTLE GOURD], probably native to tropical Africa and long cultivated in both hemispheres, and *Coccinea grandis* [IVY GOURD], an Old World species naturalized in South America, are grown for use as containers, musical instruments or ornaments.

Although primarily grown for their edible flesh or as ornamentals, the seeds of some species of *Cucurbita* yield a high quality oil which is utilized, particularly in Europe. The seeds of one mutant of *C. pepo* contain up to 50% oil.

*Common marrows, squashes and other cucurbits: 1 Watermelon; 2 Honeydew Melon; 3 Netted or Nutmeg Melon, Musk Melon; 4 Gherkin; 5 Cucumber; 6 Courgette; 7 Summer Squash 'Summer Crookneck'; 8 Pumpkin; 9 Winter Squash 'Hubbard'; 10 Custard Marrow; 11 Vegetable Marrow. 1, 2, 3, 7, 9, 11 ($\times\frac{1}{4}$); 4, 5, 6 ($\times\frac{1}{2}$); 8, 10 ($\times\frac{1}{10}$).*

**Melastoma** a genus of evergreen shrubs native to southern China, Indomalaysia and the Pacific. A number of species, notably *M. denticulatum*, with showy white flowers, and *M. malabathricum*, with large violet-pink or purple flowers, are cultivated as ornamental flowering shrubs in tropical gardens or in greenhouses in temperate climates.
MELASTOMACEAE, about 70 species.

**Melia** a small genus of deciduous trees native to Australia and the East Indies, cultivated for their fragrant inflorescences. The hard seeds of the purplish-flowered Asiatic species *M. azedarach* [CHINA BERRY TREE, UMBRELLA TREE, BEAD TREE, PRIDE OF INDIA, PERSIAN LILAC] are sometimes used as beads for rosaries. The bark, leaves and fruits of this species have medicinal uses and the fruits are a source of insecticide. A number of species, including *M. azedarach*, *M. dubia* and *M. excelsa*, produce valuable timber; that of the latter resembles mahogany and is put to a wide range of uses, including general carpentry work, furniture and veneer making.

*M. azedarach* is widely naturalized in tropical America, and widely planted in other tropical and warm temperate regions for its commercial and ornamental value. The best-known cultivars include 'Floribunda' (= *M. floribunda*) and 'Umbraculiformis' [TEXAS UMBRELLA TREE].
MELIACEAE, about 10 species.

**Melica** a genus of perennial grasses attractive spreading inflorescences native to temperate regions, except Australasia, of which *M. altissima* and *M. ciliata* are cultivated as ornamentals.
GRAMINEAE, about 50–70 species.

*The leaves of the Lemon Balm or Sweet Balm (*Melissa officinalis*) are strongly lemon-scented and are used for seasoning. (× ⅓)*

*The Field or Corn Mint (*Mentha arvensis*) is closely related to the cultivated Spearmint and is a common weed in wheat fields. (× 1)*

**Melicoccus** a genus of only two species, both from tropical America and the Caribbean. One of these *M. bijugatus* (= *M. bijuga*) [SPANISH LIME, HONEY BERRY, GENIP, MAMONCILLO], forms a sizeable tree, cultivated for its green globular edible fruits. The single seed is surrounded by a yellow, sweet, juicy pulp.
SAPINDACEAE, 2 species.

**Melilotus** [MELILOTS, SWEET CLOVERS] a genus of annual or biennial herbs with pea-like flowers, mainly native to the Mediterranean and Eurasian regions. Unlike the true *CLOVERS (*Trifolium*), they grow to 10ft tall, have mostly pinnate leaves with finely toothed leaflets, and their flowers are borne in long spikes or racemes. The pod is usually short, containing only one or two seeds.

A number of species are grown as fodder crops or green manure. Most contain coumarin and produce a smell of new mown hay when cut or grazed. Their copious nectar is the source of a good quality honey. Useful fodder crops are grown from *M. officinalis* [COMMON MELILOT, SWEET CLOVER, BOKHARA OR BUCKHARA CLOVER], *M. alba* [WHITE MELILOT, WHITE SWEET CLOVER, BOKHARA CLOVER] and *M. indica* (= *M. parviflora*) [SMALL FLOWERED MELILOT, SOUR CLOVER]. *M. officinalis* has additional uses in flavoring cheeses and as an insect repellent.
LEGUMINOSAE, about 20 species.

**Melissa** a small genus of bushy herbaceous perennials from southern Europe and Asia. The leaves are aromatic and hairy and the pale yellow to white or pinkish flowers are borne in whorls. *M. officinalis* [BALM, LEMON BALM] is cultivated for its lemon-scented foliage used in seasoning and in medicine. There are cultivars with attractive golden or variegated leaves.
LABIATAE, 4–5 species.

**Melittis** a genus consisting of a single species, *M. melissophyllum* [BASTARD BALM]. It is a perennial herb growing up to 28in tall, with ovate leaves bearing the large creamy-white, pink or purple flowers in their axils. It grows in western, central and southern Europe, extending to the Ukraine, and is cultivated as a border plant, particularly as the cultivars 'Album' and 'Grandiflorum', which are white- and creamy-white flowered respectively.
LABIATAE, 1 species.

**Melon** a name applied to two quite different species of widely cultivated plants of the cucumber family (Cucurbitaceae), **Cucumis melo* [SWEET MELON, MUSK MELON] and **Citrullus lanatus* (= *C. vulgaris*, *Colocynthis citrullus*) [WATER MELON].

*Water Melons (*Citrullus lanatus*) ready for harvest in western Texas. Most USA production is in the southern states.*

*C. melo* is an annual, trailing vine. Its angular stems bear large, alternate, kidney-shaped leaves, the unbranched tendrils and yellow flowers being produced in the leaf axils. There is a great variety of fruits. NETTED, NUTMEG OR MUSK MELONS, usually named cultivars of *C. melo* var *reticulatus*, are smaller than most melons, with smooth skins often covered with net-like markings. The CANTALOUPE (var *cantalupensis*) is a little larger and has thicker, rough to warty skin. They are widely grown in Europe and a few hardy cultivars are grown under glass in north temperate regions. The OGEN MELON exported from Israel is a member of the cantaloupe group.

The CASABA OR WINTER MELON (var *ino-*

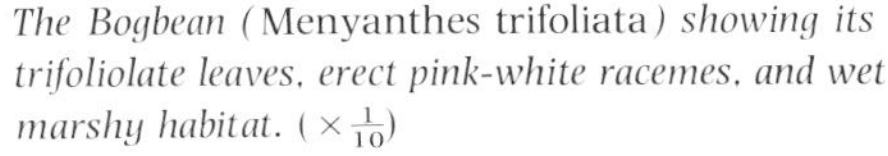

*The Bogbean (*Menyanthes trifoliata*) showing its trifoliolate leaves, erect pink-white racemes, and wet marshy habitat.* ($\times \frac{1}{10}$)

*dorus*) and the HONEYDEW (var *saccharinus*) are grown commercially but to a smaller extent. All these varieties have fruits with succulent flesh that is sweet and often scented, making a delicious breakfast or a dessert dish when served cold with a little sugar or limejuice. The ORIENTAL PICKLING MELON (var *conomon*) and the MANGO MELON (var *chito*) are used for both pickling and preserves. The SNAKE or SERPENT MELON (var *flexuosus*) has fruits up to 40in long and 3in in diameter. They may be contorted into serpent-like shapes and are mainly grown for curiosity value. The DUDAIM MELON (var *dudaim*) has large flowers which produce small highly scented fruits about the size of an orange. (See also WATER MELON.)
CUCURBITACEAE.

**Mentha** see MINT.
LABIATAE, about 25 species.

**Mentzelia** a genus of annual, biennial and perennial herbs native in tropical and subtropical North and South America and the West Indies. *Mentzelia* does not exhibit the barbed, stinging hairs so characteristic of other members of the family. The showy orange, yellow and white flowers are often particularly fragrant in the evening. *M. laevicaulis* [BLAZING STAR, PRAIRIE LILY], a bushy annual or biennial, is widely cultivated for its large golden-yellow flowers, 2.4in in diameter, produced two or three together and opening in the evening. Other ornamental species include *M. albescens* and *M. lindleyi* (= *Bartonia aurea*).
LOASACEAE, about 70 species.

**Menyanthes** a genus consisting of a single species, *M. trifoliata* [BUCKBEAN or BOGBEAN], a north temperate perennial aquatic herb usually growing in bogs, ditches or other

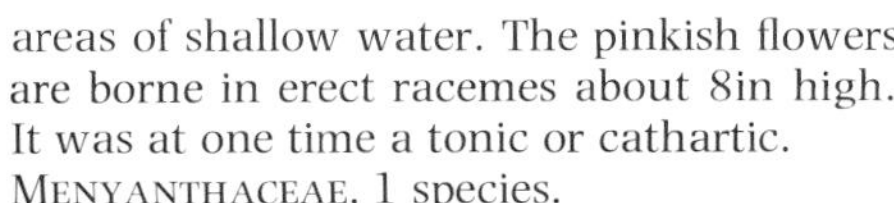

areas of shallow water. The pinkish flowers are borne in erect racemes about 8in high. It was at one time a tonic or cathartic.
MENYANTHACEAE, 1 species.

**Menziesia** a small genus of north temperate Asian and American species of deciduous, slow-growing shrubs. The alternate, entire leaves are variously pubescent and bristly, and the nodding white, pink, purple or deep red flowers are produced in terminal clusters on the previous year's growth. The Japanese group includes several cultivated species, eg *M. ciliicalyx* and *M. pilosa* [MINNIEBUSH].
ERICACEAE, 7 species.

**Mercurialis** a genus of annual or perennial herbs largely confined to the Mediterranean and Europe. *M. annua* [ANNUAL MERCURY] a weed of cultivated ground and waste places, is the most widespread, and *M. perennis* [DOG'S MERCURY] is a common woodland plant, forming pure stands on a wide variety

*A peasant crop of melons in Afghanistan, showing a wide range of form and quality – such crops contain great genetic diversity and are of importance in the future breeding of the crop.* ($\times \frac{1}{10}$)

of soils. The latter species was at one time used as a dye.
EUPHORBIACEAE, 15 species.

**Merendera** a small genus of crocus-like perennial herbs, native to the Mediterranean region, Afghanistan, the USSR and Ethiopia. They produce star-shaped flowers with narrow pink or rose petals. The best-known species is *M. pyrenaica* (= *M. montana*, *M. bulbocodium*), from the Pyrenees, Spain and Portugal. *M. filifolia*, from the western Mediterranean, is sometimes cultivated in rough grass, and the corms of *M. robusta* (= *M. persica*), from northern Afghanistan and adjacent USSR, are used as a treatment for rheumatism.
LILIACEAE, about 10 species.

**Mertensia** a genus of north temperate perennial herbs distributed as far south as Mexico and Afghanistan. The leaves are entire, often with pellucid glands. The bluish, purplish or white, bell-shaped flowers are
(continued on p. 228)

*The green-flowered Dog's Mercury (*Mercurialis perennis*) is common and often abundant in woodlands during early spring.* ($\times \frac{1}{15}$)

# Medicinal and Narcotic Plants

For most of Man's history the fields of botany and medicine were, for all practical purposes, synonymous fields of knowledge, as the leading ethnobotanist R. E. Schultes has pointed out; the witch-doctor – usually an accomplished botanist – is probably the oldest of the professions in Man's culture. The close relationship between plants and Man can be traced back to earliest times when primitive man seeking to survive in this planet had to learn to distinguish and recognize plants that were useful as food or drugs from those that were ineffectual or poisonous. It has been noted that the number of plants that have been used in folk medicine greatly exceeds those used or cultivated for food or other purposes. The first botanic gardens were medical gardens or gardens of simples (ie herbs) attached to medical faculties.

There are references to drugs of plant origin in the early Greek literature and Hippocrates listed plants according to their uses, but the first important classification of drugs plants according to their use was compiled in the first century AD by Dioscorides. His compilation of plant lore formed the basis of materia medica for centuries until the publication of the more complete works, such as the *Dispensorium* of Cordus in 1515 and the first official pharmacopeia in Augsburg in 1564, soon followed by others.

The rapid development of the field of organic chemistry in the 19th century led to a wider understanding of the chemical structure of plant drugs and to their gradual replacement by drugs of synthetic origin. While the early official pharmacopeias comprised largely drugs of plant origin, today the percentage of drugs of natural plant origin in say the British and American Pharmacopeias of the 1960s is five or six per cent.

Nonetheless, in recent years there has been a resurgence of interest in the plant kingdom as a source of drugs and there is today a deep interest in understanding plants, their physiology and chemistry and their ethnobotanical significance. No longer does the pharmaceutical industry neglect plants in favor of "coal tar" drugs, largely due to the discovery in the last 10–20 years of the so-called "wonder drugs" such as reserpine from **Rauvolfia*, cortisone precursors from **Strophanthus* and **Dioscorea*, hypertensive agents from **Veratrum*, and the use of steroids of plant origin especially in oral contraceptives, the discoveries of antibiotics, and the more recent interest in hallucinogens. As a consequence it is estimated that of the 300 000 000 new prescriptions filed in the United States each year, half contain at least one ingredient of natural plant origin. The spectacular development of phytochemical research in the past quarter of a century has only covered a small portion of the potential offered by the plant kingdom and the more extensive exploration of the tropical flora, coupled with an increasing interest in and knowledge of the plants used in folk medicines, suggests that the surface has only just been scratched.

Medicinal plants, or crude drugs as they are known commercially, are a diverse and economically important group of species belonging to many families, genera and species throughout the plant kingdom. They are used in the pharmaceutical industry for the production of drugs in the form of tablets, capsules and injections or for the preparation of tinctures, infusions and mixtures. The specific drugs contained by medicinal plants are known as "active principles". They may be divided chemically into a number of groups, principally the alkaloids (see p. 26), glycosides, volatile essential oils, resins and oleo-resins and steroids. Such drugs are isolated from poisonous plants – medicinal plants are useful as drugs because they are toxic. Toxicity does not imply fatal results – it is a matter of dosage. Indeed the difference between a poison, a medicine and a narcotic is just one of dosage. Some crude drugs with low toxicity are used in medicine in the dried form or as infusions or tinctures. An example is valerian (from **Valeriana officinalis*) used as a sedative in medicinal preparations as a tincture. In modern pharmaceutics, the active principles in poisonous plants which comprise the group of specific drugs are isolated and a standard dosage is formulated.

The alkaloids are the major group of specific drugs. They were amongst the earliest plant poisons to be isolated – morphine was isolated in a pure form in 1806 from the *OPIUM POPPY (**Papaver somniferum*) – and research into their nature and structure led to the development of the sciences of organic chemistry and pharmacology. Examples include drugs used as local anesthetics, analgesics, muscle stimulants and relaxants, hallucinogens and tranquilizers. Glycosides are widespread in the plant kingdom and many have a pronounced pharmacological effect on mammals. There are several groups of glycosides, the most widely used in medicine being the cardiac or cardioactive glycosides which have a specific effect on the heart muscle. Glycosides isolated from *FOXGLOVES (*Digitalis purpurea* and *D. lanata*) are widely used in the treatment of heart conditions. The FOXGLOVE was first introduced into medicine by William Withering in 1785 but the nature of the active principles was not discovered until 1933 by Stoll in Switzerland. Likewise, the purgative drug *cascara sagrada obtained from *Rhamnus purshiana*, was introduced into medicine in 1870, based on its use by North American Indians, but it was not until 1975 that the

NARCOTIC or HALLUCINOGENIC PLANTS

Note: Some narcotic plants are mentioned under the other sections of this table.

| Common name | Scientific name | Family |
|---|---|---|
| FLAG ROOT, SWEET FLAG | **Acorus calamus* | Iridaceae |
| FLY AGARIC | **Amanita muscaria* | Amanitaceae |
| YOPO, VILEA, SEBIL | *Anadananthera peregrina* | Leguminosae |
| BELLADONNA | **Atropa belladonna* | Solanaceae |
| CAAPI | *Banisteriopsis caapi, B. inebrians,* | Malpighiaceae |
| BOLETUS | *Boletus manicus* | Boletaceae |
| ANGEL'S TRUMPET | *Brugsimania aurea* | Solanaceae |
| ZACATECHICHI (BITTER GRASS) | *Calea zacatechichi* | Compositae |
| MARIJUANA | **Cannabis sativa* | Cannabaceae |
| *ERGOT | *Claviceps purpurea* | Hypocreaceae |
| THORN APPLE | **Datura stramonium* | Solanaceae |
| DOWNY THORN-APPLE | *D. inoxia* | Solanaceae |
| HORN-A-PLENTY | *D. metel* | Solanaceae |
| HENBANE | **Hyoscyamus niger* | Solanaceae |
| MORNING GLORY | **Ipomoea tricolor* (= *I. violacea*) | Convolvulaceae |
| OLOLOLIUQUI | *Turbina corymbosa* | Convolvulaceae |
| MESCAL OR PEYOTE BUTTON | **Lophophora williamsii* | Cactaceae |
| *MANDRAKE | *Mandragora officinarum* | Solanaceae |
| CULEBRA BORRACHERO | *Methysticodendron amnesiacum* | Solanaceae |
| *NUTMEG, *MACE | *Myristica fragans* | Myristicaceae |
| T-HA-NA-SA, SHE-TO | *Panaeolus sphinctrinus* | Agaricaceae |
| SYRIAN RUE | *Peganum harmala* | Zygophyllaceae |
| INDIAN POKE | **Phytolacca acinosa* | Phytolaccaceae |
| SACRED MUSHROOM | **Psilocybe mexicana* | Agaricaceae |
| SWEET SCENTED MARIGOLD | **Tagetes lucida* | Compositae |

## MEDICINAL PLANTS

### I Alkaloid-containing Plants

| Common name | Scientific name | Family | Alkaloid |
|---|---|---|---|
| *BETEL-NUT PALM | *Areca catechu* | Palmae | Arecoline |
| *HEMLOCK | *Conium maculatum* | Umbelliferae | Coniine |
| INDIAN TOBACCO | **Lobelia inflata* | Lobeliaceae | Lobeline |
| *PEPPER | *Piper nigrum* | Piperaceae | Piperine |
| *TOBACCO | *Nicotiana tabacum* *N. rustica* | Solanaceae | Nicotine |
| COCAINE | **Erythroxylon coca* | Sterculiaceae | Cocaine |
| BELLADONNA | **Atropa belladonna* | Solanaceae | Atropine |
| THORN APPLE | **Datura stramonium* | Solanaceae | Hyoscine |
| HENBANE | **Hyoscyamus niger* | Solanaceae | Hyoscyamine |
| *MANDRAKE | *Mandragora officinarum* | Solanaceae | Scopolamine |
| *CURARE | *Chondrodendron tomentosum* | Menispermaceae | Tubocurarine |
| *OPIUM POPPY | *Papaver somniferum* | Papaveraceae | Morphine, codeine papaverine |
| IPECAC, *IPECACUANHA | *Cephalaeis ipecacuanha* | Rubiaceae | Emetine |
| CALISAYA | **Cinchona calisaya* | Rubiaceae | Quinine, quinidine |
| HUANACO | *C. micrantha* | Rubiaceae | Quinine |
| QUININE | *C. officinalis* | Rubiaceae | Quinine |
| *ERGOT | *Claviceps purpurea* | Hypocreaceae | Ergotamine |
| MADAGASCAR PERIWINKLE | **Catharanthus roseus* | Apocynaceae | Vinblastine, vincristine |
| INDIAN SNAKEROOT | **Rauvolfia serpentina* | Apocynaceae | Reserpine |
| STRYCHNINE | **Strychnos nux-vomica* | Loganiaceae | Strychnine |
| HELIOTROPE | **Heliotropium europaeum* | Boraginaceae | Heliotrine, lasiocarpine |
| BROOM | **Cytisus scoparius* | Leguminosae | Sparteine |
| LABURNUM | **Laburnum anagyroides* | Leguminosae | Cytisine |
| LUPIN | **Lupinus* species | Leguminosae | Lupinine |
| ACONITE | **Aconitum* species | Ranunculaceae | Aconitine |
| *COFFEE | *Coffea arabica, C. canephora* | Rubiaceae | Caffeine |
| *TEA | *Camellia sinensis* | Theaceae | Caffeine |
| *KOLA | *Cola nitida* | Sterculiaceae | Caffeine |
| CHOCOLATE | **Theobroma cacao* | Sterculiaceae | Theobromine |
| EPHEDRA | **Ephedra sinica, E. distachya, E. equisitina* | Ephedraceae | Ephedrine |

### II Glycoside-containing Plants

| Common name | Scientific name | Family | Type of glycoside |
|---|---|---|---|
| *CASCARA | *Rhamnus purshiana* | Rhamnaceae | Anthraquinone |
| SENNA | **Cassia angustifolia* | Leguminosae | Anthraquinone |
| ALEXANDRIAN SENNA | *C. acutifolia* | Leguminosae | Anthraquinone |
| *RHUBARB | *Rheum officinale, R. palmatum* | Polygonaceae | Anthraquinone |
| BUCKTHORN, ALDER BUCKTHORN | **Rhamnus frangula* (= *Frangula alnus*) | Rhamnaceae | Anthraquinone |
| *ALOE | *Aloe barbadensis* (= *A. vera*) | Liliaceae | Anthraquinone |
| FOXGLOVE | **Digitalis purpurea, D. lanata* | Scrophulariaceae | Cardiac |
| STROPHANTHUS | **Strophanthus sarmentosus, S. gratus, S. hispidus, S. kombe* | Apocynaceae | Cardiac |
| OLEANDER | **Nerium oleander* | Apocynaceae | Cardiac |
| QUEEN OF THE NIGHT | **Selenicereus grandiflorus* | Cactaceae | Cardiac |
| LILY OF THE VALLEY | **Convallaria majalis* | Liliaceae | Cardiac |
| STAR OF BETHLEHEM | **Ornithogalum umbellatum* | Liliaceae | Cardiac |
| SQUILL | **Urginea maritima* | Liliaceae | Cardiac |
| PHEASANT'S-EYE | **Adonis vernalis* | Ranunculaceae | Cardiac |
| CHRISTMAS ROSE | **Helleborus niger* | Ranunculaceae | Cardiac |
| YAM | **Dioscorea elephantipes* | Dioscoreaceae | Saponin |
| *LICORICE | *Glycyrrhiza glabra* | Leguminosae | Saponin |
| GINSENG | **Panax pseudoginseng* *P. quinquefolius* | Araliaceae | Saponin |
| WORMWOOD | **Artemisia absinthium* | Compositae | Coumarin |
| MEZEREON | **Daphne mezereum* | Thymelaeaceae | Coumarin |
| BLACK HAW, SWEET HAW | **Viburnum prunifolium* | Caprifoliaceae | Coumarin |

### III Volatile (Essential) Oils

| Common name | Scientific name | Family | Primary component |
|---|---|---|---|
| ANISEED | **Carum carvi* | Umbelliferae | Limonene |
| *PEPPERMINT | *Mentha piperita* | Labiatae | Carvone |
| *SPEARMINT | *M. spicata* | Labiatae | Carvone |
| *CAMPHOR | *Cinnamomum camphora* | Lauraceae | Camphor |
| *CLOVES | *Syzygium aromaticum* | Myrtaceae | Eugenol |
| *SASSAFRAS | *Sassafras albidum* | Lauraceae | Safrole |
| WINTERGREEN | **Gaultheria procumbens* | Ericaceae | |
| *GINGER | *Zingiber officinale* | Zingiberaceae | |
| *MUSTARD | *Brassica* and *Sinapis* spp | Cruciferae | |
| CAJUPUT | **Melaleuca leucadendron* | Myrtaceae | Cineole |
| EUCALYPTUS | **Eucalyptus globulus* | Myrtaceae | Cineole |

### IV Resins and Oleoresins

| Common name | Scientific name | Family | Primary component |
|---|---|---|---|
| PEPPER TREE | **Schinus molle* | Anacardiaceae | Urushiol |
| ASAFOETIDA | **Ferula foetida* *F. rubricaulis* | Umbelliferae | Asafoetida |
| *STORAX | *Styrax benzoin* | Styracaceae | Benzoin |
| BALSAM OF PERU | **Myroxylon balsamum* | Leguminosae | Cinnamein |
| ORIENTAL SWEET GUM | **Liquidambar orientalis* | Hammamelidaceae | Storesin |
| SWEET GUM | *Liquidambar styraciflua* | Hammamelidaceae | Storesin |

detailed structures of the active principles, cascarosides A and B, could be finally elucidated. Examples of these and of other groups of drug plants are given in the accompanying table.

Narcotic or hallucinogenic plants have been defined as those which contain "chemicals which in nontoxic doses, produce changes in perception, in thought and in mood, but which seldom produce mental confusion, memory loss or disorientation for person, place and time". The term narcotic comes from the Greek *narkoun*, to benumb, and strictly speaking refers to substances which terminate their action with a depressive effect on the central nervous system. In this sense both alcohol and tobacco are narcotics. Stimulants, on the other hand, such as *coffee, are not regarded as narcotics since they do not in normal dosage lead to a terminal depression. They are, however, psychoactive, a term often used in a broad sense to cover both narcotics and stimulants. The term narcotic is also used popularly to refer to substances which are dangerously addictive, such as opium and its derivatives. It is evident that there is no one term that adequately covers all psychoactive plants, but the term hallucinogen is widely used and understood. Hofmann, following an earlier classification of Lewin, divides psychoactive drugs into five groups: analgesics and euphorics (eg opium and *coca), sedatives and tranquilizers (eg reserpine), hypnotics (eg kavakava) and hallucinogens or psychotomimetics (eg peyote, marijuana).

Most hallucinogens derive from plants. Their activity is due to a limited number of chemical substances which act on a particular part of the central nervous system in a specific way. Most of them belong to the wide class of compound known as alkaloids. Hallucinogens include well-known plants such as *MORNING GLORY (**Ipomoea tricolor*) and BELLADONNA (**Atropa belladonna*). *Ergot derives from the pathogenic fungus *Claviceps purpurea* which grows on rye and other grasses, and was responsible for the horrifying disease known as St. Antony's fire, induced by eating bread made from rye contaminated with ergot. Lysergic acid diethylamide (LSD), a highly potent hallucinogen, is a synthetic derivative of ergot. It is believed now that the only deliberate use of ergot as a hallucinogen was in ancient Greece when it is said to have played a role in the Eleusinian mysteries.

It is only in the past 30 years or so that interdisciplinary research has led to a further appreciation of the potential role of hallucinogenic plants in modern medicine and society. As Schultes and Hofmann have written: "Plants that alter the normal functions of the mind and body have always been considered by people in non-industrial societies as sacred, and the hallucinogens have been 'plants of the gods' *par excellence*".

*One of the group known as mesembryanthemums.* Lampranthus spectabilis *on the shores of the Monterey Peninsula, California.*

borne in drooping racemose or cymose inflorescences. A number of species are grown as garden plants in borders or rockeries, such as *M. virginica* [VIRGINIAN COWSLIP], the dwarf *M. primuloides* and *M. echioides*, whose creeping habit makes it suitable for ground cover. The rhizome of *M. maritima* [OYSTER PLANT] is used as a food by Alaskan eskimos.
Boraginaceae, about 50 species.

**Merulius** a cosmopolitan genus of basidiomycete fungi usually found growing on wood, with the fruiting body flat on the substrate and the fertile layer (hymenium) uppermost. Some species have recently been transferred to **Serpula*, most notably the dry rot fungus *Serpula lacrymans* (formerly *M. lacrymans*).
Corticiaceae, about 40 species.

**Mesembryanthemum** [ICE PLANTS] a genus of annual or biennial herbs with very soft, succulent and brittle stems, cylindrical or flat, expanded leaves and mostly inconspicuous pallid flowers borne singly or in inflorescences. The most obvious characteristic is the overall presence of large glossy papillae which make the whole plant sparkle in the sun as if covered in hoar frost, hence the common name. In recent years many members of the original genus have been transferred to 125 smaller genera of which *Mesembryanthemum* is but one.

Centered in the Cape region of South Africa, *Mesembryanthemum* has two widely distributed species, *M. crystallinum* [ICE PLANT], naturalized in Mediterranean regions, the Canary Isles and California, and *M. nodiflorum* found in Africa, southern Europe, the Near East, Atlantic islands, California and Mexico. *M. crystallinum* is sometimes cultivated as an ornamental for its glittering foliage. It can also be grown as a substitute for spinach where the ground is too dry for that crop, and the soft fleshy shoots have been included raw in salad. The seeds also have been used to make bread.
Aizoaceae, 40–50 species.

**Mespilus** see MEDLAR.
Rosaceae, 1 species.

**Mesua** a small genus of evergreen tropical Asian shrubs or trees. *M. ferrea* [IRONWOOD] is a handsome tree bearing fragrant large solitary flowers. The flower buds and flowers are used locally in cosmetic preparations and perfumery, and the very hard timber is used for walking sticks and cabinetwork.
Guttiferae, 3–6 species.

**Metasequoia** an unusual genus in that it was known as a fossil before being discovered in 1945 as a living tree. It is a coniferous genus consisting of a single living species of deciduous tree *M. glyptostroboides* [DAWN REDWOOD]. The fossil record of *Metasequoia* extends back to the Cretaceous period (about 100 million years) and at one time the genus was widespread in the Northern Hemisphere. Although now geographically restricted as a native tree to a small area in central China, the DAWN REDWOOD will grow successfully in a variety of climates and soils and has been planted widely as an ornamental in Europe and America. (See also p. 914.)
Taxodiaceae, 1 species.

**Metrosideros** a Pacific genus centered in Polynesia, with some representatives in Australasia. Species are either evergreen trees, shrubs or aerial-rooted climbers. They form an extremely attractive group of plants as the stiff, long stamens protrude beyond the flowers and are frequently of a vivid red or yellow. The hard wood of trees such as *M. robustus* (confused in cultivation with *M. umbellatus*), *M. collinus* (= *M. diffusus*) and *M. umbellatus* (= *M. lucidus*) (the generic name means "iron core") is used locally for boatbuilding and carving. *M. excelsus* (= *M. tomentosus*) [NEW ZEALAND CHRISTMAS TREE, POHUTUKAWA], with dark crimson flowers, is a common subtropical ornamental.
Myrtaceae, about 60 species.

**Metroxylon** a genus of stout, solitary or clump-forming tree palms native from Thailand and Malaya to Fiji. *M. rumphii* and *M. sagus* are the *SAGO PALMS widely cultivated in villages throughout the Asian tropics for their starch (marketed as sago). *M. sagus* is also a prime palm for thatching. The Pacific Islands species are known as IVORY NUT PALMS, the hard horny endosperm being the vegetable ivory that was formerly used for buttons.
Palmae, 15 species.

**Metzgeria** a genus of tropical and subtropical thallose liverworts growing on rocks, tree trunks and, more rarely, on living leaves. The

*The evergreen foliage and crimson flowers make the New Zealand Christmas Tree (*Metrosideros excelsus*) a common ornamental in the subtropics.*

*Common Millet (*Panicum miliaceum*) is widely cultivated as a food crop for Man or livestock, shown here in Hidalgo State, Mexico.* ($\times\frac{1}{15}$)

thallus consists of a conspicuous cylindrical midrib with a thin wing, one layer of cells thick, on each side of it. The sex organs are produced in highly specialized branches. METZGERIACEAE, about 50 species.

**Michaelmas daisies** short-lived perennial herbs or shrubs belonging to the large genus **Aster*. They are characterized by having tall, erect stems with alternate leaves and solitary or clustered inflorescences of small, daisy-like heads which have one or two series of white, blue, pink or red narrow strap-like ray florets and a central button of yellow disk florets.

Although there are several South African blue-flowered shrubby species of *Aster* cultivated in greenhouses, most MICHAELMAS DAISIES are tall, hardy, leafy perennial herbs of American origin. These are chiefly forms of *A. amellus*, *A. cordifolius*, *A. ericoides*, *A. laevis*, *A. lateriflorus*, *A. novae-angliae*, *A. novi-belgii*, *A. thomsonii*, *A.* × *versicolor* (= *A. laevis* × *A. novi-belgii*) and *A. vimineus*. Varieties of *A. novi-belgii* [NEW YORK ASTER] and *A. novae-angliae* [NEW ENGLAND ASTER] form by far the biggest group, although these are now rapidly being superseded by many new hybrid forms which are produced every year.

In addition to border plants there are a number of colorful dwarf species from the mountains of Europe, America and Asia well adapted for use in rock gardens. Important species include *A. alpinus*, *A. diplostephioides*, *A. falconeri*, *A. flaccidus and A. tongolensis* (= *A. subcoeruleus*).
COMPOSITAE.

**Michelia** a genus of Asian shrubs and trees very similar to **Magnolia*. A number of species, notably *M. champaca* [SAPU] and *M. doltsopa* (= *M. excelsa*), produce a rather variegated timber used extensively in India, Sri Lanka and China for joinery and house building. These and other species are cultivated for their showy, often fragrant flowers, yellow or orange in *M. champaca*, yellow in *M. compressa*, yellowish green in *M. figo* (= *Magnolia fuscata*) and yellowish white, tinged green in *M. doltsopa*. Champaca oil, obtained from the flowers of *M. champaca*, is used in perfumery in Asia.
MAGNOLIACEAE, about 50 species.

**Miconia** a large genus of tropical American shrubs and trees with one species occurring in West Africa. Some species, are grown in greenhouses for their large attractive leaves. The flowers, which are white, yellow, pink or purple, are not very conspicuous; the fruits are berry-like. Cultivated species include *M. flammea* and *M. ovata* but perhaps the most striking is *M. calvescens* (= *M. magnifica*), from Mexico, which has very large, broadly ovate leaves, up to 28in long, reddish-orange beneath with pale green or whitish veins.
MELASTOMATACEAE, about 600 species.

**Micromeria** a genus of herbs and sub-shrubs closely related to other herbs such as *THYME, *MINT and *SAGE. Some species are grown for their ornamental appearance and were formerly grown as potherbs. *M. croatica*, from Croatia, is a small herb producing pale rose-violet flowers in spring. *M. marginata* (= *M. piperella*), from the Maritime Alps has reddish-purple or violet flowers in the summer. All of these and a few other species are suitable rock-garden plants. LABIATAE, about 100 species.

**Mignonette** the common name for certain annual to perennial herbs of the genus *Reseda*, native to Europe and the Mediterranean. The terminal spike-like racemes of small flowers are usually greenish-yellow, orange or whitish. *R. odorata* [COMMON MIGNONETTE] is grown as a border plant largely for its scent, although some cultivars produce spikes of attractive red flowers. This species yields a perfume oil. A reddish-yellow dye used to be obtained from *R. luteola* [WILD MIGNONETTE, DYERS' ROCKET, WELD]. *R. alba* is known as the WHITE UPRIGHT MIGNONETTE.
RESEDACEAE.

**Mikania** a large genus of evergreen twining or creeping herbs and shrubs, mostly native to tropical America and the West Indies, but also found in Africa and tropical Asia. *M. scandens* [CLIMBING HEMPWEED] a quick-growing herb with ivy-like, bronze-olive-green leaves with brownish veins, is endemic to eastern North America, with related species pantropical in distribution. *M. apiifolia*, with softly hairy, lobed leaves is cultivated out of doors in warm climates or otherwise in heated greenhouses. The Brazilian *M. ternata*, a half-woody vine with purple hairy stems and yellowish flowers, is grown in hanging baskets.
COMPOSITAE, about 150 species.

**Mildew** see Fungi, p. 156.

**Milium** a genus of annual or perennial grasses native to north temperate regions. They have spikelets consisting of a single floret. *M. effusum* var *aureum* [GOLDEN MILLET] is cultivated as an ornamental.
GRAMINEAE, about 3–4 species.

**Millet** a loose term for a large number of cultivated grasses with small edible seeds. Most millets are believed to have originated in Africa or in Central and East Asia. Although largely replaced by other cereals, millets are still grown extensively in Asia, particularly in China, and in parts of Africa. They can produce grain under conditions of intense heat, scanty rainfall, relatively in-

Metzgeria furcata *is a small thalloid liverwort, here showing the hairy globular sheaths surrounding the male sex organs (antheridia).* ($\times 4$)

fertile soil, and a short growing season. Thus they tend to be "poor man's cereals", mainly grown for local consumption, and are therefore useful in dry areas of India, Africa and Australia.

*Eleusine coracana* [FINGER OR AFRICAN MILLET, RAGI] is the most important species and constitutes a staple food in areas of East and central Africa and in the Mysore plains of India. The small brown (sometimes white) grains are ground into a flour used for porridge, or fermented to produce beer.

*Pennisetum americanum* (= *P. typhoides*, *P. glaucum*) [BULRUSH, PEARL, SPIKED OR CAT-TAIL MILLET] is widely cultivated in Africa (particularly the Sudan) and India on rather sandy dry soils which cannot support other cereal species. In addition to the grain which is eaten unground or as porridge, this species makes a useful fodder crop.

*Setaria italica* [ITALIAN OR FOXTAIL MILLET] is an important grain crop cultivated widely in India and Japan, and in parts of North Africa and southeastern Europe. It is also grown in the USA as a fodder crop, and in parts of the USSR where other grains are unprofitable. The grain is used for food and for brewing beer, and is the millet commonly seen in bird cages.

*Echinochloa frumentacea* [JAPANESE BARNYARD MILLET] is the quickest growing millet, producing a crop in only six weeks. It is used as a substitute for *RICE in China and Japan when the paddy fails. Other millets include *Panicum miliaceum* [COMMON OR PROSO MILLET], *Digitaria exilis* [FUNDI], *Eragrostis tef* [TEFF] and *Paspalum scrobiculatum* [KODA OR KODO MILLET].
GRAMINEAE.

*A cultivated Sensitive Plant (*Mimosa pudica*) showing the leaves semi-closed – a position typical of an hour after sunset.* ($\times \frac{1}{10}$)

**Miltonia** a largely tropical American genus of epiphytic and pseudobulbous orchids which are cultivated usually in the form of spectacular multispecific hybrids. In most species, the entire flower has a pansy-like appearance (hence the common name PANSY ORCHIDS), the basic flower colors being mauve, pink and white. In many of the species and hybrids, however, there are large overlapping and regularly spaced blotches of contrasting maroon, purple and yellow. Miltonias have been widely hybridized with species from other genera such as *Oncidium* (to give × *Miltonidium*), *Brassia* (to give × *Miltassia*).
ORCHIDACEAE, 25 species.

*Most species of* Mimulus *are native to North Africa, but some are naturalized elsewhere, such as the Monkey Flower (*M. guttatus*), seen here growing in Britain.* ($\times \frac{1}{5}$)

**Mimosa** a large genus of annual and perennial herbs, shrubs, subshrubs, trees and climbers. Many are thorny or prickly and bear flowers borne in tight compact heads. The best-known is *M. pudica* [SENSITIVE PLANT, HUMBLE PLANT, SHAME PLANT], a tender subshrub native to Brazil, whose light green leaflets fold together when touched. *M. argentea* is a climber having attractive foliage with a silvery white midrib. The tropical American herb *M. invisa* [GIANT SENSITIVE PLANT] has been used as a green manure crop. The bark of the Mexican shrub *M. purpurascens* is used for tanning leather.

Florists' mimosa is *Acacia dealbata*.
LEGUMINOSAE, about 450 species.

**Mimulus** a cosmopolitan genus of annual and perennial herbs or rarely shrubs, especially frequent in North America but naturalized elsewhere. Many species are cultivated, notably *M. luteus* [MONKEY MUSK, MONKEY-FLOWER] from Chile, and the North American *M. moschatus* [MUSK PLANT], formerly grown for its musky scent which seems to have disappeared in cultivation. Many of the cultivated species, including the North American *M. ringens* [LAVENDER WATER MUSK, ALLEGHENY MONKEY-FLOWER], *M. cupreus*, from southern Chile, *M. variegatus*, from Chile, and their varieties, are grown in rock gardens, borders or beside pools, for their attractive showy snapdragon-like flowers, predominantly yellow, orange or crimson in color, variously blotched or spotted.
SCROPHULARIACEAE, about 150 species.

**Mimusops** a genus of mostly tropical Old World evergreen shrubs and trees with thick leaves and axillary clusters of whitish flowers. *M. balata* [BALATA] is a large tree, native to Madagascar (BALATA of tropical America is a different species, *Manilkara bidentata*, the source of a nonelastic latex). *M. elengi* [SPANISH CHERRY, MEDLAR] is a small tree native to India and Malaysia which bears edible, ovoid, yellow fruits.
SAPOTACEAE, about 20 species.

**Mint** the common name for *Mentha*, a well-known and widely grown genus of aromatic perennial herbs mostly native to north and south temperate regions. It includes *M. spicata* [SPEARMINT, COMMON MINT], *M. × piperita* (= *M. aquatica* × *M. spicata*) [PEPPERMINT], *M. citrata* [ORANGE OR BERGAMOT MINT], *M. arvensis* [FIELD MINT], *M. × rotundifolia* (= *M. longifolia* × *M. sauveolens*) [APPLE OR ROUND-LEAFED MINT] and *M. arvensis* var *piperascens* [JAPANESE MINT].

Mints are characterized by the small, almost regular, rather unspecialized flowers, arranged in dense many-flowered verticillasters, spikes or heads. Hybrids between species are frequent and these have resulted in the description of a very large number of variants or "species". In many areas, hybrids are more frequent than the parent species.

Mints have a long history of cultivation and they are now grown throughout the world. The much-used essential oil, menthol, is present in most species, but menthol of commerce is mainly derived from JAPANESE MINT, an important crop in Japan, China and Brazil. SPEARMINT, the culinary herb, and PEPPERMINT, widely used in pharmacy and as a flavoring, are also widely grown. Several others are grown commercially and a few, including *M. × rotundifolia* and *M. × gentilis* (= *M. arvensis* × *M. spicata*) [AMERICAN APPLEMINT] make decorative garden plants.
LABIATAE.

**Mirabilis** a genus of American annual or perennial herbs (with one Himalayan species). They have opposite leaves, the lower stalked and the upper stalkless. The inflorescence is one-to-several-flowered but normally only the large, fragrant, central flower develops within a five-lobed petaloid calyx.

*M. jalapa* [FOUR O'CLOCK PLANT, BEAUTY-OF-THE-NIGHT, MARVEL OF PERU] has white, yellow, pink, red or striped flowers which open in the late afternoon. The tuberous roots of this species are the source of a purgative drug used as a substitute for *jalap. *M. jalapa* and *M. longiflora* (white to pink or violet flowers) are among several species cultivated as tender annuals in cooler temperate regions, for their ornamental value.
NYCTAGINACEAE, over 60 species.

**Miraculous berry** or **fruit** the common name for *Synsepalum dulcificum*, a West African shrub often planted near native dwellings. The fruit is fleshy and the pulp around the seeds has a sweet taste with a curious lingering after-effect which causes acid substances to taste sweet when taken up to three hours later. It is an ingredient of palm wine and is used to improve the taste of stale food. The active sweetener (a protein) is of considerable economic interest in the search for non-sucrose sweeteners.
SAPOTACEAE.

**Miscanthus** a genus of tall graceful perennial Asian grasses, some of which, especially *M. sacchariflorus* and *M. sinensis*, are commonly cultivated in a range of varieties as ornamentals in garden borders. The fan-shaped, feathery, terminal inflorescences are also useful when dried for use in floral bouquets.
GRAMINEAE, 15–18 species.

*Mistletoe (*Viscum album*) infects trees at points where the seeds have been deposited by fruit-eating birds that eat the white berries but not the seeds. This species is harvested in Britain at Christmas time for decorations.*

*The widespread north temperate moss* Mnium punctatum, *showing the large oval leaves and pendent spore capsules on orange stalks.* (×3)

**Mistletoe** the name given to several members of the family Loranthaceae. They are semiparasites and the best-known is the Old World *Viscum album*. Other mistletoe genera include *Phoradendron* in North America, *Arceuthobium* in North America, Europe and Asia, and *Loranthus* in the Old World tropics and Australasia.

Seeds of parasitic species germinate on the host and absorb nutrient fluids from the host by means of haustoria. The commercial MISTLETOE of North America is *P. serotinum*. The much smaller *A. pusillum*, which is parasitic on conifers, is known as the DWARF MISTLETOE. The most attractive parasitic species is the tropical American *Psittacanthus elytranthe* [RED MISTLETOE], which bears conspicuous red flowers.

In Britain at Christmas the MISTLETOE is traditionally associated with the other evergreens HOLLY and IVY, their colored berries contrasting with the white mistletoe. The custom of kissing under the MISTLETOE reflects its supposed aphrodisiac powers. Extracts of MISTLETOE have been used to lower blood pressure.
LORANTHACEAE.

**Mitella** [MITERWORT, BISHOP'S CAP] a genus of perennial herbs native to North America and Japan. Most have basal heart-shaped leaves and an erect leafless flowering stalk. *M. diphylla* [COOLWORT], *M. breweri* and *M. nuda* are sometimes cultivated as border or rock-garden plants, producing numerous small, nodding flowers on an erect spike-like raceme.
SAXIFRAGACEAE, about 15 species.

**Mnium** a genus of mosses mainly distributed in north temperate regions. Several are notable for their large leaves which in texture and superficial appearance recall the fronds of filmy ferns. Damp woodland habitats are favored and several species, such as *M. hornum*, *M. punctatum* and *M. undulatum*, occur more or less throughout the north temperate zone.
MNIACEAE, about 50 species.

**Molasses** an important by-product (along with *bagasse) arising from the extraction of sugar from *Saccharum officinarum* [*SUGAR CANE]. It is a very viscous, blackish-brown, strong-smelling fluid which is separated from the crystalline sugar during the later stages of extraction in the refinement process. It is a complex mixture of substances but consists predominantly (about 30%) of sucrose which cannot be extracted economically from the remaining soluble invert sugar, gum, starch and carbonated ash.

Fermentation and distillation of molasses produces a variety of products, including a number of alcohols, acetone, citric acid, glycerol and, by fermentation, edible yeasts. Perhaps the most famous distillate is dark rum, produced mainly in the cane producing countries of the Caribbean, including Venezuela (and also in the Canary Islands). Other fermentation products based on raw molasses include ethyl, amyl and butyl acetate, vinegar and carbon dioxide.

Molasses is used in animal foodstuffs, particularly as an additive to grass for improving the palatability of silage. It is also extensively used as fertilizer and soil improver, especially on sandy soils, since it is a valuable source of potash and organic matter.

Molasses is also known as treacle and in a refined form it is sold for culinary use as black treacle. Cane syrup is a very different product from the true molasses since it is a very pure, clarified sugar product, manufactured for direct human consumption.

**Mold** see Fungi, p. 156.

**Molinia** a genus of perennial grasses of temperate Eurasian origin, the most common of which is *M. caerulea* [MOOR GRASS]. This is the characteristic species of a wet, acid, grass moor, producing valuable spring pasture and surviving fires because of its dense, tussock-forming leaf-bases. The variegated form is used as a bedding plant, having leaves with white stripes and long, erect panicles, bluish greenish or white.
GRAMINEAE, 2–3 species.

**Moluccella** a genus of annual and perennial herbs native in the Mediterranean region and extending to northwest India. The calyx is characteristically bell-shaped with relatively insignificant teeth. *M. laevis* [SHELL FLOWER, MOLUCCA BALM, BELLS OF IRELAND], with greenish calyces, is a hardy annual which dries well and is popular in flower arrangements. *M. spinosa* is a perennial, with the corolla longer than the calyx.
LABIATAE, 3–4 species.

**Momordica** a genus of annual or perennial, tendril-bearing, climbing herbs native to tropical Asia and Africa, but widely cultivated throughout the tropics for their white or yellow flowers, but principally for their round, oblong or cylindrical, bitter but edible fruits. Popular species include *M. balsamina* [BALSAM APPLE] and *M. charantia* [BALSAM PEAR, BITTER GOURD], whose fruits are used in pickles, curries and salads.
CUCURBITACEAE, about 40 species.

**Monanthes** a genus of mostly perennial, but a few annual, dwarf tender leaf-succulents from the Canary Isles, Salvage Isles and North Africa. Some of the perennials, such as *M. polyphylla*, are grown in succulent collections for their dainty miniature habit, colorful and often flossy, papillate leaves and starry flowers with conspicuous nectar scales. In addition to the purple-flowered *M. polyphylla*, cultivated species include the yellowish-flowered *M. pallens* and *M. anagensis*.
CRASSULACEAE, about 16 species.

**Monarda** a genus of annual and perennial aromatic herbs native to North America and Mexico. The flowers are in heads, usually with an involucre of bracts, which in some cases are very showy. *M. didyma* [SWEET BERGAMOT, BEE OR FRAGRANT BALM, OSWEGO TEA] is widely cultivated in gardens and there are several cultivars with flower colors ranging from white and pink to scarlet and violet.
LABIATAE, 12 species.

**Monardella** a genus of annual and perennial aromatic herbs native to western North America. The terminal heads of flowers are rose-purple, lavender or white and resemble those of **Monarda*. Some species are grown as ornamentals, particularly in rock gardens, including *M. candicans* and *M. nana*, with white, rose-tinged flowers, and the red- to yellowish-flowered *M. macrantha*.
LABIATAE, about 20 species.

*The Yellow Bird's-nest (*Monotropa hypopitys*) is one of the few saprophytic herbs.* $(\times \frac{1}{8})$

**Monostroma** a genus of parenchymatous green algae found on rocky seashores attached to the substrate by rhizoids. The plant has a ruffled thallus one cell thick, and the pale green fronds finally spread out flat, reaching a length of about 6 in. *Monostroma* is cultivated as a food plant in Japan.
CHLOROPHYCEAE.

**Monotropa** a genus of saprophytic fleshy herbs distributed over the Northern Hemisphere. They are devoid of chlorophyll and the stems and scaly leaves are yellow throughout. Their roots function in symbiosis with fungi which form mycorrhiza and thus enable the plant to absorb complex food materials. *M. hypopitys* [YELLOW BIRD'S-NEST] and *M. uniflora* [INDIAN PIPE] are the best-known species, both of them producing whitish or pinkish flowers.
MONOTROPACEAE, 3–5 species.

**Monstera** a genus of evergreen lianas from tropical America and the West Indies. They begin as climbers and have woody stems but become epiphytes with aerial roots. The leaves are thick and entire when young, but often the tissue between the veins ceases to grow and, becoming dry, tears away, leaving holes between the ribs. The most commonly grown species is *M. deliciosa* [MEXICAN BREAD-FRUIT, WINDOW PLANT, CERIMAN, SWISS-CHEESE PLANT], from Mexico and Central America, often grown indoors for its large perforated leaves. In the tropics, the inflorescence develops into a long succulent cone-like fruit smelling of pineapples.
ARACEAE, 30–50 species.

**Moraea** a genus of cormous or rhizomatous iris-like herbs native to tropical and southern Africa. The spreading flowers are usually fragrant and showy, either red, lilac, white or yellow in color, and usually borne in branched inflorescences. Cultivated species include *M. neopavonia* (= *M. pavonia*) [PEACOCK IRIS] with predominantly orange-red flowers, and the yellow-flowered *M. ramosissima* and *M. spathulata*.
IRIDACEAE, about 100 species.

**Morels** saprophytic terrestrial fungi of the mainly temperate genus *Morchella*, with fleshy fruiting bodies consisting of a hollow cylindrical stipe and a grayish to dark brown convoluted cap with interconnecting ridges and depressions lined by asci. The best-known species is the edible *M. esculenta* which grows in calcareous woodland, pasture or sand dunes in spring, and is much sought after and collected from the wild in Europe and the USA. The cap of FALSE MORELS (*Gyromitra*) is by contrast saddle-shaped or convoluted ("brain-like").
MORCHELLACEAE, about 15 species.

**Morina** a genus of thistle-like perennial herbs which make good garden-border plants, although they are not widely grown. They are found native from southeast Europe to the Himalayas and southwest China. The leaves are opposite or whorled, usually spiny. The showy flowers are borne in axillary whorls and are white, changing to crimson in *M. longifolia* [WHORL FLOWER], rose-red in *M. betonicoides* and white or purple in *M. bulleyana*.
DIPSACACEAE, about 10–15 species.

**Morinda** a genus of erect or climbing tropical and subtropical trees and shrubs. The funnel- or salver-shaped flowers are small, white or red, in heads, and the fruit is a conglomeration of berry-like carpels. *M. citrifolia* [INDIAN MULBERRY], whose flowers and roots produce a red and a yellow dye, respectively, is a small tree native to Southeast Asia and Australia. The red dye, known as "al" is used to color wood and linen. Several other species also yield dyestuffs from their flowers or roots. *M. citrifolia*, *M. bracteata* and the shrub *M. jasminoides* are also cultivated as ornamentals.
RUBIACEAE, about 80 species.

**Moringa** a genus of deciduous trees from the Mediterranean, Africa and India. *M. pterygosperma* (= *M. oleifera*) [HORSE-RADISH TREE], from India, is cultivated for an oil (ben oil) obtained from the seeds. Locally in India, the root is scraped and used in curries and pickles, and the flowers and bark

*The massive leaves of the Swiss-cheese Plant (*Monstera deliciosa*), growing here in its natural habitat in Trinidad, West Indies.* $(\times \frac{1}{30})$

*A morel (*Morchella elata*), showing the cylindrical stipe and "honeycomb" cap typical of the genus.* (×1)

have medicinal value. This species and *M. aptera* (which yields an oil from the seeds used in perfumery) are also grown for ornament.
MORINGACEAE, 5–12 species.

**Morning glory** the common name for several decorative species of the genus **Ipomoea* which bear flowers which open soon after dawn and wither by about noon. The name is also applied to species of **Calystegia*, **Convolvulus* and *Merremia*.
CONVOLVULACEAE.

**Morus** see MULBERRY.
MORACEAE, about 12 species.

**Mosses** see p. 234.

**Mountain ash** the common name given to some species of trees and shrubs of the genus **Sorbus*. **Eucalyptus regnans* is also called MOUNTAIN ASH.

**Mucor** one of the largest genera of the pin molds, usually saprophytic and fast-growing. In nature, *Mucor* species are of worldwide distribution, commonly occurring on decomposing vegetable matter, dung, soil and leaf litter. *M. hiemalis* and *M. circinelloides* can be obtained regularly from soil and soil-contaminated substrates. *M. pusillus*, a species which can grow at temperatures up to 130°F, has been reported as a pathogen of domestic animals, with feeding stuffs as the probable source of infection. It has also been reported from man. *Mucor* species are used in fermentations in China and Indonesia to make *soybeans a more palatable and digestible food.
MUCORACEAE, about 50 species.

**Mucuna** a genus of tropical and subtropical twining and climbing herbs from both hemispheres. *M. pruriens* [COWAGE, COWITCH] has intensely irritant hairs over the pods. Cultivars of this and other species, including *M. aterrima* [BENGAL BEAN] and *M. deeringiana* [VELVET BEAN], also with irritant hairs on the pods and spectacular flowers, are used for fodder and silage. Spectacular tropical ornamental species include *M. bennettii* [NEW GUINEA CREEPER], with flame-colored pea-like flowers, *M. rostrata*, from tropical America, with orange flowers, and *M. imbricata*, from India, with purple flowers.
LEGUMINOSAE, about 120 species.

**Muehlenbeckia** a genus of climbing or prostrate shrubs or subshrubs native to Australasia and western South America.

Several species are cultivated in greenhouses, hanging baskets and outdoors, mostly for their curiosity value. For example, the shiny black nutlets of *M. complexa* [WIRE VINE], a deciduous climber up to 100ft, from New Zealand, are enclosed in an expanded glistening white perianth.
POLYGONACEAE, about 15 species.

**Mulberry** the common name for members of the deciduous, woody, mainly tropical genus *Morus* and its fruits. The stems of *Morus* species contain a milky latex. The flowers are small and individually inconspicuous but are clustered into green, pendulous, male or female catkins. The mulberry fruits form around a central core in blackberry-like clusters in which the colored juicy parts have developed from the perianth segments of the individual flowers. Cultivated mulberry fruits may be about 0.8in long, but those from the wild are usually less than 0.4in long.

*M. alba* is the WHITE MULBERRY of China where its main use was to provide silkworm fodder from the soft, tender leaves and also to provide timber. The WHITE MULBERRY used to be considered one of the two most important Chinese timber trees and most Chinese homesteads had one or two planted nearby. It forms a wide-spreading tree up to 50ft tall, with gray bark, small leaves and red fruits. *M. alba* was probably the parent of the original American "DOWNING" MULBERRY, selected for its fruit yield. *M. alba* var *tatarica* [RUSSIAN MULBERRY] is a very hardy variety not grown for its fruit but as an ornamental low-growing shrub in cold northerly climates.

*M. rubra* [RED MULBERRY, AMERICAN MULBERRY] is a native of eastern North America and a common tree of American woodland. The fruits are red to purple, and drop from the branches when ripe. The fallen fruit is juicy and very sweet, and is collected to make pies, jams and jellies. The tree also provides useful timber for boat building and fences.

*M. nigra* [BLACK MULBERRY, PERSIAN MULBERRY, ENGLISH MULBERRY], from Iran and Southwest Asia, is the most common species and has been cultivated in the Mediterranean area for centuries. It attains a height of no more than 32ft and bears purple to black, juicy fruits.

*M. mesozygia* is a central African species up to 100ft tall. It is utilized as a shade tree; the top branches are removed and the lateral branches are weighted to produce an umbrella-shaped crown. It yields edible mulberries, but they are small and not usually harvested.

**Broussonetia papyrifera*, a member of the same family, is called the PAPER MULBERRY.
MORACEAE, about 12 species.

**Mullein** the common name for some species of the genus *Verbascum* such as *V. thapsus* [GREAT MULLEIN, AARON'S ROD, HAG TAPER, ADAM'S FLANNEL, JACOB'S STAFF, SHEPHERD'S CLUB, BLANKET LEAF], *V. lychnitis* [WHITE MULLEIN] and *V. nigrum* [DARK or
(continued on p. 236)

*The English or Black Mulberry (*Morus nigra*) is the most common mulberry and has the largest and juiciest fruits.*

# Mosses and Liverworts

## THE BRYOPHYTES

*A tussock of the moss* Polytrichum commune, *showing the upright capsules still with their hood-like coverings (calyptras).* ( × 1)

MOSSES ARE POPULARLY SEEN AS PLANTS OF soft texture, vaguely defined growth form and strictly limited stature. They are clearly distinct from all other types of plants except for the liverworts which are placed along with them in the same division of the plant kingdom – the Bryophyta, the mosses in class Musci, the liverworts in class Hepaticae. All bryophytes are relatively small plants, most less than 8in long, many below 0.8in. They occur most commonly in warm and temperate climates and prefer moist conditions. All bryophytes have a common, and unique, life history which entails a regular alternation between a flattened or leafy sexual phase or gametophyte (the liverwort or moss plant as we know it) and a spore-bearing plant (sporophyte) which follows fertilization and takes the form of a "fruiting body" or capsule borne aloft on the sexual plant.

Liverworts and mosses may be regarded as the amphibians of the plant world. Although they are land plants, water is essential for the male gametes (spermatozoids) to swim through to reach and fertilize the eggs that are retained within the female sex organs. In many instances a thin film of dew or rain water covering the plants is sufficient for this purpose. Bryophytes do not have true roots although they do possess root-like appendages (rhizoids) that help anchor the plants but do not absorb water or nutrients from the soil.

Having established that liverworts and mosses have many features in common, what then are the differences between them? About 15% of liverworts are thallose, that is they comprise a flattened green body that lacks leaves. These thallose liverworts are quite distinct from the erect, leafy moss plants and are thus not easily confused. The remainder of liverworts are "leafy" and may at first glance be confused with mosses. However, the leaves of these liverworts are generally arranged in two or three ranks, and are characteristically frail, often very small, and invariably without a true midrib, whereas those of mosses are spirally arranged, are of firmer texture and usually larger.

One small group of bryophytes which closely resemble thallose liverworts, and indeed were once thought to be liverworts, is now considered to be a separate class (Anthocerotae) within the bryophytes. These hornworts as they are called occur throughout the world, in moist shaded habitats. There most distinctive feature is the long cylindrical capsule which splits into two horn-like segments to release its spores. (See also *Anthoceros*.)

Although bryophytes mainly favor damp habitats, many mosses are able to survive in dry conditions. They have the power to enter a state of apparently total desiccation, remaining in it for weeks at a time only to recover with speed whenever rain comes. Bryophytes have no means of penetrating the soil beyond a depth of a few centimetres and mainly depend for the small amounts of mineral nutrients they require on water dripping from trees or even on the minute amounts conveyed by direct precipitation.

All bryophytes, but particularly mosses, are important primary colonizers of new habitats, preparing the ground for subsequent colonization by other plants. This is seen to the best advantage in the primary colonization of bare rock surfaces by species of *Grimmia*, *Andreaea* and *Camptothecium*. They are seen as helping to collect a sufficient nidus of soil particles and organic debris to make possible the eventual germination of seeds.

Many mosses and liverworts are reliable indicators of the nature of the surface rock and soil conditions. Thus species such as *Tortella tortuosa*, **Neckera crispa* and *Scapania aspera* indicate alkaline conditions while most species of **Rhacomitrium*, all species of **Polytrichum* and *Scapania gracilis* indicate acid conditions. It has even been suggested that certain mosses, such as *Merceya* species, which in some parts of the world have been found to be constantly associated with high concentrations of copper, might be of more than passing interest to ore prospectors.

Mosses occur in most types of plant community, but their importance varies greatly. They tend to be very sparse in grassland and savanna, and even in tropical forests, if there is a dry season, their role is limited. On the whole, the higher the latitudes the larger the part mosses will play within the vegetation.

*The semi-aquatic moss* Drepanocladus lycopodioides *growing with* Salix repens *and* Equisetum variegatum. ( × 5)

*A thick cover of bryophytes and lichens on the gnarled trunks of English Oak trees (*Quercus robur*) and boulders.*

Throughout the vast coniferous forests of the boreal zone of Eurasia and North America, the moss component in the ground flora is important; farther North, through the taiga into arctic tundra, the bryophytes, chiefly mosses, but with liverworts freely represented, assume dominance along with lichens. In lower latitudes much the same situation is found in mountaintop vegetation. There is a single example of a genus of mosses achieving sole dominance in a particular habitat. This is the genus **Sphagnum* (the bog mosses) whose members achieve dominance in bog communities throughout the world. More often mosses form small locally concentrated communities, as in flushes on mountain slopes or on decaying logs in woodland.

Pellia epiphylla, *a thallose liverwort that grows in moist, rich soil, particularly on banks of streams. The plants have a flattened green thallus (the gametophyte or sexual generation), from which the sporophyte (spore-producing generation) emerges, the latter consisting of a stalk (seta) surmounted by a black spore-containing capsule. After dispersal the spores germinate to form new gametophytes.* (×2)

Liverworts do not approach mosses in ecological importance. They never make up a major feature of the vegetation nor do they assume dominance over great tracts of country. In general, regions with a constantly high relative humidity and offering an abundance of "temporary" habitats for colonization are those that suit liverworts best. In temperate regions, liverworts are most prolific on western seaboards with their associated high rainfall. On boulders, rotting logs and sheltered banks in highland woods, leafy liverworts form a conspicuous part of the vegetation. In the dry tropics, liverworts only do well where there is a constant supply of surface water or where extreme shade and adequate shelter are provided. In the humid tropics, however, liverworts are found in a unique habitat – on the surfaces of large leaves, particularly those that are evergreen. Such epiphyllous liverworts share this habitat with lichens and other lower plants. They obtain no direct nourishment from the leaves and rely for their water on the saturated atmosphere.

Mosses and liverworts have remarkable powers of regeneration even from very small fragments. A fair degree of vegetative spread must be by this means, but many species also produce special vegetative propagules called gemmae.

Economically, mosses and liverworts are of limited importance. The economic role of mosses has largely been restricted to a limited range of uses in horticulture. The exception is *Sphagnum* moss, whose pronounced water-holding capacity and slight antiseptic properties have led to several uses, notably as a material for dressing wounds in World War I. There are also signs that certain mosses and liverworts may prove to be of increasing value as indicators of the extent of certain types of pollution, since many species are very sensitive to pollution, particularly sulfur dioxide in the atmosphere.

BLACK MULLEIN], once of importance in witchcraft, and the source of a dye. These species are grown as garden ornamentals, as well as others such as *V. phoeniceum* [PURPLE MULLEIN].
SCROPHULARIACEAE.

**Mummy wheat** or **miracle wheat** the usual names applied to the commonest branched form of the mealy-grained emmer wheat variety *Triticum turgidum* var *mirabile*. MUMMY WHEAT is a variety which differs from the normal *T. turgidum* by having long branches emerging from the lower spikelets instead of the normal three-to-five-grained spikelets. The name MUMMY WHEAT is also applied to various emmer wheat grains occasionally taken from sealed Egyptian tombs of the 18th dynasty. Dyed imitations are often sold in Middle Eastern markets to unsuspecting tourists.
GRAMINEAE.

**Mung bean** one of the common names given to *Phaseolus aureus*, an erect annual bean plant widely cultivated in the tropics and subtropics for its edible pods and green or yellow seeds. The germinated seeds are the chief source of Chinese bean sprouts.
LEGUMINOSAE.

**Musa** a Southeast Asian genus of large to gigantic perennial herbs, the source of the *BANANA and of *abaca fiber (Manila hemp). The basal corms are surmounted by "pseudostems" of leaf sheaths. The terminal inflorescences are thrust up through the center of the pseudostem. Most species fall into two major groups: (1) *Musa* (= *Eumusa*) and *Rhodochlamys;* (2) *Australimusa* and *Callimusa*. The former is most diverse in the region Malaysia–Indochina, the latter in the Borneo–New Guinea area. *M. acuminata* (= *M. cavendishii*) is of great importance as the primary source of the edible bananas to which the inedible *M. balbisiana* contributed by hybridity. *M. textilis* (*Australimusa*), from the Philippine Islands and Borneo is the source of abaca fiber or Manila hemp.

Both *M. acuminata* and *M.* × *paradisiaca* (= *M.* × *sapientum* (*M. acuminata* × *M. balbisiana*)) are called BANANA or EDIBLE PLANTAIN, each containing numerous cultivated forms of edible seedless bananas. *M. acuminata* contains 5 subspecies and includes such cultivars as 'Dwarf Cavendish' and 'Giant Cavendish'. Cultivars of *M.* × *paradisiaca* are of hybrid rather than of autopolyploid origin and include both dessert and cooking bananas. Another edible group of cultivars, sometimes called *M. fehi* [FEHI or FE'I BANANA], is widely cultivated throughout the Pacific.

Some wild bananas are very attractive plants and others have interestingly bizarre features. Thus *M. coccinea* and *M. beccarii* have brilliant scarlet bracts, *M. velutina* has fruits self-peeling at maturity and *M. ingens*, from New Guinea, is the largest herb known to science.
MUSACEAE, about 30 species.

**Muscari** a genus of herbaceous perennial bulbous plants native to Europe, the Mediterranean and western Asia. A number of species are commonly cultivated in gardens, the best-known being *M. botryoides* [GRAPE HYACINTH], with small globose, sky-blue or white flowers in dense racemes 1.2in long on stalks up to 10in high. *M. armeniacum* is similar to *M. botryoides;* a double form called 'Blue Spike' is often cultivated. Other popular species include *M. comosum*, the strongly scented *M. racemosum* (= *M. moschatum*) and *M. latifolium*, which is unusual in having almost black, fertile flowers surmounted by a head of bright violet-blue sterile ones.
LILIACEAE, about 40 species.

*Inflorescence of a species of* Muscari. *Such Grape Hyacinths are popular subjects for cultivation in temperate gardens.* (×3)

*Seeds of the Mung Bean* (Phaseolus aureus), *which may be eaten whole or germinated to give "Chinese bean sprouts".* (×¾)

**Muscat** or **muscatel** a variety of *GRAPE (*Vitis vinifera*) cultivated in wine growing areas throughout the world. The fruit is ellipsoidal in shape with a high sugar content. It is one of the forms of grape which are dried to form *raisins. Most muscatel wine is sweet, including dessert wines such as Beaumes de Venise, except that produced in Alsace and Bulgaria.
VITACEAE.

**Mushrooms** See Fungi, p. 156.

**Musk** or **musk plant** common names for the herbaceous *Mimulus moschata*. The MUSK MALLOW is *Malva moschata*.

**Mustard** a condiment derived from the seeds of *Brassica nigra* [BLACK MUSTARD], *B. juncea* [BROWN MUSTARD], both with dark-colored seeds, and *Sinapis alba* [WHITE MUSTARD] with yellow seeds. BROWN and WHITE MUSTARD are the main sources of seed currently used in the manufacture of table mustard. BLACK MUSTARD has now been more or less completely replaced by BROWN MUSTARD, a smaller, more compact plant whose fruits do not shatter so easily, and are therefore much more suited for mechanical harvesting.

Mustard seed has been used as a spice for thousands of years. The pungency of mustard is due to essential oils (mustard oils, isothiocyanates) which are released by the enzyme hydrolysis of mustard oil glucosides when crushed or powdered mustard seed is mixed with water. English mustard is made with cold water, not with vinegar, which allows the full development of its characteristic clean, hot flavor.

French mustards are of two basic types – the pale yellow Dijon and the darker Bordeaux. Dijon mustard is made from BLACK or BROWN MUSTARD seeds from which the coats have been removed; they are then ground with verjuice (from sour green grapes) into a fine paste. Bordeaux mustard is made from the whole seeds, including the coats, and contains vinegar, sugar, tarragon and other herbs and spices. The vinegar inhibits myrosinase enzyme action and gives a milder mustard lacking in mustard oils. German mustard is similar to Bordeaux mustard in composition. The mild mixed mustard used in the USA (and in piccalilli sauce) is made mainly from WHITE MUSTARD seeds.

Mustard seed, especially that of *S. alba*, is used in curries and pickles in the East. Mustard oil is obtained by pressing the seeds of various species of *Brassica* and is widely used in India as a cooking oil. The mustard in mustard and cress, the salad vegetable, is the seed-leaf stage of *Sinapis alba* or more commonly today of *RAPE, *Brassica napus*.
CRUCIFERAE.

**Mutisia** an exclusively South American genus of perennial herbs or, more rarely, low shrubs, which occur mainly in the Andes from Colombia to Patagonia. The flowers, borne in heads at the apex of short branches, are frequently very colorful, varying from orange or yellow to red or purple (rarely white), but only five species, *M. decurrens*, *M. ilicifolia*, *M. latifolia*, *M. clematis* and *M. acuminata*, are at all frequently cultivated. COMPOSITAE, about 60 species.

**Myosotis** [FORGET-ME-NOTS] a genus of annual, biennial or perennial herbs from temperate regions of all continents. The plants are often hairy and the small, blue, pink, yellow or white flowers are solitary or in terminal cymes. There are many cultivars of *M. scorpioides* [FORGET-ME-NOT], *M. alpestris* [ALPINE FORGET-ME-NOT] and *M. sylvatica* [GARDEN OR WOOD FORGET-ME-NOT], all of which flower best in partly shaded positions. Many of the New Zealand species in cultivation, including *M. angustata* and *M. albida*, have white flowers, and *M. australis* is yellow or white flowered.
BORAGINACEAE, 40–50 species.

**Myrica** an almost cosmopolitan genus of small, aromatic, deciduous or evergreen trees or shrubs. The best-known species is *M. gale* [SWEET GALE], from north temperate regions. Its strongly aromatic leaves are used medicinally against dysentery, as a moth-repellent, and as a flavoring for beer. *M. rubra* (= *M. nagi*), from Japan, southern China, Korea and the Philippines, is cultivated in China for its edible seeds. The evergreen North American tree *M. cerifera* [WAX MYRTLE], the shrubs *M. californica* [CALIFORNIA BAYBERRY] and *M. pensylvanica* [BAYBERRY] are three of the species which produce wax on the surface of their fruits, which is used for candles.
MYRICACEAE, about 35 species.

**Myriophyllum** a cosmopolitan genus of mainly aquatic perennial herbs commonly called milfoils. The plants have either a free-floating habit or a submerged one, in which the plant is anchored by rhizomes to the substrate. In all forms the inflorescences are borne aerially. Several species, including *M. hippuroides* and *M. heterophyllum* [WATER MILFOILS] are used as oxygenating plants in aquaria.
HALORAGACEAE, about 45 species.

*The characteristic cinnamon-colored flaking bark of* Myrtus luma *(*=Amomyrtus luma*). (×⅛)*

*Today, Black Mustard (*Brassica nigra*) is grown mainly for soil cover or grazing and produces an amazing visual display in spring.*

**Myristica** a predominantly Southeast Asian genus of evergreen trees of which the most important commercially is *M. fragrans* (= *M. aromatica*) [NUTMEG TREE] which has aromatic leaves, pale yellow flowers and brown seeds with a thin scarlet aril. It is from the seeds and aril that the spices nutmeg and mace are obtained, but the species is also grown for ornament. It is native to the Moluccas but is grown commercially mainly in Indonesia and the West Indies (Grenada) (see also Nutmeg and Mace).

The wood of the Javanese *M. inermis* is used as a fumigant and the oil of *M. simiarum*, native to the Philippines, is used to cure skin ailments.
MYRISTICACEAE, about 80 species.

**Myroxylon** a small genus of tropical American trees. The trunks of *M. balsamum* yield a *balsam (*Peru balsam from variety *pereirae*, Tolu balsam from variety *balsamum*) used for medicinal purposes and as a fixative in the perfume industry. *M. balsamum* also yields a fragrant, hard, heavy, reddish-brown timber which is exported from Brazil. It is cultivated in the tropics.
LEGUMINOSAE, 2 species.

**Myrrh** or **sweet cicely** common names for *Myrrhis odorata*, a herbaceous perennial native to Europe. It is sometimes used as a potherb, the pinnate aromatic leaves being eaten as salad, and the roots boiled and used as a vegetable. The white flowers are borne in umbels and followed by dark brown ridged fruits about 1in long. This old-time herb was also used in home remedies and for flavoring brandy.

The myrrh used in medicine, incense etc is an oleo-gum-resin obtained from the trunks of species of *Commiphora*, mainly *C. molmol*, native to Arabia and northeast Africa.

**Myrtus** [MYRTLES] a genus of fragrant evergreen shrubs with some trees, from tropical and warm-temperate regions, particularly America. The leaves are fragrant when crushed, and the small, usually white flowers are also fragrant.

*M. communis* [COMMON MYRTLE] the only European native (unless it is naturalized from Asia), has ovate to lanceolate leaves which are dark shining green above; distillation yields the perfume "eau d'ange". The globose fruit is purple-black (white in 'Albocarpa'). Var *tarentina* [TARENTUM MYRTLE] was worn by Athenian judges and victors at the Olympic games. Among ornamental species hardy in warmer temperate areas are: *M. bullata* (= *Lophomyrtus bullata*), a small tree with puckered leaves; *M. luma* (= *Luma apiculata, Amomyrtus luma*), a bush or tree to 65ft with flaking rusty bark; *M. ugni* (= *Ugni molinae*) [CHILEAN GUAVA OR MURTILLO], a small shrub with fragrant, rounded and concave, rose-tinted petals, and ripe fruits used sometimes in jam making; and, perhaps the hardiest, the prostrate shrub *M. nummularia* (= *Myrteola nummularia*).
MYRTACEAE, about 100 species.

**Najas** a cosmopolitan genus of submerged annual and perennial herbs. Some species such as *N. flexilis* when they grow profusely can be used as fertilizer or, when dried, as packing material. In Hawaii, *N. major* is eaten as a salad vegetable.
NAJADACEAE, about 35–50 species.

**Nandina** an East Asian genus represented by a single half-hardy evergreen ornamental shrub species, *N. domestica* [SACRED BAMBOO]. It is bamboo-like in habit with alternate, twice or thrice pinnate leaves which turn red in autumn. The small white flowers are borne in large terminal panicles and the fruit is a red berry.
BERBERIDACEAE, 1 species.

**Naranjilla** the common name for the subshrub **Solanum quitoense*, not known in the wild state but grown commercially in Colombia, Ecuador and Costa Rica at 3 250–8 000ft, for its small, round, bright orange, tomato-shaped, thick-skinned fruits. The rather acidic pulp is used for making drinks and sherbets.
SOLANACEAE.

*... Daffodils,*
*That come before the swallow dares, and take,*
*The winds of March with beauty ...*
*William Shakespeare*

**Narcissus** a genus of bulbous herbs of Europe and North Africa, centered on Spain and Portugal and occupying a wide range of habitats from lowlands to exposed mountain sites at elevations up to 6 500ft. The flowers have six free perianth segments, uniting into a cylindrical tube above the ovary. A distinctive shallow ring or deep cup projecting at the junction of perianth segments and tube is called the corona; it is often more brightly colored than the white or yellow perianth.

There are about 60 wild species and most hybridize freely. Most grow wild in the Pyrenees or around the Mediterranean but some occur further north, *N. pseudonarcissus* [TRUMPET NARCISSUS] extending to England and Wales. *N. tazetta* [POLYANTHUS NARCISSUS] has the widest range, from Spain eastwards to Japan. Most species are spring-flowering but *N. viridiflorus* and *N. serotinus* flower in September and October.

The popular name for *Narcissus* species is DAFFODIL, although, especially in the UK, a distinction may be drawn between those with long, trumpet-shaped coronas [DAFFODILS] and those with small or medium-sized coronas [NARCISSUS]. The genus is divided into two subgenera, *Hermione* and *Narcissus*. The former includes *N. tazetta*. The subgenus *Narcissus* includes most of the commercially important species: *N. hispanicus*, *N. bulbocodium* [PETTICOAT DAFFODIL], *N. jonquilla* [JONQUIL], *N. triandrus* [ANGEL'S TEARS], *N. pseudonarcissus*, *N. poeticus* [POET'S NARCISSUS] and *N. cyclamineus*. The most frequently grown cultivars arose from *N. hispanicus*, *N. pseudonarcissus*, *N. poeticus* and *N. tazetta*.

*Narcissus* became an important ornamental crop at the end of the 19th century and has increased in popularity ever since. In the UK, the Royal Horticultural Society list contains nearly 10 000 named cultivars classified into 11 divisions based on appearance, trumpet shape and parent species. Relatively few cultivars are widely grown commercially, perhaps three-quarters of the world cultivated area being made up of fewer than 20.

Narcissuses are grown commercially in a number of countries throughout the world with a suitable temperate climate and light soils, but the UK area is larger (13 000 acres) than all the others together. There is considerable international trade in narcissus bulbs, mainly from the Netherlands, but increasingly from the UK.

The narcissus is deservedly popular as a garden plant and requires little attention to produce an annual show of flowers. The main commercial importance is for sales of bulbs and of outdoor-grown or greenhouse-forced flowers.

Bulb growing in the field is a highly mechanized, efficient operation, with mechanical planting, harvesting and grading. Bulbs are grown in ridges at planting densities of 0.3–0.4lb/ft$^2$ and left for two years before lifting in the UK or annually in the Netherlands.
AMARYLLIDACEAE, about 60 species.

*The curious-shaped leaves of the Naranjilla (*Solanum quitoense*). The tomato-like fruits of this plant make a refreshing drink. (×2)*

**Narcotic plants** see Medicinal and narcotic plants, p. 226.

**Nardostachys** a small genus of perennial herbs from the Himalayas and western China, with fragrant rhizomes. The rose-purple-flowered *N. jatamansi* (= *N. grandiflora*) yields an essential oil, spikenard, of ancient fame and still valued as a perfume. It is also used as a black hair dye and tonic, and to treat nervous disorders.
VALERIANACEAE, 3 species.

**Nasturtium** a small genus of perennial herbs, native to the Northern Hemisphere, though now widely naturalized. It is sometimes included in the genus **Rorippa*. *N. officinale* and *N. microphyllum* are often cultivated as GREEN or SUMMER *WATERCRESS and the hybrid *N.* × *sterile* as BROWN or WINTER WATERCRESS. The name Nasturtium was applied by a number of the old herbalists to species of the unrelated genus **Tropaeolum*, and is still one of the common names [GARDEN NASTURTIUM] of *T. majus*, a strong-growing annual climber much cultivated in gardens for its attractive bright orange or yellow flowers.
CRUCIFERAE, 6 species.

**Navicula** a very common genus of diatoms usually found living on mud or sand surfaces. The cell is motile (free swimming) and this enables it to move out into the light after being buried by any disturbance of the substrate.
BACILLARIOPHYCEAE.

**Neckera** a genus of mosses from which some species have been transferred to other genera such as *Neckeradelphus*, *Neckeropsis*, *Calyptrothecium*, *Pinnatella* and others. Although *Neckera crispa* is a conspicuous moss (especially on tree trunks) across most

of the north temperate zone and *N. complanata* is distributed across four continents, the genus is primarily tropical. It is among the genera which account for the "pendent" or festooning habit found in some mosses in damp conditions in warm climates. *N. crispa*, on rock substrata, is a notable basic (alkaline) soil indicator.
NECKERACEAE, about 75 species.

**Nectarine** the reddish yellow fruit produced by the species *Prunus persica* var *nucipersica*, a form of peach. Although nectarines are usually smaller than peaches and have a distinctly different flavor, the only factor which distinguishes them without ambiguity is their smooth skin. It is believed that the nectarine first arose thousands of years ago after the spread of the peach from China to Central Asia.
ROSACEAE.

**Nectria** a cosmopolitan genus of ascomycete fungi, many species of which cause important cankers. Probably the most thoroughly studied is *N. galligena*, which causes a perennial canker on a number of hardwoods, notably apples and pears. The flask-shaped ascocarps (perithecia) are usually brightly colored and are formed in clusters on outbreaks of the canker or scattered on bark. Infection occurs in wounds of the tree, the most important being leaf scars formed when the leaves are shed in wet weather; pruning wounds, growth cracks and scab lesions are also important. *N. galligena* also causes "eye rot" of apple or pear fruit.
NECTRIACEAE, about 50 species.

**Nelumbo** a genus of two aquatic species, the pink-petaled *N. nucifera* [INDIAN, HINDU, CHINESE OR SACRED LOTUS], from Asia and northeastern Australia, and the yellow-petaled North American species *N. lutea* (= *N. pentapetala*) [AMERICAN LOTUS, WATER CHINQUAPIN]. The Asian species is sacred to Buddhists; both are prized ornamentals.

*N. lutea* has leaves 12–24in across, raised above water level. The flowers are large, up to 10in wide, yellow and fragrant. The leaves of *N. nucifera* are even larger than those of the AMERICAN LOTUS (up to 36in) and the fragrant, white-tipped rose or pink flowers may be up to 12in wide.

There are numerous old cultivars of *N. nucifera*, including ones known in the west such as 'Kermesina,' 'Alba Grandiflora', 'Alba Striata' with striped petals, as well as gold-fringed, gold-freckled, double-flowered and dwarf forms suitable for container growth.

As well as being highly valued ornamentals, both species have rhizomes that are edible, either raw or cooked. They are juicy, crisp and slightly sweet, and if ground up yield a fine, easily digested form of starch. The leaves are also used in steamed meat dishes, and the fruits (achenes) are regarded as a luxury dessert in China, also being eaten in the Americas. The achenes may also be candied or preserved in China. (See also *Lotus*.)

The Lotus of the ancients and of the myth of the Lotus-Eaters is thought by some authorities to have been *Ziziphus lotus*.
NYMPHAEACEAE, 2 species.

*Canker of an apple branch caused by the ascomycete fungus* Nectria galligena, *which enters through wounds.* (× ¼)

*The Petticoat Daffodil, one of the commonly cultivated dwarf forms, is a naturally occurring variety of* Narcissus bulbocodium. (× ⅓)

**Nemesia** a genus of annual or perennial herbs and subshrubs mostly native to South Africa, with a few in tropical Africa. A number are used as garden bedding plants. The markedly asymmetrical, two-lipped flowers are usually borne in racemes or sometimes solitary. The annual species *N. versicolor* and *N. strumosa* are commonly grown in a range of cultivars with petals in shades of white, yellow, blue, orange, scarlet, and pink.
SCROPHULARIACEAE, about 50 species.

**Nemophila** a genus of annual herbs native to North America, some of which are cultivated as spring and summer bedding plants. The most popular are *N. maculata* [FIVESPOT], which has flowers up to 3in across with white petals each tipped with a purple blotch, and *N. menziesii* (= *N. insignis*) [BABY-BLUE-EYES], with flowers of a similar size, but blue or white and lacking blotches, although cultivars with blue flowers margined with white and with blue veined with purple are also grown.
HYDROPHYLLACEAE, about 11 species.

**Neoregelia** is a genus of South American evergreen herbaceous plants, mostly native to Brazil, with one species in Colombia and Peru. They produce strap-shaped leaves in a basal rosette in such a way as to form a depression or almost a tube at the center. The compact inflorescence is sunk in the center of this depression. The leaves at the center of the rosette are often bright red and this color persists after the white, blue or violet flowers have withered (the flowers last a single night). Several species are grown as ornamental greenhouse and pot plants. *N. carolinae* (= *N. marechalii*) has many cultivated varieties and strains, and var *meyendorffii* is probably the typical form; *N. spectabilis* is also widely grown.
BROMELIACEAE, about 40 species.

Narcissus requienii *growing in the Pyrenees, where it is often found in meadows, along stream banks or on cliff ledges.* (× ½)

**Neottia** a genus of saprophytic leafless orchids indigenous to temperate Eurasia. *N. nidus-avis* [BIRD'S-NEST ORCHID] is found in deciduous woods on calcareous soils. It has no chlorophyll and is entirely of a brownish color. Species of *Neottia* have short, thick, much-branched roots which are mycorrhizal. The outer zone of each root is permeated with a network of fungal hyphae. The hyphae are able to survive and grow

Pitcher Plants (Nepenthes sp), growing in the upper montane rain forests of Malaya. (× ⅓)

near the surface of the root but towards the inside they are digested by enzymes produced by the orchid which, obtaining all its nutrients from the fungus, thus compensates for its photosynthetic deficiency.
ORCHIDACEAE, 3 species.

**Nepenthes** a genus of carnivorous pitcher plants which are common throughout the jungles of the Old World tropics (excluding Africa but including Madagascar). Most are herbaceous vine-like plants, often epiphytic, which climb by means of tendrils which are extensions of the midrib. Mature leaves may be from 12 to 40in long. The tendrils develop to form pitchers which are generally green, often blotched with red or purple, and sometimes variously ribbed. The pitchers are variable in shape and size according to species. Insects are attracted to honey and the bright color of the pitcher; once inside, the slippery surface prevents them from climbing out, and they drown in the water contained in the base of the pitcher. The plant then absorbs the products of decay.

Many beautiful species and hybrids are cultivated, including *N. albomarginata* (a plant suitable for hanging baskets), the robust *N. mirabilis*, *N. hookerana* and their hybrids *N.* × *lawrenceana* and *N.* × *morganiana*.
NEPENTHACEAE, about 70 species.

Part of a Bull Kelp (Nereocystis sp) showing the top of the tubular stipe (stalk) which provides buoyancy. Attached to this are a number of flattened blades. (× $\frac{1}{10}$)

**Nepeta** a genus of annual or perennial herbs occurring more or less throughout warm-temperate regions of the Northern Hemisphere, as well as in the mountains of tropical Africa. Their flowers have a curved, narrow corolla-tube and a two-lipped limb, the lower lip saucer-shaped and often tesselated. The best-known species is the aromatic *N. cataria* [CATMINT, CATNIP] from Europe and North Africa, a popular garden plant with gray leaves and white purple flowers, much liked by cats. *N.* × *faassenii* (= *N. mussinii* × *N. nepetella*) is used as an edging plant with silvery leaves and whorls of lavender flowers. *N. nervosa* has light blue flowers and is also cultivated for ornament.
LABIATAE, 200–250 species.

**Nephrolepis** a genus of terrestrial ferns which are widely dispersed throughout the tropics and subtropics of both hemispheres. They are commonly called LADDER or SWORD FERNS, the attractive crowns of long drooping leaves being a common feature. The genus reproduces rapidly by producing numerous runners and is one of the most important commercial greenhouse ferns. Some, such as *N. biserrata* cultivar 'Furcans', are suitable for growing in baskets.

Other commonly cultivated species include *N. cordifolia* [ERECT SWORD FERN], all cultivars of which, including 'Compacta', 'Plumosa' and 'Variegata', bear erect leaves, and *N. exaltata*, whose cultivars 'Bostoniensis' [BOSTON FERN] and its crested-leaved derivatives are extremely popular house ferns. Two other cultivars, 'Smithii' and 'Whitmanii' are known as LACE FERNS.
POLYPODIACEAE, about 30 species.

**Nereocystis** [BULL KELP] a genus of brown algae which grows in the subtidal zone along the western coast of North America. The plant consists of a sturdy holdfast from which a long tubular stipe arises. This ends in a bladder (containing carbon monoxide and carbon dioxide), bearing flattened fronds.
PHAEOPHYCEAE.

**Nerine** a genus of bulbous perennials native to southern Africa. The leaves are basal and strap-like. A number of species, eg *N. sarniensis* [GUERNSEY LILY] are cultivated as garden and greenhouse plants for their attractive inflorescences of red to crimson flowers. Other popular cultivated species are *N. bowdenii* (rose-pink flowers), *N. pumila* (bright scarlet flowers), *N. humilis* (rose-purple flowers), and *N. flexuosa* cultivar 'Alba' (pure white flowers).
AMARYLLIDACEAE, about 30 species.

**Nerium** a small genus of very ornamental evergreen shrubs, native from the Mediterranean eastwards to Japan. *N. oleander* [COMMON OLEANDER, ROSE BAY] and "*N. odorum*", a sweet-scented form of it, are widely grown as longliving street plantings in mild climates, for their attractive white, pink, rose or purple flowers. However, the plants are poisonous throughout and can be fatal if eaten. They contain oleandrin, a cardiac glycoside which is used medicinally and in rat poisons.
APOCYNACEAE, 2–3 species.

**Nest ferns** a general term applied to certain ferns where the leaves wrap around trunks and branches producing a space in which humus accumulates, eg in the Stag's Horn Fern (*Platycerium bifurcatum).

Common Oleander (Nerium oleander). (× ¼)

*The berries of the Woody Nightshade (*Solanum dulcamara*). The berries have a bitter-sweet taste and are slightly poisonous.* (×1)

**Nettle** a common name for numerous unrelated species of plants which usually have stinging hairs. **Urtica dioica* [COMMON STINGING NETTLE] is a common temperate weed which is used as a source of fiber; the leaves can be eaten as a vegetable. Several other *Urtica* species are also commonly called nettles. *U. urens* [DOG NETTLE, SMALL NETTLE] has similar uses to *U. dioica* and the leaves are used medicinally as a diaphoretic. A number of **Lamium* species are called DEAD NETTLES since the leaves look like those of the stinging nettle but do not sting. The name FALSE NETTLE is applied to several species of **Boehmeria*. The WOOD NETTLE is *Laportea canadensis*, a North American perennial herb which yields a fine strong fiber comparable to *ramie.

**Neurospora** a widespread genus of terrestrial saprophytic fungi especially common in the tropics on soil and vegetation exposed to fire. The fungus is visible as a pink powdery mass made up of chains of wind-dispersed conidia. It can be a serious contaminant in bakeries, where its ability to grow rapidly at fairly high temperature enables it to colonize warm bread; hence its common names of RED BREAD MOLD and BAKERY MOLD. It is also a contaminant of wood-drying kilns. *N. crassa* is much used in genetical studies, as many biochemically deficient mutants have been isolated.
LASIOSPHAERIACEAE, 4 species.

**Nicandra** [APPLE OF PERU] a genus comprising a single species, *N. physaloides*, a glabrous annual herb from Peru. The flowers are solitary, pale blue and drooping, and the calyx is inflated and bladder-like when in fruit. It is a weed in tropical America and the USA and has been used in the production of fly poison. It is sufficiently hardy to be grown as an ornamental border plant.
SOLANACEAE, 1 species.

**Nicotiana** a large New World genus of annual and perennial herbs (rarely shrubs), including the tobacco plant and several ornamental species. About half the species originated in South America; the remainder are natives of western North America and Mexico, Australia and certain islands in the South Pacific.

Appreciable amounts of nicotine are present in about 10 species. Of great economic importance as a stimulant, nicotine is also extracted for insecticidal purposes. Only *N. tabacum* [COMMON *TOBACCO] and, less importantly, *N. rustica* (both from South America) are widely cultivated, being grown throughout the world except in arctic and near-arctic zones. Indian tribes of North America used to smoke, sniff or chew for ritual or pleasure the leaves of *N. bigelovii* and *N. attenuata*.

Several species are cultivated for their attractive inflorescences of tubular flowers ("flowering tobaccos"), particularly *N. alata* (= *N. affinis*), a hybrid called N. × *sanderae* (= *N. alata* × *N. forgetiana*), and *N. glauca* [TREE TOBACCO].

Classic studies in genetics, cytology and physiology have been done with species of *Nicotiana*. Recently, pioneering studies on culturing and hybridization of isolated cells, generation of plants from anthers and tumor formation in hybrids have been performed with members of this genus.
SOLANACEAE, 64 species.

**Nidularium** a small Brazilian genus of epiphytic herbs with rosettes of attractively colored (often reddish or purple) spiny-margined leaves. The flowers are red, blue, purple or white, in a central compound inflorescence, surrounded by bracts which are usually colored. Many of the species are cultivated as greenhouse ornamentals, or outdoors in warmer climates, including *N. innocentii*, with several varieties, *N. fulgens*, with bright scarlet flowers, and *N. procerum* (= *Karatas purpurea*).
BROMELIACEAE, 20–25 species.

**Nierembergia** a genus of subshrubs and perennial herbs native to Mexico and South America. A number of the species, such as *N. scoparia* (= *N. frutescens*) [TALL CUP FLOWER], *N. repens* (= *N. rivularis*) [WHITE CUP FLOWER] and *N. gracilis*, are grown as border and pot plants for their large conspicuous flowers, usually whitish, blue or violet in color.
SCROPHULARIACEAE, about 35 species.

*The Stag's Horn Fern (*Platycerium bifurcatum*) forms a "nest" around the branch of a tree in which humus collects. The branched fertile leaves give this species its popular name.* ($\times\frac{1}{12}$)

*The flowers and stinging leaves of the Common Stinging Nettle (*Urtica dioica*), a common temperate weed.* ($\times\frac{1}{4}$)

**Nigella** a small genus of annual herbs, occurring naturally from Europe across the Mediterranean to Central Asia. *N. damascena* [LOVE-IN-A-MIST, DEVIL-IN-A-BUSH] has large blue flowers surrounded by an involucre of finely dissected upper stem leaves. Some cultivars have white, pink or mauve flowers. *N. hispanica* [FENNEL FLOWER] has deep blue flowers and red stamens, but lacks the showy involucre. *N. sativa* [BLACK CUMIN], a blue-flowered species, with solitary flowers without an involucre, is cultivated for its seeds which are used for seasoning.
RANUNCULACEAE, about 20 species.

**Nightshade** a common name for various species of **Atropa* and **Solanum*, some of which are poisonous. The most commonly occurring species are *A. belladonna* [DEADLY NIGHTSHADE], *S. nigrum* [BLACK NIGHTSHADE] *S. dulcamara* [WOODY NIGHTSHADE, BITTERSWEET]. Another species, **Circaea lutetiana*, is known as ENCHANTER'S NIGHTSHADE.

**Nitella** one of the most common genera of stoneworts, often found forming subaquatic meadows at the bottom of shallow lakes. The plants consists of extremely large translucent internodal cells with branches of small cells arising at the nodes.
CHAROPHYCEAE.

**Nitrobacter** a genus of soil-inhabiting bacteria, several species of which are involved in the conversion of nitrites to nitrates, the latter being available for uptake by roots of plants. (See p. 806.)

**Nitrosomonas** a genus of soil-inhabiting bacteria, several species of which are involved in the conversion of ammonia and ammonium salts to nitrites. (See p. 806.)

**Nolana** a genus of low growing, sometimes prostrate and fleshy-leaved annual or perennial herbs or subshrubs native to semidesert waste regions of America from Peru to Patagonia (Chile). A few species, including *N. humifusa* (= *N. prostrata*) and *N. paradoxa*, are cultivated as garden ornamentals for their attractive white, pink or blue flowers.
NOLANACEAE, about 60 species.

**Nomocharis** a genus of bulbous herbs native to the high meadows of northern Burma, western China and southeast Tibet. They are closely related to *Lilium* with beautiful, more or less open flowers resembling *Odontoglossum* orchids. Among popular cultivated species are the white-flowered *N. mairei* (sometimes flushed purple), the yellow-flowered *N. euxantha* (tinged red at the base) and the yellowish-white-flowered *N. saluenensis* (flushed rose-pink).
LILIACEAE, about 10 species.

**Nopalea** a genus of large cacti native to Mexico, Guatemala and Central America. They are mostly tree-like with definite trunks and flat, fleshy branches bearing spines that are very like those of the PRICKLY PEAR (*Opuntia*). The most important species is *N. cochenillifera* [COCHINEAL CACTUS] of Mexico, the principal food plant of the cochineal insect from which a scarlet food-dye is obtained. *N. cochenillifera* is also widely cultivated for its foliage and its red flowers. Other cultivated species are *N. brittoni* and *N. dejecta*.
CACTACEAE, about 8 species.

**Norfolk Island pine** the common name for *Araucaria heterophylla* (= *A. excelsa*), a tall impressive conifer native only to Norfolk Island in the South Pacific. It is, however, widely cultivated as an ornamental tree, especially in the Mediterranean region, and as a greenhouse pot plant.
ARAUCARIACEAE.

**Nostoc** a genus of blue-green algae having simple chains of cells, which may be differentiated as spores or thick-walled heterocysts, embedded in mucilage. Nostocs have a wide distribution in marine, freshwater and terrestrial habitats and are abundant from polar regions to coral atolls. They often appear as gelatinous masses on damp rocks or soil, where they are important as nitrogen fixers. They may form symbiotic associations, with fungi (as lichens), liverworts, cycads and the flowering plant *Gunnera*. Some species are eaten as a delicacy in the Far East.
NOSTOCACEAE.

**Nothofagus** an important genus of deciduous or evergreen trees ranging in South America from about latitude 33° southwards to Cape Horn and from New Zealand northwards through Tasmania and eastern Australia to New Caledonia and New Guinea. Many species are dominants or codominants in the tropical montane and lowland cool temperate forests of the Southern Hemisphere, though some grow in subtropical lowland conditions.

Several species are important providers of hardwood timber for furniture and construction. Some deciduous species, principally the South American *N. antarctica*, *N. obliqua* [ROBLE BEECH] and *N. procera*, are grown as garden ornamentals for their form and fine autumn coloring. A number of evergreen species are also favored as ornamentals, notably the New Zealand *N. menziesii* [SILVER BEECH], *N. truncata* [HARD BEECH] and *N. solandri* [BLACK BEECH], and the Australian *N. moorei* [AUSTRALIAN BEECH] and *N. cunninghamii* [MYRTLE BEECH].
FAGACEAE, 35–40 species.

*The Roble Beech (*Nothofagus obliqua*), a native of Chile and Argentina but sometimes cultivated in north temperate regions.*

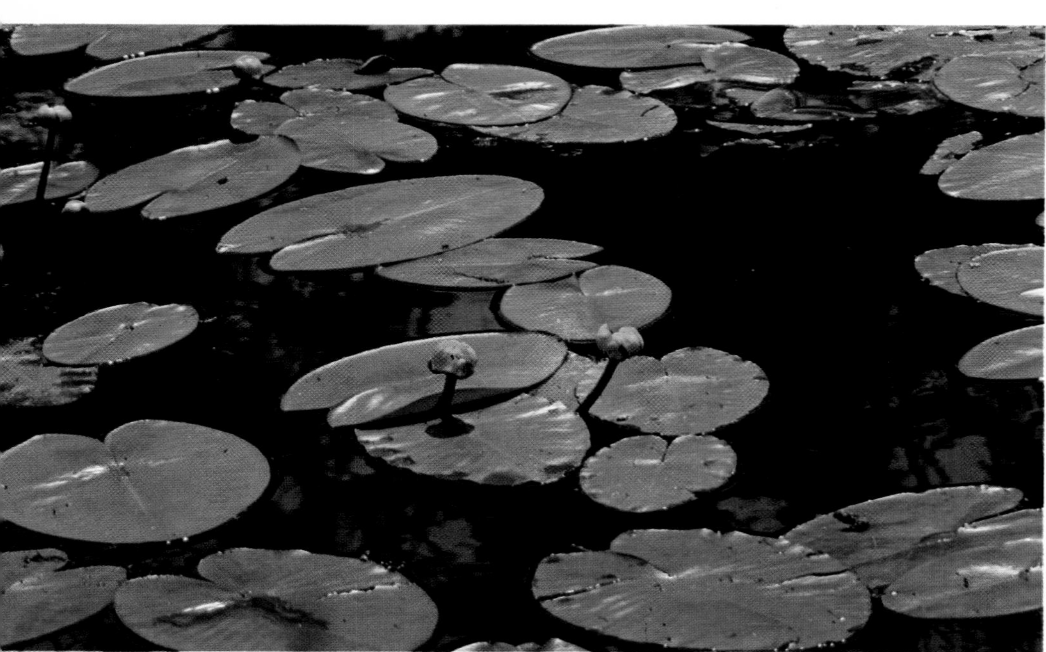

*The Yellow Water Lily (*Nuphar lutea*) is common in ponds and slow-moving rivers throughout north temperate regions.* ($\times \frac{1}{12}$)

**Notholaena** a group of rock-inhabiting xerophytic ferns [sometimes called GOLD, SILVER OR CLOAK FERNS] mainly native to warm-temperate and tropical America. They are sometimes included in the genus *Cheilanthes*. A few are cultivated, especially in rock gardens, including *N. aurea* [GOLDEN CLOAK FERN], *N. newberryi* [COTTON FERN] and *N. sinuata* [WAVY COTTON FERN], while *N. trichomanoides* with its pendulous fronds is popular for hanging baskets.
POLYPODIACEAE, about 60 species.

**Notocactus** a South American genus of small, globular to short-cylindric cacti, much in demand by specialist cactus growers. The flowers, borne near the center, are mostly large and yellow; *N. uebelmannianus* has yellow or deep wine-purple flowers, and *N. graessneri* combines golden spines with lime-green blooms. *N. ottonis* and *N. leninghausii* are old favorites, now rivaled by some superb recent discoveries, such as *N. brevihamatus*, and *N. magnificus*.
CACTACEAE, about 30 species.

**Nuphar** a genus of northern temperate aquatic plants often known as YELLOW WATER-LILIES. Many species are cultivated, usually in still water, although *N. advena* and *N. lutea* [YELLOW WATER-LILY, BRANDY BOTTLE] can be grown in slow-flowing streams. Both of these species and others such as *N. japonica* and *N. polysepala* have peltate floating leaves and large, open yellow flowers. The starchy rhizomes of some species such as *N. advena* [YELLOW POND LILY] are eaten as food by North American Indians.
NYMPHAEACEAE, about 25 species.

**Nutmeg** the common name for **Myristica fragrans* [NUTMEG TREE], from the Moluccas, from which the spices nutmeg and *mace are obtained. Its fruit resembles a small leathery skinned peach with soft yellow flesh, containing one large shiny brown seed enveloped in a bright red network of tissue, the aril. When ripe, the fruit splits into two or four segments and opens out like a star to reveal the spectacular arilate seed.

The fruit is gathered at this stage and separated into pericarp, aril and seed. The former is used to make a jelly preserve. The other parts are slowly dried and cured; the aril then becomes mace and the seed kernels nutmegs. Any broken or inferior seeds are pressed to make "nutmeg butter" for perfumery. Nutmeg and mace are toxic if taken in large quantitites due to the presence of the aromatic oil myristicin.

Today, although nutmegs are grown in various countries, the best come from the species' original home in the Spice Islands.
MYRISTICACEAE.

**Nuts** see p. 244.

**Nymphaea** [WATER-LILIES] a genus found in shallow waters of the Northern Hemisphere and the tropics, a few reaching southern Africa and Australia. The leaves are more or less circular or oval and the flowers are large, showy and, like the leaves, usually float on the water's surface.

Many species have been cultivated for millennia; they show a wide range of colors and are often hybrids, derived from *N. alba* [EUROPEAN WHITE WATER-LILY], *N. lotus* [WHITE LOTUS], *N. rubra*, *N. caerulea* [EGYPTIAN BLUE LOTUS], *N. capensis* [CAPE BLUE WATER-LILY] and *N. tetragona* [PYGMY WATER-LILY], which is small enough for aquarium use.

The seeds of many species are eaten, those of *N. lotus* being made into a kind of bread in India, and in Africa the rhizomes are eaten. The rest of the plant contains the toxic alkaloid nupharin.
NYMPHAEACEAE, about 50 species.

*European White Water-Lilies (*Nymphaea alba*) in a natural pond.* ($\times\frac{1}{15}$)

Nymphaea *'Gladstoniana,' one of the largest hardy-hybrid water-lilies in cultivation.* ($\times\frac{1}{3}$)

**Nymphoides** a genus of annual or perennial aquatic herbs, superficially resembling **Nymphaea* [WATER-LILIES]. *Nymphoides* species are found throughout the tropics and temperate regions, some of them having very wide distribution, eg *N. indica* [WATER SNOWFLAKE], which is pantropical and has yellow and white flowers. *N. aquatica*, of eastern North America, produces curious swollen banana-like root tubers. A common Eurasian species is the yellow-flowered *N. peltata*. The fruits (capsules) of all species mature under water and split by an internal swelling of mucilage.

Several species, sometimes commonly called FLOATING HEARTS, are cultivated as ornamentals, including *N. cordata*, of eastern North America, and the three species mentioned above, but their rapid growth makes them a potential weed menace in the tropics.
MENYANTHACEAE, 20 species.

**Nypa palm** the common name for *Nypa fruticans*, the only member of the genus *Nypa*. It is unique in its abundance and local dominance in mangrove forests from Sri Lanka and the Bay of Bengal eastwards to the Solomons, Micronesia and the Ryu Kyu Islands. This palm has a stem that lies horizontally below the surface of the semi-liquid mud and often branches dichotomously, but no erect trunk. Stout roots are borne on the lower surface. *Nypa* is second only to the *coconut in its importance in the domestic economies of the Malay archipelago. The fronds make a very durable thatch and the "meat" of the young nuts is edible. The young inflorescences, bound and beaten, give a copious yield of sugary liquid, which is boiled to produce a dark treacle. This exudate is then fermented into toddy.
PALMAE, 1 species.

*Rootstocks of a water-lily (*Nymphaea *sp), from a dry-season waterhole in Australia. Such roots were formerly a staple carbohydrate food for the local aboriginal people.*

**Nyssa** a genus of Southeast Asian and North American trees and shrubs. The timber of some species is used commercially, especially *N. aquatica* [COTTON GUM, TUPELO GUM] and *N. biflora* (= *N. sylvatica* var *biflora*) [TUPELO, WATER GUM, TWIN-FLOWERED NYSSA]. *N. sylvatica* [TUPELO, PEPPERIDGE, BLACK or SOUR GUM] is cultivated for ornamental purposes. It is a broadly conical tree, reaching a height of 80ft and producing scarlet and gold autumnal coloring. The fruit of *N. ogeche* [OGEECHE LIME, OGEECHE PLUM] is edible.
NYSSACEAE, 6 species.

*The Fringed Water-Lily (*Nymphoides peltata*).* ($\times\frac{3}{4}$)

# Nuts

Man has eaten nuts since the earliest times, firstly gathered from wild trees but progressively a number of species have been brought into cultivation. The nutritive value of nuts is high, most being rich in protein, oil and fat and they are often high in vitamins. In general, nuts are eaten raw, but some such as the *ALMOND (*Prunus amygdalus*) and *MACADAMIA (*Macadamia integrifolia* and *M. tetraphylla*) are also eaten cooked. The PEANUT (*Arachis hypogaea*) is normally eaten roasted and/or salted.

In a strict botanical sense, a nut is dry type of indehiscent fruit in which the single seed is enclosed in a hard bony or woody pericarp. In this sense few of the seeds known colloquially or in commerce as nuts are correctly described. Most are the stones of drupes such as ALMONDS (*Prunus amygdalus*) or *WALNUT (*Juglans regia*) or are simply seeds from other kinds of fruit container such as PINE KERNELS (*Pinus pinea* etc) and *BRAZIL NUTS (*Bertholletia excelsa*).

The true nuts which are commercially important are found in the families Betulaceae and Fagaceae. Several species from the *HAZEL genus (*Corylus*) (Betulaceae) provide nuts which are enclosed in a leafy involucre. The principle species are the HAZELNUT or COB (*C. avellana*), and the FILBERT (*C. maxima*). Most of today's varieties originated in the 19th century. They are primarily used as dessert nuts but are also used extensively in confectionery.

The SWEET *CHESTNUT (*Castanea sativa*) (Fagaceae) and its relatives in the same genus (see table) are true nuts that are completely enclosed in a very spiny involucre, which eventually opens to allow nuts to fall out. The SWEET CHESTNUT is native to southwestern Asia; it was introduced to southern Europe by the Greeks and later to Britain by the Romans. It did not reach North America until the 18th century, where it has now virtually replaced the AMERICAN CHESTNUT (*C. dentata*), which was all but exterminated by chestnut blight. CHESTNUTS have many uses, being ground into flour normally for use in soups, stews etc, or eaten whole, after either roasting or boiling. Preserved in sugar or syrup, they are used in dishes such as the famous French delicacy, marrons glacés. CHESTNUTS have also found use as livestock feed, notably for pigs. Other true nuts are the *WATER CHESTNUTS (*Trapa natans* and other species) which can be consumed, boiled or their starchy contents ground into flour.

Among the most popular nuts derived from drupes is the ALMOND (*Prunus amygdalus*). The tree is much like a PEACH in appearance, but the fruit is not fleshy, but dry and leathery. ALMONDS originated in the Near East but spread early to Europe and subsequently to North America. Two forms exist, the BITTER ALMOND (var *amara*), which is the main source of almond oil, and the SWEET ALMOND (var *amygdalus*), which is grown for its edible nuts.

The family Juglandaceae contains two genera, *Juglans* and *Carya*, that provide WALNUTS, HICKORY NUTS and PECANS where the fruits are indehiscent drupes which contain stones considered as nuts but in which the hard shell is the inner fruit wall.

The WALNUT (*Juglans regia*) native from southeastern Europe to China, is widely cultivated throughout north temperate regions. The nuts are mainly used for dessert purposes, but also in confectionery and cooking. Young green fruits are often pickled in vinegar. The North American BLACK WALNUT (*J. nigra*) produces nuts that have a tough shell, although softer-shelled cultivars have also been developed. The strongly flavored nuts are mainly used in confectionery and ice cream. The nuts of the BUTTERNUT (*J. cinerea*), another North American tree, have a rich flavor, but also suffer from having a hard shell. Several *Carya* species yield edible nuts, but the most widely cultivated is the North American PECAN (*C. illinoinensis*), which has long enjoyed popularity in North America as a dessert and confectionery nut, and is now increasing in popularity in Europe.

The PISTACHIO (*Pistacia vera*) has long been cultivated in the Mediterranean area and western Asia and more recently in the southern United States. PISTACHIO NUTS, which are the seeds contained in the bony shell of ovoid drupes, are expensive to produce but are valued for their flavor and ornamental color.

The aforementioned nuts are grown mainly in temperate regions, but a number of tropical species are also important. CASHEW NUTS are produced by *Anacardium occidentale*, native to Brazil but now widely grown for their edible kernels in South America, India and East Africa. The nuts, which are mainly used for dessert purposes, have a very high fat and protein content. The CASHEW APPLE is the swollen juicy pedicel – an accessory false fruit. One of the other best-known tropical nuts is the South American BRAZIL NUT. As with the closely related *SAPUCAIA (*Lecythis sabucayo*) and MONKEY NUT (*L. usitata*), the nuts of commerce are harvested from wild trees. BRAZIL NUTS, actually seeds, are produced in quantities of 12–22 inside a large woody, thick-walled capsular fruit that weighs up to 4lb. They have a very high fat content and are mainly used as dessert nuts, particularly around the Christmas period. The tree grows wild in the rain forests of the Amazon Basin in Brazil, Venezuela and Guiana and is never cultivated commercially. The *COCONUT (*Cocos nucifera*) is commercially important for the fiber (coir) extracted from the fruit wall, the dried endosperm or flesh (copra), the oil extracted from the copra, and as a dessert nut. The edible part is the endospermous lining to the stone or nut which encloses a central cavity containing milk when ripe. It is eaten raw and the shredded, desiccated flesh is used extensively in confectionery. Nuts used mainly as masticatories are the *BETEL NUT (*Areca catechu*) and *KOLA NUT, from various *Cola* species.

Possibly the most widely cultivated tropical "nut" is the PEANUT (*Arachis hypogaea*), an annual member of the family Leguminosae, in which fruits (pods) develop beneath the surface of the soil, hence its alternative name of GROUND NUT. The "nuts" of commerce are the seeds, but some appear on the market still enclosed in their fragile fruit cases. PEANUTS are rich in both oil and protein and are chiefly grown as an oil crop; only the best-quality product reaches the dessert market.

The only commercially important nuts contributed by Australian species are MACADAMIA NUTS. MACADAMIAS have long been a source of food for aborigines, but are now mainly consumed as dessert nuts in the United States, with some being used in confectionery. MORETON BAY CHESTNUTS (*Castanospermum australe*), the product of another Australian tree, are collected from the wild and only have local importance.

OYSTER NUTS, the seeds of a member of the cucumber family, *Telfairia pedata*, are mainly consumed in East Africa. PINE NUTS or PINE KERNELS are mainly obtained from the STONE or UMBRELLA PINE (*Pinus pinea*), grown in Italy, where they are eaten raw or roasted and salted, and also in confectionery. Many other pines yield edible seeds which are eaten locally.

PILI NUTS (*Canarium luzonicum* and *C. ovatum*), from the Philippines, and JAVA ALMONDS (*C. commune*), from Java, are the stones of drupes from trees belonging to the family Burseraceae. Along with MACADAMIA NUTS, both PILI NUTS and JAVA ALMONDS have the highest known fat content of any nut (70–72%). The seeds of the PILI NUT yield an oil (pili nut oil) that is used in confectionary, as are the whole roasted nuts. Uncooked nuts are a purgative, but they are eaten locally after cooking. Similarly the JAVA ALMOND is also used in confectionary and the oil is used in cooking and for lighting. These species are not cultivated, the nuts being collected from wild trees and only very small quantities enter international trade.

*Common edible nuts: 1 Hazelnut; 2 Walnut; 3 Black Walnut; 4 Giant Filbert; 5 Butternut; 6 Pecan; 7 Almond; 8 Pistachio; 9 Sweet Chestnut; 10 Macadamia Nut; 11 Brazil Nut; 12 Pine Nut; 13 Water Chestnut; 14 Cashew Nut; 15 Coconut; 16 Betel Nut; 17 Kola. 1 to 4, 6 to 8, 10, 12, 14, 17 (×1); 5, 9, 11, 13, 16 ($\times \frac{2}{3}$); 15, 17 (pod) ($\times \frac{1}{2}$).*

EDIBLE NUTS

| Common name | Scientific name | Main areas of cultivation |
|---|---|---|
| *HAZELNUT, COB EUROPEAN FILBERT | *Corylus avellana* | Turkey, Italy, Spain, France, England, Oregon |
| GIANT FILBERT | *C. maxima (C. americana)* | (as above) |
| TURKISH COBNUT | *C. colurna* | Turkey |
| SWEET *CHESTNUT | *Castanea sativa* | S Europe, N America |
| AMERICAN CHESTNUT | *C. dentata* | N America |
| JAPANESE CHESTNUT | *C. crenata* | Japan, N America |
| CHINESE CHESTNUT | *C. mollissima* | China, Korea, N America |
| *ALMOND | *Prunus amygdalus* (= *P. dulcis*) | Mediterranean, SW Asia, N America |
| SWEET ALMOND | var *amygdalus* | America |
| BITTER ALMOND | var *amara* | |
| *WALNUT | *Juglans regia* | Europe, Asia, N America |
| BLACK WALNUT, EASTERN WALNUT | *J. nigra* | N America |
| BUTTERNUT | *J. cinerea* | N America |
| JAPANESE WALNUT | *J. ailanthifolia* | Japan, N America |
| CHINESE WALNUT | *J. cathayensis* | China, N America |
| PECAN | **Carya illinoinensis* | N America |
| SHAGBARK HICKORY | *C. ovata* | N America |
| SHELLBARK HICKORY | *C. laciniosa* | N America |
| *BRAZIL NUT, PARANUT | *Bertholletia excelsa* | Amazon region (wild) |
| *SAPUCAIA, SAPUCAYA | *Lecythis sabucayo* | S America (wild) |
| MONKEY NUT | *L. usitata* | S America (wild) |
| CASHEW NUT | **Anacardium occidentale* | Tropical S America, India, E Africa |
| *COCONUT | *Cocos nucifera* | India, Sri Lanka, Malaysia, Indonesia, Philippines |
| *MACADAMIA NUT, AUSTRALIA, or QUEENSLAND NUT, (smooth shell) | *Macadamia integrifolia* | Australia, California |
| MACADAMIA NUT (rough shell) | *M. tetraphylla* | Australia, California |
| MORETON BAY CHESTNUT | *Castanospermum australe* | Australia (wild) |
| OYSTERNUT | *Telfairia pedata* | E Africa |
| PEANUT, GROUND NUT | **Arachis hypogaea* | India, tropical Africa, China |
| PILI NUT | *Canarium luzonicum* *C. ovatum* | Philippines |
| JAVA ALMOND | *C. commune* | Java |
| PISTACHIO | **Pistacia vera* | E. Mediterranean, India, S USA |
| *BETEL NUT | *Areca catechu* | Old World tropics |
| *KOLA | *Cola nitida* | W Africa, Caribbean |
| | *C. acuminata* | W Africa, Brazil |
| WATER CHESTNUT | *Trapa natans* *T. bicornis* *T. maximowiczii* | E Asia, Malaysia, India |
| PINE NUT, PINE KERNEL | **Pinus pinea* | Mediterranean |
| | *P. pinaster* | Mediterranean |
| SWISS STONE PINE | *P. cembra* | Europe |
| MEXICAN STONE PINE | *P. cembroides* | Mexico |

**Oak** the common name for the large and economically important genus *Quercus*, which consists of deciduous, semi-evergreen or evergreen trees and some shrubs prized for their noble aspect and autumn colors. Oaks occur predominantly in the Northern Hemisphere, with the majority in North America, but a large number in Europe, the Mediterranean and Asia. In South America, oaks occur only on the Andes of Colombia. The relatively small tropical distribution is virtually confined to high mountains.

The leaves are rarely entire, and the margins are usually cut or lobed in various ways. The fruit is a large, solitary, characteristic nut (acorn) more or less enclosed from the base upward by a cup (cupule) composed of variously shaped scales usually more or less imbricate.

Oak provides one of the finest hardwoods and is in the forefront of temperate timbers because of its great strength and durability. It is not easy to distinguish the various commercial oak timbers, but a distinction is made between the WHITE OAKS and RED OAKS, the former being somewhat harder and more durable. Both kinds are used for the same purposes: furniture, and bridge, ship and many other types of building. The wood will take a high polish and when radially cut it is a favorite for paneling because of the fine "silver grain" formed by the wood rays. Important WHITE OAK species are *Q. alba*, *Q. macrocarpa*, *Q. robur*, *Q. petraea* (= *Q. sessiliflora*); important RED OAKS are *Q. rubra* (= *Q. borealis*), *Q. velutina* and *Q. palustris*. *Q. virginiana* [LIVE OAK] is considered to be the most durable of all oak timbers. It is used for trucks, ships and toolmaking, but unfortunately is now in short supply.

The timber of some oaks is used for inlay work. For example, "brown oak" is oak timber stained by the mycelium of the bracket fungus *Fistulina hepatica*. Similarly, oak timber may be stained a deep emerald green by the mycelium of the cup fungus *Chlorosplenium aeruginascens*. The green coloring substance has been isolated and characterized as a rare type of green pigment named xylindein.

*Cork is obtained from the outer bark of *Q. suber* [CORK OAK, LIVE OAK] from southern Europe. *Q. coccifera* [KERMES OAK, GRAIN TREE] is the host for a scale insect, *Coccus ilicis*, which since medieval times has been extracted to give a fine scarlet dye. A bright yellow dye, quercitron, is obtained from the inner bark of *Q. velutina* [BLACK or YELLOW-BARKED OAK]. *Q. faginea* and the closely related *Q. infectoria* are important sources of tannins from the bark and from galls.

Both *Q. coccifera* and *Q. ilex* [HOLM OAK] are evergreen and are characteristic of the Mediterranean region, the former making impenetrable holly-like bushes, the latter trees that will form forests if left alone. The HOLM OAK is often considered a reliable indicator of the Mediterranean climate.

*Ripe Common Oats (*Avena sativa*) ready for harvesting. This species is particularly suited to cool, wet climates.* (×1)

*Two ornamental oaks – Red Oak (*Quercus rubra*) in winter dress, with behind it an evergreen Holm Oak (*Q. ilex*).*

Acorns are not generally of much economic importance, but they are eaten by small game birds and have been used to fatten pigs and poultry. They are not much used for human consumption but those of *Q. rotundifolia* are quite palatable.

Many oaks reach noble proportions and are long-lived. For this reason a number of species are grown as specimen ornamentals. Added to this, many have rich autumn tints and/or attractively cut leaves. In the former group are *Q. ellipsoidalis* [NORTHERN PIN OAK], with crimson autumn foliage, *Q. phellos* [WILLOW OAK], with yellow and orange autumn foliage, *Q. coccinea* [SCARLET OAK] and *Q. palustris* [PIN OAK], both with scarlet autumn foliage, and *Q. rubra* [RED OAK], whose leaves turn through red, mixed yellow and brown to red-brown before falling. The last three species are native to the eastern USA and make a major contribution to the magnificent autumn display of that region.

Other attractive ornamentals include *Q. alnifolia* [GOLDEN OAK], with leaves yellow beneath, *Q. castaneifolia* [CHESTNUT-LEAVED OAK], with coarsely toothed leaves, grayish beneath, *Q. frainetto* [HUNGARIAN or ITALIAN OAK], with deeply lobed leaves, and *Q. marilandica* [BLACKJACK OAK], which has almost triangular leaves. Finally, mention should be made again of the HOLM OAK, which is widely grown in temperate regions for its rounded form and glossy evergreen leaves. It thrives in most well-drained soils and tolerates clipping, shade and coastal situations.
FAGACEAE.

**Oat** the common name for several species of the mostly annual grasses of the genus **Avena*, predominantly native to temperate regions and to mountains in the tropics. Oats are a major temperate cereal and occur in the cultivated form in three groups: the diploid *strigosa-brevis* [FODDER OATS], the tetraploid *abyssinica* and, most importantly, the hexaploid *sativa-byzantina-nuda* group. The first oats to be cultivated were those of the *strigosa-brevis* group and these continued in cultivation until the 20th century at the extremes of soil and climate conditions.

The two main species of oat cultivated are the hexaploid *A. sativa* [COMMON OAT], grown in cooler and wetter regions, and *A. byzantina* [RED OR ALGERIAN OAT] which is grown in hotter, drier areas. Most cultivated oats are grown in the USA, southern Canada, the USSR and Europe, particularly in Mediterranean countries. Another cultivated hexaploid species, *A. nuda* [NAKED OAT], is Chinese in origin and may well have been derived from the other two cultivated species of this group. There is evidence that these three cultivated species were derived from *A. sterilis* [ANIMATED OAT]. *A. fatua* [WILD OAT, TARTARIAN OAT, POTATO OAT, FLAVER, DRAKE] is a weedy species evolved from either *A. sterilis*, *A. sativa* or *A. byzantina*. *A. abyssinica*, confined to Ethiopia, is a member of the *barbata* group of tetraploids and may well have evolved by autopolyploidy from the *strigosa* group diploids.

Only wheat, maize and barley are more important as temperate cereal crops than oats. As well as being adapted to cool, moist conditions, oats grow and mature rapidly, so can be grown where the season is short. The straw is a valuable winter feed for livestock and some of the crop is cut for hay or silage. The oat grain contains about 15% of protein and 8% fat, the remainder being mostly carbohydrate. It is a valuable crop for Man and his livestock, and has been esteemed for centuries as a food for horses.
GRAMINEAE.

**Ochna** a genus of deciduous trees and shrubs native to South Africa and tropical Africa and Asia. Although the yellow or green flowers are attractive, it is the clustered fleshy fruits which are the main reason for growing such species as the South African *O. atropurpurea* and *O. serrulata* as ornamental shrubs in gardens within the tropics or in temperate regions under glass.
OCHNACEAE, about 85 species.

*A marble gall (oak apple) on oak (*Quercus *sp) containing the larva of the cynipid wasp* Andricus kollari. *This gall contains tannins used in the manufacture of blue-black ink.* (×1½)

*A temperate mixed woodland of southern England comprising oak (*Quercus *sp), Silver Birch (*Betula pendula*) and Bracken (*Pteridium aquilinum*).*

**Ochroma** see BALSA.
BOMBACACEAE, 1 species.

**Ocimum** a genus of herbs and subshrubs mainly from tropical and subtropical regions, and containing several potherbs. The best-known is *O. basilicum* (see BASIL). *O. sanctum* [HOLY BASIL] is a sacred plant in the Hindu religion. *O. viride* [FEVER PLANT] is used as a tea-like infusion in West Africa and is locally used as a treatment for feverish conditions.
LABIATAE, about 150 species.

**Ocotea** a tropical and subtropical genus of trees mostly from the New World but with some species in southern and East Africa and the Atlantic islands. Several are economically important for their timber. *O. rodiaei* [BIBISI TREE, GREENHEART] yields a very hard wood used for marine work (see GREENHEART). Other New World species include the West Indian *O. leucoxylon* [MAZA LAUREL] with a soft wood used for general carpentry. *O. rubra*, from Guiana and Brazil, and the hard, heavy *O. spathulata*, from the West Indies. *O. bullata* [BLACK STINKWOOD] is locally important in South Africa. Several species, notably *O. indecora* and *O. squarrosa* (both natives of Brazil), also yield medicinal preparations.
LAURACEAE, about 300 species.

**Odontoglossum** a genus of tropical Central and South American epiphytic, pseudobulbous orchids, many species of which are prized as ornamental plants, eg *O. crispum*, with many cultivars, and *O. pulchellum* [LILY-OF-THE-VALLEY ORCHID].

Flower color ranges from purest white to deep, dull maroon-purples and bright shining chestnut browns. Usually large (up to 4in in diameter) and frequently with striking color combinations, the flowers have made odontoglossums very popular plants for cultivation both as specimen plants and cut-flowers. Many hybrids between *Odontoglossum* species, and with species of related genera such as **Oncidium*, **Miltonia*, and **Brassia*, have produced the full spectral range of flower colors.
ORCHIDACEAE, about 200 species.

**Oedogonium** a genus of widespread filamentous green algae found in ponds and streams. When young they are usually attached by a holdfast but when mature they form free-floating masses.
CHLOROPHYCEAE.

**Oenothera** a genus of herbs and shrubs native to temperate and subtropical North and South America and also represented in the West Indies. It includes the EVENING PRIMROSES, which are night-flowering, and the SUNCUPS or SUNDROPS, which are day flowering.

The flowers are either solitary or in long racemes and are normally large, showy, and white, yellow or reddish in color. Although a number of species have become widespread weeds, many species are cultivated either in rock gardens (such as *O. acaulis*, a white to

rose flowered tufted perennial) or in garden borders. Popular species include *O. biennis* [COMMON EVENING PRIMROSE], whose roots and shoots are edible, *O. nocturna*, *O. missourensis* (= *Megapterium missourense*), *O. tetragona* (= *O. youngii*), *O. bistorta* [SUNCUP] and *O. fruticosa* [SUNDROPS].
ONAGACEAE, about 80 species.

**Oil crops** see p. 250.

**Okra** the common name for **Hibiscus esculentus* (= *Abelmoschus esculentus*), a stout, annual herb which grows up to 6.5ft, native to central Africa but widely cultivated throughout the tropics and subtropics for its soft edible pod. Among other common names are GUMBO, SYRIAN MALLOW and LADIES FINGERS. The showy yellow flowers ripen to produce fruits (pods) which when full grown are up to 10in long and contain numerous brown or black seeds. The wall of the unripe pod is fleshy and extremely mucilaginous.

The fruit is usually used while still unripe and green and while in this state may also be preserved by slicing and drying. After drying it is often powdered. Okra fruits are also preserved by canning, salting, pickling and so on, but are more often used fresh or cooked as a vegetable ingredient of many regional dishes; in this form it is very slimy because of the mucilage it contains and is perhaps an acquired taste. The powdered okra is used as a thickening for soups, stews etc.

The seeds of okra are often used as a substitute for coffee while the leaves and young immature fruits have long been used as emollient poultices. Decoctions of the fruit are widely used for a variety of medicinal purposes such as the treatment of catarrh, eye complaints and diseases of the urogenital system.

The stem of okra also contains long useful fibers which can be used for rope- and sail-making, and the leaves can also be used as a culinary herb. Many varieties have been produced through its long history in several continents. These varieties differ in the size and form of the fruit, its flavor and the amount of mucilage contained in its flesh. *H. abelmoschus* (= *Abelmoschus moschatus*) [MUSK OKRA, MUSK MALLOW], is a closely related species which comes from the Indian subcontinent and, like okra, is cultivated throughout the tropical regions of the world. It is grown for its showy flowers as well as its seeds, called ambretta seeds, which have an oleo-resinous oil in the seed-coats. This has a musky odor and is often used in perfumery as a substitute for musk.
MALIACEAE.

*Okra fruits (*Hibiscus esculentus*); the pods are picked while still green and are eaten fresh or cooked. Okra is grown throughout the tropics.* ($\times \frac{1}{10}$)

Olearia stellulata *has a mass of white daisy-like flowers, from which the common name, Daisy Bush, is derived.*

**Olea** a small genus of evergreen trees or shrubs, native in warm temperate or tropical regions, from southern Europe and the Mediterranean to Africa (the main center), southern Asia, eastern Australia and New Caledonia. The best-known species is *O. europaea* [COMMON OLIVE], very widely grown since early times in areas of Mediterranean climate for its edible fruits and oil (see OLIVE). Other cultivated species include *O. ferruginea* (= *O. cuspidata*) [INDIAN OLIVE] and *O. africana* [WILD OLIVE]. The wood of these and other species such as *O. laurifolia* [BLACK IRONWOOD] is often valued.
OLEACEAE, about 20 species.

**Olearia** [DAISY BUSHES, DAISY TREES, TREE ASTERS] a genus of evergreen pubescent small trees and shrubs native to Australia, Tasmania and New Zealand, with a few species in New Guinea. The foliage is almost heath-like in *O. solandri*, extremely narrow in *O. lineata*, and in *O. nummulariifolia* the small leaves are thick and rounded and packed closely on the stems. Most species, however, have typical flat leaves usually with entire margins. In *O. macrodonta* and *O. ilicifolia* the leaves are coarsely toothed and holly-like. In *O. argyrophylla* they may be over 6in in length but in most species they are much smaller, for example 2in in *A. allomii*.

The flower heads are of typical daisy form. In *O. colensoi*, *O. forsteri* and *O. traversii*, outer ray florets are absent. Flower color is usually white or yellowish but in *O. gunniana* pink and blue forms are known and in *O. semidentata* the typical form is purple. The latter is one of the largest-flowered species, with flower heads as much as 2in in diameter. Most of the above and many other species are grown in gardens as ornamental shrubs.
COMPOSITAE, about 100 species.

**Olive** the common name for **Olea europaea*, widely cultivated in areas with a Mediterranean climate. Trees may survive for 1 500 years or more and are among the oldest trees known in Europe; it is thought that some of the clones in existence today have survived from Roman times.

Olives are hand picked when straw-colored for green table olives and when black and ripe for table use, cooking or more usually for oil. Olives are inedible as gathered from the trees, and they are subjected to various treatments such as steeping in a potash or salt solution which gives rise to a lactic acid fermentation, and they are then preserved in brine. Black olives may be stored direct in a brine solution but the best-quality table ones are preserved in a marinade of olive oil, often with various herbs such as species of thyme, rosemary etc. Green olives are often sold stoned and stuffed with sweet red pepper, anchovy or almonds.

The main producers of olive oil are Spain, Italy and Greece. The finest oil is obtained from the first cold pressing and is of delicate flavor (virgin oil); subsequent pressings are made under heat and are of poorer quality. The press cake formed may be treated with solvents to give a final extract of oil and the residue can be processed for use as cattle cake, fertilizer or in soap manufacture. Apart from a major use in garnishing salads, olive oil is widely used for medicinal purposes, for canning sardines and other preserves, in dressing wool, and in soap manufacture and cosmetics. Olive wood is decorative and can be finely worked.

The name OLIVE is also given to many

*The spectacular* Oncidium pulvinatum *is one of the many orchid species that grow in the Brazilian rain forest.* ($\times 1$)

*Cumin (*Cuminum cyminum*) sown in between olive trees (*Olea europaea*) in the Middle East.*

unrelated species such as *Canarium album* [CHINESE OLIVE], *Elaeocarpus serratus* [CEYLON OLIVE], *Sterculia foetida* [JAVA OLIVE] and *Dodonaea viscosa* [SAND OLIVE] to name but a few.

**Olpidium** a widespread genus of plant-parasitic chytrid fungi. *O. brassicae* in the roots of crucifers is thought to carry certain plant viruses such as tobacco necrosis virus. At maturity, the total protoplasm of the thallus is converted into one spherical, ellipsoid or cylindrical zoosporangium, one to several in a host cell. A discharge tube usually penetrates the host cell wall to the exterior. The released zoospores reinfect other plants.
OLPIDIACEAE, 25–30 species.

**Omphalodes** a genus of annual, biennial or perennial herbs found in damp shady places in mountain crevices or maritime rocks and sands through southern Europe, North Africa, southwestern Asia and Mexico. The flowers, which are solitary and axillary or in terminal cymes, are blue or white in color with a short tube and five prominent scales at the throat. Several species are cultivated, particularly the perennial *O. verna* [BLUE EYED MARY, VENUS NAVELWORT, CREEPING FORGET-ME-NOT], a popular plant of cottage gardens, and *O. cappodocica*.
BORAGINACEAE, about 24 species.

**Oncidium** a large tropical Central and South American genus of epiphytic pseudobulbous orchids all with markedly similar flowers, both in shape and color pattern, but of considerable vegetative variability. The basic flower color is bright canary-yellow for the petals and sepals, while their bases are a unique combination of the basic yellow, overlain, speckled, blotched or dotted with shades of brown. The plants can be upright, pendulous or scrambling, generally with a long strap-shaped leaf arising from each pseudobulb. Densely mottled blackish-green leaves are characteristic of plants such as *O. krameranum* [BUTTERFLY ORCHID], from the damper and warmer regions from Costa Rica to Ecuador. Species such as the West Indian *O. altissimum* and *O. papilio* (also BUTTERFLY ORCHID), from Venezuela to Peru and Brazil, are widely grown and hybridized. Other attractive cultivated species include *O. cheirophorum* [COLOMBIA BUTTERCUP], from Costa Rica to Panama, and the Brazilian *O. flexuosum* [DANCING-DOLL ORCHID].
ORCHIDACEAE, about 400 species.

**Onion** the common name for species of **Allium*, the best-known of which is *A. cepa* [COMMON ONION], grown throughout the world as an annual crop, although it is ordinarily a biennial. The COMMON ONION probably originated in Central Asia, possibly Afghanistan, and there are references to its cultivation in the Middle East dating back at least 3 000 years.

With the spread of onion culture, numerous cultivars (such as the *shallots) have appeared, differing in size, shape, color, flavor, adaptability in bulb formation in relation to temperature and day-length, keeping qualities, pungency and resistance to pathogenic diseases such as *Botrytis* neck-rot and leafblight, *Sclerotium* white rot, and onion yellow dwarf virus. World production of onions is approximately 12 million tons, principal producers being the USA, Spain, Japan, Turkey, Italy and Egypt.

The COMMON FIELD ONION is propagated from seeds, but other races are propagated as sets, ie small onions arrested in their development from seed, ripened off and planted out the following spring as multipliers where the bulb can be divided into separate plantable portions. The onion bulb consists of a mass of swollen leaf-bases. They form by the lateral expansion of leaf-base cells and the subsequent differentiation of swollen and bladeless bulb scales instead of bladed leaves. Compared to other fresh vegetables, onions are high in digestible carbohydrate and intermediate in protein content. When onion tissue is wounded, an enzyme reaction releases sulfur-containing volatile compounds that give onions their characteristic flavor and lachrymatory properties. This reaction takes some time and treatment which rapidly disrupts enzyme proteins (eg boiling) will prevent the development of full flavor.

Another widely cultivated species, also Asian in origin is *A. fistulosum* [WELSH ONION, JAPANESE BUNCHING ONION], which is leafier and has a softer bulb; the long leaf-bases form the edible part. It is the principal garden onion of China and Japan. (See also CHIVES, GARLIC, LEEK and SHALLOT.)
LILIACEAE.

*Onions (*Allium cepa*) growing commercially in Lincolnshire, England.*

# Oil Crops

Economically important vegetable oils form two main groups: the essential volatile oils (see p. 136) and the fixed or fatty oils. It is probable that all seeds contain some fixed oil but only about a dozen contain sufficiently large quantities of oil of a suitable type, and are cultivated easily enough to be major crops (see accompanying table). The fixed oils are divided into: (a) drying oils which are used in the manufacture of paints and varnishes; (b) semidrying oils used for foods and in soap manufacture; and (c) nondrying oils which remain liquid at ordinary temperatures and are used for edible purposes.

In organized industrial situations vegetable oil is extracted from plant material by hydraulic and screw presses or solvent extraction systems, but throughout the tropics there are many local simple methods of extraction. The residue remaining after oil extraction (oilcake) is rich in protein and is therefore employed in the manufacture of animal foods. In certain cases the residues contain toxic factors and then the material can only be used as a fertilizer. Although oil has been extracted from the seeds of many species, there are only about twelve major oil crops which, in the main, are cultivated in the tropics.

Oils used mainly as cooking and salad oils and in margarine manufacture include those from the *SUNFLOWER (*Helianthus annuus*), *MAIZE or CORN (*Zea mays*), GROUND NUT (*Arachis hypogaea*), *SOYBEAN (**Glycine max*), *OLIVE (*Olea europaea*), and SESAME (**Sesame indicum*). *Rape oil (*Brassica campestris* and *B. napa*) is also used in margarine manufacture and in industry as a lubricant. *Castor oil (**Ricinus communis*), in addition to its medicinal properties, is largely used in the

OIL CROPS

| Common name | Scientific name | Family |
|---|---|---|
| **I Major oil crops** | | |
| *SUNFLOWER OIL | *Helianthus annuus* | Compositae |
| *RAPE OIL | **Brassica campestris*, (*B. rapa*) *B. napus* | Cruciferae |
| *CASTOR OIL | *Ricinus communis* | Euphorbiaceae |
| *MAIZE OR CORN OIL | *Zea mays* | Gramineae |
| PEANUT, GROUND NUT OIL | **Arachis hypogaea* | Leguminosae |
| *SOYBEAN, SOYA OIL | *Glycine max* | Leguminosae |
| *LINSEED OIL | *Linum usitatissimum* | Linaceae |
| *COTTON SEED OIL | *Gossypium* species | Malvaceae |
| *OLIVE OIL | *Olea europaea* | Oleaceae |
| *COCONUT OIL (COPRA) | *Cocos nucifera* | Palmae |
| PALM OIL | **Elaeis guineensis* | Palmae |
| AMERICAN PALM OIL | *E. oleifera* | Palmae |
| SESAME OIL | **Sesamum indicum* | Pedaliaceae |
| **II Minor oil crops** | | |
| BABASSU OIL | **Orbignya barbosiana* (*O. speciosa*) | Palmae |
| COHUNE OIL | *O. cohune* | Palmae |
| BEN OIL | **Moringa pterygosperma* (*M. oleifera*) | Moringaceae |
| *BRAZIL NUT OIL | *Bertholletia excelsa* | Lecythidaceae |
| CANDLENUT | **Aleurites moluccana* | Euphorbiaceae |
| CHINA WOOD OIL | *A. fordii* | Euphorbiaceae |
| TUNG OIL | *A. montana* | Euphorbiaceae |
| JAPAN WOOD OIL | *A. cordata* | Euphorbiaceae |
| CARAPA, ANDIROBA | *Carapa guianensis*, *C. procera* | Meliaceae |
| CASHEW NUT KERNEL OIL | **Anacardium occidentale* | Anacardiaceae |
| *CHAULMOOGRA OIL | *Hydnocarpus wightiana* *H. anthelmintica* *Taraktogenos kurzii* | Flacourtiaceae |
| *COCOA OR CACAO BUTTER OIL | *Theobroma cacao* | Sterculiaceae |
| *COLZA | *Brassica rapa* *B. napus* | Cruciferae |
| CROTON OIL | **Croton tiglium* | Euphorbiaceae |
| ENG OIL | *Dipterocarpus tuberculatus* | Dipterocarpaceae |
| GORLI OIL | *Oncoba echinata* | Flacourtiaceae |
| GURJUM, GURJUN OIL | **Dipterocarpus lamellantus* *D. turbinatus* *D. alatus* | Dipterocarpaceae |
| HEMPSEED OIL | **Cannabis sativa* | Moraceae |
| ILLIPE NUT OIL | **Shorea macrophylla* *S. stenoptera* | Dipterocarpaceae |
| *KAPOK SEED OIL | *Ceiba pentandra* | Bombacaceae |
| *MACASSAR OIL | *Schleichera oleosa* | Sapindaceae |
| MAW SEED OIL | **Papaver somniferum* | Papaveraceae |
| *MUSTARD OIL | *Sinapis alba* *Brassica nigra* *B. juncea* | Cruciferae |
| NIGER SEED OIL | **Guizotia abyssinica* | Compositae |
| OITICICA OIL | *Licania rigida* | Chrysobalanaceae |
| *PEACH OIL | *Prunus persica* | Rosaceae |
| PERILLA OIL | **Perilla frutescens* (*P. ocymoides*) | Labiatae |
| PISTACHIO OIL | **Pistacia vera* | Anacardiaceae |
| *WALNUT OIL | *Juglans regia* | Juglandaceae |

*Major oil-yielding plants: 1 Castor Oil; 2 Coconut; 3 Sesame; 4 Olive; 5 Oil Palm; 6 Sunflower. Fruits: 1, 3, 4, 5, 6 (×½); 2 (×¼). Fruiting head: 5 (×⅙). Shoots: 1 (×1/15); 3 (×⅙); 5 (×1/120); 6 (×⅛).*

*Two major oil crops in mass cultivation.*
Above *Olive groves* (Olea europaea) *near Toledo, Spain. The oil, which is extracted from the fruit wall and seed kernel, is mainly used for cooking, salad dressings, soap manufacture and in food preservation.*
Right *Sunflowers* (Helianthus annuus), *the seeds of which yield oil that is used in cooking and in the manufacture of margarine.*

preparation of paints, enamels, soap and lubricants.

*Linseed oil (*Linum usitatissimum*) is the most important of the drying oils and is used in the manufacture of paints and varnishes. *Cotton oil (*Gossypium* species) is a by-product of commercial cotton production for fiber and is used in foodstuffs. The dried kernel or copra of *Cocos nucifera* [*COCONUT] is one of the major sources of vegetable oil in world trade. Fruit of the West African *Elaeis guineensis* [OIL PALM] yields two oils: palm oil from the mesocarp and palm kernel oil from the kernel. Both are used in food and soap manufacture. Some other commercially valuable minor oil crop species are listed in the accompanying table.

**Onobrychis** a genus of herbs or spiny subshrubs from Europe, North Africa and western Asia. They have tufts of odd-pinnate leaves and racemes or spikes of pink, purple or white, pea-like flowers, and are an important constituent of grazing pastures and poor vegetation in southeastern Europe. *O. viciifolia* [SAINFOIN, ESPARCET or HOLY CLOVER] is used as a fodder crop, although its use has declined with the introduction of improved strains of *CLOVER and *LUCERNE. Some species including *O. laconica* and *O. radiata* are grown as garden ornamentals.
LEGUMINOSAE, about 60 species.

**Onoclea** a genus represented by a single species of fern, *O. sensibilis* [SENSITIVE FERN], native to northern Asia and North America, and cultivated in gardens for its two kinds of foliage: deeply pinnatifid sterile leaves up to 40in long and the smaller erect bipinnate fertile fronds with the pinnules rolled up into bead-like segments which open to discharge the spores.
ASPIDIACEAE, 1 species.

**Ononis** a genus of annual, biennial and perennial herbs and subshrubs mainly from Europe and the Mediterranean region. Most have pink or purplish pea-like flowers. They will thrive in the poorest stony and sandy soils and species like *O. spinosa* [SPINY RESTHARROW] were at one time a serious weed of arable land. Two attractive garden subshrubs are *O. rotundifolia* and *O. fruticosa*, with pink flowers and grayish foliage.
LEGUMINOSAE, about 70 species.

**Onopordum** a genus of annual and biennial herbs native to Europe, North Africa and western Asia. Several species are cultivated in garden borders, such as *O. acanthium* [COMMON COTTON OR SCOTCH THISTLE] and *O. tauricum* (= *O. virens*). They are tall, erect plants, up to 10ft high, with silvery jagged leaves and reddish purple or blue, thistle-like flower heads.
COMPOSITAE, about 40 species.

**Onosma** a genus of evergreen annual biennial or perennial herbs or subshrubs with rough bristly hairs, native from the Mediterranean region to the Himalayas and China. They have tubular, pendent flowers and usually gray-green leaves. Of several cultivated species *O. alboroseum*, with white flowers turning deep red then bluish, *O. tauricum*, with yellow flowers, and *O. echioides*, with pale yellow flowers, are among those grown in rock gardens.
BORAGINACEAE, about 150 species.

**Oomycetes** see Fungi, p. 156.

**Ophioglossum** a cosmopolitan genus of primitive terrestrial ferns, the most common species, including *O. vulgatum* and O. TONGUE]. In *Ophioglossum* the stem is short with a sterile frond which is normally ovate although in some species, such as the epiphyte *O. pendulum*, the sterile frond may be elongated into a long strap-like hanging leaf. The fertile frond in this genus is of interest and appears as a double row of large sunken sporangia and usually arises from the junction of a sterile blade and its petiole. Several species, including *O. vulgatum* and *O. pendulum*, are cultivated for their attractive foliage.

Local medicinal uses of members of the genus include a cough remedy (*O. pendulum*) and an aphrodisiac (*O. spicatum*). *O. ovatum* and *O. reticulatum* are used as fuel in Madagascar and parts of the Moluccas respectively.
OPHIOGLOSSACEAE, 30–50 species.

*In the orchid genus* Ophrys, *the flowers of different species resemble female insects of the particular species involved in pollination. Shown here are:*

Left *the Fly Orchid* (O. insectifera)*, from Europe* ($\times 2$) *and* Right *the Late Spider Orchid* (O. fuciflora)*, from central and southern Europe.* ($\times 4$)

*The Restharrow* (Ononis repens) *is a widespread weed of pastures and coastal areas, with attractive pea-like flowers.* ($\times \frac{1}{3}$)

**Ophiopogon** a small genus of perennial stemless herbs with grass-like leaves, native from India to Japan, including the East Indies. A number of species are cultivated for their attractive racemes of white or bluish flowers followed by conspicuous berries. They include *O. intermedius* (= *O. spicatus*), *O. jaburan*, with various cultivars, and *O. japonicus* [LILYTURF, MONDO GRASS]. The tubers of the latter species are consumed as a vegetable in Japan.
LILIACEAE, 10–20 species.

**Ophrys** a small genus of herbaceous perennial orchids with ovoid tubers, native to Europe, North Africa and East Asia. The flowers are similar to those of **Orchis*, but are without a spur. They often bear a striking resemblance to insects, and some species are in fact pollinated by attracting male insects which try to copulate with the flowers, a phenomenon described as pseudocopulation.

*O. apifera* [BEE ORCHID], is a particularly attractive species about 12–16in tall with few flowers. The sepals are pink, the petals greenish, and the brown labellum is curiously marked and very hairy. It is very widely distributed but always rare. *O. insectifera* [FLY ORCHID] has rather small flowers showing a striking resemblance to a fly. *O. speculum* [MIRROR ORCHID, MIRROR OF VENUS] is a common, attractive Mediterranean orchid with a labellum of reflective brilliant metallic-blue surrounded by gold (hence the common name). (See also p. 767.)
ORCHIDACEAE, about 30 species.

**Opium poppy** the common name for **Papaver somniferum*, an erect, glaucous annual with coarsely lobed or toothed leaves, sometimes spiny, and large showy flowers with white, red or purple petals which have a dark spot at the base.

The OPIUM POPPY probably originated as a cultivated plant in Turkey and has been cultivated since ancient times in much of Europe and Asia for its medicinal narcotic latex, opium. The seeds (sometimes called maw seeds), which contain no alkaloids, are used as a condiment and in baking, often being sprinkled on bread or confectionery. They are also the source of a drying oil used in the manufacture of paints, varnishes and soaps. The cultivars used for seeds belong to the subspecies *hortense*, which more recently has gained popularity as a garden plant.

Today the main areas of opium production (obtained from subspecies *somniferum*) are the Middle East, Turkey, India, China and the Balkan peninsula. Latex is extracted from the capsules by making incisions with a special knife. The latex exudes from the cuts as a white fluid and rapidly coagulates, turning brown. The following day the coagulated drops of latex are scraped off the capsule and then dried or mixed with water and boiled till thick. They are then kneaded into balls of crude opium which can be kept for years.

Opium contains over 25 alkaloids, and also oils and resins. Morphine, the most important alkaloid, is a powerful and medically important analgesic and narcotic. Opium, however, poses very serious problems of addiction, leading to socially harmful effects and often mental and physical deterioration and breakdown. This has led to restrictions on its cultivation but with only limited success.
PAPAVERACEAE.

*Opium poppy cultivation in northern Thailand, where opium is an important cash crop. Here the seed capsules are being cut to release the latex.*

**Opuntia** a large genus of prostrate to tree-like cacti native from temperate North America to the southern tip of South America. Most opuntias have at least some of their stems jointed. The shape of the stems may be obovate, cylindrical, globular or flattened into round pads, and the leaves are cylindrical to conical, usually small and deciduous.

*Species like* Opuntia basilaris, *seen here growing in Death Valley, California, can survive temperatures as high as 158°F.* (×⅓)

Most species bear spines and all bear tufts of barbed bristles (glochids) on each areole. The flowers are usually large and spreading, with yellow the predominant color, although orange, white and purple forms occur.

Economically *Opuntia* has a mixed reputation. As a weed, certain species invaded Australia and by 1920 dominated considerable areas of agricultural land. Parts of South Africa became similarly infested. However, in frost-free countries, species of *Opuntia* can be grown as hedges, and African farming communities commonly plant a few as fodder reserves in times of drought (the spines are cut off or burnt). *O. ficus-indica* [INDIAN FIG] is a widespread species now extensively cultivated commercially in the tropics, subtropics and Mediterranean countries for its large, juicy fruits which are eaten raw after peeling, or made into jam, jelly or various confections. The young stems are diced after removal of the spines, and eaten in salads or cooked as a vegetable. The reticulate woody skeletons of the cylindrical-stemmed CHOLLAS are used for making trinkets and rustic ornaments.

The genus has been divided into four subgenera: *Brasiliopuntia*, *Consolea*, *Cylindropuntia* and *Opuntia*, on the basis of vegetative, floral and fruit characters. *Brasiliopuntia* contains species with a tree-like habit with unjointed primary stems. The jointed branches close to the main stems are cylindrical, those further away are flattened. Seeds are solitary or few in number and have a woolly texture. These features are to be seen in such species as the Brazilian *O. brasiliensis* which grows to a height of about 20ft and bears yellow flowers 2in in diameter and subglobose yellow fruits.

*Consolea* also consists of mostly tree-like species with cylindrical stems bearing oblong or flattened joints. The seeds bear hairs on the sides only. Members of this subgenus are native to Florida and the West Indies and include the cultivated *O. rubescens*, which grows to about 21ft, the joints bearing close-set areoles but few or no spines. The flowers are about 0.8in across, yellow to red in color and give rise to obovoid to globose reddish fruits.

*Cylindropuntia* contains prostrate to tree-like species with globose to cylindrical jointed or unjointed stems, smooth or tubercled. The seeds are glabrous. This subgenus is further subdivided into five sections, of which *Austrocylindropuntia*, *Cylindraceae* [CHOLLA], and *Grusonia* contain mostly erect species. Species in *Corynopuntia* have a prostrate and spreading habit and those of *Tephrocactus* are clump-forming with stems having globose to short-cylindrical joints.

*Austrocylindropuntia* includes such cultivated species as *O. cylindrica* [DANE CACTUS], from Ecuador and Peru, *O. subulata* [EVE'S PIN CACTUS], from Argentina, and the Bolivian

Opuntia leucotricha *is a tree-like species with brilliant yellow flowers and white to red edible fruits.* (×¼)

On the Canary Island of Fuerteventura, the Indian Fig (Opuntia ficus-indica) is commonly used as a hedging or barrier plant.

*O. vestita* [OLD MAN OPUNTIA, COTTON POLE CACTUS], whose areoles bear long white hairs almost covering the stem. *O. clavariodes* [CRESTED OPUNTIA, SEA CORAL, FAIRY CASTLES, GNOME'S THRONE, BLACKFINGERS], possibly Chilean in origin, is most often grafted on another *Opuntia* or **Cereus*. *O. salmiana*, from Brazil, Paraguay and Argentina, with its freely branching habit and sprawling cylindrical stems which bear yellow bristles, short spines and numerous white flowers, is an attractive houseplant.

Most of the *Cylindraceae* are North American in origin but a number are cultivated as ornamentals there and elsewhere. Their primary stems are normally unjointed but they bear cylindrical, jointed branches. Cultivated species include *O. acanthocarpa*, a densely spiny shrub with laterally compressed tubercles, straw-colored spines and red to yellow flowers, *O. cholla*, with sheathed brownish spines and large pink flowers, *O. bigelovii* [TEDDY-BEAR CACTUS], with a short erect trunk bearing tubercles hidden by a dense mat of pale yellow spines which later turn black. The flowers are greenish yellow and about 1.6in across. Other species in this group include *O. tunicata*, *O. prolifera* [JUMPING CHOLLA] and *O. ramosissima* [PENCIL CACTUS].

Species in the section *Grusonia* have erect stems, more or less divided into cylindrical joints. The tubercles are confluent into ribs. They are mostly north Mexican in origin.

*Corynopuntia* species are mainly native to Mexico and the southwestern USA. The better-known cultivated species include *O. schottii* [DEVIL CACTUS], with yellow flowers, and slender brownish-gray spines tinged pink or red, *O. vilis* [LITTLE TREE OPUNTIA, MEXICAN DWARF TREE CACTUS], with purple flowers and club-shaped joints bearing white to red spines, and *O. stanlyi* with yellow flowers and short club-shaped joints bearing flattened brown or reddish spines.

The clump-forming species of *Tephrocactus* include the Argentinian *O. articulata*, with many cultivars such as 'Inermis' [SPRUCE-CONE], with few spines (sometimes none), and 'Syringacantha' [PAPER CACTUS, PAPER-SPINED PEAR], whose brownish spines are papery in texture. Other cultivated species in this section include *O. sphaerica* [THIMBLE CACTUS], native to the Andes of Peru and Chile, with broad, low tubercles, areoles brown and woolly with spines brown becoming gray, and orange flowers (violet in cultivar 'Violaciflora', and *O. floccosa* [CUSHION CACTUS, WOOLLY SHEEP], native to the Andes of Peru and Bolivia, the oblong joints of which have areoles covered with long white hairs that almost conceal the stems.

The largest number of cultivated species in this genus belong to the subgenus *Opuntia* [PRICKLY PEAR, TUNA]. *O. ficus-indica* belongs to this group as well as a large number of attractive ornamentals, including flat-padded species such as *O. leucotricha*, from Mexico, and *O. erinacea* var *ursina* [GRIZZLY BEAR CACTUS], from the southwest USA, with white curling bristles, and *O. scheeri* with golden-yellow bristles. Especially commendable for miniature bowls and window sill culture are certain dwarf cultivars of the Mexican *O. microdasys* [RABBIT EARS, BUNNY EARS], with tiny pads covered in soft white-yellow bristles that can be handled without discomfort.
CACTACEAE, about 300 species.

**Orach** or **orache** the common name for **Atriplex hortensis*, an annual herb growing to a height of 6.5ft, with angled, toothed leaves. It is native to Asia, and is sometimes cultivated in Europe and North America for the leaves and young stems which are used as a vegetable. Cultivars with red or coppery tints are grown as ornamentals.
CHENOPODIACEAE.

**Orange** or **sweet orange** the fruit of **Citrus sinensis*, by far the most important commercial citrus fruit. It originated in north-eastern India and adjacent regions of China and is now grown in subtropical and tropical zones all over the world, principally in the Mediterranean region (Spain, Italy, Israel), Florida and California (USA), Brazil and South Africa. World production of oranges represents over 82% of the world's total production of citrus fruit.

All sweet orange varieties can be eaten fresh or pressed for their juice, but eating oranges of high quality must be easy to peel and juicing oranges must have tough membranes and adherent peel so that debris does not easily pass into the juice. Typical examples of eating and juicing oranges are 'Shamouti' and 'Valencia Late' respectively. Most of the world's crop is eaten fresh, but over 40% of the US crop is pressed.

More than 160 orange cultivars have been described, but only a few are commercially important. Oranges can be classified into four main groups.

*The fruit of the Sweet Orange (*Citrus sinensis*) is known botanically as a hesperidium; its flesh is rich in vitamin C.*

*The Bird's Nest Orchid (*Neottia nidus-avis*) contains no chlorophyll and relies for nutrition on its symbiotic association with fungi.* ( × ½)

I. COMMON ORANGES. A group including 'Bernia' ('Vernia'), an important late Spanish variety of fair quality, also grown in North Africa, 'Biondo' ('Comuna'), the common name for several seedy, local varieties, still widespread in Italy and Spain, 'Ovale', the oval, seedless Italian cultivar of high standard and 'Shamouti' (better known as Jaffa orange) the early to mid-season variety of Israel. 'Valencia Late' (including Jaffa late) is the most important seedless late orange cultivar grown in both hemispheres, accounting for probably more than 15% of the total world orange production.

II. SUGAR OR ACIDLESS ORANGES. This group includes local cultivars (eg 'De Nice') insipid in taste and of minor importance.

III. PIGMENTED (BLOOD) ORANGES. This group owes its pigmentation to anthocyanins dissolved in the cell sap. Its cultivars succeed well in cool areas (Italy and Spain), where the color becomes deep wine red. Important cultivars are 'Moro' and 'Tarocco' (Italy); 'Sanguinilla Negra' (Spain); 'Ruby' (California).

IV. NAVEL ORANGES. The name derives from a small rudimentary fruitlet embedded at the stylar end of the main fruit. It is not an unusual feature in other species, but here it becomes recognized as a "trade mark" of this group which originated as sport of a common cultivar. 'Washington' ('Bahia'), which originated in Brazil, is now one of two main commercial oranges of California.
RUTACEAE.

**Orbignya** a South American genus of slow-growing slender palms with dense crowns of large pinnate leaves. Although widely applied to the genus, the common name BABASSÚ PALM refers in fact only to *O. barbosiana* (= *O. speciosa*). This species is very productive but the seeds have a very hard endocarp which creates problems in commercial extraction. However, when processed they yield a valuable vegetable oil (babassu oil) which is used primarily in margarine production and also in the local soap industry. *O. cohune* [COHUNE PALM], of Central America, is also a source of kernel oil.
PALMAE, 25 species.

**Orchid** a term applied to members of the family Orchidaceae, many of which are cultivated as garden, house or greenhouse plants or for cut-flowers. Most orchid greenhouse plants are of tropical origin; a few are terrestrial (ie ground-inhabiting) but most are epiphytes growing naturally on the bark of trees. In greenhouse cultivation the epiphytic orchids can be grown successfully in pots containing substantial amounts of peat or other natural fibrous materials.

Under natural conditions, development of orchids grown from seed depends on the infection of the root with specific fungi and the establishment of a symbiotic relationship. Commercially orchids are vegetatively propagated by division of the rhizome (which may be pseudobulbous), by cuttings, by apical meristem culture, or by germination from seeds, which are extremely small and undifferentiated. Interspecific and intergeneric hybridization is commonly used by growers to obtain a greater richness and beauty of floral form and color.
ORCHIDACEAE.

*The Lady Orchid (*Orchis purpurea*); each flower has a large deep-purple veined lip (labellum), two back-swept lateral petals, with one of the sepals forming a hood.* ( × 1)

*The Green-winged Orchid (*Orchis morio*) is a locally plentiful, though declining, species of old calcareous pastures.* ( × ¾)

**Orchis** a genus of temperate terrestrial orchids native to North America and Eurasia, usually found on open grassy slopes and in woodlands. *O. simia* [MONKEY ORCHID] and *O. militaris* [MILITARY ORCHID] are two species in which the common names are an accurate description of the flowers' appearance.

Morphologically, all species are typical of the average terrestrial temperate orchid with few- to many-flowered racemes of purple, mauve, lilac, crimson or white flowers more or less surrounded by a basal rosette of oblong-ovate to lanceolate and elliptical leaves. In some species the leaves are dark purplish-black spotted and in *O. mascula* [EARLY PURPLE ORCHID] spotted and unspotted leaf forms occur.

*The Dwarf Orchid (*Orchis ustulata*) is also known as the Burnt Orchid since the hood is brown or dark purple.* ( × 1)

Species grown in damp situations in the garden include the European *O. militaris*, with large fragrant rose or red-violet flowers, the Eurasian *O. morio* [SALEP ORCHID, GANDER-GOOSE, GREEN-WINGED ORCHID] with purplish (rarely white) flowers, the North American *O. rotundifolia* [SMALL ROUND-LEAVED ORCHID, SPOTTED KIRTLE PINK], with white to mauve flowers, and *O. spectabilis* (= *Galeorchis spectabilis*) [SHOWY ORCHID, WOODLAND ORCHID, PURPLE HOODED ORCHID, KIRTLE PINK], with showy, pink to mauve (rarely white) flowers.
ORCHIDACEAE, about 50 species.

**Origanum** a genus of perennial herbs and small shrubs native to Europe, the Mediterranean region and Central Asia. *O. majorana* (= *Majorana hortensis*) [SWEET MARJORAM, COMMON WILD MARJORAM] and *O. vulgare* [POT MARJORAM] are popular kitchen herbs, also known as OREGANO. Other species used as herbs include *O. compactum* and *O. glandulosum* in North Africa, *O. creticum* [SPANISH HOPS], *O. heracleoticum* and *O. onites* [POT MARJORAM] in southern Europe. *O. dictamnus* [DITTANY OF CRETE] is a popular ornamental white-woolly dwarf shrub with fragrant, pink, drooping flowers and reddish shiny bracts.
LABIATAE, 15–20 species.

**Ornithogalum** a largely temperate genus of bulbous herbs mainly native to the Mediterranean region and South Africa. The narrow leaves are produced in a basal rosette with a racemose or corymbose inflorescence of white, greenish-white or yellow to orange-red flowers arising from the center. Most species have white flowers with a green central stripe on each segment. *O. thyrsoides* [CHINCHERINCHEE, CHIN-CHIN], has beautiful white, long-lasting flowers in a dense raceme, and is popular as a cut-flower or pot plant.

Other cultivated species, usually known as STAR OF BETHLEHEM, include *O. arabicum*, *O. nutans*, *O. pyrenaicum* and *O. umbellatum*.
LILIACEAE, about 150 species.

*The parasite* Orobanche crenata, *one of the largest and most destructive of the Broomrapes, seen here completely killing its host, a Broad Bean (*Vicia faba*) plant.* ($\times \frac{1}{5}$)

*The Military Orchid (*Orchis militaris*), so called because of the resemblance of the hanging labellum to a soldier-like figure.* ($\times 1$)

**Orobanche** [BROOMRAPE] a genus of temperate Eurasian and subtropical annual to perennial herbs parasitic on the roots of other flowering plants (usually herbaceous dicotyledons), for example *O. ramosa* on cultivated plants such as **Cannabis sativa* [*HEMP], **Nicotiana tabacum* [TOBACCO], **Solanum* species etc. They contain little or no chlorophyll and thus derive all or most of their organic nutrients from their host.
OROBANCHACEAE, about 140 species.

**Orris root** the common name for the rhizome of the perennial herb **Iris × germanica* var *florentina* (= *I. florentina*), which is cultivated on a commercial scale in some Mediterranean countries and in Iran and northern India. Orris, the dried and powdered tissue, which has the sweet scent of violets, is used in the perfumery and cosmetics industries.
IRIDACEAE.

**Ortanique** a hybrid derived from a chance cross in Jamaica between **Citrus sinensis* [SWEET *ORANGE] and *C. reticulata* [*TANGERINE, *MANDARIN]. The fruit looks like a thin-skinned orange, is juicy and has a pleasant flavor. It is now grown on a considerable commercial scale.
RUTACEAE.

**Oryza** a genus of annual, sometimes perennial, tropical grasses centered in the wet tropics of Asia and Africa, and characterized by their large spreading paniculate inflorescences with flexuous branches and small, one-flowered spikelets. The important cereal *O. sativa* [*RICE] belongs to this genus.
GRAMINEAE, 15–20 species.

**Osage orange** the common name for *Maclura pomifera* (= *M. aurantiaca*) [also known as BOW WOOD], a fast-growing spiny deciduous tree reaching up to 60ft, from the southern and southeastern USA. It is the only species of its genus. The fruits are orange-shaped, yellowish green and very decorative, and it is grown in the USA and Europe as an ornamental tree and hedging plant. The wood is bright orange-colored, strong, hard and durable, and was formerly used by the Osage Indians and other tribes for bows and clubs. The bark yields a yellow dye.
MORACEAE.

**Oscillatoria** a genus of blue-green algae having simple, unbranched, unsheathed filaments of similar cells. The filaments are motile and often show an oscillatory movement, to which the name is due. Species are common in soil, freshwaters and in littoral marine habitats.
OSCILLATORIACEAE.

**Osmanthus** a genus of evergreen shrubs or small to medium trees native mainly to East Asia and the USA, with a few species in the Pacific area (Polynesia). They have white or yellowish flowers in axillary or terminal clusters. The fruit is a drupe, more or less oval, usually blackish-blue or violet. Species such as *O. armatus*, *O. delavayi* and *O. suavis* are useful ornamentals for their evergreen

*Fruits and leaves of the Osage Orange (*Maclura pomifera*).* ($\times \frac{1}{6}$)

habit and holly-like appearance. The flowers of *O. fragrans* [SWEET OLIVE] are used in China to flavor tea. It has long been cultivated.
OLEACEAE, 30–40 species.

**Osmunda** a genus of temperate and tropical ferns of Europe, Asia and North and South America. They are intermediate between the primitive and the more advanced ferns. The leaves are bipinnate and have a separate distal part of the frond for the fertile area, which is dark brown and reduced. The massive sporangia are borne marginally on short, thick stalks on the reduced fertile part of the frond. The most common species, *O. regalis* [ROYAL FERN], is widely cultivated as an ornamental. The young shoots (croziers) of *O. cinnamomea* [CINNAMON FERN] are eaten locally.
OSMUNDACEAE, 8–10 species.

**Osteospermum** a genus of herbs and subshrubs native to southern Africa, tropical East Africa, with others in southwest Arabia

and Jordan. Several are cultivated as ornamentals, such as *O. ecklonis*, a subshrub or shrub with narrow, shallowly toothed leaves and daisy-like flower heads up to 2.8in across; the outer ray florets are bluish to violet below and white above, the inner disk florets blue.
COMPOSITAE, about 70 species.

**Ostrya** [HOP HORNBEAMS] a genus of medium-sized deciduous trees with wide-spreading horizontal branches. They are found throughout the temperate regions of the Northern Hemisphere. The leaves closely resemble those of the true *HORNBEAMS (*Carpinus*) while the fruit clusters have a hop-like appearance.

Species occasionally cultivated are *O. carpinifolia* [EUROPEAN HOP HORNBEAM], native to southern Europe and Asia Minor, and *O. virginiana* [AMERICAN HOP HORNBEAM] from the eastern USA. The wood of the AMERICAN HOP HORNBEAM is extremely hard and tough – hence its popular name of IRONWOOD – and is widely used for tool handles and fence posts.
BETULACEAE, about 10 species.

*Harvesting rice (*Oryza sativa*) by hand in the Philippines, a method still widely employed by subsistence farmers of Southeast Asia.*

*The Royal Fern (*Osmunda regalis*), showing the brown fertile fronds with the larger sterile fronds behind.* ($\times \frac{1}{20}$)

**Ourisia** a Southern Hemisphere genus of herbaceous, tufted or rhizomatous plants occurring in temperate forests and alpine areas of South America, New Zealand and Tasmania. The New Zealand and Tasmanian species are characterized by delicate, irregular, white, yellow or purple-centered flowers. The South American species include red, long-tubed, hummingbird-pollinated species. The white-flowered *O. macrocarpa* and *O. macrophylla*, both from New Zealand, and the red-flowered *O. coccinea* are widely cultivated.
SCROPHULARIACEAE, about 25 species.

**Oxalis** a very large genus of annual to perennial herbs with creeping or erect, sometimes woody stems; they are sometimes stemless, often bulbous, tuberous or rhizomatous, and rarely shrubs or subshrubs. They are widespread in temperate regions, but most abundant and diverse in South America and South Africa. The leaves are trifoliolate to many-foliolate, or sometimes reduced to one or two leaflets. The leaflets can often move in response to changes of temperature or light. The yellow or white to pink or purple flowers are borne singly or in umbellate cymes on leafless stalks. Some species can reproduce by bulbils and may, like the South African *O. pes-caprae* (= *O. cernua*) [BERMUDA BUTTERCUP], become pernicious weeds of cultivated ground. In the tropics, subtropics and the Mediterranean area, the bulb of this species, like the tuberous stems of the high Andean *O. tuberosa* [OCA], are used as food.

Several species are cultivated as garden ornamentals, including the stemless, lilac-pink-flowered *O. adenophylla*, and the erect, much-branched, rose-flowered *O. rosea* and *O. rubra* (white-flowered in cultivar 'Alba'). *O. corniculata* [CREEPING OXALIS, CREEPING LADY'S SORREL], a profusely branched perennial is a cosmopolitan weed often found on the floor of greenhouses. The trifoliolate leaves of *O. acetosella* [CUCKOO BREAD, WOOD SORREL] are sometimes substituted for *SHAMROCK.
OXALIDACEAE, about 800 species.

**Oxydendrum** a genus comprising a single species, *O. arboreum* (= **Andromeda arborea*) [SOURWOOD, SORREL TREE], native to the eastern USA. It is a small deciduous tree with deeply fissured bark and bears many pendulous panicles of small, white flowers. It is widely cultivated in warmer temperate climates for its foliage which turns brilliant scarlet in autumn.
ERICACEAE, 1 species.

**Oxytropis** a genus native to mountainous and cold regions of North America, Asia and Europe. The species are perennial herbs, with purple, violet, white or yellow pea-like flowers, produced in spikes, racemes or borne directly on the stem. A number of dwarf species including *O. campestris*, *O. jacquinii*, and *O. pilosa* (= **Astragalus pilosus*) are cultivated as rock-garden plants.
LEGUMINOSAE, 250–300 species.

Oxalis enneaphylla *in flower in Tierra del Fuego, Chile. This species is also grown in cultivation.* ($\times \frac{1}{5}$)

# P

**Pachysandra** a small genus of perennial herbs or subshrubs native to East Asia, with one species in North America. Two species are grown for ground cover: *P. procumbens* [ALLEGHANY PACHYSANDRA], with spikes of purplish-white flowers, and *P. terminalis* [JAPANESE PACHYSANDRA], with shorter spikes of greenish-white flowers, tinged purple.
BUXACEAE, about 5 species.

**Paddle wood** a very hard, compact, close-grained wood, derived from the tropical American tree *Aspidosperma excelsa*. It is yellowish-white, tinged with pink, and has an elasticity which makes it suitable for paddles.
APOCYNACEAE.

**Paeonia** a genus of perennial herbs and shrubs mainly native to the north temperate region. The genus includes a number of very popular ornamental species such as the European *P. officinalis*, which has large, showy flowers up to 5.5in across, varying in color from white through pink to crimson, and single or double depending on cultivar, the European and southwest Asian *P. arietina*, with reddish-pink flowers, the Caucasian *P. mlokosewitschii* with yellow cup-shaped flowers, and the Siberian and Chinese *P. lactiflora* (= *P. albiflora*, *P. chinensis*) [CHINESE PEONY, COMMON GARDEN PEONY] and its hundreds of garden derivatives.

Of a number of attractive shrubby species ("tree peonies"), the most popular are the Asiatic *P. suffruticosa* [MOUTAN, TREE PEONY], with large bluish-purple flowers, and the Chinese *P. lutea* with fragrant yellow flowers.
PAEONIACEAE, 33 species.

**Paliurus** a genus of deciduous shrubs or small trees native from southern Europe to East Asia, some of which are grown as ornamentals. The stipules are usually modified as spines which in *P. spina-christi* (= *P. aculeatus*) [CHRIST'S THORN, JERUSALEM TREE] are either straight or bent backwards. The flowers are small, greenish-yellow, borne in axillary clusters or terminal panicles.
RHAMNACEAE, 6–8 species.

**Palmetto** the common name given to palms belonging to the genus *Sabal*, native to warm America and the West Indies. Many are cultivated, eg *S. minor* [DWARF, SCRUB or BUSH PALMETTO], *S. mexicana* (= *S. texana*) [TEXAN PALMETTO] but the most useful is *S. palmetto* [CABBAGE TREE, BLUE, CABBAGE or COMMON PALMETTO], whose leaves are used for thatching houses and supply an edible palm cabbage.
PALMAE, about 25 species.

**Panax** a small genus of perennial herbs mainly native to East Asia and North America. The best-known species is *P. pseudoginseng* (= *P. ginseng*) [GINSENG], which is cultivated for its rhizomes and fleshy roots, especially in Manchuria and Korea which is the main exporter. The North American *P. quinquefolius* [AMERICAN GINSENG] is also cultivated for its roots and rhizomes.

The dried and powdered rhizomes and roots of these species have long been esteemed, particularly in Chinese medicine, for their restorative powers. Ginseng is gaining increasingly in popularity as a stimulant in the Western world, where it is marketed under various trade names. The active principles are glycosides, one of which is panaquillon.

*Modern Garden Pansies (*Viola × wittrockiana*) are all highly complex hybrids derived principally from* Viola tricolor *(Heartsease) and* V. lutea. (× ½)

The original wild ginseng root (known locally as zansami or man root) was first found in the Korean mountains some 5 000 years ago. In Korea, intensive botanical research, coupled with selection of roots of the appropriate age (about six years) and careful quality control, has led to the worldwide marketing of a superior product. Ginseng may be consumed from the powdered root, compressed into a palatable tablet, as a tea-like infusion, or as an elixir in an aqueous alcohol base.
ARALIACEAE, about 6 species.

*The fragrant flowers of* Pancratium maritimum, *a Mediterranean species known as the Sea Lily or Sea Daffodil.* (× ⅓)

**Pancratium** a genus of bulbous perennial herbs mainly from the Mediterranean region to tropical Asia and tropical Africa. Several species are cultivated for their white flowers but are scarcely hardy. *P. canariense* from the Canary Islands is 2ft tall with flowers 4in across; *P. illyricum* is shorter with very fragrant flowers, and *P. maritimum*, from the Mediterranean also has very fragrant flowers. *P. zeylanicum* is only 12in tall, with solitary flowers.
AMARYLLIDACEAE, about 15 species.

**Pandanus** a large genus of trees and shrubs from the Old World tropics. The common name of SCREW PINES given to some species derives from the fact that the branched stems are often twisted and bear cone-like fruits that resemble *pineapples. *Pandanus* species have aerial prop roots and are conspicuous trees growing to a height of 65ft or more.

The best-known species is *P. odoratissimus* [PANDANG, BREADFRUIT, THATCHSCREW PINE], which is found on sea coasts from Southeast Asia to the Polynesian islands, and many cultivated forms are known. They make handsome greenhouse plants, as do other species, including *P. vertchii*, *P. baptistii* and *P. candelabrum* [CANDELABRA or CHANDELIER TREE]. In addition to their ornamental value,

certain species such as *P. furcatus* (Bengal to Burma), *P. odoratissimus* and *P. utilis* (Madagascar) are valued for their leaves which are woven into hats, floor coverings, baskets etc. The fruits of some species are soft, sweet and edible.
PANDANACEAE, about 650 species.

**Pandorea** a genus of woody climbing shrubs native to Australia and Malaysia, two of which are cultivated as ornamentals. *P. pandorana* (= **Bignonia australis*) [WONGA-WONGA VINE] produces panicles of numerous pinkish-white flowers and *P. jasminoides* (= *B. jasminoides*) [BOWER PLANT] has much larger pinkish-white flowers in fewer-flowered panicles.
BIGNONIACEAE, about 10 species.

**Panicum** a large genus of tropical and warm temperate annual and perennial grasses. Many of these species are termed *millets, and as such are of economic importance, especially in southern Europe and India, as human food and animal fodder. *P. miliaceum* [COMMON OR PROSO MILLET] is the true millet of history and is still grown in eastern and southern Asia, and in the USA. The grain is used in the same way as *rice, or as porridge, and as flour. The leaves and stems are also used for fodder. *P. sumatrense* [LITTLE MILLET] is grown extensively in India as a substitute for rice, for flour and for animal fodder. *P. maximum* [GUINEA GRASS] is a 10ft high perennial grown in tropical Africa, India and America as one of the best fodder grasses of the tropics. *P. molle* [MAURITIUS GRASS] and *P. purpurascens* [PARA GRASS] are also important fodder plants. A few species are grown for ornamental purposes, including *P. virgatum* [SWITCH GRASS]. In contrast *P. repens* is one of the most troublesome weeds of tea plantations in Asia.
GRAMINEAE, about 500 species.

Paphiopedilum rothschildianum. *Seen here are two of the three striped sepals, one of the dotted lateral petals and the pouch-shaped, red-colored dorsal petal or labellum.* ($\times \frac{1}{3}$)

*Bud of a Corn Poppy (*Papaver rhoeas*), showing the two protective sepals still folded round the developing flower.* ($\times 1\frac{1}{2}$)

**Pansy** the common name for a group of species, varieties and hybrids of the genus **Viola*, favorites of gardeners for centuries. PANSIES have many common names, such as HEARTSEASE, LOVE-IN-IDLENESS, FLOWER OF LOVE, CUDDLE-ME-TO-YOU, HERB TRINITY, THREE FACES UNDER A HOOD. The GARDEN PANSY is *V. × wittrockiana*, a hybrid of mixed origin, derived from *V. tricolor* [TRICOLOR PANSY] and including *V. lutea* [YELLOW MOUNTAIN PANSY], and possibly *V. altaica*.
VIOLACEAE.

**Papaver** a genus of mainly annual and a few perennial herbs mainly native to Europe, Asia and other parts of the Old World, but with a few in western North America. The flowers are borne solitary on leafless stalks as in *P. nudicaule* [ICELAND POPPY, ARCTIC POPPY] or on leafy branching stems as in *P. rhoeas* [FLANDERS, COMMON or CORN POPPY], *P. glaucum* [TULIP POPPY] and *P. somniferum* [*OPIUM POPPY]. Although many species, such as *P. rhoeas* and *P. dubium*, have flowers with red petals, the numerous cultivated varieties of other species, such as *P. nudicaule*, *P. alpinum* and *P. orientale* [ORIENTAL POPPY], have petals in a range of colors, including white, yellow, orange, red, crimson and purple. The fruit is a capsule opening by pores immediately below the persistent stigmatic disk. (See also OPIUM POPPY.)

The SHIRLEY POPPIES are a strain of *P. rhoeas* with white and pink, single or double flowers. Pigments from these have been used to color medicines and wine.
PAPAVERACEAE, about 100 species.

**Papaw, pawpaw, papaya** or **melon tree** common names for **Carica papaya*, a sparsely branched small tree perhaps originating in Mexico or Costa Rica, though now cultivated throughout the tropics for its delicious fruits, which may weigh up to 20lb. The fresh fruit is eaten with lemon or lime juice or in fruit salad; it may be tinned, crystallized or made into jam, ice cream, jellies, pies or pickles; when unripe, it is used like marrow or apple sauce. The young leaves of *C. papaya* are sometimes eaten as a vegetable and the seeds used as a vermifuge, counter-irritant and abortifacient.

The green fruit is scarified for the latex which contains papain, a proteolytic enzyme much in demand as a tenderizer for meat, and in the manufacture of chewing gum and cosmetics, in tanning, in degumming silk and in giving shrink-resistance to wool. Papain is widely produced in tropical Africa, notably Tanzania and Uganda and in Sri Lanka, although most of the exported latex comes from Hawaii.

*Asimina triloba* [AMERICAN PAWPAW], which belongs to the family Annonaceae, is a small tree of the eastern USA. It bears purple flowers and small yellow-green pulpy fruits which are a local delicacy.

**Paphiopedilum** a genus of tropical and subtropical, mostly terrestrial or epiphytic Asiatic orchids without pseudobulbs and closely related to the temperate northern hemisphere genus **Cypripedium* [LADY'S SLIPPER ORCHIDS]. They are tufted plants bearing strap-shaped to ovate leaves. The flowers are borne on upright stems, and colors vary from white, yellows, greens and browns to violet, deep crimson to purple. As well as being streaked and shaded in various colors, the flowers are further distinguished by their hairy margins and deep red or green shining warts.

Paphiopedilums have been extensively hybridized to produce larger and larger, more

*A Papaw tree (*Carica papaya*), showing a cluster of developing fruits which are large berries containing numerous seeds.*

heavily colored flowers, and are, perhaps, the most popular of all cultivated orchids. *P. insigne*, from the Himalayas, contains a range of cultivars and is a parent of several hybrids in cultivation.
ORCHIDACEAE, about 50–60 species.

**Paprika** a bright red powder made from the dried and ground fruits of certain varieties of **Capsicum annuum*. Types produced range from sweet to pungent but typically paprika lacks the pungency of *chillies. Lower quality paprikas include seed and sometimes parts of the flower, which increase the pungency. Paprika is produced mainly in Spain (where it is known as pimentón), Portugal and Hungary. The finely ground powder is used to flavor and garnish food, including ketchup and other sauces. It is the national spice of Hungary.
SOLANACEAE.

**Paradisea** a small genus of rhizomatous herbs native to the mountains of Europe, and eastern Tibet. *P. liliastrum* [ST. BRUNO'S LILY, PARADISE LILY] is cultivated for its racemes of conspicuous funnel-shaped white flowers about 2in long.
LILIACEAE, 2 species.

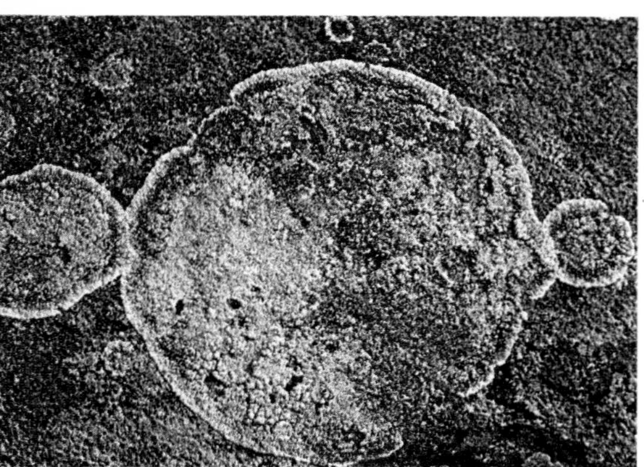

*Parmelia is one of the many genera of crust-forming lichens that grow on bare rocks slowly building up an organic substrate.* (×1)

**Paris** a small genus of perennial rhizomatous herbs native to Europe and temperate Asia, with a single stem bearing four or more net-veined leaves in a whorl at the top. The solitary, erect flowers are greenish and inconspicuous. *P. quadrifolia* [HERB PARIS] was formerly used medicinally for such complaints as headaches and rheumatism. This species and *P. polyphylla* are sometimes grown as ornamentals, particularly for their attractive bluish-black or bright scarlet fruits.
LILIACEAE, about 20 species.

**Parkia** a genus of tropical leguminous trees, some with edible pods or seeds. The seeds (beans) of *P. biglobosa* (= *P. africana*) [AFRICAN LOCUST, NITTA TREE] are rich in protein and are embedded in a mealy pulp which is eaten raw. The seeds are used to make a drink, or like those of *P. filicoidea* [FERN-LEAVED NITTA, WEST AFRICAN LOCUST], *P. javanica* of Indonesia and *P. speciosa* of Malaysia, powdered as condiments.
LEGUMINOSAE, about 40 species.

**Parkinsonia** a small genus of American and African tropical and subtropical trees or shrubs bearing short racemes of large yellow flowers. The only cultivated species is the fragrant-flowered *P. aculeata* [JERUSALEM-THORN, MEXICAN PALO VERDE, RETAMA], from tropical America, which requires greenhouse conditions in cooler temperate regions. However, it is widely cultivated as an ornamental shrub in tropical and subtropical gardens.
LEGUMINOSAE, 2–4 species.

**Parmelia** a large genus of lichens, either leaf-like or forming leafy crusts on trees and rocks. The genus has a worldwide distribution. *P. omphalodes* is very abundant in western parts of Scotland and was once a common source of dye for tartans.
PARMELIACEAE, about 550 species.

**Parnassia** a north temperate and arctic genus of perennial herbs with saucer-shaped flowers, characteristic of marshland and upland bogs. Among the cultivated species are *P. palustris* [GRASS OF PARNASSUS, WHITE BUTTERCUP], *P. glauca* (= *P. caroliniana*) and *P. parviflora*. All of these species have white flowers with spreading petals and contrastingly colored green, pink or purplish veins.
SAXIFRAGACEAE, about 15 species.

**Paronychia** a cosmopolitan genus of small annual or perennial herbs, often tuft- or carpet-forming. Several species are grown in rock gardens, such as *P. argentea* and *P. kapela* (including *P. serpyllifolia*), both with conspicuous silvery bracts concealing the flowers. *P. argentea* and *P. capitata* yield Algerian tea, which has various medicinal uses.
CARYOPHYLLACEAE, about 50 species.

*Virginia Creeper (*Parthenocissus quinquefolia*) is a fast-growing creeper with spectacular autumn colors.*

*St. Bruno's Lily (*Paradisea liliastrum*) growing in an alpine meadow. This hardy species is commonly cultivated.* (×⅓)

**Parrotia** a genus comprising a single species, *P. persica* [PERSIAN IRONWOOD OR IRON TREE], native to Iran. It is a small deciduous tree, often grown as an ornamental for the attractive autumn tints, gold and crimson red, of its ovate leaves.
HAMAMELIDACEAE, 1 species.

**Parsley** the common name for *Petroselinum crispum*, a biennial or short-lived perennial with aromatic leaves, rich in vitamin C. It is probably native to southern Europe and western Asia but is now widely cultivated in most temperate countries as a herb, garnish and flavoring. Most modern cultivars have curled and crisped leaves but varieties with

*Grass of Parnassus (*Parnassia palustris*), a plant of marshes and bogs with beautiful, faintly honey-scented flowers.* (×1)

flat leaf segments (eg var *neapolitanum*) are still widely grown. Var *tuberosum* [TURNIP-ROOTED PARSLEY], with swollen roots which are eaten boiled, is grown in some European countries.
UMBELLIFERAE.

**Parsnip** the common name for *Pastinaca sativa*, a hardy biennial usually grown as an annual root vegetable, with long tapering cream-colored roots with a sweet taste and somewhat larger and coarser than the related carrot. The plant is native to the Mediterranean region and western Asia but is now cultivated throughout the temperate regions of the world. It is normally eaten boiled or roasted.
UMBELLIFERAE.

**Parthenocissus** a small genus of climbing vines native to North America, Mexico and temperate Asia. It is closely related to the genera **Vitis* and **Ampelopsis*. They are deciduous, vigorous plants with tendrils or adhesive pads. Many of them develop rich autumn colors on the leaves and some are widely grown to cover walls and fences, especially *P. quinquefolia* (= *A. quinquefolia*, *V. quinquefolia*) [VIRGINIA CREEPER, WOODBINE, AMERICAN IVY, FIVE-LEAVED IVY]. This is a vigorous species native to the USA and Mexico, with five-lobed leaves, brilliantly colored in the autumn. *P. tricuspidata* (= *A. tricuspidata*) [BOSTON IVY, JAPANESE IVY], from China and Japan, is a widely planted, self-clinging climber with adhesively tipped tendrils, and is also endowed with brilliant autumn colors. *P. henryana* (= *V. henryana*), native to China, is another self-clinging species, bearing three- to five-lobed leaves with silvery-white veins over dark green and bronze.
VITACEAE, about 15 species.

**Paspalum** a large genus of mainly tropical American, mostly perennial grasses with erect stems and an inflorescence consisting of one or more spike-like racemes. *P. scrobiculatum* [KODO MILLET], grown in India, especially in the barren hill regions, is hardy and drought-resistant. *P. notatum* [BAHIA GRASS], grown as fodder from Mexico to South America, has been introduced, as var *saurae* [PENSACOLA BAHIA GRASS], into the southern USA as a lawn grass.

The South American *P. dilatatum* [DALLIS GRASS], known as a pasture grass in the USA, has also been introduced into India, and *P. mandiocanum* is an important fodder crop in Brazil. The Mexican and South American *P. malacophyllum* [RIBBED PASPALUM] has been introduced into the southern USA for use as a hay crop and for soil conservation.
GRAMINEAE, about 400 species.

**Passiflora** a large tropical genus of vines which climb by means of tendrils. They are chiefly native to tropical America, with a few species in Asia, Australia and Madagascar. The genus is noted for its fruit and its flowers, thought by early Spanish Christian missionaries to represent the instruments of the Crucifixion. The most striking features of the flower is the corona, consisting of one to six rows of filamentous structures arising from the base of the corolla, each conspicuously banded with contrasting colors.

Among the most common cultivated species, *P. caerulea* [BLUE PASSION FLOWER] is a vigorous climber with fragrant white, blue and purple flowers 4–7in across. The flowers are followed by attractive orange fruits. Garden hybrids between this species and others including *P. alata* and *P. racemosa* have been produced. *P. coccinea* [RED PASSION FLOWER, RED GRANADILLA] has flowers 4–5in in diameter with vivid scarlet to orange sepals and petals. The corona is purple, pink or white. *P. manicata*, with its vivid scarlet petals, is also commonly called RED PASSION FLOWER. *P. edulis* [PURPLE GRANADILLA], from southern Brazil, and *P. quadrangularis* [GIANT GRANADILLA] are commonly cultivated in tropical and subtropical countries for their edible fruit. *P. quadrangularis* is also cultivated for its flowers which have an attractive shaggy corona, white with zones of blue and purple. The yellow or purple berries of *P. edulis* are the source of passion fruit juice, and the species is grown commercially for this purpose in Australia, New Zealand, South Africa, Hawaii and Kenya. It is the variety *flaviocarpa* [YELLOW PASSION FRUIT] which is particularly cultivated for this purpose. A juice used in beverages is also extracted from the fruit of *P. maliformis* [SWEET CALABASH, SWEETCUP, CONCH APPLE], which is cultivated for this purpose in the West Indies.
PASSIFLORACEAE, about 400 species.

**Paulownia** a small genus of vigorous, fast-growing, deciduous trees from China which are often grown as ornamentals. *P. tomentosa* (= *P. imperialis*) [PRINCESS, KARRI, EMPRESS OR FOXGLOVE TREE] has large, felty, heart-shaped leaves whose size decreases with the maturity of the tree, and huge clusters of purple-blue, foxglove-like flowers. *P. lilacina* has a similar habit but bears drooping lilac foxglove-like flowers with yellow throats. The wood of *P. tomentosa* is used in Japan for furniture making and other purposes. The genus is sometimes placed in the Scrophulariaceae.
BIGNONIACEAE, 6–8 species.

*Flower and fruit of* Passiflora vitifolia. (×½)

**Pavonia** a large genus of tropical, subtropical and temperate herbs and shrubs. A number of species, including the shrubby tropical American *P. spinifex* and *P. hastata* are grown as ornamentals, while the bark of *P. bojeri*, from Madagascar, and *P. shimperiana*, from tropical Africa, yields a fiber used to make cloth. The tropical African tree *P. hirsuta* yields a mucilage from its roots which is used in butter-making by the natives because of its capacity to coagulate milk.
MALVACEAE, about 200 species.

**Pea** a term applied to the plants and the seeds of many members of the family Leguminosae (itself often called the PEA family). The most familiar are from the genus **Pisum*: *P. sativum* var *sativum* (= *P. hortense*) [CULINARY, GARDEN OR COMMON PEA] and *P. sativum* var *arvense* [FIELD PEA]. The former has white flowers and green or yellow seeds, the latter has red or purple flowers and dark seeds. Var *macrocarpon* is the SUGAR or SNOW PEA with edible young pods.

The FIELD PEA is an important crop, providing valuable feed for stock and improving the soil by the action of its nitrogen-fixing root nodules. It is grown either alone or mixed with a cereal, and may be cut green for fodder or left until maturity and the seeds harvested for a protein-rich dry feed.

The dried peas of *P. sativum* var *sativum* were once one of the staple foods in Western Europe, but nowadays, with proteins obtained mainly from dairy products, peas are used immature as a green vegetable. The recent increased demand for tinned and

*A field of the Common or Cultivated Pea (*Pisum sativum *var* sativum*), showing the white flowers which distinguish it from the Field Pea.* (× 1/3)

frozen vegetables has led to the selection of cultivars which will retain the shape, color, flavor and texture of the peas and ripen at different seasons so that canning factories can receive a steady supply. There are innumerable named cultivars of peas based on particular character combinations such as tall, dwarf, color (green or yellow) texture (smooth or wrinkled) etc.

Other peas include **Psophocarpus tetragonolobus* [*ASPARAGUS PEA], **Cicer arietinum* [*CHICK PEA], **Vigna* [*COWPEAS], **Lathyrus* [*GRASS PEA, SWEET PEA] and species of **Abrus* [ROSARY PEA], **Cajanus* [PIGEON PEA], **Chorizema* [FLAME PEA], and **Clitoria, Centrosema* [BUTTERFLY PEAS].
LEGUMINOSAE.

**Peach** a drupe fruit similar to the *plum and *cherry, produced by **Prunus persica*. The peach, after the apple, is the world's most widely grown fruit tree and they may also be grown as ornamentals for their blossom. Although the peach is native to China it is now grown in the warmer areas of the temperate zones, in the USA, the Mediterranean countries, the Far East, Central and South America, South Africa and Australia.

Peaches are of two main types – "freestones" (used mostly for fresh consumption) and "clingstones" (used mostly for canning); they may also be classified on the basis of flesh color – yellow or white. Since peaches can only be stored for a few weeks a very high proportion is processed. Most peach varieties are grafted on rootstocks grown from peach seeds – either wild types or selected commercial varieties of other *Prunus* species such as *P. tomentosa*. In France peach × almond (*P. amygdalus*) hybrids have done well as rootstocks for peaches on poor soils subject to lime-induced iron deficiency.

New genetic material from China has been a major contributor to changes in varieties. Thus CHINESE CLING, introduced to America from China via England in 1850, was the parent of such well-known varieties as 'J. H. Hale' and was involved in the ancestry of a high proportion of present-day varieties.
ROSACEAE.

**Pear** the common name for the popular edible fruits produced by the 15–20 species of the genus **Pyrus*. They evolved in Central Asia with secondary centers arising in both China and the Caucasian region. In China and Japan *P. pyrifolia* (= *P. serotina*) [ORIENTAL OR SAND PEAR], a species with hard crisp fruit, formed the source, with *P. nivalis* and *P. communis*, from which cultivated varieties were selected, with perhaps *P. syriaca*, *P. ussuriensis* and *P. longipes* as additional donors. Because cultivars of *P. pyrifolia* are gritty (due to stone cells) and have little flavor, they are mostly used for culinary purposes.

In Asia Minor the important pear type now known as the EUROPEAN OR COMMON PEAR, was first selected from *P. communis*. *P. pyrifolia* crossed with *P. communis* (*P.* × *lecontei*) has given rise to important commercial cultivars such as 'Leconte', 'Kieffer' and 'Garber'. These are more resistant to fireblight (caused by the bacterium *Erwinia amylovora*) than the standard European pears but have fruit of poorer quality, which makes them more suitable for canning than for fresh consumption.

*Ripe Peach fruits (*Prunus persica*) ready for harvesting.* (× 1/4)

In North America, pears have usually been grafted on pear seedlings obtained from commercial varieties such as 'Bartlett' (known in Europe as 'Williams' Bon Chrétien') and 'Beurre Rose'. On such rootstocks large trees are produced which are able to withstand cold winter conditions. In contrast, in Europe *Cydonia oblonga* [QUINCE], including vegetatively propagated selections such as 'Quince A', are used as rootstocks because of their ability to dwarf and to induce trees to fruit early in their life.

Pear decline caused by a mycoplasma has caused the death of millions of trees in the USA. Seed from the Chinese species *P. calleryana* and *P. betulifolia* and from European pear varieties has provided a source of rootstocks that render grafted trees resistant to the mycoplasma.

The present world production of pears is over 7 million tons per year. Major producers are Italy, China, West Germany, the USA, France and Japan.
ROSACEAE.

**Pearl barley** the hard, pearly pellets left after removal of the adhering floral organs or husk from the *barley grain. It is used in soups, stews and casseroles.
GRAMINEAE.

**Pecan nut** the fruit of the tree **Carya illinoinensis* (= *C. pecan*), a native of the southeastern USA and Mexico. The wild trees produce edible fatty nuts (dry drupes), which were eaten by the Indian tribes in these areas. Now on a commercial scale, the pecan industry in America is of considerable importance and large plantations of trees are

*A dwarf Pear tree (*Pyrus communis*) in full flower and trained along wires in the form of an espalier. Such dwarf forms are high yielding.*

cultivated in states of the southern USA.

More than 500 varieties are now grown, mainly selections from wild seedlings, and named cultivars are usually propagated by budding or grafting on seedling stocks. The quality of the nut is dependent on a high kernel percentage. Most of the harvest is shelled mechanically and used for confectionery, sweets, ice cream and the fresh and salted nut trade.

The food value of pecans is high, and the nuts contain a higher fat content than any other vegetable product (over 70%). Oil from rejected and moldy nuts is used for cooking and cosmetic production.
JUGLANDACEAE.

**Pediastrum** a genus of microscopic colonial green algae with a distinctive plate-like form, found in freshwater ponds. A colony consists of 16 or 32 cells, each with a cup-shaped chloroplast and large pyrenoid. The marginal cells are drawn out into two projections.
CHLOROPHYCEAE.

**Pedicularis** a large genus of semiparasitic, usually perennial herbs native to the north temperate regions, with one species in Andean Ecuador and Colombia. A few species are cultivated for ornament in the border or rock garden but the seed must be sown with that of a suitable host plant – usually grasses. Most have cylindrical or swollen tubular, hooded, purplish or reddish flowers, although white and yellow are also known.

Well-known cultivated species include *P. delavayi*, with white markings on the rose-purple corolla, *P. palustris* [SWAMP OR MARSH LOUSEWORT], an annual suitable for damp places, *P. sylvatica* [LOUSEWORT], with bright red flowers, and *P. verticillata* with pink or white varieties.

Cultivated North American species include the perennials *P. canadensis* [COMMON LOUSEWORT, WOOD BETONY], with yellow or reddish (rarely white) flowers and *P. densiflora* [INDIAN WARRIOR], with crimson flowers.
SCROPHULARIACEAE, about 400 species.

**Pedilanthus** a genus of succulent cactus-like shrubs native to warm regions of North, Central and South America and the West Indies. Two species, *P. macrocarpus* and *P. tithymaloides* (= **Euphorbia tithymaloides*) [REDBIRD CACTUS, RIBBON CACTUS, SLIPPER SPURGE OF FLOWER, JEW BUSH, DEVIL'S BACKBONE, JAPANESE POINSETTIA], are cultivated as ornamentals, the latter with zigzag stems and densely clustered flowers enclosed by bright red or purple bracts.
EUPHORBIACEAE, about 30 species.

**Peganum** a small genus of shrubs native from the Mediterranean region to Mongolia and from the southern USA to Mexico. The seeds of *P. harmala* [HARMAL, HARMELA SHRUB] are narcotic and in parts of the East they are burnt and the smoke inhaled. Other local uses are to treat eye diseases and nervous complaints, as an aphrodisiac and to stimulate the appetite. A red dye is extracted from the fruits.
ZYGOPHYLLACEAE, 4–5 species.

**Pelargonium** a large genus including the "geraniums" of cultivation. Almost pantropical, the genus is particularly abundant in southern Africa, and extends into some warm-temperate areas. Mostly herbaceous and often somewhat succulent, many of the wild species have small flowers; breeders have enlarged them in cultivation.

The use of pelargoniums as ornamentals is varied, and they are grown as subshrubs, bedding plants or in hanging baskets. Almost all found today in gardens are of hybrid origin. *P. fulgidum* hybrids such as *P. × ignescens* are the commonest subshrubs. The 'Regal' or 'Domesticum' pelargoniums listed under *P. × domesticum* [SHOW GERANIUM, FANCY GERANIUM, MARTHA WASHINGTON GERANIUM, SUMMER AZALEA, REGAL GERANIUM], with beautiful flowers and often colored leaves, are mostly developed from *P. cucullatum*, *P. angulosum* and *P. grandiflorum*. Further hybridization with *P. quercifolium* has produced more cultivars.

*P. × hortorum* [FISH GERANIUM, ZONAL GERANIUM, HOUSE GERANIUM, BEDDING GERANIUM], of complex hybrid origin, mainly derived from *P. inquinans* and *P. zonale*, constitutes another important section in the genus, often with patterned leaves, and both single or double-flowered. The IVY LEAVED or HANGING GERANIUM group of pelargoniums are based on *P. peltatum* and are the most popular for hanging baskets.

Some species are grown commercially, mainly in Madagascar, Sri Lanka, East Africa and Algeria. The young shoots are distilled to produce an oil, geranium oil, used in perfumery.
GERANIACEAE, about 250 species.

*Pecan nuts (*Carya illinoinensis*) are grown almost exclusively in the USA, where they are extremely popular.* ($\times 1$)

Pelargonium *species are commonly called Geraniums. The red Geraniums, such as shown here, belong to the group of "zonal" hybrids known as* Pelargonium × hortorum. ($\times \frac{1}{5}$)

**Pellia** a small genus of thallose liverworts, all of which occur in the temperate and boreal climates of much of the Northern Hemisphere. They are found, often in great abundance, in moist habitats in forests, along streams and in open marshes and fens. The thallus is flat, bright green or with a purplish tinge, irregularly branched, and with an indistinct broad midrib which is simply a thicker area. The sporophytes are often numerous, with a long seta and a spherical capsule.
PELLIACEAE, about 4 species.

**Peltigera** a genus of leafy lichens, mostly found growing on the ground. In almost all species the algal symbiont is blue-green. *P. canina* and other species sometimes infest lawns on poorly drained soils.
PELTIGERACEAE.

# ILLUSTRATION CREDITS

Unless otherwise stated below, all illustrations are © Equinox (Oxford) Limited (photographer Eric Crichton). Reference numbers denote page number followed by position on page (reading left to right and top to bottom). (t = top, b = bottom, r = right, l = left, c = center)

Photographs by:

A-Z Botanical Collection (AZ)
Alvin, K. L. (KLA)
Barrett, S. C. H. (SCHB)
BASF
Bateman, G. (GB)
Burras, J. K. (JKB)
Cook, C. D. (CDC)
Dodge, J. D. (JDD)
Duckett, J. G. (JGD)
Dunlop Ltd (D)
Food and Agriculture Organisation (FAO)
Fox, D. J. (DJF)
Gibbons, R. B. (RBG)
Government of Jamaica (GoJ)
Grey-Wilson, C. (CG-W)
Harris, D. (DH)
Harris, E. (EH)
Hepper, F. N. (FNH)
Heywood, V. H. (VHH)
Hora, F. B. (FBH)
ICI Plant Protection Division (ICIP)
International Rice Research Unit (IRRU)
Jury, S. L. (SLJ)
Keith-Lucas, D. M. (DMK-L)
Lacey, W. S. (WSL)
Mabberley, D. J. (DJM)
Mathew, B. (BMa)
Matthews, G. A. (GAM)
Moore, D. M. (DMM)
Morely, B. (BM)
Natural Science Photos (NSP)
Norrington-Davies, J. (JN-D)
Oxford Scientific Films (OSF)
Proctor, M. C. F. (MCFP)
Rowley, G. D. (GDR)
Seddon, B. (BS)
Spectrum Colour Library (SCL)
Weed Research Organisation (WRO)
Whitmore, T. C. (TCW)
Whitmore, W. A. (WAW)
Woodell, S. R. J. (SRJW)
Wright, J. O. (JOW)
Zefa (Z)

127cl FNH, 128tl DMK-L, 128br GDR, 129tl bc SCHB, 130tl MCFP, 130br FNH, 131tr FNH, 132tl SLJ, 132br GDR, 133tr CG-W, 134tl RBG, 134br SLJ, 135tl DMK-L, 135tr FNH, 137tl bc GB, 138cl EC, 138bl MCFP, 139bl RBG, 139tr FNH, 140tr MCFP, 142tr MCFP, 143bl DH, 143tr FNH, 148bl DJF, 150tl BM, 154bc NSP, 155tl NSP, 155bl GDR, 155tr RBG, 160cl BMa, 160bc BS, 160tr NSP, 161bl RBG, 161tc MCFP, 162tr SLJ, 163cl EH, 164bl NSP, 164tc MCFP, 164br NSP, 165 GB, 166 GB, 167tl GoJ, 167cr CG-W, 168bl BMa, 171bc RBG, 172tc NSP, 172br GAM, 173tl GAM, 176t D, 177bl NSP, 177tr GB, 178tl MCFP, 178bl DMK-L, 179bl GAM, 180cr JGD, 180bc MCFP, 181tl MCFP, 181b GAM, 181tr GB, 182bl JOW, 182tr FNH, 183tl GAM, 183cr GAM, 184tl MCFP 184bc cr RBG, 185tl GAM, 185br RBG, 186bl JKB, 186tr GAM, 187bl CG-W, 187tr GAM, 188br GAM, 189br NSP, 190t WRO, 191tl CG-W, 191cr GAM, 192tl DJM, 192bl GAM, 193bl DH, 193tr GDR, 194bl AZ, 195bl GAM, 196bl RBG, 196tr GAM, 197bl OSF, 197tr KLA, 198bl NSP, 198tr GB, 199bl DH, 199tr DMK-L, 199br ICIP, 202cl RBG, 203bl GAM, 203tr KLA, 204bl RBG, 205tl BMA, 205cl GAM, 205br DMK-L, 205cr NSP, 206bl CDC, 206tr FNH, 207cl GAM, 207tr CG-W, 208bl WAW, 208tr RBG, 209tc DJM, 209b NSP, 210bl RBG, 210bc GDR, 211tl RBG, 211br WRO, 212bl tr DMK-L, 212br MCFP, 213bc RBG, 213tr NSP, *214bl tr GB, 215tr GB, 216tl JN-D, 216br GAM, 217tl Z, 217cr GDR, 218b WSL, 219tl MCFP, 219br DH, 221tr CG-W, 222bl JKB, 224bl RBG, 224cr NSP, 225tl bl GAM, 225cr FAO, 228tl NSP, 228br FBH, 229tl DJF, 229br MCFP, 230bl BASF, 231tr MCFP, 232tc GAM, 232br NSP, 233tl NSP, 233br RBG, 234bl tr MCFP, 235t bl MCFP, 236bl NSP, 236bc RBG, *237bl GB, 237tr NSP, 238tr JKB, 239tc RBG, 239cr CG-W, 240tl TCW, 240bl JDD, 240br SLJ, 242bl RBG, *242tr GB, 243bl WSL, 243tc GAM, 243tr DH, 243br RBG, *246tr GB, 247tr GAM, 248br RBG, 249tl FNH, 251t SCL, 251br Z, 252bc CG-W, 252tr RBG, 253bl DJF, 253tr NSP, 254tl DJF, 255 RBG, 256bl WRO, 256tc CG-W, 256cr GB, 257tl IRRU, 257bl DMK-L, 257br DMM, 259bl NSP, 259br DJM, 260cl RBG, 260br EH, 260tr NSP, 261tl RBG, 261tr NSP.

(*courtesy The National Trust)

Artwork panels for Economic Plant Special Features: R. Gorringe.